Mark II

JOHN NICHOLSON & JOE PADUDA

50 Years of Syracuse University Rowing

Commissioned and Published by:
Syracuse Alumni Rowing Association (SARA) and
SARARowing.com
Syracuse, New York, USA

Syracuse Alumni Rowing Associaiton

The mission of the Syracuse Alumni Rowing Association (SARA) is to support, promote, and celebrate the sport of rowing at Syracuse University and grow the legacy of Syracuse University Rowing around the country. SARA builds on the century-plus tradition of rowing at SU by connecting alumni, parents, rowers and friends at races and events; by coordinating fundraising initiatives; by honoring athletic and organizational achievements and post-graduate successes of the SU rowing community; by keeping SU rowing alumni in touch through various communications media; and by keeping and celebrating the history of Syracuse University Rowing.

Mark II
50 Years of Syracuse University Rowing

John Nicholson & Joe Paduda

Table of Contents

3

4

In 1874, rowing at Syracuse University was born. The oldest sport on the SU campus, rowing has a rich and storied 140-year history. The legacy of Syracuse Rowing has been created by over 6,000 men and women athletes who pulled an oar or steered a shell over the waters of Onondaga Lake while their coaches provided a steady hand to guide these crews.

As alums, we remain proud to be part of a program that has been continuously recognized as a leader in collegiate rowing. Syracuse Rowing has produced Olympians, coaches, doctors, engineers, artists, teachers, business and community leaders, politicians, fathers and mothers. Undoubtedly, the time spent training and competing for Syracuse has influenced every one of our successes. Grit, determination, teamwork, a strong work ethic, integrity, leadership and humility are traits that distinguish a Syracuse rower.

The sport of rowing and Syracuse University Crew have significantly evolved since the publication of *Mark of the Oarsmen* in 1963. Rowing, a sport once reserved for the elite and wealthy, has grown exponentially since the 1960s with the emergence of women's inter-collegiate rowing, juniors, masters and para-rowing. Yet the dedication of the Syracuse University athletes, the boathouse they use and the water they row on have remained constants. Wooden racing shells and oars have been replaced by carbon fiber. A coxswain's megaphone has been replaced by an electronic sound system. Women's rowing began–grew to become a NCAA varsity sport–and now surpasses men's rowing in number of programs as well as number of athletes. Boats are faster, athletes are stronger and coaching and training are much more sophisticated. Rowing at Syracuse has been at the forefront of all of these evolutions.

Syracuse Alumni Rowing Association (SARA), founded in 1953 by Dr. Bruce Chamberlain '41 and Dr. Thomas Kerr '39, has been a driving force in that evolution. Preserving the history of Syracuse Rowing is one of the most important roles of SARA. The original *Mark of the Oarsmen*, authored by Malcolm

Alama and first published by SARA in 1963, documents Syracuse Rowing's first 85 years. This narrative account of the birth of Syracuse Rowing through 1962 has been a "must read" for all Syracuse oarsmen and oarswomen. All of us, having read *Mark of the Oarsmen*, cherish the history of Syracuse Rowing and we are proud to have been a part of a founding institution in collegiate rowing.

When the idea for *Mark II* germinated during a monthly SARA Executive Board conference call in 2011, everyone agreed that *Mark II* was overdue and needed to be written.

Commissioning the writing of *Mark II* seemed like an obvious idea and one that was consistent with SARA's mission to preserve the history of Syracuse Rowing.

We are blessed to have as part of our SARA family Joe Paduda '80, a previously published author of *The Art of Sculling*, and John Nicholson '68, is a graduate of the School of Speech and Dramatic Arts (now VPA) and a professor at the SU Newhouse School of Public Communications, as well as an Emmy-winning news reporter, sports event host and "The Voice of Syracuse Rowing."

Both Joe and John immediately stepped up to the plate to produce this volume of Syracuse Rowing history. *Mark II* picks up where *Mark of the Oarsmen* left off and captures the most recent 50-year history of Syracuse Rowing.

Balancing demanding careers and home lives, Joe and John worked as a team to undertake this daunting task. Their effort took nearly four years and three SARA administrations to complete. There were countless interviews, as well as extensive research through University and newspaper archives to capture the facts and recreate the spirit of the crews from those eras. Undoubtedly, capturing a precise and indisputable record is impossible and we thank Joe and John for the balanced and objective recording of our history.

Mark II chronicles a half-century of the highs and lows of Syracuse rowing–including the 1978 IRA Men's National Championship, the moving of the IRA Regatta out of Syracuse, appearances at the Royal Henley Regatta, grand finals appearances at the Eastern Sprints Regatta, the emergence of women's rowing as an NCAA varsity sport, Big East Championships and NCAA National Championship Regatta appearances. Many racing shirts were won and lost over these years.

For the Syracuse rower, what was more important than the wins and losses, were the life experiences, the indelible friendships, and the personal fortitude necessary to row for Syracuse. *Mark II* rekindles many fond memories for many of us and confirms our devotion to Syracuse University Rowing. It reminds us of the importance of our men and women alums and program supporters. We are proud; we are honored; and we are humbled to have raced wearing orange and eagerly await the generations to come who will embrace the heritage of Syracuse University Rowing.

Mark of the Oarsmen and *Mark II* serve as a reminder to all current and future Syracuse rowers of the responsibility they have to uphold the integrity, spirit, fight and competitiveness of Syracuse Crew. Each of them is continuing the legacy and writing the next chapters of Syracuse Rowing history.

We owe a huge thank you to Joe and John, and all of those that have contributed in creating *Mark II*.

Enjoy a great read.

"Pull Hard, Go Fast–Go Orange!"

Tracy Brown '90	Joe Kieffer '88	Lynne Pascale '81
SARA President	SARA President	SARA President
2010–2011	2012–2013	2014–2015

Acknowledgements

T he authors would like to thank the many people who gave of their time and memories to make this book possible.

We thank alumni and / or coaches: Bill Sanford, Nancy Sanford, Kristen Sanford, Gary MacLachlan, Paul Dudzick, Ned Kerr, Dan Hogan, Giles van der Bogert, Ted Kakas, Larry Laszlo, Drew (Andy) Harrison, Ken Hutton, Alan More, Paris Daskalakis, Jason Premo, Josh Stratton, Joe Peter, Dick "Pappy" Yochum, Tom Rouen, Jim Kries, Tom Denver, John Hession, George Chapman, Mark Lyvers, Barry Weiss, Hugh Duffy, James (Jamie) Bettini, Chris Ludden, Adlai Hurt, Dave Reischman, Peter Romano, Justin Burgess, Dan O'Shaughnessy, Rick Holland, Martin Etem, Tyson Bry, Mike Gennaro, Tyler Toporowski, Mike Dietrick, Chris Lutz, Kate Modolo, Alicea Kochis, Helen Tanger, Anna Goodale, Colin Goodale, Kate Todd, Justin Moore, Molly Tibbetts Scannell, Matt Morrow, Lynne Della Pelle Pascale, Rick Tremblay, Gerry Henwood, Art Sibley, Jeff Pesot, Chris Lang, Jen Sacheck, Tracy Brown, Sheila Roock, Charlie Clark, Martha Mogish Rowe, Dan Hanavan, Andy Papp, Bob Price, Bill Bater, Don Plath, Steve Anthony, Tom Darling, Bill Purdy, Mac McNamara, Scott Baltazar, Charlie Gibson, Bob Donabella, Krista Karns, Justin Stangel, Ken Schmidt, Eric Fudo, Walt Kehm, Peter Kruse, Mark Vyzas, Jeff Harriman, Odette Mitchell-Servilio, Paul Buff, Murray Lukoff, Austin Curwen, Jennifer Sanford-Wendry, Rich Kortright, John Hilfinger, and Jan Palchikoff.

Sue Edson and her staff at the Syracuse University Athletics Department were particularly patient, helping us locate and pick through dozens of paper and digital files, find race results, and figure out where to find obscure bits of information. Susie Mehringer, Dave Gunn, Larry Kimball, Goran Buckhorn, Bill Miller and Tom Weil provided access to information and resources we could not have located on our own.

The authors greatly appreciate the generosity of the many-times unknown oarsmen and oarswomen, as well as alumni and family members, who graciously donated photographs to the Syracuse University Athletics Department throughout the years. The inclusion of photographs in *Mark II* establishes a more meaningful and vivid history of Syracuse Rowing. We sincerely thank you.

As the organization dedicated to the support and success of Syracuse University Rowing, the Syracuse Alumni Rowing Association has been instrumental in the writing, publication, and dissemination of *Mark II.*

The patient persistence of SARA Presidents Tracy Brown, Joe Kieffer and Lynne Pascale kept things moving forward.

Finally, we would like to thank our lovely brides, Susan Nicholson and Deb Paduda. Why they put up with this–and us–will never be known. This book would not have been possible without their understanding and constant support.

– John Nicholson '68 & Joe Paduda '80

T here is a bond among the men and women who pull sweep oars and those smaller in size–but not in stature–who steer their shell, call their cadence and urge them on. No one who has never been involved in rowing is likely to truly understand it, and no one who has rowed competitively will forget it.

Likewise there is a bond among those who have competed for a particular university's crew even if the history of the program has its ups and downs; perhaps especially if it does. Such is the case with Syracuse University Rowing.

In his introduction to the reissue of *Mark of the Oarsmen* in 2011, Dr. Bruce Chamberlain wrote, "Those who know and love sports understand that history is critical to their appreciation. In no sport is this truer than in rowing. The Syracuse Alumni Rowing Association, of which I am privileged to have been a founder, has always understood the importance of history to keeping crew alive at Syracuse. That is why we commissioned the book."

That too, is why SARA has commissioned this book, the history of the oarsmen and oarswomen, coxswains, managers, coaches and administrators who have made their mark on Syracuse University Rowing since publication of the original volume in 1963.

This story is in part the story of the Sanfords. But it is also the story of other coaches who came and went and of hundreds of athletes, some of whom stayed four or five years and some who didn't get past year one.

It is a story of great triumphs and crushing defeats, of battling wind and rain, ice and snow, sleet, wakes, floods, and breakage.

There are the great rivalries with Cornell and Navy, Dartmouth, Boston University, Penn, Temple, Georgetown, Notre Dame, Rutgers and Brown. And of course the Big East, Eastern Sprints and Intercollegiate Rowing Association (IRA) / National Collegiate Athletic Association (NCAA) foes: the 'Cliffies, Crimson and Eli, Huskies (Washington) and Huskies

(Northeastern), Cardinals, Quakers, Badgers, Lions, Tigers and Bears. Oh my!

Mark II also tells of the emergence of women's rowing, the path blazed by a hardy group of women in the early seventies who wanted nothing more than a chance to row for Syracuse. And it describes the constancy of rowing against a backdrop of enormous societal change. Yes, our sport, and our school, have evolved so dramatically we can scarcely believe the SU of our day is the same school that sits on The Hill today. But through the five decades, the essence of rowing at Syracuse has remained the same.

Both of the authors have a personal role in the story, though we've tried not to make much of it. This has been a labor of love. A longer labor, quite honestly, than we had expected. The inspiration we both have gained from our involvement with Syracuse University Rowing and the friendships we have made are more than enough compensation.

We have a copy of *Mark of the Oarsmen* that belonged to a team member from 1919–1922. He wrote notes in the margins, sometimes exclaiming over memories and sometimes offering words that are the equivalent of "bunk" indicating that the story as told was not exactly the way it was. No doubt readers of this volume will have similar reactions. Fair enough. This is the story as best we've been able to put it together based on records, clippings and recollections of the men and women who lived it.

We hope you enjoy it!

– John and Joe

Chapter 1
1978 – National Champions

C oach Bill Sanford stood near the victory dock at the IRA finish line on Onondaga Lake, waiting for the start of the last race of the day–the men's varsity eight. As the tall, gangly coach listened for the announcer's call that the race had started, the north wind ruffled his thinning hair, foreshadowing a rough start and long race for the big boats. After a season that had started out with a poor showing in a home loss to Harvard, the crew had come together, improving seemingly every week. With a solid string of wins in dual meets, a decent showing at the Eastern Sprints, and strong talent up and down the boat, Sanford felt confident his crew would be among the medalists.

Less than an hour before, coxswain Ozzie Street had launched the varsity from the dock at Long Branch. Walking down the boat, shaking each man's hand before they pushed off, Sanford had seen little of the banter that normally marked the pre-race launch. Instead, he felt a quiet confidence coming from the crew. Normally sophomore stroke Art Sibley and his classmate and bowman Gerry Henwood would be bouncing around, annoying the upperclassmen on the crew, but this was different–the guys were "wired, they were ready to go but they seemed relaxed and happy they were in the finals … they were quiet and I think that was because they were focused."

Finals day had dawned hazy and a good bit cooler than Friday; a steady headwind was predicted and conditions on Onondaga Lake looked to be a bit choppy, especially near the start of the 2,000-meter course on the lake's eastern shore. As the boathouse bunkroom came to life, most of the guys came out on the balcony to check conditions before heading into the dining room / Sanford living room for Sandy Pisani's pre-race breakfast. With all three Orange eights in the grand finals along with an SU entry in almost all the small boat events, the SU faithful had much to be excited about, even if the competition was looking very, very strong.

Buzz Congram's Northeastern crew also had boats in each of the eight-oared finals, and the Huskies, along with Brown and California, the guest from the West, were looking like serious competitors for the top of the podium.

There was a good deal of confidence in all of the SU boats. The JV was coming off a very solid season, the frosh were looking for a third-straight title and the varsity had seen strong results late in a season that had been a bit unsatisfying for the Orange early on.

It started with that loss to powerful Harvard on a Syracuse course shortened by the weather, then a Goes Cup win over Cornell, as Navy stayed home. The Eastern Sprints saw Yale upset the Harvard varsity, with SU finishing third.

The Orange looked to have another shot at Yale with the Eli joining Dartmouth and MIT on Packard Cup race day in Syracuse. But Orange stroke Sibley was nursing a pulled scapular muscle after the Sprints, forcing a change in the varsity lineup. Henwood moved from bow to the other end of the boat to stroke, with fellow soph Steve Anthony coming up from the JV to row in bow.

Alas, Dartmouth deprived SU of its shot at Yale by upsetting the Eli in the morning, as the Orange dispatched MIT. SU had to be content with taking care of the Big Green and winning the Packard Cup in the afternoon.

By all accounts, the boat had been flying in the Packard Cup race, with Anthony's mental toughness and power contributing to the dominant performance. Still, Sibley's recovery was a big concern. While no one discounted Steve Anthony's ability and will to move a boat, Sibley was the varsity's guy and he had worried he wouldn't be ready for the IRAs.

He wasn't the only one wondering; a local reporter had asked Coach Sanford about Sibley's status. The coach's response had been unequivocal, "We need Art in the boat at the IRA." That opinion was shared by the crew. Seven-man Bill Reid had insisted they go out in a pair while Art was working his way back, and the row had done wonders for Art's confidence. Art recalled that Bill had told him he wanted nothing more than to get Art back in the boat, and he had come back to the dock at the end of the row with renewed confidence.

Soon after, Sibley returned to his spot facing Ozzie Street.

In spite of Sibley's return the varsity hadn't moved well in Thursday's opening heat. The boat had felt out of sync and heavy. Trying to get some swing in the boat, Street had called the stroke rating down from a 34 cadence to a 32 cadence "… to settle the crew down. I hoped dropping the cadence would get them in a rhythm, but it backfired and Cal began to move out on us," and when the rhythm stumbled, the crew couldn't get it back together. Despite holding on to the lead for the first part of the race, SU couldn't maintain it. Cal pulled away in the last forty strokes, earning a spot in the finals and consigning the Orange to a trip to the repechages. After the race, the crewmen were a bit dispirited; they'd worked very hard in the race but the boat hadn't moved like it had in practice, and now had to race again on Friday.

Attitudes brightened when the crew learned that six-man Tom Evancie had been suffering from dehydration most of the race and thus had little left in the last 500. Evancie was hustled into the care of the trainers, who administered intravenous fluids. He started feeling much better before the day was over. As for Evancie's teammates, they knew they had a much better race in them, and began to focus on their next race; the reps.

The crew would have to race well on short rest to make the grand finals.

Talking with his crew before launch on Friday, Coach Sanford reminded them that, "as bad as the boat felt and as bad as you rowed you all know what the boat feels like when it's going well." He told the guys to remember what it felt like when they were going well, "… don't put any extra pressure on, just go out and row how you've trained to row and you'll be fine."

Off the starting line, and pretty much throughout the race, Northeastern set a furious pace; SU was content with a solid and comfortable second. The top two would qualify. The day was hot, with temperatures near ninety degrees, and the decision to not go all out may have been influenced by Evancie's dehydration the day before. Whatever the reason, at the end of the Friday morning racing, SU's varsity was into the finals, albeit without the benefit of a win in either the heats or the reps.

The local press wasn't overly impressed with the race, with one reporter noting, "Syracuse was overhauled in the stretch for the second-straight day and Syracuse winds up second behind Northeastern." Both Northeastern and Syracuse were going to qualify comfortably, as third place Princeton was a solid two lengths behind the Orange and wasn't a real threat at any time. The reporter noted that after the hard row in the previous day's heats, Sanford's crewmen were more than content to qualify without expending any additional energy, energy they'd certainly need in the finals on Saturday.

Less than 24-hours later they were at the starting line.

Despite having to work their way into the grand finals via the repechage, varsity bowman Henwood and the rest of the crew knew the lineup was comprised of guys who had won at the IRAs before in Frosh Coach Drew Harrison's victorious 1976 and 1977 freshman crews, along with seniors Bill Reid, Andy Mogish, Jr., future Olympian Bill Purdy, Tom Evancie, and Dave Townsley who all had won silver as freshmen. If anything, the reps had helped the crew get just a bit more racing experience, a big help after the late-season injury to sophomore stroke Sibley had resulted in a line-up shift for the Packard Cup against Dartmouth.

Weather for the finals featured a headwind causing the first thousand to be either "pretty" or "very" choppy depending on who was recalling the conditions. The varsity grand final would be the last race of the day, and there was lots of racing to be done before the closing event. In the first of the eights races, Drew Harrison's freshman eight successfully defended its national championship, handily defeating Northeastern with Cornell coming in third.

This was becoming a typical SU freshman performance, with the crew gaining considerable speed at IRA Camp and defeating crews that had beaten them earlier in the season. Northeastern had won the Sprints, and the victory was sweet indeed for the Orange frosh. As the bemedaled and beaming freshman eight pulled away from the awards dock, the finish line crowd roared its approval of the first of what they hoped would be an Orange sweep of the eights. The freshmen had delivered, now it was up to the JV and varsity.

Alas, while the JV was able to finish with a podium spot, it was not the top place. Capturing bronze behind Penn in front followed by the Northeastern Huskies, the second eight acquitted itself well, staying in contention throughout the race in conditions that were slow–and getting slower as the headwind seemed to build.

With the small boats and lower eights out of the way, it was time for the marquee event–the varsity eights.

Before the race, cox Ozzie Street and Sibley had discussed the crew's weak point–the third 500. All season this had been a bit of a problem, and the other crews that had raced successfully against SU had usually made their move there. Sibley and Street decided they had to break that pattern. For the finals, the plan was to start well, stay among the leaders, then pull all out the stops in the third 500 and break away.

The finals featured Penn, Cornell, Northeastern, SU, Brown, and California with the Orange in "lucky lane five," where Henwood, Street, and Sibley had been a year before when they won the second of Drew Harrison's three consecutive IRA frosh titles. It turned out to be a classic Syracuse IRA race–a bit of chop, good headwind and a tight pack with no clear favorite.

"Are you ready? Ready all. Row!" They were off.

The pack was pretty tight off the line. Then it settled into a dogfight. Henwood felt a lot of splashing at the start, the pace settled, the legs started pounding down, and while the boat wasn't the smoothest it had been, it was moving. It felt stronger and more powerful somehow, definitely different than the feeling in the heats and reps of the last two days.

The good feeling in the boat wasn't felt by SU fans on the shore. Listening to the race announcer, they heard the Orange in fifth place after 500 meters. Out in lane five, the conditions were somewhat rougher than the more-protected inside lanes, and that may have helped the near shore crews open up an early lead. But Syracuse was under-stroking the field at a 33 cadence, waiting for conditions to improve.

Coming to the 1,000-meter mark, the Orangemen were right where they wanted to be, behind Penn, Cornell, and Brown all in the inshore lanes, but well within striking distance. Cal wasn't handling the conditions as well and seemed to be faltering just a bit, while Northeastern's hard effort the day before in the heat seemed to have taken a toll; NU fell off the pace in the second

500.

Ahead at the finish line, the crowd may well have groaned upon hearing Syracuse was in fourth at the midpoint, but Sanford wasn't concerned. He was thinking, "just keep a steady pace as the water gets better, up your stroke and you're going to go faster and faster and so at the 1,000-meter mark we were in fourth place and then we just went through the rest of them in the last 1,000 just by swinging and rhythm and taking the stroke rating to a 34–35 as the water got better. And we were long as hell. We were the longest crew out there and into that headwind that paid off because then they just went by–just motored away."

The Orangemen were determined to make this their strength; for weeks they'd been focusing on driving through the third 500, and the crew dug in. As the Orange entered the third 500, from the bow-seat Henwood saw the engine room in the middle of the boat "moving a wall of water with each stroke."

With the powerful Purdy, Evancie, Shamlian and Townsley driving the boat into the headwind, they started to move away from Penn and Cornell. Halfway through that 500, SU had broken clear of Penn and Cornell, leaving Northeastern and California further back. The power kept coming, and with 500 meters to go it was SU in front of Brown by almost a length.

Syracuse had gone from well back in fourth to well out in the lead in just 500 meters. The Orangemen had taken the worst part of their race, that dreaded third 500, when the legs are screaming and there's so far to go and it is so easy to cut back just a hair, and they had made it theirs.

While the third 500 was the key, Street knew that Coach Vic Michalson's Brown was a very good headwind crew and their fitness would be a factor in the last quarter of the race. This was shaping up to be a very long 2,000 meters, and his guys would have to go very, very hard to hold Brown off. After the effort of the third 500, that was a tall order indeed. Brown evidently knew it had to go early, as the SU lead was too big to overcome in the last thirty strokes. About ten strokes into the last 500, Street saw Bruno begin to go. He told his crew, "Here comes Brown, just relax." Waiting for a few beats, the boat noticeably relaxed, the tension seeming to dissipate. Ozzie called the sprint, the rating came up, the boat was flying, and Brown's push into the Syracuse lead halted, then reversed.

With twenty strokes to go, the Orange bow was in front and moving away from Bruno.

Years later Henwood would say that during those last twenty strokes, he knew they would win, and despite the utter exhaustion, there was an incredible feeling of accomplishment, of joy. So much had gone into those six-and-a-half minutes, so many hours of training and so much effort and struggle, and now, in that instant, it was coming together just as they'd pictured it so many times.

As the Orange varsity eight crossed the finish line, the stands erupted. The hometown crowd had watched and listened and cheered, dismay turning to exuberance as SU had driven through the field in that key third 500, held off Brown, then moved out again to win convincingly. Now, as the Orange crew waited its turn to pull into the awards dock, there were handshakes up and down the boat, back-slapping, yells of congratulations and a celebratory dive into Onondaga Lake by Gerry Henwood. With bronze and silver medals awarded, SU pulled into the dock, Ozzie Street called the "one foot, up and out" and the oarsmen faced a roar from their coach, teammates, families, friends, and fans.

They had done it! They were the 1978 IRA Varsity Champions!

For Coach Sanford, the victory was sweet indeed. Walking down to the awards dock, he ran into the *Syracuse Herald-Journal's* Bob Snyder. Earlier, Sanford had heard Snyder was going to write Sanford's epitaph if the varsity didn't come home with the trophy. Spotting Snyder, Sanford told him, "Looks like you're going to have to rewrite your story."

Pedaling his bicycle the short distance back to the Ten Eyck Boathouse from the finish line, Sanford recalled the difficult path they'd trod on the way to the podium. That season-opening loss to Harvard on a course shortened by a blizzard, the injury to Sibley, his decision to keep Street–at 146 pounds, by far the heaviest coxswain at the regatta–in the varsity boat, the pressure to produce after two years of freshman championships, the prior year when SU should have won. The memories flooded back, halted only when he pedaled up to the dock.

There, Ozzie Street was in full voice. Sanford remembers Street talking to the press, saying, "I told everybody we had this thing back in April and nobody wanted to listen to me; now maybe in the future you'll listen to me." Recalling that moment, Sanford said, "I can remember him going off and everybody laughing at him. He had a good time with it and he took full credit. He took full credit for it, which every one of them should have.

"But you've got a guy like [two-man Andy] Mogish who sees a camera or a recorder and ducks away and he wouldn't want to talk–and then you'd see [seven-man] Bill Reid, who came out of his shell and he starts talking. The guy you couldn't get that close to over the years, all the time he was feeling the same thing everybody else was. And he was a real big part of that whole thing."

The crew threw Street into the river in celebration. And then they threw Sanford in also.

After 58 years, the Syracuse varsity eight was finally back on top.

This was the 1978 IRA-winning varsity eight crew's line up:

Cox	Ozzie Street
Stroke	Art Sibley
No. 7	Bill Reid
No. 6	Tom Evancie
No. 5	Bill Purdy
No. 4	Dave Townsley
No. 3	John Shamlian
No. 2	Andy Mogish, Jr.
Bow	Gerry Henwood

Chapter 2
Coach Loren Schoel – The Bear

1920 was the last time the Syracuse men's crew had won the varsity eights in the IRA Championships.

After four decades of ups and downs, Syracuse's 1959 varsity eight had come tantalizingly, but heartbreakingly close. A crew whose seniors had won the IRA freshman race three years earlier, went into the 1959 IRA on Onondaga Lake favored to win, only to come in second to Wisconsin. That crew regrouped, won the right to represent the USA at the Pan American Games and then went on to win gold and become one of the most honored Syracuse crews of all time.

The Pan Am Games gold-medal-winning crew consisted of Chuck Mills at stroke, Captain Jim Kries, Nelson Miller, Ed Montesi, Mike Larsen, Tom Rouen, the coach's son Bob Schoel, Jim Edmonds and cox Jerry Winkelstein. Their coach was known as "The Bear."

Loren W. Schoel was not called The Bear because he was cuddly. He was a big–6'4"–burly man, with a fishing hat clamped on his head and a cigar clenched in his teeth–a U.S. Navy veteran, outwardly gruff and unbending. Some never saw past that. The guys on that Pan Am eight did.

"He was a father image to all of us," Tom Rouen says. "We all loved him. We played games with him. We pulled tricks on him and he'd get even with us by taking us down to the tanks … that's going to the end of the lake." Rouen lived with the Schoel family at the SU boathouse as a senior.

His son Bob, who rowed in the two seat says the Pan Am Championships, meant everything. "My dad did not like to lose so his Pan Am experience meant the world to him."

"He was a larger than life guy," the Captain, Jim Kries says. "I kind of was afraid of Coach Schoel and then at the same time I was delighted to be in his company."

"He was the world's largest marshmallow," Nelson Miller adds. "I loved him dearly. Loren was probably more of a father to me than my real father. He had some quirks. He was a little

23

stubborn in a way and that didn't work out too well for him in the end but he was a wonderfully dedicated man."

Schoel, a Washington state native, had coached Cornell's freshman crews to championships and the leaders of the newly formed Syracuse Alumni Rowing Association and the SU Athletics Department were looking for similar results at the varsity level when they brought him in in the fall of 1955 at the age of 45. He'd kept Vic Michalson on as freshman coach and "Mike" in turn handed over well-prepared athletes to the varsity coach.

Success had come quickly as the 1950s turned into the 1960s.

But it would not last.

Chapter 3
1962–1964 – A Feisty Bunch

When Coach Schoel looked over his returning crew squad in the fall of 1961, the memories of his 1959 Pan Am gold medal crew were still fresh. In 1960, an eight with most of the same men had just missed qualifying for the Olympics. But the victorious Pan Am Games veterans were gone to graduation and only senior Captain Gary Gardener remained from the Olympic Trials eight.

The other returning juniors and seniors had not come close to those heights, as the JV had finished last in the 1961 IRA and the varsity finished ninth.

For the sophomores it was a different story. They had just won the Eastern Sprints as freshmen and were third in the IRA–a disappointment to them. "We couldn't get alignment and the starter missed Dick's [coxswain Dick Hersh] hand–with 13 boats lined up that can happen–and the field left without us," stroke Dan Hogan says. "The race was a scramble from there and we ended up behind Washington and Cornell."

They were a feisty bunch.

A long-standing tradition had Orange frosh submit to having their heads shaved by varsity team members during Spring Camp at the boathouse. This group would have none of that, Giles van der Bogert recalls. "Gladstone, who was our number-seven-man, went nose-to-nose with the varsity. Steve dared one or all of them to try to cut his hair and told them to keep their hands off of his crew."

Fisticuffs were avoided in favor of a one-mile race between the varsity and freshman eights. If the freshmen won there would be no head-shaving.

The frosh kept their hair.

"Needless to say, our freshman boat had a very aggressive personality," van der Bogert says. "We believed, to a man, that it was our inherent right to cross the finish line first, regardless of the competition. It was really great."

Those freshmen beat good crews and survived adversity in 1961, winning over Harvard but suffering on the Severn River

25

at Annapolis a week later in miserable conditions as they lost to Cornell and Navy.

The frosh and varsity dealt with food-poisoning on a trip to Dartmouth, most of them having eaten bad stew packed for the trip. The Orangemen gutted it out to beat the Big Green but it was not easy. "It is a fact that the Catholics held the squad together as we had fish instead of beef stew and were able to pull the crew down the course," stroke Dan Hogan says.

The performance at Annapolis stuck in the Orangemen's craw but provided an opportunity and a powerful lesson, van der Bogert remembers. "A Navy launch passed us during the race and we were swamped by its wake. We were outraged, but Vic (Michalson) told us 'that's racing' and assured us that we would have an opportunity to reverse the results. A few weeks later we did just that, catching Navy on the last stroke of the Eastern Sprints final, with Cornell a very close third. It was a sweet victory for us replete with tons of trading shirts, but the sweetest part of all was Vic, later in the year, telling us that our performance was the reason that he was selected as the head coach at Brown. That kind of thing is difficult for a college freshman to appreciate but, looking back that may have been our most significant accomplishment as a crew."

Now Michalson was gone to Brown where crew had just been granted full varsity status and he was the first full-time coach. It wouldn't take long to bring Bruno to a position of strength. Gene Perry who had rowed in the seven seat in the 1957 Orange crew deemed the "Best in the East" had succeeded him as freshman coach at SU.

And those feisty freshmen were sophomores ready to assume their place at the varsity level.

It was never that simple.

Struggles

It doesn't happen often that a freshman crew moves up to the varsity level and into the first boat intact and it didn't happen this time. But it was close. The preseason report had six sophomore oarsmen in the first boat along with coxswain Dick Hersh. Hogan was stroke, Carl Parlato, who'd sat out the year before, was at 7, Ted Kakas at 6, Gladstone at 5, Donald Dick at 4 while van der Bogert held down the two seat. Only juniors Bill Sanford at 3 and Walter Barber at bow were able to crack the lineup, although senior Captain Gary Gardener was said to be pushing Sanford for the three seat.

The Bear was described as "looking for his finest sophomore crop since 1957 to engineer an upward swing in Syracuse crew fortunes this spring."

"As I recall we had very high aspirations after our frosh year and we were aware that our senior year was an Olympic year," Ted Kakas says.

Veterans including Tony Johnson, Jerry Van de Water, Chuck Rayfield and Gardener found themselves in the JV.

"The sophomores wouldn't let anybody in the boat," Bill Sanford says. "They wanted the same boat as their freshman year. They were a close crew and so I had to battle like hell to be in there." Sanford says certainly Johnson and Gardener had the experience, strength and fitness to be in the first boat. "I think that there were probably better rowers that were not in the boat but because of the chemistry and the psychology of that sophomore boat and the way they felt but you weren't going to prove it by going out there because they were a group together. They were a 'band of brothers,' if you will."

Looking back from the perspective of 50 years, van der Bogert had noted some animosity between the frosh and varsity in '61. Hogan clarifies it this way, "There was a lack of respect on our part. There were several upperclassmen with good high school and club experience and they were frustrated and negative. We did not understand the reasons at that time and mistook their attitude for a lack of competitiveness. When we went to the varsity, our attitude also changed."

The season opened with the Orangemen continuing their mastery over Dartmouth winning the Packard Cup again at home, with the JV and freshmen completing the sweep in two-mile races. But Cornell won the Goes Trophy in Ithaca for the first–of what would become nine years–in a row. The Orangemen were second, ahead of Navy. SU's JV was also second and the freshmen were third. In New Brunswick, the Orange varsity rebounded, taking the measure of Rutgers and Columbia. The JV was second and the freshmen again were third. The Eastern Sprints saw the SU varsity eight get through to the grand final only to finish sixth in a race in which Penn and Yale crossed the line in a dead heat for the championship.

The Orangemen had been third behind Penn and Yale in the morning heat, edging Navy for the last spot in the grands. The JV showed strong, finishing third in its event.

But the freshmen did not qualify.

At the IRA, SU's JV8 again finished in the top-three, taking bronze medals behind Navy and Cornell. Cornell won the freshman two-miler, with Rutgers and Washington next. SU was tenth.

The IRA varsity three-miler also went to Cornell, with Washington taking silver and California the bronze.

Syracuse wound up in an ignominious eleventh place.

Schoel had made changes in the lineups over the course of the season but when the official photo for the IRA was taken, only two upperclassmen were in the first boat; junior Walter Barber was now at seven and senior Captain Gary Gardener at three. Seven of the men from that freshman eight were in the varsity. Hogan stroked, Kakas was at 6, Gladstone at 5, Dick at 4, van der Bogert at 2 and Dave Norris was at bow. Hersh was the cox.

They'd had another season's experience.

Perhaps 1963 would be better.

1963

With support from the Class of '64–the 6'7" local boy and U.S. Army veteran–Bill Sanford was elected team captain for the 1962–1963 season. "I think it was based on my approach to rowing and also my approach with Loren who was the coach because there were times with Loren, with the coach, that I had to speak up and give the opinion of either the crew or myself in regard to something that was going on," he says.

He'd gotten into it with The Bear on one occasion as a junior, after getting permission to help paint a married teammate's apartment and coming back early to discover the varsity eight he normally was in was already out on the water. After practice, Sanford says he confronted the coach in front of the team, using "some vocabulary I shouldn't have."

The Bear pulled him into his office, Sanford says, and apologized. "At that point I think that the guys knew that I wasn't going to take a lot of guff if it's unfair." He wound up getting the team award for outstanding junior.

"My senior year we went out there and there was an awful lot of turmoil within the crew," Sanford says, "because of 'musical chairs' basically. There was always a different lineup and that was really where I think it started with Loren in terms of people wondering what was going on because he'd done an outstanding job with getting the '59 crew together and that sort of thing."

Along with a handful of seniors, most of the veterans of the '61 freshman champion eight were back as juniors. The sophomore class included sizable oarsmen such as Tom Prindiville and Bob Jackson, plus the very talented coxswain Jim Segaloff.

The names would change, class by class, year by year, but the results on the water looked familiar.

The Orange went to Hanover and came home again with the Packard Cup after a win over Dartmouth. The JV and frosh also won.

In the Goes Trophy race SU trailed two of the best collegiate crews that year in Cornell and Navy–a disappointment but no shame. The JV and freshmen also were third.

But a week later in New York, Columbia and Rutgers both out-rowed the Orangemen. "Beaten by two crews that we should have buried, and did in later races," van der Bogert notes. The JV managed a second-place finish but the freshmen were third.

That wasn't all that went wrong in New York City that weekend. "Our chartered Greyhound was stripped to the bone, tires and all, as it sat overnight on the mean streets near the Columbia campus!" van der Bogert remembers. "I can still see our driver sitting on the curb with his face buried in his hands as he contemplated the phone call that he needed to make to Greyhound. Ouch."

The team photo of the 1963 V8 has van der Bogert at

stroke, Tom Prindiville at 7, Kakas at 6, Bruce Buckley at 5, Dick at 4, Bill Sanford at 3, Hogan at 2, Barber at bow and Hersh at cox. But once again there were changes to these seatings from week to week. "We rarely sent the same V8 lineup out to race two weeks in a row," van der Bogert says.

Eastern Sprints: West Germans and Ithacans

Cornell's Big Red varsity was good enough in 1963 that it trailed only the guest Ratzeburg Crew from West Germany at the Eastern Sprints and actually out-rowed the defending Olympic champions in the morning heat.

"Facing high winds in the morning trial heats, the high-stroking Germans barely qualified," the *Harvard Crimson* reported. "They lost to Cornell by half-a-length, and just nosed out Wisconsin by two feet for second place and a ticket in the finals. The race was their first defeat in America.

"There wasn't much doubt about the German victory in the finals, however, as they welcomed the afternoon's smoother conditions for their extremely high stroke and never gave the Big Red a chance."

Since Ratzeburg was not eligible for the title, it went to Cornell. Yale took second and Princeton took third. Then it was Wisconsin, Brown and the Orangemen of Syracuse in sixth place.

Neither the SU JV nor the freshmen qualified for the grand finals.

"We rowed very well in the morning heats to qualify for the final," van der Bogert says. "Unfortunately, we had a very bad start in the final and never recovered. We improved throughout the season to the point that we were in the thick of things by the Sprints and rowed quite well in the IRA."

Orange Sixth at the IRA

In the week leading up to the IRA the Orange varsity was listed as a dark horse crew and came in for some praise in the *Syracuse Herald-American*. "The Syracuse varsity has looked very impressive to me," Brown's Vic Michalson said. "They're moving the boat well."

Schoel himself seemed optimistic. "The kids have been rowing well," he declared. "I'd say that our timing right now is better than anything I've seen in quite a while."

Better, but not enough to get the Orange into the medals, or even close.

Cornell completed its banner year by winning the varsity eights' championship. The Big Red covered the three miles in 17:24. Navy was second and MIT third. The Orangemen took sixth behind California and Wisconsin and was four lengths back of the Big Red.

van der Bogert stroked the SU eight, with Tom Prindiville at 7, Kakas at 6, Bruce Buckley at 5, Dick at 4, Bill Sanford at 3, Hogan at 2 and Norris in bow. Hersh was the cox.

The SU frosh also took sixth in their two-miler but were five lengths behind the winning Navy Plebes, who beat Washington by an eyelash.

The JV was tenth with Navy in front, fifty seconds ahead of the Orange oars.

Looking back decades later, some veterans of those teams say they were frustrated because the coach continually changed the lineups, looking for just the right combination instead of letting eight men work together to gain the swing and the confidence that would bring the needed speed. Ted Kakas, who'd been named captain for his senior year, recalls going to visit the coach in his apartment to talk about picking a lineup and sticking with it, but being turned away by the coach's wife and not getting to speak with The Bear.

Steve Gladstone, who would go on to great success as coach at Princeton, Harvard, Brown and California, left the squad after the Eastern Sprints that year, because of his frustration over the lack of consistency.

"He came to my room as captain at the Eastern Sprints," Bill Sanford says, "and told me that this was going to be his last race. And he told me that the reasons why is that he wasn't happy with the rowing at all and wasn't getting along with coach and hadn't liked some of the things that Loren had done, that coach had done, that affected him a great deal like when his mother passed (the year before). And there was a headline 'Rower's Mother's Last Wish: That He Row in the IRA.' And apparently it had come from Loren and Steve didn't know anything about it."

Gladstone confirms the story saying, "I was at a funeral in the morning and flew up and raced in the afternoon. Who knows? In retrospect it was not a good thing to do but that's what I did."

And the part about it being his mother's wish? "He (Schoel) made that up."

Gladstone says he indeed was frustrated when he left the team after the Sprints in his junior year. In retrospect "I think I could have been more tolerant but I wasn't and I can't replay it now. It was very difficult working with Loren. If I'd been more tolerant and mature I would have stayed through the IRA. My discontent was too transparent."

He says he might have come back senior year but he spent much of that year in France and when he returned he was married with a baby on the way.

1964

Big change was coming to America in the fall of 1963. Before it was over President John F. Kennedy would be assassinated. American involvement in Vietnam was beginning to grow. Hair was getting longer and drug experimentation and "sexual liberation" were just around the corner.

But for Syracuse Rowing, the only big change was the departure of freshman coach Gene Perry and the hiring of last year's varsity Captain Bill Sanford to take his place. Sanford had spent two years in the Army before coming to SU, so he had a couple of extra years on the incoming freshmen, but not many.

"Bill is a mature boy," Schoel declared in an SU news release. "He was a fine oarsman and leader as an undergraduate. He'll do just fine."

Perry, who was pursuing a doctorate, went to work in the Dean of Men's office.

"In my senior year as captain I apparently was doing some things that the coach liked," Sanford says, and "… during IRA Camp he took me into his apartment one evening where he had some guests. One of them was Dr. Tom Kerr. So Loren said we are going to talk to you and see if maybe you can coach the freshman crew next year if you'd like. And I said, 'man I'd love to do that and so I went in and talked to those folks and came out.'

"And then later that evening I was walking down the hallway and Edith [Schoel] came out and told me that I was going to be the freshman coach next year. So then the next morning Loren asked me if that would be OK and I said it absolutely would be and was very happy and couldn't wait."

The salary was $3,800, an amount Sanford says went a long way in those days and he supplemented it with a newspaper distribution route Vic Michalson helped him get with the *Post-Standard*. "I got a paper route district that had 38 paper boys and had to get the papers out there at three o'clock in the morning so they could get the papers delivered but it worked out well because I was making $125 a week off of that."

Red-Blooded He-Men

The attitude in the program was old school, straight-arrow. In a special bulletin from the Syracuse Alumni Rowing Association to incoming freshmen Coach School wrote, "Rowing is not an easy sport. It takes red-blooded he-men to participate in it."

The SARA publication added, "The 'Old Oars' say that rowing is the king of all sports. It breeds men of self-discipline, strong character and determination."

The freshmen who received those words included experienced oarsmen such as James "Ned" Kerr, Bill McCusker and John Campbell, all from Philadelphia, and Paul Dudzick of Buffalo. Dudzick had rowed well enough for the West Side Boat Club to have made *Sports Illustrated's "Faces in the Crowd"* feature. Kerr's father, Dr. Tom Kerr had co-founded SARA and named his son James for Jim and Ned Ten Eyck.

Among the walk-ons was a 6-foot-six-inch, 205-pounder from Jamesville-DeWitt High School, Gary MacLachlan. He had tried out for the SU football team but learned a hard lesson in an encounter with a great SU fullback.

"The first scrimmage we had as we were getting into early August was with the varsity and late in the scrimmage they sent me in as a defensive end and Jim Nance came around left end and I was wearing kneecaps for the rest of the day [having been run over by the powerful fullback] and shortly after that decided that football was probably not going to be my sport at Syracuse and packed it in."

At registration Big Mac found he could not walk beneath the oar set at six-feet-high at the entrance to Archbold Gym's basketball courts. Bill Sanford was right there to grab him up and MacLachlan soon was bitten by the rowing bug.

"I can remember starting to drool when I saw this guy," Sanford says. "I didn't waste any time in getting to him and telling him all the tremendous benefits of being on the crew and helping him through registration."

The freshman class looked solid in Sanford's first year. "They were a rambunctious group," Sanford says.

"They'd do anything you asked them to."

The varsity continued to be troubled under The Bear.

Winter and Spring of Discontent

The coach and his first boat coxswain butted heads at the end of fall practice. Dick Hersh tells it this way, "I went to him in confidence and explained that we had a terrible morale problem because the guys felt he was not boating the best guys on the basis of on-the-water evidence. This issue was a culmination of several years of the same situation but getting cumulatively worse and I felt an obligation to at least give him honest feedback. He blew up at me and suggested he knew better than I did what was needed and that I could forget ever being in the varsity boat again. I left the squad."

Senior John Reed would take over at cox, eventually to be replaced by junior Jim Segaloff in the spring.

SU started Spring Camp in typical fashion by clearing the floats in front of the boathouse of three-inches of snow, then heading up the Seneca River. The temperature was thirty-three degrees.

"It was miserable rowing into the wind and the boys came in with cold faces and fingers, but we got in a pretty good morning workout," Coach Schoel told a newspaper reporter. "I'm sure the coaches minded the weather a lot more than the kids did."

To get ready for the spring racing season the squad hosted a variety of crews at home on a single day, rowing six races and winning them all. The varsity eight beat the Detroit Boat Club and the JV topped Undine Boat Club of Philadelphia in 2,000-meter races. The third varsity beat St. Joseph's School of Buffalo, while the frosh and second frosh beat West Side Boat Club.

A varsity four made up of members of the Syracuse first eight beat the Undine spares later in the day over 2,000 meters so those spares could get a race in.

Schoel noted that he had plenty of port oars but not enough starboard oars. He also noted some problems with the release and said he had the crews working in fours to improve that.

Spring Season

The official season opened at home with the now traditional Packard Cup race against Dartmouth. Pete Gardner was head coach of the team still often called "The Indians" and Orange alum Andy Geiger was coaching the Dartmouth frosh.

Schoel had installed team Captain Kakas at stroke after starting the spring with Giles van der Bogert there. Giles was now at six. Dave Norris was at seven and Don Dick at five, for a Class of '64 stern four. Bob Jackson, Tom Prindiville, Bob Whyte and Paul Brown made up the bow four with John Reed coxing. Dan Hogan had dropped to the two seat in the JV, but would soon return to stroke the varsity eight.

The SU varsity got off to a bad start after a week of practicing quick starts. "It was horrible … the worst start in the world," coxswain Reed told the *Syracuse Herald-Journal*. "Water was splashing and we were rocking all over the place."

SU settled down and opened it up, spacing power moves between the rollers on Onondaga and won by seven lengths. Reed was rewarded in the traditional way. His teammates threw him into the water.

35

"Dave Norris at number 7 really came through for us," Schoel said. "If there'd been a tailwind today we'd have tried for a record." The headline read, "SU Crews Outsplash Dartmouth Rowers."

The JV and freshmen also won.

The Goes Trophy race again was a different story. The races would be rowed at Annapolis on the always troublesome Severn River over the Olympic distance of 2,000 meters. Harrison "Stork" Sanford's Cornell crew was defending IRA and Eastern Sprints champion, losing only to Ratzeburg before the Henley Regatta.

"This is the one we've been aiming for since fall," Schoel told *The Herald*. "We're going down there to win."

No such luck.

The Big Red took the varsity eights by more than three lengths, with Navy third even though Cornell's six-oar John Rothschild caught a crab near the finish. That made it three straight Goes Trophies for Cornell and its first win at Annapolis since 1952.

Schoel said afterward that a power boat wake hurt SU and missed Cornell, "Just as we were getting going, we shipped about three inches of water." The coach described himself as bitterly disappointed with the outcome but pleased with the way his varsity fought back.

Cornell took the JV race by rowing through Navy with Syracuse well behind.

The Cornell cubs completed the sweep by a length over SU. Navy was well back. The Orange had led after a quarter-mile but couldn't keep the lead. Bill McCusker had stepped in to stroke just before the race when it was determined that Paul Dudzick just couldn't go with a pulled muscle in his back.

The next week Syracuse took on Rutgers and Columbia in what was scheduled to be another 2,000-meter race at home, but with winds on Onondaga gusting to 50 miles-per-hour, the races were moved to the Seneca River at twilight. The makeshift course was described as being the "Henley distance" of 1-5/16th miles. In spite of under-stroking SU's 36 at 32, Rutgers nipped the Orange varsity eight by a one-tenth of a second, with Columbia well behind.

It was an evening of very tight racing. The Syracuse JV beat Rutgers by half-a-second, with Columbia third.

Columbia won the first freshman eights by a full second over SU, with Rutgers six seconds back.

SU's 3V beat Columbia, and Columbia's second frosh out-rowed the Orange.

At the Eastern Sprints Schoel had shaken up the varsity eight again. Sophomore Bob Whyte was now the stroke, with Ken Hafner was at seven, then Kakas and Dick were at six and five. Soph Bruce Wilson was at four, football running back Norm Magers, who'd decided to try crew, was at three, van der Bogert was at two and Bill Todd was in bow. Segaloff was the cox.

Going in Schoel felt Bill Sanford's lads had the best shot at success. "Our freshmen have as good a chance as anyone to qualify," he told a reporter.

Sanford put it this way, "If we can get by the morning heat I think we can take the afternoon one." Yale was favored to win it all and was in the heat with SU. After missing a couple of races with that bad back, Dudzick was at stroke once again, backed up by Jim Gulnac, Gleed Thompson, MacLachlan, Dale Cutler, Alex Pregnar, Dave Tousignant, and Kerr. Geoff Headley coxed.

The competition proved too stiff and the frosh did not get through to the grand final. Cornell won it over Harvard, BU, Brown, Yale and Princeton. Both the JV and varsity eights did make it to the grand finals and each wound up sixth. The varsity was second in the morning heat behind Harvard and edging Wisconsin.

It was Harvard's turn to move to the front in the varsity eights' grand finals. Cornell was second and Yale third. Then it was Wisconsin, MIT and the "Schoelmen."

The IRA

1964 was an Olympic year so the IRA at Syracuse was set up as a two-day event with races at 2,000 meters. Qualifying would be on Friday with the grand finals and consolations on Saturday.

A local newspaper reporter called SU's effort to that point "a fair-to-middling season," but said, "Syracuse is expected to be a definite threat this year."

Coach Schoel sounded ambitious, saying if the varsity eight finished first or second or within a length of the winner it would compete in the Olympic Trials in New York City July 8th–11th.

Instead SU did not make the grand final, finishing third in the consolation race, ninth overall. California, Washington and Cornell were the medalists.

The JV suffered the same fate–third in the consolation race. Washington won the grand finals over California and Cornell.

The Orange freshmen had the best finish, getting to the grand final where they were sixth behind Wisconsin, Brown, Columbia, Washington, and Cornell. Schoel now saw the men in that boat, the Class of '67 as they key to success in the coming years.

It's Not Over 'til It's Over

The promising Class of '64 was finished at Syracuse, its remaining members in a varsity eight that finished ninth in the IRA.

Decades later Ted Kakas expressed his frustration. "Four of our seniors returning for our senior year had won the National 4+ Championship that summer beating the Pan Am gold medal four, (including Ted Nash) by a length," he wrote in an e-mail. "When you add in Gladstone, Hogan, Don Dick and Paul Eckhardt (all from our frosh crew) we had a very strong core group even going into our third varsity campaign. Coach Schoel continued to put people into the varsity that I don't think any one of us had any confidence in. In our three varsity campaigns we finished last in the grand final every year."

But several of its members had more rowing to do that summer. Kakas, Norris, Dick and van der Bogert along with junior coxswain Segaloff were invited to take part in the "Laconia Plan." As van der Bogert describes it, it was organized to produce two collegiate all-star boats to compete in the 1964 Olympic Trials.

"Oarsmen were drafted from many other college programs, including Cornell, Wisconsin, Brown, etc. Scores of fine oarsmen descended upon the sleepy little town of Laconia, New Hampshire and camped out on cots crammed into the local high school gymnasium. It was right on the lake, but had no air conditioning.

"The coaches were Jack Frailey from MIT and Norm Sonju from Wisconsin.

"There were not enough boats available to get us all on the water," van der Bogert says. "So much of the initial competition was centered on running, isometrics, and other forms of torture. Coxswains with clipboards reported our every weak moment. You know the drill! Some oarsmen began to leave for home, longing for a kinder and gentler place to spend their summer. The first week culminated in a two-mile group run on the cinder track. It was a real mob scene, but the thing that really sticks in my mind is that the SU oarsmen all finished in the top five. I seem to recall that Norris and Kakas were the top two. This was early proof that SU was well represented, despite our lackluster collegiate season.

"Then the seat racing began. For the next two weeks we competed morning and evening for the sixteen coveted seats and the two cox positions. When all was said and done, all five Orange athletes were selected to row in the Olympic Trials! This was far more than from any other crew. I believe that the next most was Cornell with two. Several oarsmen from crews that had beaten us during the season remarked to me about this fact. They could not believe the talent level from SU in contrast to our mediocre race seasons of the past few years."

The coach and his new captain were looking for ways to improve on those mediocre results.

Chapter 4

1965–1966 – Confidence and Dashed Hopes

T he senior coxswain Jim Segaloff was the captain as the Orangemen prepared for the 1965 season and he had a message for his teammates heading into the fall semester in 1964. In a letter to team members, Segaloff wrote, "It appears to me for the first time since I can remember all the seats are wide open. The competition will be keen and you can be sure that those in the varsity eight surely deserve that distinctive label."

Fresh off the summer in Laconia, Segaloff wrote, "I feel that the experience I picked up this summer opened my eyes to many things. I rowed with and was coached by some of the finest coaches in the country; among them Harvard, Wisconsin, and MIT coaches. I also had the chance to cox some of the oarsmen who have been beating us for the past few years: this includes men from Cornell, Harvard and Wisconsin. I can honestly and sincerely say to you that I was not overly impressed. Here at Syracuse we are at no disadvantage–either in manpower or in coaching. I have found Coach Schoel's ability to be matchless. His ability, plus your desire and determination to improve your rowing, should add up to a fine season.

"Of course it's very easy to sit back in early September and contemplate the fine successes in the spring. The potential is there, but no one is going to hand out victories. We've all got to improve ourselves. Syracuse has not been where it belongs for more than three years. It's time for a change!"

In his preseason letter to the squad, Coach Schoel offered similar sentiments. "The whole squad needs to develop themselves physically, especially in the arms and shoulder girdle. So do your isometric exercises as well as the calisthenics. You know your weaknesses so start in now to correct them. We have had two or three very mediocre years. They have been quite frustrating, but I am confident that we are on our way back up again. With your help and determination we can, and will."

Schoel's men wrapped up the fall season with an Intrasquad Regatta, splitting up his thirty-five men into three eights. "We've had a good fall practice," the coach told the *Syracuse Post-*

Standard. "We've made a lot of progress."

The fall had included experimenting with the new shovel blades that Ratzeburg had popularized with its 1960 Olympics win. "The catch felt more solid with the spade blades," coxswain Jim Segaloff said.

Sophomores the Key

"We've got depth," Schoel said at the end of fall practice, "but the squad is going to be a young one."

Besides Segaloff only three other seniors were on the spring roster: Bob Jackson, Tom Prindiville and Dick Foreman. The junior veterans were Bob Whyte, Bruce Wilson, Dennis Zutant, Bill Rossell, Tom Denver and Virgilio (Vic) Ciullo. Fifteen sophomores were listed including Dudzick, Gulnac, MacLachlan, Pregnar and Kerr who'd been in that sixth-place IRA boat as freshmen and three coxes–Headley, Pat Nalbone and Ted Horowitz.

"Sophomores will be the key to success," Schoel told a reporter as the spring season neared. At least the biggest of them was paying careful attention to what the coach had to say. Asked about The Bear nearly 50 years later, Gary MacLachlan sighs. "Yeah," he says. "Scary. Intimidating. And with some kind of fear of God making you want to work as hard as you possibly can. I don't remember him as a huge tactician other than working us incredibly hard. You know, Baldwinsville and back in a snowstorm, as soon as the ice went out.

"He would critique your style occasionally but mostly it was pounding your legs and getting your arm strength and coordinating your arm strength and your leg drive so that you got your maximum power, but–and I remember the stubby cigar. And I remember his gruffness … and the hat, the big duffle hat."

"A Dismal 1965 Season"

That's what *Herald-Journal* columnist Arnie Burdick called that spring in retrospect. It is fair to say the Orangemen did not get as far as they and their coach has hoped. They would have no home races that spring until the IRA in June.

There had been the usual friction between the freshmen and varsity with the yearlings winding up with shaved heads during Spring Camp and wise guy John Nicholson winding up getting a tetanus shot after an unsuccessful effort to fight off the upperclassmen led to a scrape against one of the bunks crammed into the boathouse dormitory area. All in good fun, more or less.

There was also some resistance to the tradition of freshmen having to wear SU beanies and bow ties on road trips until their first win. Coach Schoel let it be known that any freshman who refused would not get on the bus to Dartmouth to open the season. Frosh Coach Bill Sanford worked out a compromise where the frosh could choose beanies or bow ties.

Everybody traveled.

Junior Bob Whyte had emerged as the varsity stroke heading into the spring, with Kerr at 7, Gulnac at 6, MacLachlan at 5, junior Bruce Wilson at 4, senior Tom Prindiville at 3, Bill McCusker at 2 and senior Dick Foreman in bow. Dudzick stroked the JV and Nalbone had won the cox position.

The Orange varsity, JV and first freshman crews came out ahead in the two-milers on the Connecticut River. In the varsity race, with Whyte stroking and wearing an old brown derby hat, SU trailed early then turned on a powerful sprint in the final 500 yards to defeat Dartmouth by one length.

The JV took the Big Green by a length-and-a-quarter, the same margin of victory the first frosh came up with. The frosh covered the two-miles in 10:01.2, just two-tenths of a second slower than the varsity. That was that for the beanies and bow ties. Dartmouth salvaged a win in the second frosh race.

"Schoel's eager young varsity looked ragged at the start but recovered to lead by 3/4 of a length at the halfway point," a newspaper report said. "It was our sprinting that did the trick," the coach opined. "Of course it was a brand new boat for us too. The boys were a little tense and they didn't settle down too well for three-quarters of a mile. But I feel they're rarin' to go now … we want the next one."

The next one was the Goes Trophy race against Navy and Cornell on Cayuga Lake. However, as much the Orangemen may have wanted it, they didn't get it. The varsity finished four lengths behind the Big Red, which topped the Midshipmen by half-a-length. Navy returned the favor in the JV race, with the Orangemen again well behind. The Big Red took the first frosh easily over Navy and Sanford's frosh were never in it. Cornell also beat the second frosh in a one-miler.

The varsity went to Boston looking for redemption and found anything but that. "Last week we weren't putting the power on right," Schoel said, "but now I think the kids' sprints are pretty good."

He'd moved Paul Dudzick into the varsity stroke seat, saying he'd be more effective in a 2,000-meter sprint race. Prindiville was now at 7, Gulnac at 6, MacLachlan at 5, Wilson at 4, Pregnar at 3, McCusker at 2 and Kerr in bow. Segaloff was the constant at cox.

Racing on the Charles River, the Orangemen finished last behind MIT, Boston University, Wisconsin and the previously-beaten Dartmouth. SU was more than a length behind the Big Green and four lengths behind the Engineers who ran away with the race.

Eastern Sprints

Dudzick and Prindiville stayed at stroke-seven for the Eastern Sprints, but Schoel moved Dennis Zutant into the six-seat and dropped Gulnac back to two and McCusker to the JV. "It's gonna be a tough one," he said, "but I think we'll be rowing our best in the Eastern Area Competition."

At the Eastern Sprints, the SU varsity eight came close to a taste of that redemption it had missed in Boston. "Lightly-regarded Syracuse almost managed to eliminate Cornell," a newspaper story said. But "almost" was the key word. Cornell took SU by half-a-length in the morning heat and grabbed the second spot in the grand final, behind Brown. Apparently out of gas, the Orange varsity was last in the "Reserve Section Races" in the afternoon.

The freshmen also were last in the second level race, having finished fourth in the morning.

The JV never got that far, being eliminated from further racing by a last-place finish in the heat, half-a-second behind Brown.

Harvard swept the grand finals.

IRA – A Non-Factor

The 14th annual Syracuse Regatta of the Intercollegiate Rowing Association was held June 19th on Onondaga Lake. The host crews were guaranteed a spot in the finals but that was only because the IRA had returned to the 3-miler for varsities and JVs and two-milers for freshmen, after going to the Olympic distance of 2,000 meters with qualifying heats in 1964.

Coach Schoel was working his crews twice a day leading up to the IRA and as other crews arrived early, their coaches took the same approach.

Visiting crews stayed free of charge in the Boys and Girls Building at the State Fairgrounds, taking a ten-minute bus ride between there and the SU Boathouse. The Orange crews also bused over for meals, driving the security guard at the entrance nuts by shouting "Excelsior!" out of the bus windows. He apparently never caught wise that they were calling out the state motto, which was writ large on a sign above the guard shack.

A local columnist noted "a new plaything" the Wisconsin oarsmen were using to pass the time between workouts. "It's called a 'flying frisbee' and is similar to a plate in form that whisks around the air much like a glider."

The Orange crews did not show up in the Coaches Poll leading into the IRA. Cornell was the prohibitive favorite in the varsity and freshman races, with Navy seen as the likely JV winner.

The Herald's Arnie Burdick reported that Paul Quinn's Navy oarsmen "shocked the rowing world" on Saturday afternoon, sweeping all three races. The Plebes took Dartmouth by a length-and-a-half in the freshman race. The favored Middies won by the same margin over Wisconsin. And to top it off, the Navy varsity, stroked by "local boy Fred Boberg" of Cazenovia, took the lead off the start and never gave it up, beating the favored Big Red by a full length. Cornell was closing in about 100 yards from the finish when six-man John Rothschild, rowing his first race of the season, caught a boat-stopping crab.

Syracuse's freshman boat wound up ninth, as did the JV. The varsity eight was 13th, beating only Princeton and Columbia.

Coach Schoel's fall season confidence that "we are on our way back up again," had been dashed. Instead the "two or three very mediocre years" had added another.

1966

The lackluster spring season of 1965 did not discourage many of the athletes from coming back that fall although the senior class again was thin in numbers. Bob Whyte returned and now was captain, joined by Dennis Zutant, Norm Magers, Vic Ciullo and Tom Denver. The junior class was the deepest and it included John Campbell, Paul Dudzick, Jim Gulnac, Ned Kerr, Gary MacLachlan, Alex Pregnar, Gleed Thompson and cox Pat Nalbone among others.

Sophs moving up included Joe Driscoll, Andy Harrison, John Nicholson, Wally Okenica, Mark Sprague, Dick Yochum, and cox Alan Bell.

The Bear said his only key loss was the excellent coxswain Jim Segaloff who had graduated.

The coach wanted his men in shape but told a reporter he was counting on them to set and follow their own standards so he did not give them a set of training regulations. "Crew is a sport that has to come from the inside anyway," he told *The Herald's* Arnie Burdick. "It has to come from right here (he taps his heart). And you know what? The leaders of this squad ... the older boys have taken the bull by the horns. They had a lot of discussions and they've come up with a set of training regulations that hardly varies one iota from what I would have written for them. But these come from the inside (tap ... tap ... tap) and this is good."

School had praise for his Captain, Bob Whyte. "Whytey's a fine boy," he offered. "He's doing a real good job, and so is Tommy Denver, the President of the Crew Club. The two of them are giving us leadership and working together nicely as a team.

They've helped pick up the spirit and attitude this year."

Weighty Issues

The Orange spent the winter months as usual, rowing in the tanks in the Crew Room in the basement of Archbold Gymnasium, running stairs inside the gym and outside in Archbold Stadium and doing calisthenics and isometrics. The Bear frowned on weight lifting and those who engaged in it did so surreptitiously.

He expressed concern about his oarsmen being too heavy, telling a reporter that light crews–like Rutgers University's "Rabbits"–seem to get into shape faster and as a result can learn to pull together as a team much earlier. "Yeah," Gary MacLachlan recalls. "6'6" and 200 pounds, 210 maybe at my most and I would always say to him, 'Coach, I think my bones weigh 210 pounds. There's nothing else I can do.' But I was always in a sweat suit and always working out other than the lovely tanks and the hydraulic rowing machines we had back then, that was about it, and running the Archbold Stadium stairs. That was a nightmare."

Yet when the coach began to construct his first varsity in the spring it was mostly the big strong guys in the first boat. Captain Bob Whyte was stroke at 6'2" and 190 pounds. 6'1" and 200-pound Alex Pregnar who liked weightlifting was at 7, at six was Jim Gulnac, 6'2" and 190, Big Mac was 6'6" and 205 at five, and Bruce Wilson 6'4" and 195 was at four. Even the bowman, Ned Kerr came in for praise from Schoel, partly for getting bigger. "The boy is a real tiger," the coach said. "He's put on weight since coming to Syracuse and certainly has improved greatly." Kerr was listed at 6'2" and 190 pounds.

The JV and third boats were considerably lighter but would irk the coach during practice throughout the season by deliberately over-stroking and often beating the varsity in practice pieces.

SU was trying some new equipment during spring practice.

The Bear had a new "Italian-rigged shell" coming and was trying out spade oars. "The wider blade should mean you can move more water after the catch," Schoel told a reporter. "And

47

here's another little gimmick. It's a push-button or adjustable control. You'll remember the old oar used to be locked in the rig. Now you can move it back and forth here, depending upon the wind.

"If you're riding into a headwind you can use a longer sweep. Then, if the wind is with you, shorten up and row a faster beat."

"How much faster will the new spade blades and rig make the boats go?" the inquiring reporter wanted to know.

"That's a good question," Schoel replied. "That's what we're all hoping to find out ourselves."

A Diamond in the Rough

Early in the preseason Schoel had experimented with Whyte, Dennis Zutant and Paul Dudzick as varsity stroke and was never entirely happy. Then one day all three were not able to make it to practice, so he tried another junior in the seat. To The Bear, Doug Kraai looked like the answer. Kraai had rowed in the JV two seat the previous year. He was a mere 6'1 and 180 pounds, but he was strong–sculpted–in a time before the term became popular.

With the junior from Fairport stroking, Schoel saw the varsity boat coming together. With Pregnar at 7 behind him, the boat found timing. Columnist Arnie Burdick opined that "a healthier attitude, an early spring, coupled with the discovery of an able pace-setter, Doug Kraai has put some kick back into the Orange Navy."

"The funny thing is," Schoel said, "Kraai is such a modest kid that he keeps referring to himself as 'the poorest oarsman' on the squad. In fact at one point, he came to Bill Sanford and said he was going to quit because he just didn't feel that he was good enough." The coaches begged to differ.

Spring – A Young Oarsman's Fancy

Syracuse Alumni Rowing Association co-founder Dr. Tom Kerr was a surgeon in Philadelphia and had brought crew to Drexel Institute there. He brought his Drexel squad to Onondaga for a set of preseason races in the spring and while there was glad-handing all around, the bigger, stronger Orangemen made quick work of the visitors, winning every race. Dr. Kerr's son Ned, of course, was in the SU varsity bow-seat. The best race of the day was between SU's second and third varsities, with Dennis Zutant stroking the 3V to a quarter-length win over the 2V as Drexel trailed well behind. SU started what Schoel called "the toughest schedule in years" by welcoming Dartmouth and Northeastern for the Packard Cup on April 23th.

The varsity flew over the two miles, beating Dartmouth and the Huskies in the near-record time of 10:00.6. Timer Dr. Bruce Chamberlain, the other SARA co-founder, checked his watch and whistled. The time was just three seconds off the course record set by the Navy eight that went on to Helsinki and won Olympic gold in 1952.

The Orange JV, 3V and second frosh also won, but the first freshmen could not complete the sweep, trailing both Northeastern and Dartmouth.

The varsity was psyched. Burdick reported that "the varsity was so charged up they came out for a spin on Sunday morning." Schoel said he found a note tacked on the bulletin board. "We're coming out Sunday morning, Coach. Be ready.

"They all showed up and we took a light spin. We rowed three-four miles. So we were able to start right out on Monday and get in a full week of work."

He pointed out the success of three local products in the varsity eight, MacLachlan, Pregnar and three-man Dick Murray. And he said "the win Saturday has given [the team] a little 'oomph.' They've got plenty of enthusiasm now." During the week the crew christened its new $3,000 shell, the "Orange Challenger."

Close But No Cigar

That next Saturday SU was home again for the Goes Cup races and this time gave Cornell's Big Red a fight. It just wasn't quite enough. Rowing through a constant drizzle, the Orange got a jump but the Big Red fought back. The traded the lead at least three times as cox Pat Nalbone upped the cadence for SU and

Cornell answered. In the last 30 strokes, Cornell out-sprinted SU and won it by half-a-length, with Navy well behind the Orange. Neither crew had ever gained open water and a newspaper report called it "one of the most exciting contests on Onondaga Lake."

"It was some horse race," Schoel said. "We'll be in there pitching against Cornell next week."

With a revised lineup that saw some moves up from the 3V, the SU JV, stayed unbeaten with a length win over Cornell and Navy well back. Cornell was going after the Orange 400 yards from the finish when a Big Red oarsman caught a crab and SU rowed home safely.

After a 45-minute delay because of weather–waves sometimes peaked at a foot-and-a-half–the first frosh, with Frank Doble stroking, came to life and knocked off Cornell by a length-and-a half with Navy third. The Orange cubs got credit for handling the choppiest water of the day and cox Rich Kortright got credit for solid steering.

The varsity and frosh rowed with spade oars, while the JV stuck with standards.

The third varsity edged Cornell by a second and the second frosh lost badly to Cornell.

Strike Two

As Schoel had indicated, the Orange had another shot at Cornell the following Saturday as invited guests in the traditional Carnegie Cup races with Yale and Princeton on Cayuga Lake. He changed the lineup again, moving Dennis Zutant and Jim Fullerton up to two and bow from the JV, swapping them with Captain Bob Whyte and Ned Kerr. Bruce Wilson also was bumped to the JV in favor of Wally Okenica, "a Vestal [New York] lad and one of SU's top rookies," according to a newspaper report.

"It's not that the kids didn't try their heart out all the way against Cornell and Navy," Schoel commented, "but I can tell you one thing–they weren't as sharp for the entire two miles as the showed with that terrific time [against Dartmouth and Northeastern] the week before."

It was a two-mile race along the west shore course on

Cayuga Lake and Cornell was not a gracious host once the crews were on the water. SU took the early lead, stroking at 35 but quickly fell back in favor of the Big Red and the Eli who drew even then took the lead. Princeton meanwhile had moved through the Orangemen. Down the stretch Cornell was strong and Yale ran out of gas. The finish had Cornell a length over Princeton, with Yale next and Syracuse last.

The Orange JV lost its unbeaten status as Cornell lost its rudder and collided with the SU riggers mid-race. Yale, already in the lead, cruised to the finish two lengths ahead of Princeton with a determined SU crew another length back. Cornell had to stop and be towed in. The freshman race also saw Yale take it over Princeton with Cornell third and Syracuse last.

Eastern Sprints Bring More Changes

The Bear changed up his varsity for the Eastern Sprints, moving Paul Dudzick into the stroke seat and Dick Yochum into seven from the JV while switching Kraai back to two. "The Sprints are run over a 2,000-meter course," Schoel said. "I feel that Dudzick will have good power and control over the shorter distance. He teams up well with Yochum. Kraai stabilizes the boat nicely at two." Gulnac and MacLachlan and Okenica remained at six, five, and four but sophomore Andy Harrison was now at three. Ned Kerr was back in the bow and Nalbone coxed.

The weather on Onondaga Lake was anything but good as SU prepared to go to Worcester. All the previous week "waters were too rough for rowing," the paper reported. "Tuesday, with waves breaking over the boathouse pier, Schoel had no choice but to make his charges run. Wednesday things were calm enough to allow the team to drag its shells out again."

The Orange varsity went after it on Saturday morning but just couldn't keep pace with Harvard and Yale. The Crimson took their rivals by a second in the heat, but both qualified, leaving SU a length or so behind and consigned to the Reserve Section Races in the afternoon. SU got it done there, taking Navy by half-a-length. Wisconsin, Northeastern, BU and Dartmouth followed. The Orange time would have been good for fifth in the grand final, which Harvard won over Brown and Cornell.

The JV struggled in its heat, finishing fourth behind Harvard, Rutgers and Dartmouth. In the consolation final the Orange was third, in a terrific fight with Brown, Cornell and Dartmouth. Bruno beat the Big Red by half-a-length, with SU two more seats back and Dartmouth another half-a-length behind.

Sanford's freshmen missed the grand final by a length, coming in third behind Harvard and Northeastern. The Orange cubs also capitalized in the afternoon consy, squeaking by Columbia, as Navy, Brown, Princeton and MIT followed.

IRA – Wounded Orangemen Struggle to the Finish

Being on home water was about the only thing Loren Schoel's varsity had going for it in the 1966 IRA. "Syracuse … impressed in early outings but haven't had much success lately," *The Herald's* Bob Snyder wrote. Apparently the seventh-place finish at the Sprints didn't count for much.

IRA Camp had brought more V8 changes with Kraai back at stroke and the muscular Alex Pregnar in at seven. But soon The Bear had lost Kraai, Pregnar and six-man Gulnac to injury. Schoel called them "the guts of my crew" and talked of possibly having to scratch his JV. Still, "the varsity will be represented on race day," he said. "We'll give a pretty good account of ourselves."

By the time the crew headed for the starting line on June 18th, the continuing shifts had brought Okenica into the stroke seat, Yochum to seven, Captain Bob Whyte to six, Zutant back into the V8 at two, and sophomore John Nicholson up from the JV and into the bow.

In the pre-IRA Coaches Poll, the Orange frosh got a pair of votes for third and the JV got one vote. But the varsity got none. Still the Orange eight were at least called a dark horse in what was considered "a wide open affair." California and Princeton shared that dark horse label.

The SU freshman wound up with the best showing of the day, finishing fifth. Penn, Princeton and Wisconsin took the medals.

Dartmouth, which was said to have switched its V8 with

its second boat, wound up winning the JV title, with Penn and Cornell next. The Orange boat was eighth in the three-miler.

The varsity struggled to a tenth-place finish out of 15 boats. Rutgers took ninth by a fraction of a second, while Washington, Dartmouth, UCLA, MIT and Columbia were behind.

It was Wisconsin's day to be champions as the Badgers beat a hard-charging Navy crew by half-a-length. Penn was third.

Some Kind of Obligation

The Bear and his big five-man were already looking ahead. "It probably wasn't until the end of our junior year," Gary MacLachlan says, "that he began to take me under his wing, kind of as a–I don't know what I'd call it, probably a quasi-parent–but, you know, grooming me to do something my senior year. And as it turned out over the summer between junior and senior year it was to be captain. And we corresponded a lot over the summer and I became his last captain. And with that there was kind of an obligation to, 'Jesus. Let's make our senior year something here. Let's … .'"

Chapter 5
1967 – The Bear's Last Stand

The Orange crew had a deep group of seniors and some promising sophomores heading into Spring Camp in 1967. Senior Captain Gary MacLachlan was back along with the experienced Philadelphia contingent of Ned Kerr, Bill McCusker, and John Campbell, veteran stroke Paul Dudzick, and Gleed Thompson, Pete Schmeckebier and Jim Fullerton. Senior cox Pat "Nails" Nalbone was back as well.

Frosh stroke Barry Singer, another Philadelphia guy returned along with Big Roy Sea, Lynn "Gunn" Gardner, Alan More, John Clark, Nick Entrikin and Frank Doble as sophomores.

The junior class was depleted with several veterans of the 1966 varsity and JV having decided they were no longer committed to the time and work that crew demanded. But Andy Harrison, was aboard along with fellow oarsmen Dick Yochum, Mark Sprague, Joe Driscoll and Vic Meyen plus coxswain Alan Bell.

So The Bear seemed to have reason for optimism. Could he have foreseen that this would be his last season as SU's head coach?

Bill Sanford says he had a sense of it. "I had a more and more difficult time with the rowers in defending The Bear," he says. "They would say a particular problem or a specific problem or the lineup changes and all of this stuff, and I'd say if the boat's going fast there'd be no reason to make any changes if the boat was going to be competitive and be fast and so the coach is trying to find that magic lineup that is going to be fast that he feels is going to be competitive. And I kept trying to say that and I did say it and it got to the point where some of the guys weren't listening anymore."

On the Water

After an icy winter, the squad got on the water for the first time on March 22nd, the day before the beginning of Spring Camp, although a few of the athletes missed practice because

55

of midterms. The next day, with Nalbone on a week's leave of absence, Bell coxed the varsity eight with Kraai at stroke, then Campbell, Harrison, MacLachlan, Sea, More, Singer and Entrikin. Joe Peter was the JV cox with Dudzick stroking, then Kerr, Thompson, Yochum, Schmeckebier, Steve Rogers, Driscoll and Fullerton.

The lineups would change almost daily through the rest of camp and leading up to the opening races. When the crews rowed a two-mile time trial the morning of April 1st, Nalbone was back in the V8 with Singer now stroking. Rogers was at seven, then Kraai, MacLachlan, Harrison, Campbell, Frank Doble and More. The V8 covered the distance on flat water into a headwind in 12:11 with the JV way behind at 12:40.

A week later the crews rowed the eleven-mile round trip to the south end of Onondaga and back, taking a half-mile and a mile time trial along the way. The frosh won the miler, with the V8 third. Coach Schoel's log read "202 miles rowed, 85 behind last year." There was concern among the troops that not enough work had been put in.

The Bear continued to experiment with spade oars (known as Macon style) and with shaving the handles of standard oars.

Dudzick, McCusker, Singer and Kraai moved in and out of the varsity stroke seat, with combinations behind them varying until two days before the season-opening Packard Cup race at Dartmouth, Schoel settled on Singer as his varsity stroke. Now it was Rogers at seven, then John Clark, Yochum, Sea, Campbell, Kraai and More.

"Every day we seem to play musical chairs," Schoel told *The Daily Orange*. It didn't help that senior Captain MacLachlan was sidelined by back spasms and wouldn't make the trip.

The Bear wasn't worried about the Big Green but MIT was another matter. "I think we can beat Dartmouth, but MIT will be tough," he said.

His words would prove prophetic.

Packard Cup

On what the *Syracuse Herald American* described as

a "dark, dreary afternoon on the Connecticut River," MIT out-rowed the Orangemen by two lengths, with the Big Green another length-and-a-half back. Tech blasted off with a 40-stroke start and then rowed the body of the race at 33 strokes-per-minute, two higher than Syracuse. It ended a nine-year winning streak for SU in the Packard Cup competition.

The JV, with Dudzick stroking, also trailed MIT by a little over a length, but beat Dartmouth easily. The SU frosh were the only bright spot, with Bill Sanford's lads taking the Engineers by a couple of lengths and Dartmouth, which had hit some debris on the way to the starting line, well behind.

MacLachlan returned to the V8 engine room on Monday, starting the week when Syracuse would head for Annapolis for a showdown on the Severn with Navy's Midshipmen and the Cornell Big Red in the traditional Goes Trophy race. But on Thursday, The Bear made four changes in the varsity midway through the team workout, moving Dudzick and Yochum from the JV to stroke-seven in the varsity, and moving John Clark up to the six-seat, swapping Roy Sea back to four. The JV had clobbered the varsity on the way out.

A frustrated Pat Nalbone was ready to quit the team but reconsidered, not wanting to leave his teammates in the lurch. When The Bear heard about it, he booted the coxswain from the squad. Alan Bell moved up to cox the Orange varsity.

Goes Trophy

The Severn was not well-policed and all three varsity crews found that out the hard way on Saturday. Pleasure boats set off wakes that blasted all three shells about a half-mile into the two-miler, with Navy in the lead. They kept rowing and when the wakes had passed, Stork Sanford's Big Red had a lead it held onto, winning over the Orange by more than three lengths and taking the Goes Trophy for the seventh-straight year. SU and Navy battled to the finish and the Orange edged the Middies by exactly one second. Schoel said his crew "rowed a real gutsy race."

One SU oarsman described rowing on the Severn as "like riding the pipelines at Malibu."

SU was third in the JV, way behind Navy and Cornell. Bill Sanford's frosh remained unbeaten, whipping Cornell by a couple of lengths, with Navy trailing. Nalbone returned to the fold on Monday and was inserted into the third varsity the following day.

Vic Michalson's Brown crew was coming to Syracuse on Saturday and The Bear decided to keep his varsity eight intact, including leaving junior Alan Bell in the coxswain seat. "I think we can probably come out on top," Schoel told *The Daily Orange*. Citing the swamping on the Severn, "We really don't know how fast we are," he said.

But some crew members worried among themselves that they had not worked hard enough as a team and were not in the shape they needed to be to stay with solid crews. Whatever the reasons, Syracuse would prove to be no match for the Bruins' varsity.

Battered by Brown

A *Herald American* account called the result of the varsity race "embarrassing." With Dudzick stroking, the Orangemen rowed high at 34–35 strokes a minute, the paper reported and "appeared to be rushing its slides while not settling" well after the start.

Brown, on the other hand, rowed "only a straight up, smooth 31 but was gaining open water with every stroke." The margin of victory was more than nine lengths over the two-mile course. "How could we stay close to Cornell and edge out Navy, then flop so badly against Brown?" The Bear wondered in *The Post-Standard's* account.

The Jayvee did better, but still was not close, as Brown out-rowed SU by three-and-a-half lengths. Again, the Orange Frosh provided something to cheer about, remaining undefeated with a nine-and-a-half length victory of their own. Bill Willson stroked it and the frosh used spade blades to propel the boat.

Wholesale Change

On Monday, Pat Nalbone was back coxing the varsity

eight and Schoel had shaken up the crew. Six sophomores were now pulling the oars. Barry Singer was stroke, Steve Rogers at seven, then the two seniors, Kraai and MacLachlan, Sea, Gardner, Doble and More. Only Big Mac and Big Roy kept their seats. Dudzick was demoted to third boat stroke. The Eastern Sprints were less than a week away.

"All right! I think we're on our way," Schoel called out repeatedly according to an article in *The Daily Orange* the next morning. "You've all earned your spurs," he told the sophomores. Former Vesper Coach Al Rosenberg turned up and rode in the coach's launch, offering some advice on drills and rigging.

On Wednesday, Sea was out of commission with a case of gout and replaced at four in the varsity by fellow soph John Clark. After the workout Nalbone said the boat felt the best it had all season.

On Thursday the varsity, JV and freshmen took a 2,000-meter time trial together. The frosh won.

On Friday the feathers hit the fan.

SU Crew Adrift in Mediocrity

That was the title of the two-part article written by Bob Snyder and published in *The Herald-Journal* as the Orange squad headed for Worcester and the Eastern Sprints. "Why is the Syracuse University crew picture so bleak as Loren Schoel prepares his oarsmen for Saturday's Eastern Sprints at Worcester, Mass.?" it began. It cited recent success. "There was the '56 frosh ... that went all the way in the IRA. Then that '59 shell ... that went on to win the Pan American Games. In '60, SU reached the Olympic Trials Finals, and in '61 the frosh set a still-standing Eastern Sprints record.

"But what about the past half dozen seasons? A sixth-place finish was The Hill eight's top IRA showing during that span and being an also-ran doesn't satisfy a lot of people.

"Even School admits things aren't looking good," the article went on. "'That loss to Brown last Saturday was the most humiliating I've ever suffered,'" he was quoted as saying.

The story cited aging facilities and lack of interest among

the student body hurting the crew program. And it pointed out morale as a problem that former oarsmen mentioned, and "the mortality rate between freshman and sophomore year."

Schoel was compared to Northeastern's Ernie Arlett, who'd turned the Huskies' varsity into a two seed behind Harvard at the Eastern Sprints. The Bear had his defenders in the article. "He's a fine teacher of rowing," said Andy Geiger, the Assistant Athletics Director who'd been a spare oar for the '59 Pan Am Crew. "He brought us back from the bottom of the heap [after coming to Syracuse from Cornell]," Geiger said.

"Loren teaches the old school of rowing and we did all right with it when we won the Pan American Games title," said Tom Rouen, who was the three-oar in that boat. "But there's plenty of room for improvement," he said.

"The new style used by Vesper, Harvard, Princeton and others can only be used by 'physical giants' and our boys aren't that big," Schoel said. "We've experimented with spades, but we use the standards now. And Stork [Sanford at Cornell] has gone back to them too."

"It's true that for some time, crewmen have talked about the communications problem between coach and crew," Snyder wrote. "But no one ever said that Ben Schwartzwalder [football] or Fred Lewis [basketball] have been running popularity contests on The Hill. And they've won more than their share."

It concluded with this: "The problems are many and the solutions varied. But one thing is agreed upon. An IRA victory would make for a happy crew family on The Hill."

Struggle at the Sprints

SU's varsity opened in a morning heat against Penn, Northeastern, Princeton and Rutgers with the top two to advance to the grand final. The Orange finished fourth, a length behind third place Princeton, but edged Rutgers for a spot in the consolation final. Penn took Northeastern to win the heat and both advanced to the top level.

The afternoon consolation race went to Princeton, with the Orangemen again in fourth behind Wisconsin and Brown.

There was some small solace in that SU defeated MIT. Navy trailed. Harvard clobbered Penn to win the grand final.

The Orange JV also was fourth in its morning heat but rallied in the consolation final to win by a second over BU.

Navy edged Sanford's frosh in the morning qualifier–the first time they'd tasted defeat, although the point was to get to the grand final and they did. Once there the Orange cubs were up against their toughest competition yet. Harvard won by open water, with a surprising Rutgers crew edging Princeton for second and Syracuse fourth, nearly two lengths back. Navy and Penn trailed.

The Orange squad returned to Long Branch to prepare for the IRA.

Letters to the Editor

Decades later, Captain Gary MacLachlan would look back on his senior season and concede there were serious problems. "We knew Loren was having disappointments and troubles and wasn't progressing the team and the program like he had at Cornell as a frosh coach and that he had anticipated and certainly did with the '59 crew. We weren't going in that direction for some reason–whether it was recruiting–or whether it was the competition was doing something different and getting better."

There was continued grumbling among some of the troops and finally senior Paul Dudzick decided to give voice to it in a letter sent to and published in *The Herald-Journal*. Following up on Bob Snyder's two-part article, Dudzick wrote "I believe that our problem begins with, as your article suggests, the rapport that exists between Coach Schoel and his oarsmen."

Dudzick conceded it is the coach's job "to dictate policies on style, techniques and methods of training." But, he wrote "It becomes increasingly difficult to believe in them when we see ourselves 'standing still' in relation to other college crews."

At the Sprints, he wrote, "any layman could observe every better-than-average team using the faster, smoother easier to row European style. Yet when a Syracuse oarsman attempts to question the coach on his thoughts concerning the new style, technique or methods he is marked as a rebel and his question remains unanswered. This is where the rapport breaks down."

Dudzick's fellow senior Ned Kerr also wrote a letter that apparently never was sent, in which he said, "I believe that Mr. Schoel is afraid to try something new, afraid that it may mean his job if it doesn't produce some winning crews. Well, if this present trend of losing continues it won't make much difference anyway."

When Coach Schoel posted the list of team members invited to stay for IRA Camp Dudzick's and Kerr's names were not on it. Their SU Crew careers were over.

The IRA

With final exams done, the squad settled into life at the boathouse, a spot the Orange athletes had pretty much to themselves until the rest of the IRA crews began arriving the week of June 11th.

The squad expecting to return in the fall voted for the next year's captain and with only a handful of juniors and a large group of sophomores involved, sophomore Frank Doble won the leadership position.

The sophomores were now veterans of a season's competition and with a remaining corps of seniors, including Captain Gary MacLachlan, Schoel was talking optimistically. He and senior cox Pat Nalbone were cited in a *Herald-Journal* article two days before the regatta as feeling that "… the Orange varsity would finish among the top five."

Alan More recalls the varsity eight had done an excellent timer (time trial) four or five days before the regatta.

Coaches polled by the newspaper didn't see it that way, ranking SU in a five-way tie for seventh place with Cornell, Brown, Princeton and Washington. Each of the crews received a single vote for third place.

Joe Burk's Penn squad was considered a slight favorite over Wisconsin, the defending champion.

The Orange JV also had a lone second place vote in the poll, while Bill Sanford's frosh were ranked fifth with one vote to win it all. The frosh were cited as "impressive in workouts at the regatta site and ... gaining backing daily."

MIT and Penn were the last of 16 squads to arrive, coming into Syracuse on Thursday.

The New York Times reported temperatures in the high 80's on Friday with no relief in sight.

Saturday, June 17th

Some 15,000–20,000 spectators lined the shore, according to newspaper accounts. The freshman eights strung out across the lake, two miles from the finish line waiting for the start. The water was flat.

"Are you ready? Ready all!" Then the boom of the cannon and the Orange frosh bolted out to the lead. It would not last.

Princeton and Rutgers pushed past Syracuse by the halfway point with Washington and Ted Nash's favored Penn frosh next. With a half-mile left, Penn took it up to 38 and moved into second. Then, with 300 yards to go the Quakers went to 42, and took it home, successfully repeating Penn's 1966 freshman win. The Orange slipped to seventh, behind Rutgers, Washington, Princeton, Wisconsin and Navy.

What had happened to the Orange cubs only came to light when the race was over. Two-man Jim Russell had passed out in the middle of the race but communication consisted of a cox with a megaphone in those days so only the oarsman behind him, bowman Duane Hickling knew it. He could only take half strokes and his attempts to rouse his teammate failed. Burdened by the dead weight and puzzled as to why the boat wouldn't go faster the Orange struggled to the finish. When it was over Hickling was finally able to shout to the rest of the boat what had happened. Coxswain Lew Brindis jumped in and swam down along the boat to help tend to his teammate.

Skies were threatening by the time the JV boats lined up for the three-miler. A third of the way in those skies opened up. Thunder boomed, lightning flashed and the wind howled in from the northwest, rolling waves across Onondaga. The 15 crews had no choice but to keep rowing. They were no longer visible from the shore and had a hard time seeing one another.

63

Fittingly it was Navy's Midshipmen who handled the awful conditions best, battling past the favored Quakers to win by open water. Schoel's Orange JV managed to take a respectable sixth, behind Wisconsin, California and Washington.

The varsity eights were already out in the starting area when the storm hit. "Meanwhile we're out sunk in the middle of the lake along with several other crews, but I'm going as captain, this is my final race, 'This is a great fitting end to my career at Syracuse,'" V8 five-oar MacLachlan recalls.

"We are swamped, soaking wet. The boat is down right to the riggers and we paddle and walk it over to the railroad bridge by the French Fort, get out of it, tip it upside down, tip it out, drain it out, and get back in and row to the starting line for our final race as Syracuse oarsmen."

Most of the other crews also rowed to shore and bailed, but Washington and Northeastern had gone back to the boathouse. The varsity eight three-miler was postponed 45 minutes, waiting for the weather to calm and for the two Huskies' squads to row back out to the start. This was the Syracuse varsity's last shot at redemption in the turbulent 1967 season.

When the cannon boomed just after five o'clock, Penn grabbed the lead and never let go, winning over Wisconsin by two lengths, Penn's first IRA varsity eight win since 1900. Wisconsin was second, followed by Cornell, Princeton, Navy, California, Rutgers, Brown, and Syracuse in ninth place, just ahead of previously unbeaten UCLA.

"The varsity felt really solid off the line and settled well," then-sophomore Alan More recalls. But the sophomore stroke Barry Singer kept the rating low–30 to 32 strokes-per-minute–for the first mile or so, and the boat was never able to catch up with the leaders. "You just can't row that low," More says. "By the time we took it up it was too late."

Aftermath

When it was all over, trophies awarded, shirts exchanged, winning coxswains tossed into the water, Schoel called his team together and looking a bit teary-eyed said everybody would have to work together to get back on track. Then the SU team members gathered up their belongings and headed for home.

The senior Captain MacLachlan made his way up to the coach's apartment in the rear of the boathouse, to thank him personally and to say goodbye. He found The Bear sitting on his bed, weeping disconsolately. He could not understand what had gone so wrong.

Rising junior Frank Doble had been elected the new captain, to the surprise of some on the team who'd expected rising seniors Andy Harrison or Dick Yochum to get the position, maybe both as co-captains. Doble was an experienced and perceptive oarsman with a strong prep rowing background.

Soon after it was reported that Doble and his father visited Athletics Director Jim Decker to voice their dissatisfaction with the coach and although he'd already been given an agreement to return for another year, by August The Bear was gone from the boathouse and Syracuse Crew.

The team members didn't learn of the visit until sometime later.

"There was a lot of dissatisfaction about how he had handled it," Alan More says.

But the Schoel era at Syracuse was over.

Chapter 6
1968–1970 – The Sanford Years: Beginnings

Bill Sanford had no interest in being an interim head coach. He says he was as surprised as anybody when Loren Schoel, the man he'd rowed for and who had hired him suddenly was gone. But with the summer half-over and not much time to find a new coach, Athletics Director Jim Decker was in a tight spot.

He was interested in Northeastern's Ernie Arlett and Tony Johnson, the SU alum who was then training for the Olympics, but even if they were interested, neither was about to make a move on such short notice. So when Decker asked Sanford to take the head job on an interim basis, Sanford rolled the dice and turned him down flat.

"I walked into Decker's office and put my resignation on his desk," Sanford says. "I'm all done because I want the head job. You have other plans so I've got to move on with my life."

Decker told the 28-year-old coach to hold onto that resignation letter. The next say he was hired.

"We're going to bring Syracuse crew back up to where it belongs," the new coach told *The Daily Orange* that fall. "This year's team has depth, size and spirit and the kids are working hard."

Hiring Big Mac

One of the first orders of business was to hire an assistant to coach the freshmen and Sanford didn't have to look very far. Like Sanford, Gary MacLachlan was a local guy who'd walked onto the SU Crew and had fallen in love with it.

"He was pretty much a rock in the crew as a freshman that I coached," Sanford says. "I thought he was a big, stable guy that could add local (knowledge) and be very helpful."

As an undergrad and eventually as captain, Mac had proved that he had a good sense of humor along with his knack for leadership. In a skit often played out on the team bus to and from practice, he would take on the role of a big, not so bright

67

and very naïve guy. Teammates would try to convince him to buy into ridiculous schemes to which he would eventually reply, "I am not that easily duped." That brought laughter all around and for MacLachlan, the sobriquet "Big Duper."

"You know, I don't remember promoting myself for this job or lobbying for it but sometime before September I was the freshman coach of crew at Syracuse," MacLachlan says. He says prominent alums Tip Goes ('14) and "Jock" Stratton ('26) spoke up for him. "I remember the salary being four-thousand dollars and it being a part time job. They wanted to step up recruiting. Bill had done a little bit of it. They wanted somebody to go on the road a little bit more."

Big Mac inherited a squad largely recruited by Sanford, but "I really, really, really got into coaching and loving freshmen and it was 'I'm now five years older than these kids and beginning to get a little bit more mature' and liked the challenges of dealing with kids that were away from home for the first time. And what little technical aspects I'd learned or knew about rowing–beginning to impart it to them training-wise and practice-wise."

Juniors Lead

Sanford had been popular enough as freshman coach that some seniors who'd left the team the year before considered coming back to row for him, but soon realized they were not in shape to do it. He was left with a thin senior class–Andy Harrison, Dick Yochum, Mark Sprague, Jim Fullerton and coxswain Alan Bell. As senior head manager, Cyrus "Sandy" Lepp held the title of Commodore, a title of respect for a senior team manager.

Captain Frank Doble was at the head of a fairly deep group of juniors that included Nick Entrikin, Alan More, Roy Sea, Barry Singer, Ken Hutton and Joe Casamento, who would go on to fame in Central New York as head football coach at Christian Brothers Academy.

Don Plath, who had walked on as a junior after being challenged by fraternity brothers who said he wasn't tough enough to row, also was on the squad along with junior coxswains Rich Kortright and Joe Peter.

Sophomores included Paul Buff, Jeff Harriman, Chuck Harris, Gary McKinney, Nils Peterson and Bill Willson, plus cox Lew Brindis.

"I had to get control of the squad," Sanford says, decades later. He brought Al Rosenberg, who had coached and won the Olympics gold medal in the eight in 1964, out in the launch during fall practice to offer some advice and that seemed to click. "The crew really responded to that and I learned an awful lot in those very brief sessions that we had," Sanford says.

The Orange went to the Head of the Charles three eights strong and came home with a gold-medal finish by the JV and a second-place finish by the varsity eight. The SU four with cox took bronze in its race. "Many of the coaches including Harry Parker said, 'Wow! What's going on there?'" Sanford says.

Parker had good reason for the comment. Then-sophomore Paul Buff recalls "… we [the varsity eight] finished the three-mile race second by only one-tenth of a second to the Cambridge [Harvard] Boat Club in the October darkness."

"The only problem we had was some residual of people who had been used to not training," Sanford says. Some of them would be gone from the squad that fall while others lasted through the spring before finding or being shown the door. "It caused me to lose some very good potential people, but I had to take them off the team in order to have a team."

Changing the Culture

While Loren Schoel had taken criticism for resisting modern training methods and rowing techniques coming from Europe, Sanford was buying in. Germany's Ratzeburg Club broke through in 1960, winning the Olympics with restyled shells, adjusted rigging, wider-bladed shovel oars and a rowing technique that applied physics and was designed for speed over 2,000 meters rather than the long haul of two or three miles. Harvard was the first to get on board among US collegiate programs and others eventually followed.

In a preseason column, *The Herald-Journal's* Arnie Burdick noted Sanford had gone for the shovel oars that Schoel had tried and rejected, and a sleek new Italian Donoratico shell he had bought from Al Rosenberg. "This baby," Sanford said, "has a curved bottom rather than a flat one like those old ones over there. It'll cut through the water, rather than just plane on it. That makes it faster."

The new coach is quoted as saying "The long, slow 10 to 20 mile training pulls are out now. We've concentrated on interval training, like trackmen; milers. We sprint hard for 10 to 20 strokes then settle. Sprint hard then settle. So that means the mileage doesn't mean what it once did. Rather, it's the kind of miles."

The rowing style now emphasized "faster hand action, more leg drive, shorter layback in order to impart a more continuous run to the boat." Burdick noted, "How well the not-too-robust Orange can master this new technique, no doubt, will determine how far they'll go this season, which seems to have more appeal and excitement than usual."

High Hopes and Early Success

A press release from SU Athletics said Sanford was starting his first season as head coach with high hopes. "If SU is out-rowed in any race this spring, it won't be because of spirit or conditioning."

In fact, Sanford had started taking his crews south during the winter, Paul Buff recalls, "So we could get out on the water in January. Our first trip was to Philly's Boathouse Row, staying in the UPenn stadium dorm and rowing sprints against John Campbell's Club [Penn AC], as well as Ted Nash's boats at Penn."

The season began on April 20th, with what had become the traditional opener, the Packard Cup which included Dartmouth and MIT. It was SU's turn to host the races on Onondaga Lake.

Because it was an Olympic year what had traditionally been two-mile races were shortened to 2,000-meter sprints.

The Orange crews had prepared with 1,000-meter time trials on Wednesday and some 500s on Thursday before tapering off. "We are coming along," Sanford told *The Daily Orange*. "I am expecting good things."

Things did not start well on Saturday afternoon as

MacLachlan's frosh fell by a length to Dartmouth, covering the course in 6:54.6 to the Green's 6:50.9.

But the JV gave Sanford his first eight-oared win as varsity coach, by a length-and-a-half over MIT in 6:44. Mark Sprague stroked it, with Rogers, Harrison, Gardner, Plath, Hickling, Willson and More behind him. Kortright was the cox.

Sanford sent Doble out as stroke of the V8, backed up by Entrikin, McKinney, Buff, Yochum, Sea, Harris and former-stroke Singer in the bow. Alan Bell was the cox.

6:47.5 after the start, Sanford had his first V8 win as coach. MIT was second about a length back and Dartmouth trailed by another three lengths.

SU's varsity four consisting of Nils Peterson, Ken Hutton, Joe Casamento, Jim Fullerton and coxswain Joe Peter also was victorious beating Dartmouth by several lengths. And the SU second frosh outrowed Dartmouth and MIT easily.

The Sanford Era was off to a solid start.

Tougher Competition

A week later the Orange crews headed south to Ithaca to take on host Cornell and Navy for the Goes Cup. This time the competition was much stiffer and the conditions much more difficult. High winds delayed the racing into the evening and it was after 7 p.m. when the freshman race got underway. It turned out to be a nail-biter. The Navy Plebes won by half-a-length and the Orange cubs edged Cornell by 0.2 seconds.

SU was second behind Cornell in the JV race. The Big Red was 3/4 of a length ahead of the Orange, who just edged out Navy.

By the time the varsity eights lined up it was dark. The SU varsity took off at 44 strokes-per-minute and had open water over Navy 500 meters in. But the Orange ran out of gas as Cornell rowed through and took the lead at the halfway point. Navy charged at the end but could not catch the Big Red. The finish had the Orange behind Cornell by more than two lengths and the Middies by a length, finishing in 6:30. It was the seventh-consecutive Goes Cup win for Cornell.

A *Daily Orange* article noted, "Still adjusting to the new Italian shell, the crew, under Coach Bill Sanford will have to work on the stamina which is needed to pull steadily after the driving start."

Navy won the varsity fours with Syracuse third.

The Syracuse second frosh fell by just over a second to Cornell.

A week later Sanford's varsity eight went to Providence where Vic Michalson's Bears walloped them by seven lengths on the Seekonk River.

The Orange JV's took Brown by half-a-length and MacLachlan's frosh broke through for their first win by a length of open water.

Eastern Sprints and IRA

The trip to Worcester for the Eastern Sprints and the IRA on Onondaga did not bring reason to celebrate for the Orange. None of the SU crews qualified for the finals at the Sprints. At the IRA, the JV did get there but finished sixth in 6:40.7.

The varsity eight had problems with that sleek Italian Donoratico shell both in Worcester and during the IRA. An oarlock sheared off during the Sprints qualifier and the Orange crew struggled to move the shell through wind and rough water on Onondaga. "The boat was, it turned out, a flat water boat," Sanford recalls ruefully.

Looking back on that first year and the two that followed, Sanford sees the struggle at least in part due to the times. "In the late 60s it was so difficult to have a team because of the Vietnam War," he says. "Guys were not training or they were hiding what they were doing and there was no focus and so we were just floundering–status quo–probably lower third of the league."

1969

By the time Spring Camp began in 1969, that year's senior class, once so deep, had been reduced to a handful. Frank Doble remained as captain, along with Steve Rogers, Alan More, Don

Plath and the coxswains Rich Kortright and Joe Peter.

The season opened on April 26th at home with the Goes Cup races and Sanford had a heavy concentration of juniors in his varsity eight. Bill Willson was at stroke with Duane Hickling at 7, Gary McKinney at 6, Paul Buff at 5 and Chuck Harris at 4. Plath was at 3, Rogers at 2 and Captain Doble in the bow. Kortright was the cox.

The result was not what SU was hoping for. The Big Red powered to a two-length win over Navy with the Orange another length behind in third.

The JV also trailed in its race, with the Midshipmen winning and the Big Red second. Nils Peterson stroked for SU with Jeff Harriman, Willis Duncan, Alan More, Steve Wheadon, Bob Fergerson, George Norcross and Tony Valdini backing him up. Joe Peter steered and called out the cadence.

MacLachlan's frosh kept SU from being shut out, taking Navy by almost a length open, as Cornell was half-a-length farther back. The frosh were Pete Washburn, Tom Gilbert, Gordon Scott, Ted Schueler, who tipped the scales at 260, Reed Augliere, John Hession, Tom Sawyer, Roger Reed and cox Larry Gersten.

The second frosh also chipped in with a length victory over Cornell.

John Hession recalls that the second frosh constantly pushed the first boat in practice and both benefitted. "Our main cox was Larry Gersten, but he had to fight off Dave Rosenthal (Rosie) to hold on to the megaphone. Jim Breuer, Terry Light, Paul Blacharski, Roger Reed all rowed well and were always pushing the team."

Holding Trophy

Vic Michalson's Brown squad came to Onondaga next and went home with the newly established Holding Trophy, but SU stayed close, losing by just over a length. Tip Goes had set up the trophy to honor Robert Holding, a Brown Trustee and President of the Brown Rowing Association.

The margin and the result were the same in the JV race but MacLachlan's first freshman eight remained unbeaten, topping the Bruin cubs easily.

Brown's second frosh got past SU.

Sprints

For the Eastern Sprints, Sanford shuffled the deck, moving Doble back into the stroke seat, where he'd spent his junior year. Nils Peterson and Jeff Harriman moved up from the JV; Peterson to the varsity four seat and Harriman to bow. When the Orange lined up it was Doble, Hickling, McKinney, Harris, Peterson, Buff, Plath, and Harriman. Kortright stayed in the coxswain's seat.

The varsity did not qualify for the grand final, which Harvard won.

Both the JV and the freshmen did get to go for the top, with the JV finishing fifth behind Harvard and MacLachlan's frosh coming in third, although more than 20 seconds behind Penn which edged Harvard for the win.

The JV and freshman performances brought the Orange squad into a tie for fourth place in the Rowe Cup standings with 18 points.

Packard Cup

After opening the season for a number of years the Packard Cup race was pushed back in 1969 to a spot where it has stayed since, a late season weekend usually between the Sprints and the IRA. Rowing this time on its home water, the Connecticut River, Dartmouth walloped SU, which just edged out MIT for second place.

Again it was Syracuse in the JV and freshman races. The second eight won easily over MIT with Dartmouth finishing third. The order was the same in the freshman race as SU took it by more than a length open.

IRA – June 12–13–14

The Orange freshmen went into the IRA seeded third

74

and looking strong, but not strong enough to get a direct pass to the grand finals. Only one crew would do that from the Thursday heat and it was top-seeded Penn. Rutgers edged Syracuse for the second spot but both would have to try to advance through the repechages.

Syracuse did it, beating Northeastern and Penn. Rutgers did not, trailing Brown in the rep, so it was Penn, Brown, Washington, Syracuse and its old rivals Navy and Cornell in the grand final.

The battle for gold was a battle for the ages. And nobody won. Penn and Washington crossed the line in a dead heat at 6:27.4. Brown got third by less than a length over SU, which edged Cornell by a bow ball and Navy by a seat or so.

Three-man John Hession recalls it as, "bitter disappointment."

The JV struggled in its opening heat, trailing Penn and Wisconsin, and then fell well out of contention in the Friday rep, trailing Navy, UCLA and Princeton.

In the petite final the Orange second boat was third behind Princeton and Washington and ahead of Columbia and Brown for a ninth-place finish overall.

Sanford's varsity eight finished behind Washington, Northeastern and Stanford in its opening heat, then third in the rep, a couple of lengths behind Cornell and a half behind Princeton.

In the petites on Saturday, SU was fourth behind Brown, Princeton and Georgetown.

In the grand finals, Penn took the varsity eight gold medal over Dartmouth and Cornell won the JV race over Wisconsin.

The SU varsity eight's tenth-place finish overall turned out to be one spot lower than that of Loren Schoel's final crew two years before.

1970

As the 1960s turned into the seventies the culture was changing, both nationally and on The Hill. In September of 1969 Chancellor William P. Tolley, who'd taken office in 1942, gave way to John Corbally. The peace, love and rock and roll of that summer's Woodstock Festival were turning to student demonstrations across the country as the Vietnam War expanded. Syracuse was no exception, as anti-war demonstrations filled the quad.

In the midst of all this Bill Sanford continued his effort to get the Orange crews back into the upper echelon of collegiate rowing. Every collegiate coach was going through a similar situation. Certainly the traditional "crew cut" had given way to considerably longer hair and the "free spirit" thinking that came with it at the Ivies. California's Berkeley campus was arguably the capital of student protest. Even Madison, Wisconsin, became a magnet for the "hippie culture."

While men still came out and rowed, many with traditional dedication, Sanford suggests some, perhaps more than usual, were not as dedicated as their coaches would have liked.

Spring Season

The Midshipmen of Navy, still sporting military haircuts, hosted the Goes Trophy races in 1970 but once again it was Stork Sanford's Cornell varsity that went home with the hardware. Navy was second with the Orangemen third. The freshmen also finished third, but the JV took second.

Bill Sanford had a veteran group in the varsity eight with seniors Lew Brindis at cox, Bill Willson, Duane Hickling and Paul Buff at stroke, seven and six, and Roy Clark who'd returned to school after a stint in Vietnam at five. The bow four were juniors Steve Wheadon, Bob Fergerson, Paul Blacharski and Tony Valdini.

But what that crew didn't have was clear separation from the JV.

Sophomore Pete Washburn was the second-boat stroke at 5'11" and a mere 150 pounds. But with experience at St. Andrew's Prep, he was "tough as can be," according to teammate Jeff Harriman, who was behind him at seven. The varsity and JV lineups had changed often leading up to the season and between the Goes Trophy meet and the upcoming battle with Brown, Harriman recalls there was a time trial. "The JV beat the varsity. Coach Sanford was frustrated with juggling the line-ups so he made the

JV the new varsity and made the varsity the JV. Brown beat the new varsity by open water while the new JV won handily."

The frosh lost to the Bruin cubs. That was May 2nd.

Two days later, with anti-war protests in full swing at SU, National Guardsmen shot and killed four students during a demonstration at Kent State. Protestors at Syracuse, with headquarters in the basement of Hendricks Chapel, planned and successfully took over the Administration Building. Chancellor Corbally would be briefly trapped in his office. Classes were canceled several weeks before the scheduled end of the semester and students were given the choice of taking the grades they had at that point or going pass / fail.

"It was my freshman year," George Chapman says. "I remember attending rallies on the quad listening to various speakers urging us to 'shut it [SU] down' and work to end the war. We 'occupied' the Administration Building, but only after dutifully attending practice on Onondaga Lake. Many wondered if their right-wing parents would pull them out of school. Once the University officially closed, you couldn't get a bus, train or plane ticket out of town. Students abandoned the 'cause' and left town in waves." The crewmen stayed.

Eastern Sprints

Coach Sanford switched his first two boats back to the way they'd been as they prepared for the Eastern Sprints. The bottom line seemed to be that either boat was pretty strong at the JV level, but neither was in the top tier among varsity eights.

SU gave it a shot in the morning heat but wound up third behind Penn and Brown. The varsity took second in the Reserve Section Races behind Wisconsin, beating Navy, Yale, Columbia and Rutgers. Harvard won the grand final.

The JV got into the grand final with a third-place finish behind Wisconsin and Penn in the heat. Penn took the championship with Harvard next, then Wisconsin, Brown, SU and Navy.

The freshmen also were third in their heat and in the Reserve Section Races, behind Cornell and Wisconsin.

Packard Cup

Conditions forced the Packard Cup races off of Onondaga Lake and onto the Seneca River course, where a strong Dartmouth varsity took the race with the Orange second by open water and MIT well behind. The JV, hitting its stride, Harriman says, picked up another win and the frosh were second.

On campus there were no classes to attend and few students around, Chapman recalls. "The few remaining student protesters, including the entire SU crew, were consolidated into a couple of dorms for the remaining six weeks or so. Eventually, we were joined by most of the crews participating in the IRA Regatta, which then was typically the first weekend in June. They too became homeless after their respective universities shut down. The boathouse was like a busy airport with various boats departing and arriving on the crowded dock. Because there were no classes, most crews worked out twice a day, adding to the confusion. We made a lot of friends with guys from all over the country including Brown, Cornell, Wisconsin, Navy, California, Penn, BU, Dartmouth, etc. It was an exciting time to be a student and oarsman."

IRA

The 1970 IRA brought 63 crews from 25 colleges and universities to Onondaga Lake, the most ever to that point. Cornell was "the strong sentimental favorite" with Stork Sanford, no relation to Bill Sanford, having announced his retirement. His final varsity eight would wind up fourth, trailing Washington, Wisconsin and Dartmouth. Syracuse's Bill Sanford was more concerned about getting his boats into the grand finals and perhaps the medals. He succeeded with one.

Frosh

1970 was the last hurrah for Gary MacLachlan as SU freshman coach. He had decided to step down to take a job with the Syracuse Parks and Recreation Department, feeling he couldn't get by on the $4,000 annual salary he was earning in what was a part-time job. His new job paid twice that.

"I'll always remember that night," MacLachlan says. "The last Friday night before the last IRA–I took Kathy [his wife] with me in the boat and we did a late night row out on the placid lake with the sun setting and I was like "Holy s**t! This is my last night with the guys and my last night coaching."

The guys were Mike Minor at cox–stroke George Chapman, Ricardo Herrera, Dave Fergusson, Tim Sprague, Mike Kalisewicz, Jim Lastowka, Chris Weldon, and Walt Hubbell. They had missed a shot at the grand final that afternoon, trailing Cornell in the repechage. The next day they'd be third in the petite final. Brown was the freshman champion.

"We were a decent middle-of-the-pack freshman crew and beginning to produce guys that were experienced in high school and prep school and easily transitioning into the varsity level at that point," MacLachlan says. "I think it was probably the beginnings of the middle and late '70s that would make us a winner."

MacLachlan would go on to become Onondaga County Commissioner of Parks and Recreation as well as Co-Director of the IRA in Syracuse. His policies on traffic and alcohol in Onondaga Lake Park would change the face of the IRA.

Orange JV Shines

The JV was made up of stroke Pete Washburn, Jeff Harriman, Paul Blacharski, John Hession, Nils Peterson, Bob Fergerson, Roger Reed, bow Tony Valdini, and cox Larry Gersten. "The JV boat seemed to be getting faster every day," Harriman says. But it had to face favored Penn in the Thursday heat and the Quakers came away with an open water victory over SU. While Penn and the other qualifier winner Washington rested on Friday, SU's JV led the whole way and knocked off Wisconsin by half-a-length to win the rep and make the grand final.

On Saturday, Harriman recalls, "We got off the line fast and smooth and led the race at the 1,000-meter mark by about a 1/2 boat length over Penn. Penn had pulled even at about the

500-meter mark when the extra race on Friday began to take its toll. Penn won (by about 1/2-length), with Washington just beating us as we held on for third." Washington had edged the Orange by two-tenths of a second. SU in turn had held off Northeastern by one-tenth of a second. Brown was another seven-tenths of a second back in fifth.

Varsity Gets Close and Sanford Gets Close To Quitting

The Orange varsity eight looked solid. Sophomore Dave Rosenthal was now the cox with Willson and Hickling at stroke-seven, then Reed Augliere, Paul Buff, Gordon Scott, Chuck Harris, Steve Wheadon, and Henry Ridgeley. It just wasn't solid enough to stay with Penn and Dartmouth in the Thursday morning heat. The Quakers out-dueled the Big Green for the automatic grand final spot, with SU ten seconds behind. In the repechage it was Vic Michalson's Brown taking on Sanford's Orange and Bruno got the best of it by half-a-length, consigning SU to the petite.

Navy took the petite over Princeton and then SU. Northeastern, Georgetown and Kansas State trailed. It was another ninth-place finish for the Orange varsity.

While there had been positives along the way, for Bill Sanford it had been a challenging first three years–so challenging that he and his wife had talked about giving it up in frustration.

"That was a critical part of my career because Nancy and I had decided … with what was going on and I was not happy, that I was going to get out because we just weren't going anywhere," he says.

Then came the freshmen in the Class of '74–the class Sanford says turned the SU Crew program around.

Chapter 7
1971–1973 – Struggle and Strife

A familiar face took over as freshman coach for Syracuse that fall. Over the summer Sanford and the alumni pushed for and got a full-time slot for a freshman coach and the then not quite princely salary of $8,000 a year–double what Gary MacLachlan had been making and perhaps ironically, the same pay he got in his new job with Parks and Recreation. The coaching slot went to Dan Hogan, who was a year behind Sanford on the SU team and had stroked the Sprints-champion freshman eight in 1961.

Hogan had been living in Buffalo with his wife and young son and worked with junior and high school crews at West Side Rowing Club. "In 1969 I was the manager of the Junior National Team that went to Italy," he says. "Two of my crews were second place to those crews. I decided that was something I would really like to try so that was sort of my entrée into it."

Back at Syracuse, Hogan used much the same tactics his predecessors had to add depth to the freshman squad. The freshmen who came into the crew room in the fall of 1970 were, as usual, mostly walk-ons.

"We recruited guys off the quad," he says. "When they'd come through registration some of the varsity would help pull them off the floor and get them to sign their names."

Hogan had known stroke Ken Schmidt at West Side but Paul Garbaczeski, Art Daley, John Duckworth and the rest of the Class of '74 were new to the sport.

"That class was the one that came in and turned us around for our crew and started getting us better," Coach Bill Sanford says.

Spring 1971

There were just three seniors on the varsity roster in the spring of 1971, Bob Fergerson, Captain Tony Valdini and Steve Wheadon. There were fifteen juniors and eleven sophs.

The Olympic racing distance of 2,000 meters was now the

collegiate standard.

The Orange crews opened the season at home on April 17th, taking on Georgetown and the University of Massachusetts. It was a solid start for the freshmen and JV but not for the varsity eight. The Hoyas edged the Orangemen by less than a deck, with the Minutemen another length behind.

The JV eight took UMass by a length open, with the Hoyas third.

The freshmen followed suit with a five length clobbering of Georgetown as UMass trailed.

"They really did catch on fast," Hogan recalls. "We had a great core of kids–good athletes, really hard working. It was really joyful to work with them. They did more than anybody could expect. They were driven by their own personalities."

A week later the varsity fared far worse against much greater competition on the flood control channel off Cayuga Lake in Ithaca. Navy romped to the win over Cornell with SU well behind. The JV also finished a distant third. Navy's victory broke a nine-year Big Red winning streak in the Goes Trophy race.

The SU freshmen were not able to keep up with the Navy Plebes, but they were only a length behind and finished the 2,000 meters in a time that was faster than the varsity or JV.

The Orangemen were home again on May 1st hosting Brown.

The lineups looked like this: Varsity–Mike Minor cox, stroke Paul Blacharski, Roger Reed at 7, Gordon Scott at 6, John Hession at 5, Reed Augliere at 4, John Lambert at 3, Steve Wheadon at 2, and Tony Valdini in bow. JV–Larry Gersten cox, stroke Pete Washburn, Bob Fergerson at 7, George Chapman at 6, Bob Halpin at 5, Jim Breuer at 4, Tom Sawyer at 3, Chris Weldon at 2, and Dave Fergusson in bow. Frosh–cox Dick Handler, stroke Ken Schmidt, Art Daley at 7, Paul Garbaczeski at 6, Eric Rogers (Steve's brother) at 5, Charles Lee at 4, Joel Augenblick at 3, Pat Huey at 2, and Greg Palladino who rowed at Liverpool in bow.

The freshmen again came up the only winner for SU, drubbing the Bruin cubs by three lengths. Brown's varsity eight took SU by a length and the JV finished three lengths open ahead of Syracuse.

Sprints

1971 was Navy's year in the varsity and freshman competitions at the Eastern Sprints. For Syracuse only the freshmen carried the Orange banner into the grand finals.

The SU varsity failed to qualify for afternoon competition, finishing way back in last place in the morning heat. A strong Rutgers team was second in the grand final with Harvard third.

SU's JV was second in the afternoon's consolation race after coming in third behind Penn and Harvard in the morning heat.

The Orange cubs beat Cornell for second place by one-tenth of a second in the morning heat to get into the grand final. Harvard won the heat.

Hogan's frosh then took third in a final Navy won by open water over Harvard. Syracuse was half-a-length back of the Crimson. Northeastern, Brown and Wisconsin followed.

Hogan was not satisfied. "I can't remember anything about the heats," he says. "Finishing third in the afternoon was a loss as far as I was concerned. Not because the crew rowed badly. Maybe it was the times. Finishing third just didn't make much difference in those days. It's more important now."

The Packard Cup was at Hanover and Dartmouth's varsity eight kept it there, in a three-way race that saw the Orange a length behind and MIT's Engineers open water back in third.

Dartmouth also won the JV race by just three-tenths of a second over SU, with the Engineers trailing.

But the Orange frosh won easily, taking MIT by open water, with Dartmouth well back.

IRA

The IRA boasted yet another record field in 1971 with 75 crews representing 27 colleges and universities. Navy and Washington were seen as the teams to beat with Navy having won the Eastern Sprints and Washington dominating the West and looking to repeat its 1970 IRA title.

There was plenty of flavor, some of it literal. Hinerwadel's hosted the annual IRA clambake, offering clams, salt potatoes, fried chicken, vegetables, coffee and kuchen, beer and soft drinks and more for $8.00 per person.

The Herald-Journal's Arnie Burdick called the Saturday finals "a 13-race jamboree." The change to 2,000 meters in 1968 and the added small boat competitions made for more action, closer finishes and shorter times between races, although Syracuse University fielded only three eights that year.

Hogan's freshmen showed more promise at the IRA but fell just short of a medal and the JV fought through to make the grand final. But the varsity finished a less-than-stellar season with a third-level final, finishing second there–14th overall.

There'd been a number of changes over the course of the season. Pete Washburn was now the varsity stroke with John Hession at seven, George Chapman at six, Roger Reed at five, Jon Schmitz at four, Bob Halpin at three, Paul Blacharski at two and Terry Light in bow. Larry Gersten coxed.

In the varsity eight grand final it was neither Navy nor Washington, although the Huskies came within eight-tenths of a second. Cornell pulled off the upset. The Middies were sixth.

The Syracuse JV battled through the repechage to get into the top tier and then wound up sixth on Saturday, just two ticks ahead of Cornell in a seven-boat final. Navy was the winner.

Gordon Scott stroked the SU second eight, backed up by Bob Fergerson, Reed Augliere, John Lambert, Jim Quattrochi, Tom Sawyer, Jim Breuer and Dave Fergusson. Dave Rosenthal coxed.

The frosh finished second to powerful Penn in the Thursday heat but won its Friday repechage to make the grand final. Schmidt was the starboard stroke, backed up by Daley, Garbaczeski, Rogers, Augenblick, Lee, Palladino and Richard Reinwald in bow, with Handler again handling the coxing duties.

On Saturday it was the Quakers first across the line, a length ahead of the next four tightly-bunched crews. Cornell took silver by about a second over Navy which edged SU for third by just over a second. Northeastern was another second or so behind the Orange and Wisconsin finished sixth.

"I can remember not being able to pick the winner until

they were virtually at the grandstand," Hogan says. "The kids were awfully disappointed. They felt, and I felt they had rowed a good race–that they had rowed well."

He continued, "I felt as if things had gone pretty well–I guess I didn't think ahead as much as what we had done and what we could have done better. I guess I felt that we could have done things a little better. I don't think I've ever coached a season when I didn't think that."

1972

In the fall of 1971 Hogan handed off those rising sophomores to Sanford and they advanced to the varsity eight in short order.

"Those crews in those days were filled with walk-ons," Sanford says. "Garbaczeski was a football player. Daley, he was a real muscular-type kid. And all those guys except for Ken Schmidt who came out of West Side. Duckworth was a walk-on."

Sanford chuckles at the memory of a race against the Coast Guard Academy in New London, Connecticut that fall. It was supposed to be low-key, but Coach Bill Stowe had brought out the fleet. Coast Guard brass and a good-sized crowd in uniform lined up in vessels along the course. "These guys are really psyched for this thing down here," Sanford says he told his coxswain. "It would be the biggest thing in the world if they could beat Syracuse." He decided to use psychological warfare.

"Are you ready?" The referee called out. "Ready All. Row!" The Coast Guard crew took off. On his instructions Sanford's men sat at the start. "They can't disqualify us," Sanford had told his crew.

"There's only two crews. We've got to have the race." He was right.

When the race was restarted the Orange blasted off at a furious pace, leaving the Coast Guard eight flummoxed and far behind. Stow, the IRA-winning Cornell stroke and Olympic gold medalist, had less than kind words for Sanford afterward.

Later that fall Sanford recalls finishing well at the Head of the Charles and heading through the winter and into the spring of

1972 with confidence.

"That crew then started asking for and demanding people [team members] to train–getting away from … the marijuana and all the stuff that was going on and started getting people training and it kept me in the game," Sanford says. "From that point on we started competing at a higher level in the league," he says.

Spring 1972

That higher level of competition was not reached immediately. 1972 would turn out to be a tough season for Sanford's varsity when it came to wins. There were none.

The spring season opened with the Orange varsity closer to Rutgers but not quite there. Rowing on the Raritan River the Scarlet Knights edged SU by a second-and-a-half. Syracuse's JV and freshmen started the season with easy wins over Rutgers.

It was SU's turn to host the Goes Trophy races but it was Navy's turn again to win in the varsity and JV. The Middies got the oars in the water last to edge Cornell by one-tenth of a second in the varsity race. SU was three lengths behind.

The Middies won the JV easily with SU in third a length behind the Big Red.

SU's first frosh were second to Cornell by a length and the second frosh returned the favor, winning by a length over Cornell.

Brown continued its dominance of the Holding Trophy, beating SU on the Seekonk River by two lengths open. Brown's JV also won, but the Orange first and second frosh both defeated the Bruin cubs.

"The first freshmen were just better than Brown was," Hogan says. "They rowed a good solid race the way they were supposed to. What I recall even more–the second freshmen had a couple of kids with good experience just on the verge of being in the first boat–the rest of the guys were typical second frosh–and they were good. They pushed the first frosh."

At the Sprints the frosh had the most success, winning the consolation race for a seventh-place finish overall. The varsity and JV did not qualify to race in the afternoon.

"We had a poor race in the morning," Hogan says. "For

some reason we just weren't well prepared–but they took a great attitude into the afternoon–probably a better attitude than I did. I think in the old days the coaches didn't have the concept of planning for peaks and valleys."

Northeastern upset Harvard to win the varsity title, while the Crimson took the JV and freshman finals.

Back home for the Packard Cup, the SU varsity fell just short of a win, with MIT taking it by a second-and-a-half and Dartmouth a length behind. The Orange did win the rest of the day's races, with the JV and freshmen way ahead of MIT and Dartmouth, and the second frosh whipping MIT.

IRA

Once again it was Hogan's freshman crews that had the most success for Syracuse at the IRA.

After finishing third in its opening heat, the freshman four won its repechage and wound up fourth in the grand final. Princeton won easily, with Santa Clara, UCLA, SU and MIT in a tight bunch behind.

Rowing in choppy water and winds so bad that Marist's and Coast Guard's boats sank, the Orange freshman eight went right to the grand final with a heat win over Navy and Brown. "That was a race that the coxswain won," Hogan remembers.

"The cox knew the lake. With the wind off shore he went right for the bank, found some better water and that's how they qualified."

Paul Sugnet–who rowed at West Side–stroked the eight with Liverpool's Jim Lough at seven. *The Post-Standard's* Neil Kerr noted, "Coach Dan Hogan's winners may also give Central New York partisans something to cheer about Saturday," although the winning time was the slowest of the three frosh victors. His words proved prophetic. The Orange struggled in the grand finals. Wisconsin won by a length, followed by Cornell, Navy, Cal, Washington and the Orange were sixth.

"I don't recall that race," Hogan says. "It was a mental thing and I think we all shared in it. That day is the worst day of coaching I've ever had. Kids went away feeling as if they let me down, let Bill down. It was poorly handled on my part. I didn't give them the reinforcement that they needed after the race."

The JV was second to Cornell in the qualifying but finished last in a three-boat rep behind Orange Coast and Brown and wound up third in the petite final. Navy won it easily and Brown again edged the Orangemen. Washington edged Wisconsin by a second to win the grand final.

The varsity was third in the rep, well behind Wisconsin and MIT. In the Petite Final SU finished fourth behind Navy, MIT and Coast Guard by a second, but did avenge the early season loss to Rutgers by four-tenths of a second.

Penn was the winner of the grand final with Brown and Wisconsin taking silver and bronze.

Wisco's overall finishes won the Badgers the Ten Eyck Trophy and an observation from columnist Arnie Burdick that Ned Ten Eyck had coached at Wisconsin before coming to take over for his father Jim at Syracuse in the 1930s. Winning the Ten Eyck Trophy for the first time, Burdick noted, was likely to help a crew program that had been "under fire recently as a heavy financial burden. Even when there's no dollars coming in, it's easier to support a winner," he wrote.

Syracuse Crew was not yet at that level.

1973

While Dan Hogan's freshmen had been successful in his first two years coaching at Syracuse, there was conflict between the head coach and his former teammate who'd been a year behind him when they were undergraduates. Sanford says Hogan wanted the job of head coach and that that was not going to work.

"Unfortunately, the third year of Dan's being the freshman coach, he and I had a real big problem and I had to tell him he wasn't going to coach anymore," Sanford said decades later. He went to Hogan's home and fired him.

Hogan concedes that he and Sanford disagreed. "I'm not saying I was an easy guy to get along with. We definitely had a personality issue and I didn't feel that–it's hard to articulate– from day-to-day-to-day he didn't put the pressure that he needed to on his crews. As a result they lost their competitive edge over a period of time. That was the thing that kind of bothered me a lot. Kids going up to varsity level weren't being given the opportunity to compete at the level they were capable of."

"It's not entirely true that I wanted his job," Hogan says. "Of course I did but I didn't make any active overtures in that respect. There were alumni who were agitating to get rid of Bill whether or not they wanted to put me in his place. I didn't encourage that or discourage it."

Hogan says he and his wife were tired of trying to get by on an assistant coach's salary and had looked at moving on, maybe out of coaching and he doesn't know if he'd have taken the job had it been offered.

"What he [Sanford] perceived is what he perceived but ... it's not true."

Sanford says the two repaired their friendship as the years passed, but "... back then it was the most difficult thing in my life to go up to the house and my wife and kids and everybody were all friends ... but Dan and my relationship had gone too far and Dan was seeking to be the head coach and that was just unfortunate."

Hogan went into advertising and eventually moved to Owego working for General Electric. He got back into rowing at the masters level with former-SU-teammates and national team rowers such as Ted Kakas, Jim Edmonds and Frank Benson. Eventually he became coach of the crews at Binghamton University.

For the rest of the 1973 spring season Bill Sanford took over coaching the freshmen in addition to the varsity crews.

The Season

George Chapman was captain in 1973 and the senior class also included Tim Sprague, Jon Schmitz, Walter Hubbell and coxswains Dave Preis and Mike Minor. The Class of '74 were now juniors and a major part of the varsity and JV.

Although there was still a long way to go, the wins began to come for the varsity and JV. It would be a tough season for the freshmen.

SU opened the season at home, welcoming Marist College although "welcomed" might not be exactly the right word. The Orangemen swept the Red Foxes with the freshmen winning by five lengths, the varsity by seven and the JV by nine. Marist had a strong freshman crew but the program was not at the level of other EARC (Eastern Association of Rowing Colleges) squads.

The Scarlet Knights of Rutgers were up next in another home meet and this one was competitive at all levels. The Orange freshmen won by half-a-length as did the varsity eight. Rutgers prevailed in the JV race by a heartbeat–seven-tenths of a second.

The Goes Cup Trophy races were at Annapolis where the conditions on the Severn were almost always dicey and where the only thing certain tended to be that nothing was certain. The races were rowed over a 3,000-meter course and the Orangemen's best finish was second in the varsity eight in a very close race. The Middies won it by 3/4 of a length over SU, which in turn took the Big Red by 3/4 of a length. Cornell took both the JV and freshman races with Syracuse well behind in third in both.

At the Eastern Sprints the Syracuse crews all wound up in the consolation finals. The JV won the consolation race for a seventh-place finish overall. The frosh were sixth in the consy with the varsity fourth behind Rutgers, MIT and Navy. Northeastern repeated as varsity champions, with Harvard taking the JV and Dartmouth the frosh championship.

The JV continued its winning ways beating MIT by a length open in Hanover, with Dartmouth two seats farther back. But MIT took the varsity race by a length-and-a-half over SU and the freshman race by 3/4 of a length over Dartmouth. The SU Frosh were never in it against the Sprints Champions.

IRA 1973

Back home for the IRA, The varsity was third in its heat behind Penn and Rutgers, then last in the rep. In a rematch of the Goes Cup, Cornell won the petite final, with Navy a length behind and SU back another length. Kansas State and Columbia trailed.

The JV was fourth in its heat and then last in the rep. It wound up third in the petite finals behind Navy and Rutgers.

90

The SU frosh without a coach of their own, struggled to finish the season, trailing the field in their opening heat and the repechage, then coming in sixth out of eight in the petite finals, ahead of only Navy and Kansas State.

The freshman four, after finishing second to UCLA in its heat, got clobbered by Cornell in the rep and wound up fifth in the petite finals.

The top priority seemed to be coming up with a new freshman coach. Sanford found a gem who would be a huge force in bringing Syracuse Crew back to the top at last.

Chapter 8
1972 – SU Women's Crew – The Early Days

The Syracuse University Women's Crew Club was established in the fall of 1972, with Mark Casey listed as the Director. Casey founded, organized, and coached the program for its first two years, beginning with a dozen athletes in 1972, adding eight more the next year, and more than doubling in size to 45 in the fall of 1973. Practice in those early days was primarily focused on the spring, with some fall rowing added in 1973. Casey was succeeded by two volunteer coaches, former Cornell rower Dan Fisher and John Duckworth, a graduate assistant and SU Men's Crew alumnus.

Across the country, women's rowing was quite new, with just a few Northeastern schools fielding teams in the early 1970s. Some high schools also had crews, with most concentrated in northern Virginia and Philadelphia along with the Northeastern prep school programs. In a situation reminiscent of the old women's half-court basketball and no track events longer than 800 meters, college crews raced a thousand or fifteen hundred meters in the early days.

Equipment was a little thin in the early 1970s, as the SU women possessed a single four donated by the estimable Fred Emerson, and a small launch and outboard purchased with funds raised in the 1973 one-hundred-mile rowathon. The men's program provided access to two shells as well, although the boats were built for the much heavier men, were "not always available" for practice, and the crew had to borrow equipment from its hosts at away races. This was not the optimal situation to be sure.

Emerson's contribution to the program, and women's rowing overall, was not limited to donating one four. In large part, he was the driver behind the Eastern Association of Women's Rowing Colleges (EAWRC), an organization founded in 1974. He also ran the first EAWRC Championships–a single, eights-only regatta–on Lake Beseck in Middlefield, Connecticut, that spring.

Competition for the club began with a scrimmage October 18, 1972 against Liverpool High School's women. The young Syracuse team faced off against Radcliffe on April 7, 1973

93

on the Charles, with the women from Cambridge victorious. On April 18th, the women found themselves back in Boston, this time competing with MIT and Wellesley in addition to the 'Cliffies in two fours races. Things went pretty well, as the Orange rowed to a pair of second-place finishes in races against four or five competitors.

Just three days later, the Orange women finished third out of five crews entered in the varsity fours event and fifth out of seven eights at the Davenport Regatta in Lowell, Massachusetts. The competition included Williams, Connecticut College, Wesleyan, Assumption, and Worcester Tech.

After the three hotly-competitive early season races, the women took a breather, regrouping, trimming the roster, and then focusing on preparing for the inaugural Eastern Women's Sprints Championships. At that time, the Sprints were run under the auspices of the Northeastern Association of Women's Rowing Colleges, the predecessor organization of the EAWRC. The race was held on the Charles River in 1973, a 1,000-meter course by this time quite familiar to the women from Syracuse. A single Syracuse four was entered, which succeeded in making the finals where it finished sixth, a credible showing for the first-year program in a field of 12 crews.

More than a month later, the four, broken down into two pairs, was in Philly for the National Women's Rowing Championships, held June 15th–17th on the Schuylkill. Again a Syracuse crew made the finals and finished sixth. The long season had been successful despite the lack of financial support and equipment challenges. With its inaugural season complete, the SU's Women's Crew Club was established.

The program took a big step up that fall as the Orange women took home top honors in the women's four in the Head of the Charles, an event that appears to have been run as an adjunct to the men's lightweight four.

With a successful fall campaign and winter training sessions just completed, the women headed to Washington, D.C. for spring break. Eighteen athletes contributed $30 apiece for food, transportation, and lodging and Coach Mark Casey's crews had five solid days on the water. While it wasn't Florida, it was far

94

better than the late winter conditions in Syracuse.

The 1974 sprint season began on Onondaga, as the Williams Ephs headed west to take on the Orange women in mid-April. Their trip was successful for the Ephs as they won the lone race. The Davenport Regatta was next up on the schedule, and SU's club took fourth out of nine in Worcester. The number of crews attending the regatta had increased significantly, a sign that women's rowing was growing in popularity throughout the northeast.

Next up for SU's Orange women was a rematch with Radcliffe in Boston, with the locals again coming away victorious. The following weekend SU defeated Worcester Tech in a race held on Onondaga Lake in what was a final tune-up before the Women's Eastern Sprints. The varsity finished just out of the medals at the Sprints, following that with the same result at the Lowell and Philadelphia Regattas later that season. The club program had made great strides, competing well against what were becoming the top programs in the nation.

That was all well and good, but to have a shot at medaling at the Sprints, they would need better equipment and more financial support from the University. That would prove to be as much of a challenge for the SU women as any crew they'd encounter on the race course.

As a club, the women got funding for their operations from various entities; a small contribution from the SU Student Association, funds from the Women's Athletics Association, dues from each rower and money earned ushering at various on-campus concerts and athletic events, with most of the funding from SU's club sports program. As funding from these sources was tenuous at best after the 1974 season Club Treasurer Julie Fagan led an effort to seek additional money and support from the Student Association. That effort was unsuccessful, but the women were nothing if not persistent.

In the fall of 1974, the nascent SU Women's Crew again applied to the Student Association Finance Board for funds for a shell, transportation, oars, and operating funds to begin a crew club. The decision, rendered by the board in December, was rather less than supportive; the initial request was for $6,761 and the amount allocated for the spring of 1975 was $130. The records of the process indicate the board found that uniforms, transportation, gas and oil were "personal items that do not benefit the entire campus," while maintenance fell in the "administration's funding realm" and oars and a boat were "expansionary items" and had to be requested in the spring. Notably absent were any funds for a coach. This was a strictly volunteer position and as such contributed to the program's "organizational difficulties."

Needless to say, the funds were less than adequate. Undaunted by the less-than-enthusiastic response, the women came back to the board early in 1975, better prepared and with a very detailed five-page budget request for the 1975–1976 season. Mileage to and from the boathouse was calculated at $0.06 per mile; uniforms at $2 per person, and the request recounted the effort put in to pay for their new fiberglass shell; a one-hundred-mile rowathon and additional fundraising that had covered half of the $5,000 needed. President Anne Lederhos and Treasurer Julie Fagan asked for a total of $2,899, most of which was for equipment. Regrettably, the Student Association's response was lost to history. However, it really didn't matter, as SU women's rowing was about to become a full-fledged varsity sport.

Chapter 9
1974–1975 – Drew's Crews

Andrew P. Harrison was one of only four men in the Class of '68 who'd completed four years on the SU squad. The others were Dick Yochum, Mark Sprague and coxswain Alan Bell. He'd come to Syracuse and tried rowing at the urging of Scott Sanford, Bill's younger brother who was his contemporary on the SU crew. Scott Sanford had been Harrison's teacher at Jordan-Elbridge High School in the rural western area of Onondaga County. "He was nice enough to bring me up to campus and introduce me to Bill and Loren Schoel and that seemed kind of interesting and I ended up going to school there and that was the introduction for which I have always been grateful," Harrison says.

Some called him "Andy," but friends soon discovered he preferred "Drew." He also picked up the nickname "The Rifleman" because of his resemblance to Chuck Connors, the former-major league baseball player who was the star of the popular TV show at that time. Harrison was 6'4" and by the time he was a senior, listed at a solid 198 pounds. Crew was a good fit, physically and mentally.

"It suited me–the hard work, I don't know what you want to call it. The working hard, the pulling hard, the attempt to put it all together when you race, the attempts to beat other people during practice–that's me. So the feeling of moving on the water–that whole bit–I fit right into that. So that for me was a pleasure."

But while he was a first-boater as a freshman and in-and-out of the varsity eight under Coach Schoel, he never did crack the varsity in his senior year, Sanford's first as head coach. Still Drew had developed a passion for rowing and decided he was going to continue.

"When I finished Syracuse as an undergraduate I felt like I was still improving as a rower and the challenge of being a good rower and being a winning rower was still alive and I wanted to continue competing so I started rowing for a couple of different clubs and over the next four or five years competed and learned to row in small boats and learned to compete in small boats and learned to be more … as an individual athlete instead of one of a unit of eight and in a pair, in a single, in a four and competed–trying to make the national team and not quite making it but nonetheless continuing to develop individual skills," he recalls.

Taking various jobs to pay the bills, he rowed at Potomac Boat Club in Washington, D.C., and then moved to Rochester to row. He also did some coaching on the side at Georgetown and in Rochester.

In fact, he says he'd been asked about interest in the freshman coaching job at SU in 1970 but passed because the rules then meant coaching for pay would take away his amateur status as an oarsman. Three years later the rules had changed.

"I was working in Rochester, New York, for the YMCA as an outreach worker which was kind of like working with street gangs or loosely affiliated gangs and trying to create something positive and also competing at Rochester Rowing Club and I applied and was offered the position and that was fantastic and it was just a whole new chapter–or chapters, plural, it was an opening to a fantastic nine years of coaching at Syracuse University."

Sanford recalls that Harrison had been an ROTC cadet as an undergrad but a physical problem kept him from being commissioned and he eventually grew out his hair, marched against the Vietnam War and got into acting on the side. In Rochester he played Buffalo Bill on stage and teammate and longtime friend Dick Yochum recalls, "When he came on … in his buckskins, naturally grown long hair and beard, he embodied every idea I ever had of Buffalo Bill."

All along he continued his passion for rowing and Sanford says by the time he got back in touch with him, Harrison was "squared away."

Sanford says Harrison showed up for his interview in a white suit and gave "a tremendous performance in the interview and I was pretty much sold on him." Harrison had brought his wife Lee along and Sanford says she was another plus. "Lee was a very positive force. She was just the kind of person you wanted to be around."

The head coach was especially sold on the belief that Harrison would attract young people to the program.

1974

Sanford took the crews to Washington, D.C., for some open water during spring break and while there took on the Georgetown Hoyas in scrimmages. "We went against Georgetown in a series of sessions and beat them every time at every distance while the frosh won four of six," the coach reported. But as was often the case, weather was a problem for the Orange back in Syracuse. "I felt we were coming along very nicely but the weather has been lousy since we returned home," Sanford said.

Spring Season

Harrison's first eight did not exactly burst out of the gate in the spring of 1974. The crews traveled to Poughkeepsie to take on Marist and Columbia on the Hudson River April 6th, and the frosh got the win by less than a length over Marist, with Columbia out of it. Marist was a top Dad Vail crew at the time, so the close win was no shame for SU.

It wound up being a sweep for the Orangemen as the JV cruised over Marist and the varsity did the same against the Red Foxes and the Lions.

Two weeks later on the Raritan River, Rutgers frosh got the better of SU by about 3/4 of a length. The Scarlet Knights' JV took SU by less than half-a-second, but the Orange varsity came through with a half-length win.

On April 27th the squad headed down the road to Ithaca and while the varsity took its first loss, it was close. Cornell prevailed by half-a-length, with Navy another half-a-length back. In fact it was a sweep for the Big Red as Syracuse was well behind in the JV race and Harrison's frosh, like the varsity could only get close. Cornell won it in 6:07 to SU's 6:10.9. The Navy Plebes were third. Perhaps most notably, the SU freshman time was only four seconds slower than the varsity and seven faster than the JV.

Sprints at Worcester

The Syracuse crews went to Worcester unseeded. Harvard

was the choice in the varsity and JV and Yale was the top freshman seed. Interestingly, the Navy Plebes whom SU had beaten in Ithaca were the second seed.

The SU freshman eight was made up of coxswain Murray Lukoff, Mark Lyvers at stroke, Pat Seaney at 7, John Hilfinger at 6, Elliot Sussin at 5, Tom Brown at 4, John Watson at 3, John DeWolf at 2 and Bill Peck in bow. Harrison's crew went through to the grand final where it finished fourth.

Lyvers, an experienced oar out of Hyde Park's Franklin D. Roosevelt High School, recalls just missing a medal, losing third in the last few strokes. "We were learning how to row and race," he says.

The Orange JV had a distinctive person in the boat. Coxswain Randy Poe was a 16-year-old sophomore, almost certainly the youngest collegiate cox in the country. Bill Mabie was stroke, backed by Joe Begley, Bill Pfeil, Mike Zapanick, Bob Halbig, Jim Constantino, Gary Jordan and Charlie Lee in bow.

The JV did not qualify for the grand final.

Matt Kirchoff stroked the V8, with Schmidt at 7, Daley at 6 and Big Mike Plumb at 5. The bow four included Duckworth, Garbaczeski, Andy Washburn (Pete's brother) and Tim Martin. They had some size, averaging 192 pounds. Senior Tom Corcoran coxed at 5'9" and 120 pounds.

The V8 wound up in the petite finals where it finished second.

Packard Cup

Dartmouth's Trustees banned the use of the nickname "Indians" for its teams in 1974, saying it was disrespectful to Native Americans. In fact, Dartmouth's teams had always been "the Green" or "the Big Green" but newspapermen had dubbed them "Indians" in reference to the College's founding mission in 1769–the education of American Indian youth in the region.

Four years later Syracuse would drop its Saltine Warrior mascot after Native American protests. Coincidentally, as a brother of Lambda Chi Alpha, Drew Harrison had played the role of the Saltine Warrior at SU football games during his undergraduate days.

MIT's Engineers and Dartmouth's Big Green came to Onondaga for the Packard Cup races in 1974 and MIT won the cup the third year in a row, using a smooth, low stroke cadence to beat the Orangemen by half-a-length. Dartmouth was several lengths back. MIT had started at a 43 cadence to Syracuse's 40, but then settled at 32–33 for the body of the race and opened a length lead. The Orange started cutting into the lead with 400 meters left, but MIT sprinted to a 39 cadence and held off Sanford's men. MIT's JV and freshmen also won over SU and the second frosh had the only SU win on the day.

MIT's first frosh got a restart when the three-man's seat broke in the first 25 seconds of the race. Once underway again, the Engineers jumped SU off the start and held the Orange off the rest of the way for a half-a-length win.

IRA

Lyvers remembers IRA Camp as "good and long" and occasionally eventful. The frosh raced the varsity in a 1,000-meter piece and were ahead and the coaches were–or were not–excited, depending on the point of view. The cox clipped a buoy, broke a few oars and riggers, and rolled the boat into the Erie Canal. The coaches were not thrilled about that.

Once the racing got underway the frosh finished fifth in the Thursday heat but came back on Friday to take second behind Cornell in the rep and qualify for the grand final. It was a dogfight in the final with Cornell winning and Wisconsin half-a-length back. SU outfought Penn for third by three-tenths of a second. It turned out to be the lowest any of "Drew's Crews" would finish in the next five years.

Harrison reflected decades later that whatever he was doing, it obviously was working. "Even though the first race in 1974 was probably ... if there was a ranking then, which I don't think there was, we would have been far, far, far from anywhere near the top at that point but we got better and better and better and better and the guys were listening and then everybody goes home with medals at the end of the season and that led to a lot of believers, including me."

The freshman four wound up third in the petite finals behind Penn and Kansas State.

Rather than compete in the JV eights, SU broke into a four and two pairs. The varsity four without cox finished fourth in a four-boat final behind Coast Guard, Penn and Princeton.

The Syracuse pair without cox won its Thursday heat, then was third behind Santa Clara and Coast Guard on Saturday. The pair with cox also took bronze in the grand final behind Penn and Cornell.

The varsity eight made the most of the IRA. While Sanford's men were third behind Wisconsin and Brown in the opening heat, they came up big in the repechage, beating Dartmouth by one-tenth of a second for the second spot behind MIT. That got them into the grand final.

In the grand finals, SU plainly had nothing left and finished sixth as Wisconsin won it all. Still it was a significant step up and there were reinforcements coming from the freshman team.

1975

Three of the sophomores who had medaled as frosh the year before were in the varsity eight as SU opened the spring season. John Watson was in bow, Pat Seaney at 3 and Mark Lyvers at 4. Veteran Matt Kirchoff stroked the eight with Tim Martin right behind him. Then it was Bob Halbig at six, Big Mike Plumb at five and Captain Andy Washburn at two, Craig Hoffman coxed and they raced in a shell named for SU alum Sidney Mang, '25. Despite the relatively diminutive Martin and Washburn, the crew averaged 6'3" and 187 pounds.

Sanford said he expected his boat to be faster than the previous year's boat, although not necessarily right away. He was high on Harrison's frosh. "This will be a big, strong and fast boat," he said.

The first frosh also averaged 187 pounds but were an inch taller than the varsity eight, averaging 6'4". Rick Tremblay was stroke with Dave Townsley at seven, then Paul Jirak, Andy

Mogish, Jr., Rod Jones, John Eisenbray, Jim Tapscott and Jim Remele in bow.

The Syracuse crews started 1975 with a sweep at Brown. Harrison's frosh took the Bruin cubs by two-and-a-half lengths. The JV won by a length and the varsity eight won by half-a-length.

But Rutgers turned the tables two weeks later on the Seneca River. The Orange frosh finished three lengths back of the Scarlet Knights. The finishes were close in the JV and varsity races but Rutgers completed the sweep, winning the JV race by a couple of seats and the varsity by just under a length.

Cornell won the Goes Cup with an open water win over Sanford's varsity with Navy third. SU's JV was a distant third behind Cornell and Navy. But the Orange frosh out-rowed the traditional rivals in an open water win over the Navy Plebes, with Cornell well back.

Sprints

The V8 had started all its races well but except for the Brown race couldn't get the job done in the second 1,000 meters. In an effort to solve the problem Sanford decided to move three guys up from the JV. Brian Mosoglo came in at bow, Joe Begley at 3 and Tom Brown at 4. Pat Seaney moved up from 3 to 7.

Lyvers went down to stroke the JV.

The Eastern Sprints were held in Princeton in 1975, but the Orange crews struggled as they often did in Worcester. The revamped varsity eight was fourth in the consolation finals and Harrison's frosh second in the consy behind Yale. Penn won the grand finals.

But with Lyvers at stroke the JV pulled off a surprise, finishing second in its heat to qualify for the grand finals and then edging MIT by seven-tenths of a second for fifth place. The order of finish was Harvard, Cornell, Navy, Northeastern and then SU and MIT.

The Packard Cup Stewards decided to mix things up a bit in 1975 and brought in Yale to join SU, MIT and Dartmouth in Hanover. Morning race winners would face off for the title and the losers would race for third place. SU's varsity eight drew the Eli in their heat and beat them by less than a second in a speedy 5:38.6. MIT took Dartmouth by a length, covering the 2K in 5:40.6.

MIT was nowhere near as fast in the afternoon but it didn't have to be. The Engineers took SU by open water, finishing in 5:56.4 to win the Packard Cup. Yale edged Dartmouth for third.

IRA

The Syracuse varsity eight was not yet in the top tier but got closer than shouting distance in the opening heat at the IRA. Powerful Wisconsin rowed through to the grand finals with Rutgers and SU next.

But things did not go well in the next day's repechage and the Orange finished behind Cornell, Brown and Princeton, leaving the crew in the petite finals. It was a fight on Saturday and Brown won it, a half-a-length ahead of Dartmouth, with SU another half-a-length back.

Yale, Princeton, Penn, Kansas State, and Nebraska followed.

Wisconsin was the IRA Varsity Champion.

Sanford's JV missed getting straight through to the grand finals with a second-place finish behind MIT in the Thursday heat. The Orange won the rep the next day by less than a second over Coast Guard, which also qualified. On Saturday, the Orange JV was ten seconds behind champion MIT, but there were four other crews–Northeastern, Wisconsin, Cornell and Coast Guard between them and SU was sixth.

Harrison's freshmen again took the repechage route to the grand finals. After finishing third behind Penn and Rutgers on Thursday, they won on Friday over Northeastern and MIT. Again, the Orange cubs saved the best for last. There was no catching Penn. The Quakers won by open water but it was SU in second, followed by Wisconsin, Rutgers, California and Princeton. This time it was silver for the young Orangemen.

And Harrison's freshman four? They won their heat and finished fourth in the grand finals.

Another group of frosh who knew how to win was headed for the varsity level. Having set the bar higher for their successors under Harrison, they were ready to move Sanford's crews into the top tier.

Chapter 10

1976 – Freshman Gold

Aﬁter a third-place ﬁnish at the '74 IRA followed by a
second-place ﬁnish in 1975, third-year coach Drew
Harrison's freshman crew was clearly on a path to the top of the
podium. If the '76 frosh could make the required next step, the
future would be bright indeed for the entire Syracuse Men's Crew.

There were several experienced guys coming onto
campus for the fall, with Bob Devlin and John Shamlian from
Philadelphia and Bill Purdy and Pete Gaines out of Liverpool High
School forming the core of the new class. While there had been
experienced rowers on the squad before, notably Mark Lyvers,
this was something of a new thing for Syracuse Rowing.

Back in the pre-recruiting era, rowing coaches would
bring in as many experienced high schoolers as they could, but
many programs relied heavily on walk-ons, Syracuse perhaps
more than most. While there were active high school and prep
school rowing programs in the Northeast and Mid-Atlantic areas,
there wasn't much rowing to speak of in many large cities. Some
areas including the South, Southeast, and Midwest were almost
devoid of high school or club rowing.

With the SUNY Forestry College providing a few big,
strong and tough freshmen each year, SU had a bit of an advantage
over the other EARC schools as it also drew from a student body
that was larger than most. Harrison had proved his ability to mold
the mix of experienced rowers, SU walk-ons, and "Stumpies" (the
term of art identifying Forestry College students) into very fit and
very strong crews, that while not the most technically adept were
certainly tough and fit enough to compete with the best in the
league.

The cup season went quite well for the Orange, with the
varsity undefeated. The JV and first freshman eights also defeated
Cornell at the Goes Cup and swept the Packard Trophy races as
well, where Dartmouth took second and MIT third in the three
eight events.

The varsity was stroked by the estimable Mark Lyvers,
with Dave Townsley in seven, Tom Evancie in six and Tom

Brown in five. Four-man Gary Jordan and John Watson in three filled out the engine room, with Paul Jirak in two and Bill Reid at bow. Murray Lukoff coxed the varsity. The lineup was pretty stable all season, with a few moves up and down the boat but little switching between the varsity and second eight. And with the results to date, the formula seemed to be working as planned.

While the program was enjoying much success in the duals and three-way events, that did not carry over to the Eastern Sprints. In addition to the Sprints falling at the end of finals week, under Bill Sanford, Syracuse Crew didn't focus on the Sprints, seeking to peak instead for the IRA. Nonetheless, the results for the eights were disappointing. None qualified for the grand finals, although the second eight won and frosh eight took second in the petites. The varsity's performance was subpar, and even the timing and SU's traditional emphasis on the IRA couldn't explain the poor showing, especially after its dominant performance in every race leading up to the Sprints.

It turned out there was a reason; the Sprints result was undoubtedly affected by Lyvers' previously-undiagnosed case of mononucleosis. The varsity stroke had been pushing hard all season, trying to push through what seemed to be fatigue and exhaustion from training. The crew was working very hard, and everyone was spent after practice; as the stroke, Lyvers was also the heart and soul of the boat, and he expected a lot from himself. While Lyvers battled through the season, in hindsight it was clear the illness had taken its toll.

While it was something of a relief to know what had led to the varsity's poor results, that knowledge didn't make it any easier to take. The diagnosis had come through right after Sprints, the crew had backed off the hard training during IRA Camp, and Lyvers felt "more normal" by the time IRAs rolled around.

The IRA Regatta came later than usual in 1976, with Thursday's heats scheduled for June 3rd. The Orange pair without was one of eight entries in what was a particularly challenging event; most oarsmen had little experience rowing coxless boats. With the added technical challenge inherent in rowing a pair coupled with the lesser ability of most of the pair rowers (most likely spares for the second and varsity eights) the result often depended as much on ability to adapt to rowing in the pair as any other factor.

In '76, Rutgers and Boston University forewent entering a varsity eight, opting instead to break their top boats down into small boats. The result of the heats seemed to demonstrate the wisdom of that decision, as both crews won their heats; SU's pair came in 27 seconds behind BU.

SU failed to qualify in the reps, but was able to win the two-boat petite. Rutgers won the grand final with Trinity and Penn following.

The Orange was also entered in the freshman four event, where SU's second boat found itself matched up again with a BU crew, this likely comprised of the best four from the Terriers' first freshman eight. Not intimidated one whit, Syracuse pressed BU all the way down the course before losing by less than a half-second; the third-place Cornell crew was a further 12 seconds back.

The rep was an entirely different affair as SU won by more than a length of open water over Yale. In the championship finals, SU's frosh four rowed to a silver medal with BU winning the Stork Sanford Trophy for freshman fours.

Rowing in the second heat, SU's freshman eight was matched up against Wisconsin, Cal, Penn, Dartmouth and Columbia. With the exception of Dartmouth, the frosh hadn't faced off with any of the crews in their heat in a dual race. The other six-crew heat looked to be somewhat faster, but with SU and Wisco traditionally late-blooming crews, the field looked to be wide open.

After Yale won the first heat by a length, the Syracuse freshmen found themselves in what was essentially a two-crew race for the lone qualifying spot for Saturday's grand finals. The Orange prevailed, crossing the line just a second in front of the Badgers with California a length-and-a-half back in third.

Harrison and his crew relaxed on Friday, watching Penn and Brown qualify, with Brown edging California by a half-second to squeak into the grands. Wisco qualified easily in the other heat, while Princeton also edged Dartmouth for the last spot in the finals by the same half-second margin.

The second place in the frosh four was a praiseworthy finish indeed for Drew Harrison's men, and one which boded well for their classmates in the eight, just then pulling up to the stake boats as the four paddled away from the awards dock. Conditions were a bit slower on championship day as the Onondaga headwind had increased a bit. That suited the low-stroking, hard-pulling SU frosh just fine. The order of finish for the grand final was Syracuse in first by a couple seconds over Wisconsin, with Yale securing the bronze.

This was the 1976 IRA-winning freshman eight crew's line up:

Cox	Miles Ianacone
Stroke	Bob Devlin
No. 7	Bill Purdy
No. 6	John Shamlian
No. 5	Paul Dierkes
No. 4	John Moyer
No. 3	Pete Gaines
No. 2	Jim Zimmerman
Bow	Dave Hess

With Drew Harrison's first Stewards Cup in hand, the racing would now turn to crews manned by upperclassmen.

1976 was a lean year for second varsity eights as only seven answered the call for entries. Syracuse finished last in its four-boat heat before qualifying for the grand finals by virtue of its third-place finish in the repechage on Friday. Facing the same slightly slower conditions didn't seem to benefit Bill Sanford's Jayvee, as the crew ended the race in fifth, a bit over two lengths behind winner Penn.

Eleven varsity eights rowed out to the start of the heats on Thursday morning, greeted by fast conditions and good water. There was no question which heat was viewed as faster, and by the luck of the draw it was the heat Sanford's crew found itself in. Wisconsin, Cal, Penn, and Brown all looked to be serious contenders for the finals, with the first three legitimate medal threats. The heat times bore out the handicapping with four crews in SU's heat beating the winning time in the second heat of the varsity eights. SU's fourth-place finish relegated the crew to the next day's reps, where it faced off with the Golden Bears again, as well as Dartmouth Cornell and Yale. California won with SU a half-length back in a comfortable second place. Penn and MIT qualified from the other heat, and the lanes for the grand finals were full.

After racing well in the heats and reps, SU's performance in the finals was disappointing at best. After losing to California by 1.8 seconds on Friday, Syracuse found itself nine seconds in back of the Varsity Challenge Cup-winning Golden Bears as they crossed the finish line in the finals. Reflecting back on the race decades later, it is tempting to chalk it up to the physical demands of three races in three days wearing down the varsity stroke, still not recovered from his months-long bout with mononucleosis.

Lyvers' illness may well have been a factor, but it wasn't an excuse. Syracuse crew had come to expect more.

Chapter 11
1977 – The Year That Wasn't

Nineteen seventy-seven was going to be "The Year," the year that Bill Sanford's varsity finally brought the IRA championship back to Long Branch after 57 long years. The freshmen under Drew Harrison had won the regatta the previous year after a second in 1975 and a third in '74.

The program was growing also, with three full varsity eights and more than two freshmen boats on the water when what passed for a Syracuse "spring" began. The talent was there, and the big eight, led by captain and stroke Mark Lyvers, was determined to deliver on its promise.

Lyvers had been in the '74 frosh eight, which had finished third behind Cornell and Wisconsin at the IRA. The atmosphere at the end of the 1974 IRAs was exciting; the varsity had improved dramatically from previous years and the team had grown in numbers and commitment. Half of the freshmen stuck around for the summer and rowed in the Syracuse Chargers program, and their effort paid off; SU's 1975 varsity eight boated four sophomores.

Apparently this wasn't what the upperclassmen expected. According to Lyvers, the insertion of four sophomores into the varsity eight created a bit of tension between those new guys and those who had been there before. Before 1975, there'd been a sense–not quite an unwritten rule or tradition, more of a feeling that you earned your spot–at least in part–through seniority. Upperclassmen somehow "deserved" those varsity seats more than sophomores, a concept that was foreign to the new guys on the varsity squad.

Whether it was the tension, a lack of maturity, or just not enough talent, the varsity didn't really come together as a crew in 1975. 1976 was considerably better, particularly in the cup races where SU swept all races in the Goes and Packard Cups, won the varsity and frosh races against Rutgers and both varsity races over Brown. Despite all of that success, when the championship regattas began, something was amiss. The varsity failed to make the finals at the Sprints, and made it into the IRA grand finals by virtue of a second-place finish in the rep, only to finish sixth.

While the varsity stroke's sickness likely affected the crew's result it didn't make the results any easier to swallow.

There were six seniors on the squad in 1977, but for whatever reason, Lyvers was the only senior who had come into the program with high school rowing experience who was still on the team in '77. Recalling the foundation they had built, Mark said "there were six people who went all the way through the four years. Not all were on the varsity, but there was a core group of non-recruited people who did something for the rowing program while they were there, and their passion and love for the sport brought success." One of those seniors, John Watson, would deliver a remarkable–and very rare–performance at the IRA.

The 1977 varsity eight was a pretty stable boat. The lineup didn't change after Spring Camp, the boat made up of medalists–and champions–from frosh crews in previous years. Still, despite the evident talent in the boat, early in the racing season it just didn't seem to completely gel, to come together and make the leap from freshman national champion to varsity national champion. It wasn't a personality issue, as Lyvers remembers the crew had "good chemistry." It certainly wasn't a lack of power–the crew had that in spades. What was missing, what they needed to make the transition from fast freshman crews to winning at the varsity level was technique.

In retrospect Lyvers deemed a lack of finesse, technical proficiency and polish were the limiting factors. He recalled the boat had a "tremendous amount of power … we won races by overpowering other crews, but that only got us so far when we got to the elite level; we needed a different level of expertise. That was the difference maker in that crew. Physically, [we were] probably more powerful than any other crew in the nation but we lacked on the technical side."

The team stayed at Long Branch for Spring Camp, trading the trip south and warmer weather for more water time. While it was typical early-March weather for upstate New York (chilly, cloudy, and one day of steady rain), the snow held off and the crews piled up the miles. After breaking camp, SU's first race was scheduled for early April in Boston, and the competition was none other than the legendary Harry Parker's Harvard Crimson. Coach

Sanford had been talking with Parker for several years about the possibility of an early season race as a way for both crews to test their speed. Things had finally come together in early 1977 with the coaches agreeing to a home-and-home series. The 1977 race was held in Boston at the unusual distance of 2,500 meters, the race lengthened to allow for Syracuse's lack of water time.

While the day started out well enough with the second freshman eight rowing steadily away from Harvard for a 2.5-second win, it was to be the only crew to head home with new shirts in its bags. Harvard managed to sweep the rest of the events, defeating the JV and first freshman by more than ten seconds. Due to an injury, the first frosh had a last minute lineup change that resulted in only one row together for the crew before race day. The varsity event was considerably closer, with SU trailing the Crimson by 3.2 seconds, proving it could compete with the cream of the EARC.

The weather gods were kind to the Orange during the week after the trip to Boston, with unseasonably warm weather and placid conditions on Onondaga. The freshmen began the week with Coach Harrison's dreaded "Tour of the Lake," a circumnavigation of Onondaga that began with Drew loudly encouraging his second boat, proclaiming them Crimson Beaters. Thus began what was to be one of the fastest freshman tours ever recorded as the first boat sought to erase a bit of the sting from the loss while the now-very-confident second frosh cut every turn and sought every advantage. The tour ended with the first boat in front, and two very tired crews. Years later, stroke Art Sibley recalled that after the row, Harrison told the first boat they would be fine, they just needed to work every day to close the gap a bit at a time.

The Goes Cup was another disappointing race for the SU varsity. Despite the beautiful conditions on the Cayuga Inlet and a fast start by the Orange that saw it with the lead well into the second 500 meters, Cornell took the Cup with Syracuse nine seconds back in second and Navy trailing. The third varsity managed to take Cornell by just over a second, the freshman and second freshman eights won convincingly, and the JV also took second, a bit more than a length behind Navy as Cornell finished third. The frosh win and the two varsity eight seconds were enough to give SU the points it needed to win the Norman Stagg Trophy for best overall performance.

Commenting after the race, Coach Sanford said: "We were rowing at altogether too high a rate during the middle of the race–36 to 36-½–and it seemed as though we ran into a brick wall during the final 800 meters."

The Orange's next competition was Rutgers at home in Syracuse. The Scarlet Knights were going through a low period, with a thin roster and dearth of talent. Without enough athletes to enter a JV, Rutgers was clearly outclassed by the deep Syracuse crew. The varsity won in a laugher, with Rutgers finishing more than 23 seconds behind the Orange. The first freshman race wasn't quite as bad, although Harrison's crew did win by just under ten seconds.

The week before final exams saw SU take to the road to race Brown and what was a very strong crew from the U.S. Coast Guard Academy. The varsity continued to improve, making technical refinements that were beginning to pay off. The Seekonk River, always a tough course with wind, tides, and current all working to confuse and confound coxswains, was solved by varsity cox Murray Lukoff, as he brought the Orange across the finish line over a length in front of Bruno, with the Coast Guard crew another length back. This was a bit of revenge for the Coasties' three-second win over SU in the JV eight race, with Brown back by just a bit of open water.

The freshmen from Onondaga made it down the course in fine fashion, dominating both of their opponents to win by over five seconds over Brown. The third varsity and second frosh stayed home, as there weren't any Brown or Coast Guard entries for them to race.

Things were coming together. The good weather and lots of miles were beginning to show their effect, as both the varsity and freshman crews were picking up more speed every week.

Heading into the Sprints, SU's varsity was looking strong. The crew was coming together, steadily making the small technical improvements it needed to win. This "technical deficit" hadn't prevented Drew Harrison's freshman crews from ever-increasing levels of success; although according to Lyvers, technique wasn't "the highest priority in Drew's mind, but from a physical standpoint he really got the most out of a crew." That was freshman rowing, but for the varsity, pure pulling wasn't enough. On the varsity level, the oarsmen were rowing against more technically proficient crews. Syracuse had to put out more energy to overcome the other crews' advantage in efficiency. Good-enough technique wasn't good enough when rowing against the likes of Cornell and Harvard, but over the course of the season things were coming along.

In 1977, the Sprints were again held in Princeton, with the 3V and 2F racing the evening before in what was then an informal event that went by the sobriquet "Saturday Night Sprints." Not an official part of the EARC Championships, this event was organized and put on primarily by the coaches. SU's second frosh, rowing under a 30 cadence for most of the 2,000 meters, finally raised the rating and came charging up on Northeastern in the last 500, but it was too little too late. NU won by less than a half-second. SU's third varsity, stroked by IRA freshman champion Rick Tremblay, rowed a very aggressive race plan and was rewarded with a Sprints championship and betting shirts from Penn and Harvard.

Years later, Tremblay would recall, "[Coxswain] Neil [Prete] and Coach Sanford played significant roles to enable the SU third varsity boat to be Eastern Sprints champions [Harvard and Penn were the other entries]. We decided to go out strong at the beginning of the race to take a significant lead. Then Neil took over. He made a sharp turn to starboard to cut off Harvard. Harvard couldn't figure out how to get around us before the finish line. I'm pretty sure we won the race by open water, at least that's the way I remember it. Then the most critical part of the race was Coach Sanford convincing Harry Parker to allow our little lane shifting and consider the race legal. Rumor has it Bill treated Harry to a steak dinner later that weekend."

With Tremblay in the SU third varsity were cox Neil Prete, Dan Hanavan, fellow IRA frosh champion Pete Gaines, Pete Hausman, Andy Papp, Walter "Pappy" MacVittie, Fred Gliesing, and Bill Samios. Hanavan also has great memories of the win. He remembers: "Looking over to the shore after the race at the finish line. The SU crew team cheering, wearing the bright orange SU suit jackets!! What style."

On Sunday morning, May 15th, the other crews took to the water. The morning heats were a success for SU as, for the first time on record, all three eights qualified for the grand finals. But qualifying was one thing; defeating crews that had beaten them handily earlier in the season was an entirely different matter. Once again, Harvard won the varsity event followed by Penn and Cornell with Syracuse just out of the medals in fourth. While SU had indeed gotten faster since the meeting in Boston, Harvard had done that and more. Notably, the third-place medalists were none other than the Big Red, and while they had beaten SU again, this time the margin had shrunk to barely a second. SU had made up a full two lengths on Cornell in three weeks.

The big boat wasn't the only crew that was faster. The JV eight, stroked by Bob Devlin, closed a bit of its gap to Harvard in finishing fifth in the grand finals. Even more impressive was the performance of the fourth-place Syracuse freshman eight, which finished just over a length behind first-place Penn while beating Harvard by a second. Princeton and Yale, silver- and bronze-medalists, both finished within a half-second of Penn. Drew's crew had gained twelve seconds on the Crimson in a month.

With final exams and the Sprints behind them, the crews were looking forward to the camaraderie of IRA Camp at the Long Branch Boathouse. This was the time when Syracuse Crew made big improvements—with school over, great weather, and intense but shorter workouts, all focus was on the IRA Regatta.

But before the IRA, SU would take on Dartmouth and MIT at the Packard Cup in Hanover, New Hampshire. 1977 wasn't a great year for the Big Green, and MIT's excellent crews from the early seventies had graduated most of their horses. The result was the SU varsity taking the Packard Cup, defeating MIT by nine seconds and Dartmouth by over thirteen seconds.

The IRA finals were rowed in typical Onondaga conditions, namely a headwind that varied from stiff to soft throughout the day. As a result, some races were considerably longer than the usual 6:00–6:25, putting a premium on conditioning and strength. That would prove to be perfect for SU's freshman eight.

Freshman coach Drew Harrison's previous three seasons

had ended with consecutive bronze, silver, and gold medals; there wasn't anyplace to go but down from there. The 1977 crew, stroked by Art Sibley and coxed by Ozzie Street was loaded with power and size, and for the first time, more than half of the crew–Street and Sibley, Gerry Henwood in seven, Peter Henriques in the three seat and Kevin Rung in bow–were experienced rowers. The other four oarsmen–two-man Dave Fish, John Stockwell in four, Jeff Braun and Steve Anthony manning the engine room in five and six–were prototype Drew Harrison freshmen–big, tough and strong. Their IRA campaign started with promise as they recorded the fastest time of any freshman crew in the heats, defeating second-place Northeastern by a bit of open water in 6:50.2, earning a bye on Friday as they advanced directly to the grand finals.

The slow time of the Orange freshman eight was indicative of the strength of the headwind on Thursday, which wouldn't let up for the rest of the regatta.

Meanwhile, the freshman four, comprised of guys from the second frosh eight, finished a very creditable second in its heat on Thursday in a time that would have garnered first place in the other fours heat. Things didn't go as well the next day, as the four faced a three-boat repechage where only the winner would make it to the grand finals. Coming in second behind Yale, SU didn't make it to the grand finals, but did win Saturday's petite finals by three-tenths of a second over Wisconsin in what would prove to be the closest race of the finals.

In addition to the two varsity eights, Coach Sanford had a pair with cox, a pair without, and a four without cox entered. Manned by the same athletes who had just won the Eastern Sprints in the third varsity, the three crews would prove to be tough competitors.

Throughout most of the seventies and eighties, the small boats at the IRA came from three different talent pools; third varsity heavy eights; varsity lightweights, primarily from the Ivies; and varsity heavies and lights from schools outside the EARC such as Marist, San Diego State, Oregon State, Coast Guard, and Worcester Polytechnic Institute. Occasionally IRA / EARC schools that were facing lean years would break their varsity eights into small boats, a practice that has fortunately fallen out of favor.

119

The four without cox was always an exciting race where bowmen, unaccustomed to steering, managing a race, and handling the myriad of tasks so ably handled by coxswains could prove to have an effect on the outcome far more significant than their efforts with one oar might imply. With Walter MacVittie, Fred Gliesing, Dan Hanavan in bow, and Andy Papp at stroke, the oarsmen needed to get a race under their belts before they were really ready to go. After failing to win its heat, the Orange four without cox stormed into the finals, winning the rep by open water. In the grand finals it finished just out of the medals in fourth.

If the four without cox was a potentially very exciting race due to the steep learning curve facing bowmen in the four (almost all steering was handled by bowmen in those days), the pair without cox added another complication. Balance and timing, so critical in a pair-oared shell, were not typically among the strong suits of the denizens of the third boat. And with just over two weeks to get familiar with each other, learn to steer, develop a bit of rhythm and coordination, establish some sort of communication process, and develop a racing start, settle, and sprint, the workload was high indeed. And success would only accrue to the boat that managed to do this consistently in two, or perhaps three, consecutive races.

The pair without cox proved to be challenging for SU's Pete Hausman and Bill Samios, as they finished well back in the heats and rep. Racing in the petites on Saturday, SU found its groove, rowing a great race to finish second, with no open water separating the pair from winner Cornell. A pair from Wayne State won the grand finals convincingly over two oarsmen from Rutgers' varsity eight.

If there's one event that was not meant to be rowed in the conditions facing all crews, on all days, in all lanes that year, it was the pair with coxswain. Likened to doing leg presses for eight minutes, the usually-interminably-long pair with cox event was going to be a marathon at the 1977 IRA. Each crew's oarsmen would have to contend not only with the drag of the coxswain lying in their bow, but the headwind which varied from stiff to very strong throughout the three days would make for a tough row.

Syracuse's pair with cox, manned by the redoubtable Rick

Tremblay and Pete Gaines, with Neil Prete in the coxswain "seat," qualified via the repechage on Friday by finishing fourth, thereby gaining the last qualifying spot for Saturday's finals. An indication of the conditions was the time registered by Yale, winner of the rep, who crossed the finish line in 8:35. The conditions worsened by Saturday morning, and they proved far too much for SU's gallant crew to handle. In a race won by Yale in 9:15, the Orange entry finished sixth after struggling with the rough conditions.

With the small boat racing wrapped up, it was time for the eights to head into their stake boats.

First up were the freshman eights.

Drew Harrison's crew, rejecting any idea that there would be a let up in the dominance of the Orange in the freshman eights, crossed the line with more than a length separating the new champions from the silver-medalist crew. SU, winning with a time of 7:23.2, was followed by Cornell (7:28) and Sprints champion Penn (7:29).

This was the 1977 IRA-winning freshman eight crew's line up:

Cox	Ozzie Street
Stroke	Art Sibley
No. 7	Gerry Henwood
No. 6	Steve Anthony
No. 5	Jeff Braun
No. 4	John Stockwell
No. 3	Peter Henriques
No. 2	Dave Fish
Bow	Kevin Rung

But it hadn't seemed like it would go that way on the way out to the stake boats. The north wind was strong enough to build a bit of a chop, and the practice starts the crew had done headed into the wind hadn't gone well. Sibley and coxswain Ozzie Street talked just before they pulled into the stake boat in lane five (well out in the choppier water). Violating a cardinal rule of racing, the cox and stroke changed the race plan then and there, agreeing to back off just a bit on the start, cut the number of high strokes and focus on getting away clean. This was a significant change from the race plan and counter to the way they'd started all their other races. And a major gamble for a freshman crew, albeit one coxed by a supremely confident U.S. Junior National Team veteran.

It worked, perhaps better than they could have hoped. Coming clean off the stake boat, the Syracuse freshmen settled to a 32 cadence well before the end of the first 500, a full eight strokes-per-minute under their usual pace for the first 500 meters. Despite the low rating, the Orange had a full length when they passed the black-and-white poles on shore marking the end of the first five hundred meters, and open water at the halfway mark. Keeping the rate at what felt like a very solid 32, they were able to maintain that advantage throughout the third 500, in large part due to Ozzie's unflappable and very vocal confidence. Despite Ozzie's–later admitted–surprise at how well his guys had handled the start and the rough water in the first 500, that surprise never showed. Listening to him during the race, seven-man Gerry Henwood recalled it was as if Oz completely expected to be where they were–out in front and on their way to winning a national championship.

That confidence, combined with the crew's superb conditioning and Harrison's ability to get his crew to perform at its best in the biggest race of the year, made the championship race a great one.

The JV's path to the finals was a different story. After its solid performance in the Sprints, the second boat looked to challenge for a medal as Harvard, third place in Worcester, wouldn't come to the IRAs. Unfortunately, the Orange JV appeared to have lost something since the Sprints, and the crew underperformed. Finishing well back in third place in its heat on Thursday, Bill Sanford's second boat faced a four-boat rep on Friday morning. The Orangemen would have to finish first or second to make it to the grand finals. Yale and Wisconsin were too much for the Orange, and SU finished third, well back of winner Yale. Saturday morning saw the crew gain a bit of redemption, winning the petites in a close one over Brown which was less than half-a-length back at the finish. Sprints champion Penn repeated, winning the JV grand finals in a headwind-slowed time of 6:31.4, with California in second and Navy picking up the bronze.

For the varsity, it was to prove to be a bittersweet end to

what had been a frustrating season.

After the fourth-place finish at the Sprints and convincing win in the Packard Cup, the top boat had continued to make progress during IRA Camp. And, with the Crimson at their Red Top Boathouse on Connecticut's Thames River training for the Harvard-Yale four-miler, Syracuse looked to be in solid medal contention.

Thursday's heat saw the Orange lined up with Sprints champion Penn in conditions that had steadily worsened throughout the day, with their race the last one held on Thursday afternoon. Penn took SU by 3.3 seconds, and Lyvers and his teammates were headed to the reps, scheduled for late Friday afternoon.

They would have to do without bow oar Dave Townsley. In what would prove to be a foretaste of what was to come in '78, Townsley had become severely dehydrated after the heats on Thursday, to the point where he wasn't able to row in the reps. Due to the weather conditions on Onondaga, races were delayed and it was hoped Townsley would recover in time to make the varsity launch for the reps. He wasn't, so Sanford had to call on John Watson, bow in the JV to sit in for Townsley. This wasn't an easy task. Watson would race in the JV reps before jumping into the varsity and racing again a couple hours later. That this was even possible was due to the IRA Officials authorizing a special exception to the rule that no athlete could compete in two events. Given the circumstances, they agreed to the switch.

What followed was described by Bill Sanford as his "biggest disappointment in that time ... we were in a position [to win the grand finals] and turned in a better time than Cornell [winner of the grand finals] but we were in the petite finals." And the fact that SU's varsity was in the petites, and not the grand finals, was due to a delay in racing, the glare of the sun, a clash of oars, and an officials' decision.

The Friday schedule was a mess. With windy conditions concerning officials, the lead official decided to push some races to very early in the morning, and delayed others till near sunset. SU's varsity, complete with its replacement bowman finally launched more than an hour after it was originally scheduled to race, rowing out for an eight p.m. start, just as the sun came close

123

to the horizon.

The day was clear, the race course pointed directly into the setting sun, and the glare off Onondaga made it very difficult for coxswains to see their navigational points. This was one of those rare days when the team would have been only too happy to see the clouds of March return. As the crews lined up on the stake boats, Syracuse was in lane two, just off Onondaga's shore. Yale was in three, with Boston University, Columbia, and Kansas State filling out the card. The Orange would have to win to qualify for the grand finals, but off the start, SU just didn't seem to have it. Whether it was the change in lineup just before the race, the conditions, or just a bad day, the Orange was struggling to stay in contention at the halfway mark.

Out in lanes five and six, referee and SU alum Chuck Mills was dealing with errant steering on the part of Columbia and Kansas State. That's when disaster struck.

Just past the thousand-meter mark, BU was in the lead, with Yale behind and SU running in third. According to contemporary press reports, "Yale was about a full boat length ahead of Syracuse 1,200 meters into Friday's repechage heat. Since only the race's victor would advance to Saturday's final, every stroke was significant." SU cox Murray Lukoff was quoted saying, "Yale moved into our lane … The conditions were really bad, the sun was right in the [Yale] cox's eyes. I'm not sure if their stern hit our bow, but the officials definitely ordered them out of our lane."

Unfortunately, Mills didn't see Yale cross over into SU's lane, and wasn't there to steer the Eli straight before they fouled Lukoff's crew. By the time the officials got control of the situation, the damage was done.

Lukoff wasn't sure SU could have made up the length on the Eli over the last 800 meters, saying, "We were having a bad race, Yale had rowed through us, so I'm not sure we could have come back. But whatever the case, they gave us a wake for at least ten strokes, maybe even more."

Finishing third, 5.4 seconds down to heat-leader Yale, Syracuse filed a protest immediately after the race. The IRA Officials debated the issue till well into the night, but their final conclusion was bad news for the Orange. Officials John Garnjost and Anthony Antin ruled that although Yale had crossed into SU's lane, SU was "not impeded enough to alter the outcome of the race." Talking to the press after the decision was announced, Sanford said, "I'm disappointed in the officials' judgment. Regardless of the amount of momentum you lose, be it one stroke or three strokes, if you're impeded, you're impeded. There are all kinds of position changes in this sport, so who's to judge how much a boat is actually hindered."

Coach Sanford went on to point out, "Sure the conditions were bad Friday, and you've got to feel sorry for the coxes. But our cox stayed well within his lane." As always, Sanford made a compelling case, but the officials ruled otherwise, and SU was relegated to the petite finals.

In fairness to the officials, in taking second to Yale, BU finished a full five seconds up on the Orange who crossed the line in third. While Yale may have impeded SU, the fact that BU and Yale were both well up on the Orange at the time of the foul may well have influenced their decision. More importantly, if SU had put together a solid first one-thousand meters, it would likely not have been in a position where an officials' decision would determine its fate.

With the decision rendered, bowman Townsley recovered and was back in the boat, and a very big incentive for the SU varsity to show the officials just how wrong their decision was, SU blew through the competition in the petite finals, winning by more than ten seconds. Despite rowing against little competition, SU finished in a time of 6:33.1, more than ten seconds in front of second place Northeastern, and barely seven-tenths of a second slower than Cornell's gold medal performance in the grand finals, in a race where Cornell was pressed hard by Penn.

Talking about it years later, Mark Lyvers recalled it was a "very good final row for the crew. It gave a lot of maturity to the underclassmen ... how you deal with adversity and changes, this paid off the next year with Sibley missing [from the varsity] after the Sprints." Stroke Art Sibley was injured and out of the varsity for more than a week.

For Sanford and his varsity crew, a grand finals and a

shot at gold would have been so much sweeter. Steeled by the 1977 season's experiences, and strengthened by another class of freshman champions, the 1978 crew would find out how sweet it could be.

Chapter 12
1977 – Women Achieve Varsity Status!

D riven by a confluence of factors, varsity status arrived in 1977 for Syracuse University Women's Crew. Title IX of the Higher Education Act of 1972 was beginning to transform college sports, led by rowing. Early in 1976, nineteen members of the Yale women's crew had shocked the world when they marched into the women's athletic director's office and promptly disrobed. With "Title IX" written on their chests and backs, the message was clear; they were no longer content to sit on the bus in their soaking workout gear, waiting for the men to finish their showers.

At Syracuse, the efforts of Lori Barnett, the program's captain and manager, along with the dogged persistence of the women who had come before Barnett, were instrumental in making women's rowing one of the first new women's sports. With a large contingent ready to take to the water as varsity athletes, women's rowing would help the University demonstrate it was moving quickly to comply with Title IX.

Title IX required universities receiving federal monies to provide equal opportunities to both men and women in all areas including sports.

Title IX had a dramatic effect on college sports as many schools have interpreted the law as requiring institutions to provide opportunities for male and female athletes that are consistent with the percentage of men and women at that institution. Thus, schools, especially those with football programs, looked for ways to increase the number of women's sports to balance the participation of men and women.

The Syracuse women's crew's first head coach was Mark Lyvers–a 1977 SU graduate–varsity stroke and team captain. Lyvers was a leader who would later be credited by *The Daily Orange* for "rocketing the team from the equivalent of Division III to one of the better Division I teams in the nation." That improvement took a lot of time, enthusiasm, and persistence in recruiting, planning, logistics, and coordination with the University and the men's program.

Lyvers made an immediate impression on the women; Lynne Della Pelle Pascale's memories of Lyvers were echoed by other alumnae. She recalled, "Mark was very organized, very bright, just a few years older than the women, he did his job very well, we felt like we could trust him and he was fair; it was rare to see a whole crew unanimous in their opinion of a coach."

Lyvers' and the crew's first recruited athlete was Kaja-Anne Jezycki of Tuxedo Park, New York. Jezycki, a 5'7" starboard oar, had rowed at the Kent School in Connecticut for four years, and would become a key contributor during her four years at Syracuse. But Jezycki, her older colleagues and fellow recruits, weren't enough to get SU's Women's Crew off to the start the coach sought.

In an interview years later, Lyvers recalled he "… hit the quad to recruit anyone, pick out the high school athletes coming in, and see what you could do from there." The recruiting efforts of Lyvers and the women were almost too successful, as he had six full eights when the rowing started in mid-September. Normal attrition shrunk the count to 3 or 4 eights by the end of the fall. With just 12 experienced rowers, the Syracuse women headed to Boston for their first race as varsity athletes–the 1977 Head of the Charles. They performed competently, finishing 19th out of 40 crews in the women's four and 15th out of 40 in the women's eight.

The Daily Orange reporter may have been just a bit hyperbolic with that "rocketing" remark, but the improvement in the team's performance over one season was remarkable. While the 1978 Sprints were canceled due to weather conditions, the women were competitive in their dual races. The race at Cornell was particularly memorable, as the crews faced white caps on the course, and the Orange women finished with five inches of water in their boat. That didn't prevent them from defeating Cornell, although Yale was well out in front.

The 1979 campaign saw some excellent racing, including a loss by a deck to Rutgers in the varsity eight in the squad's opening race, with SU taking both the JV and novice races in the Raritan River contest. Stroked by Kate Sibley, sister of SU men's varsity rower Art, the lineup included Lynne Della Pelle at seven,

128

Shari Hersh in six, Leslie Weber at five, Diane Kulpinski in four, Irene Marx at three, Kaja-Anne Jezycki in the two seat and Kristin Brodie in bow.

In the Penn-BU-Syracuse race, the Orange varsity placed second, well back of Penn but a length up on BU. The second season for the varsity program ended with a tenth-place finish for the varsity and a grand final appearance and sixth overall for the JV at the '79 Sprints. Yale repeated as champions, a testament to the tenacity of the women who had brought equality to intercollegiate women's rowing.

1980 was looking to be a breakout year. With Robbi Needham assisting as novice coach, Lyvers wasn't stretched quite as thin. The program had lost one coxswain and two rowers to graduation, and had nine juniors returning for the 1980 season. The women's challenge was to improve even more than the other programs in the EAWRC, acknowledged as the strongest women's league in the nation. In an interview in an April 1980 issue of *The Daily Orange*, Lyvers was guardedly confident, saying "We should improve greatly on that this year ... whether we can get in the top six this year depends on a number of things, especially how quickly we mature as a team ... I don't think it would be unrealistic for us to make the top six ... of the Eastern Sprints with the varsity." That optimism was tempered by his personal experience as an athlete: "It's funny because you could have a really good team one year and come in third or fourth in the championships, but in any other year that crew might be able to win everything." The team would benefit from off-season competitive experience as well; Della Pelle had been in the winning lightweight women's crew at the National Championships in 1979, and varsity coxswain Megan Waldron had coxed several championship crews as well.

Those crews would be rowing in new shells, a major improvement over the castoff equipment from the men's program they'd used previously. Two new lightweight Kaschper shells occupied racks in the Long Branch Boathouse, one, named La Meilleure (French for "the best") donated by the SU Men's Athletics Department and Office of Student Affairs and another a gift of ORANGE PLUS, the SU women's athletics support organization and Leo Jezycki, father of Kaja-Anne. The

University's contributions may have been due in part to the years of persistence exhibited by the founders of the SU Women's Club and the new awareness of the impact of Title IX.

Penn was deemed the favorite for the 1980 varsity eight championship, with Williams and Yale also highly touted. SU's women wouldn't have to wait long to see how they matched up; their opening race featured defending national and EAWRC champion Yale along with a strong Cornell crew. While the results of that bell-ringer would be one measure of progress, the Orange women's lack of water time–they had not gotten into the shells until March 19th, and had only seven miles of training on the water during spring break–would temper any dissatisfaction from a less-than-stellar showing.

The Quakers proved their press wasn't hyperbolic, beating SU by almost 14 seconds on their home course in Philadelphia in the Orange Challenge Cup.

Partway through the season, Lyvers departed unexpectedly. There appear to have been several factors involved in the departure, including issues related to equipment. Lyvers was replaced on an interim basis by Robbi Needham; who was assisted by a committee of coaches including men's Graduate Assistant Jay Printzlau and Men's Head Coach Bill Sanford.

Penn returned to the top of the podium at the EAWRC Sprints, with SU far back in the field.

Two-time women's Olympic team member Jan Palchikoff was named the new women's head coach in August, and was excited about the opportunity. In an interview, she said, "SU has all the ingredients for a strong women's crew and I expect SU will be among the best." Palchikoff hit the ground running. Palchikoff was assisted by novices coach Debra Quinn. Quinn came in with excellent credentials, having coached Radcliffe's lightweight eight to an undefeated season and EAWRC championship.

Relying on the women's version of an age-old recruiting tactic, she and new assistant Deb Quinn put tape on the wall at class registration marking 5'9", and buttonholed any woman hitting that mark. In an interview with *The Herald-American,* Quinn described the result of their efforts, "You should have seen the girls when we sent them out for the first time on a two-mile run. Ten minutes went by. Fifteen minutes. Did they get lost? we wondered. Forty-five minutes later the last one came struggling in with one newcomer proud when she completed two miles without stopping, walking, or throwing up."

The 1981 racing season was predicted to be a good one for SU's women. Lyvers' recruiting efforts had resulted in "... two of what [Lyvers] considered the top six recruits in the country ... people right off of last year's U.S. Junior National Team."

The schedule kicked off in October of 1980 with the National Women's Invitational Regatta. Hosted by Mount Holyoke College, the novice-only event featured crews from six programs competing in a 2,800-meter time trial followed by a head-to-head format for the four-boat finals. The results were encouraging, as the SU women's A boat won the time trial by 14 seconds and the grand finals by 13 seconds, while the B crew won the petite final by 18 seconds.

The Head of the Charles saw two SU women's crews competing in the Championship 4 and Championship 8 events, the eight finishing 30th with the four taking the 33rd spot in its event.

When the spring season came around, the crew looked quite different from the one that had finished the 1980 season. The new boats were crewed by many new faces. Of the 21 non-seniors who rowed at the EAWRC Championships back in May, only eight experienced rowers were on the roster, with the rest of the 40-woman roster made up of newcomers to the program. The normal drop-off may have been exacerbated by some athletes' dissatisfaction with the way the departure of Lyvers was handled as he was well regarded by the entire team. Others likely had their own reasons. Varsity basketball center Martha Mogish (Andy Mogish's sister) had jumped into a boat right after her basketball season had ended, with her last year in the JV. She had met with Palchikoff in the fall to discuss the same arrangement, but Palchikoff had rebuffed her only to ask Mogish to row on the novice crew in the spring. Mogish declined.

As a result, for much of the season Palchikoff boated a varsity and two novice eights, along with a JV 4. The new coach was "especially enthused" about the novices, saying, "We have size in our favor, strength, and the fact that they just won't quit. There are no weak links in the novice boat." The JV would be filled primarily with novices; although the novice eight was the priority and thus the rowers in the JV would be those who failed to make the first novice boat, Palchikoff opined they'd be "very competitive." The varsity, while smaller and lighter than many of the crews they'd face, were nonetheless "skilled oarswomen" and "tough."

The crews would be tested quickly; on April 4th in Derby, Connecticut, Palchikoff's women took to the water for a three-way race with Yale and Cornell. Cornell and Yale had begun the competition–that would become the Cayuga Cup years later–in 1976, with SU added to the event in 1978. The novice eights finished poorly–a second novice verdict of "easily"–and with the first novice seven seconds behind winner Cornell and a half-length back of Yale. The JV and varsity 8's also finished third in their races, with SU seven-plus-seconds behind Yale in the varsity.

The next week saw the crew in Philadelphia for the Orange Challenge Cup race, a new cup race initially involving Penn and SU; Northeastern would be added in 1990. For the first edition Syracuse, Penn and BU faced off on the Schuylkill. Conditions were challenging. While a stiff headwind and steady rain persisted during all four races, the "Syracuse weather" seemed to favor the guests from upstate. SU won the first three races (entering two crews in the 2nd novice race), but couldn't close out the day with a sweep, losing to Penn despite a good start and a solid settle. The Quakers pulled steadily away, finishing 14 seconds up on the Orange women, who were paced by stroke Lynne Della Pelle.

MIT and Northeastern in Boston were next up on the schedule, followed by Williams, the final away race of the season. The Orange women weren't able to break through in either of these events, and were looking forward to getting back on their home course.

The only home race of the year featured Rutgers, and the notoriously fickle weather Onondaga was becoming famous for. A stiff headwind and whitecaps on the course forced the women onto an alternate course past the Ten Eyck Boathouse. Rutgers handled the rough water better than Palchikoff's varsity, but the calmer waters spelled doom for the guests. As the crews passed the boathouse, coxswain Megan Waldron called the rate up to 34, and the Orange steadily pulled away to an open water victory. Commenting on the race, the coach said: "This was a nice win for us. We have been close and we've had some injuries and illnesses but today we were very patient." Quinn's novices dropped their second race of the season, taking some of the glow off Palchikoff's first varsity victory.

At the fifth annual Athletic Awards Banquet, held a few days after the Rutgers race, Lynne Della Pelle was honored as the 1981 Verhulst Sportswoman of the Year for Crew. She was lauded for her athletic excellence, team spirit, and fair play. She has gone on to play a key role in Syracuse Alumni Rowing Association and as of the writing of this book is President of SARA. Two of Della Pelle's teammates, Linda Zembsch and Kristine Jensen, were invited to the US Women's Rowing Development Camp that summer. This was especially notable as both rowed on the novice A crew that spring, and both are Liverpool High School graduates.

The plethora of talented novices paid dividends for Syracuse, as the first novice crew was ranked first in the EAWRC Coaches Poll just before the Rutgers race after amassing a 5-and-2 record. With the loss to Rutgers' novices, SU dropped to a no. 3 ranking; the varsity, with four freshmen and only two seats occupied by rowers with more than one year's experience was ranked ninth and the second novices were ranked seventh going into the Sprints.

On the waters of Lake Waramaug in Connecticut, the SU women acquitted themselves well. The lightly-experienced varsity finished tenth overall, while the novice crews rowed to their ranking. The first boat finished third, just 1.5 seconds back of winner Yale and a deck back of silver-medalist Cornell; the SU second novice crew won the petite finals.

For the first time, SU sent a crew to the National Women's Intercollegiate Rowing Championships, held in San Diego on a 1,000-meter course. Breaking down into fours, the women, mostly veterans of the varsity eight, failed to make the finals. Shrugging off the poor results, the Orange women joined forces and won bronze in the senior eight behind the Eastern Selection Camp and

133

Pioneer Valley crews.

In another first, former-SU-rower Rosalyn Bandy was named to SARA's Board of Directors in 1981, becoming the first woman to serve on the board.

Recruiting was becoming commonplace in women's rowing; Quinn added Sheila Roock out of Liverpool High School and Melissa Entwistle from the Kent School to the roster for the fall of 1981.

Roock and Entwistle were two of the experienced rowers coming to campus that fall, where they would face a full racing season before heading indoors for winter training. The women raced in the Head of the Charles Regatta as well as the Head of the Schuylkill Regatta, and took part in the first annual Princeton Chase. The eight took 19th on the Charles and the four finished somewhat better, coming in 14th out of 40 crews. Of note, the Charles limited events to 40 entries in those days. Both coaches sculled in the women's single event as well, with Palchikoff finishing 10th and Quinn 26th.

A week of work produced much improvement for the eight, as it earned a fourth place out of 20 on the Schuylkill. The novice / JV eight was 13th, and the novice eight 15th in their races. It was a short drive over to Princeton for the four-crew chase; SU took second and fourth, with the host Tigers in the top spot and Cornell splitting the two Orange crews.

With the fall over, Coach Palchikoff sat down with an SU sports information representative to give her take on the coming season. "The team performed beautifully in 1980–81. Phase II starts now. Syracuse has all the elements of a winning program … and the proven ability of our novices, who finished third at the 1981 Eastern Championships and Syracuse has the nucleus of a top-level varsity crew. This year should see the Orange women stroking at the front of the fleet."

Leading the effort were three former-U.S. Junior National Team athletes–Colleen Waldron, Clair Berg, and Julia Grant–plus senior Kaja-Anne Jezycki and returning varsity coxswain Megan Waldron–sister of Colleen–who'd spent the summer with the U.S. National Team. After the fall season and early spring workouts, the women headed to Tampa for spring break before a racing

134

season that would feature many of the East's top programs.

The spring started well enough for the novices, who eked out a half-second victory over Rutgers on a 1,600-meter course on the Raritan River in New Jersey. This was the last of the racing that day, as thunderstorms and wind gusts up to 39 miles-per-hour forced the cancellation of the rest of the morning's races. The next weekend's racing took place on the Onondaga Lake Inlet as winds averaging 15 miles-per-hour made conditions on the lake course challenging at best. Once again, the novices led off with a victory in a squeaker. Deb Quinn's rookies bested Yale by seven-tenths of a second, with Cornell a mere three-tenths of a second behind the Eli on the 1,500-meter course. That win, and another in the novice four, proved to be the only victories on the day for the Orange as Yale swept the rest of the events, with Cornell bringing up the rear. None was close.

The Waldrons, Jezycki, Linda Zembsch, Kris Jensen and their fellow varsity rowers next took on Penn and Northeastern on home waters. Again the novices were successful, this time winning by more than ten seconds. As the morning wore on, conditions worsened to the point that two of the three fours' events were reduced to racing over shortened courses as the racing moved in off the lake; the novices competing over 900 meters and light four over 700 meters. Penn showed why it was considered a favorite to win it all, defeating Palchikoff's varsity by eleven seconds on Onondaga Lake. Northeastern was another 20 seconds in back of the Orange.

SU came in second in each of the remaining races as the Quakers also won the JV four while the Huskies took the second novice eight and the two other four races. Again, none was close.

The Charles River was the site of the next regatta, with Palchikoff's women taking on Radcliffe, BU, and Dartmouth. Boston University dominated the varsity events with SU in third, eight seconds back of the Terriers in the varsity eight and six seconds behind BU in the JV eight. Coach Quinn's second novice eight was overmatched in its event, coming in almost 30 seconds behind BU.

The program was off to a solid start, albeit one with much to do to become consistently competitive. Most programs were feeling their way along; women's collegiate rowing was evolving rapidly and administrators, coaches, and athletes alike were struggling a bit. Strong support was evident at some schools, with Dartmouth's Pete Gardner an early and committed supporter of Dartmouth's women's program. Other schools were more reluctant to get behind the sport, and athletic directors were in a bit of a quandary about coaches, budgets, recruiting and scholarships.

After several years of essentially zero support for women's rowing, Syracuse University had committed to a major investment in women's rowing. Now that the program was established, it would be up to the athletes and coaches.

Chapter 13
1978 – The Rest of The Story

The varsity eight wasn't the only national champion wearing orange in 1978. Drew Harrison's frosh crew won as well, continuing what was becoming a tradition for the Orange first-years, winning the Stewards Cup for the third-consecutive time.

This was the 1978 IRA-winning freshman eight crew's line up:

Cox	Bob Donabella
Stroke	Jerry Jacobi
No. 7	Steve Buergin
No. 6	Tom Darling
No. 5	Rick Ritter
No. 4	Andy Groch
No. 3	Dave Pistacchio
No. 2	Charlie Feuer
Bow	Mark Bickford

In retrospect, it was almost as if a freshman IRA championship was expected, and this somehow diminished the significance of the accomplishment. Familiarity bred–if certainly not contempt–at least expectation.

For both the varsity and freshman crews, and the entire men's roster, 1978 was a year ripe with opportunity and built on a fiercely competitive program. The fall season had seen two eights race at the Head of the Charles, with both performing well, finishing in the top ten in the Club and Championship Eight races.

When the team came off the water in November, there were more than thirty varsity oarsmen competing for spots as well as the usual four-plus freshman eights. While attrition would cut the frosh to two boats by the time the crews were back on the water, there wasn't much of a reduction in the varsity ranks. The steady diet of eight-mile runs to Peck Hill, an hour of weight circuits modeled after the East German program–where the goal was to lift a total of fifty tons in sixty minutes–long steady-state pieces in the Archbold tanks and the much-hated hour of stadium steps three times a week did little to keep the athletes away. When the ice broke on the Seneca River, four eights remained, perhaps the largest contingent of varsity rowers to take the water at Syracuse in recent memory. Sanford recalled years later "I thought that with that conditioning no one in the nation would have better winter conditioning than we could have had that year."

The combination of the workload, the depth of the team, and the quality of the last few freshman classes gave Sanford confidence; in an interview in 2011, he recalled, "One thing I did have was probably thirteen people that could make the varsity (chuckles). We had the depth and so the quality work we got on the water with the varsity and JV going against each other and people being able to look at those seats and say, 'Hey, maybe we can get there,' can cause an intensity that you don't normally see between a varsity and a JV at that caliber, at that level and I thought that brought us along faster for sure and I can remember moving people in, moving people out and the varsity would be within a second."

There wasn't much water time before racing began; while the team had gone south, it had only traveled as far as Philly for Spring Camp, where conditions weren't very conducive to long rows and lots of practice sessions. With the combination of a lack of water time, the deep roster, and a surfeit of talent, there was a good bit of seat shuffling, with guys shuttling among the V, 2V, and 3V on a regular basis as Sanford sought the best combination of power and technique.

The first race was to be a repeat of the season-opener in 1977, as Harry Parker's Harvard Crimson made the long drive to Long Branch from Boston in mid-April. Staying in the Ten Eyck Boathouse, the Crimson bedded down on Friday night, looking for a good night's sleep before taking to the boats in the morning. Unfortunately, a couple of "visitors" entered the boathouse in the wee hours, making off with a Harvard oar and a couple of sweatshirts. When the mischief was discovered, Coach Parker made it known that there would be no racing until and unless the purloined possessions were returned. Fortunately, good sense combined with a display of fury the likes of which had never been seen before on the part of Coach Sanford prevailed and the "missing" items were located and restored to their rightful owners.

Conditions on the lake merited a small-craft warning, forcing the coaches to shorten the course to 1,600 meters, starting the race just outside the channel and heading past the boathouse to the finish line just beyond the John Glenn Boulevard bridge. Harvard was even more riled up than the lake while SU's rowers were angry, embarrassed, humiliated, and completely distracted. Again, Coach Sanford, "I'm not giving them a race plan, I'm giving them hell!"

The outcome was all too predictable: "Harry's strategy–because he told me this afterwards, he says 'the first thousand meters,' which turned out to be 600 because we moved in, he said 'just–it's a water fight, just survive' to his crew. 'Just survive. When you hit the river that's when you go. Just survive at first. We can overcome anything if we just do that.'

"As I remember it, Harvard's varsity had a length going into the river because he survived better than we did. And what happened with us, and all the guys talked about it afterwards, if their arms would tighten up so much because of hitting the water with the oars and they were not like a goose's neck with their arms. They were fighting it and so they all tensed up so when it came time to perform their arms just didn't have anything. So they beat the ... it was a hell of a battle and we should have rowed it better. But I ... as I said, I was distracted, my team was distracted, everybody was distracted."

With that debacle to chew on, and the knowledge that the Orange was about nine seconds slower than Harvard, the crew prepared for the Goes Cup.

Things turned around nicely for the Orange, rowing on the same conditions-shortened 1,600-meter course. With Navy absent, the top eights swept Cornell, winning the varsity by a length-and-a-half for SU's first Goes Cup win in 20 years. While Cornell had lost several of the guys who had powered them to an IRA-varsity-eight victory the previous year, this wasn't an easy win over a mediocre crew. The Big Red was stroked by U.S. National Team rower Chip Lubsen, with two fifth-year seniors in the boat as well.

Next up was the Holding Trophy contest on the Seekonk. While the venue changed, the result didn't. It was the Orange over

Brown by a bit more than a length in a tide-aided 5:53.3. Knowing they'd be rowing with the current, Sanford had increased the load on the oars by moving the buttons in a bit. As a result, Syracuse under-stroked Brown by a couple of strokes-per-minute, and was able to raise the stroke for a clinching sprint.

With the early season duals out of the way and final exams coming up, it was back to Long Branch to prepare for the Eastern Sprints. The convincing wins over the last couple of races had started just a glimmer of hope that perhaps Syracuse could break the curse of the Sprints; SU had never won gold in the varsity, second varsity, or freshman eight events at the Sprints.

The varsity qualified relatively easily, and found itself facing off with top-ranked Yale and its old nemesis Harvard in the final. The plan was to stay within striking distance for the first 1,250, keep "wood-on-wood," stick with the leaders, and with 750 to go … GO!

Sanford recalls, "We had it in our head that it would be like the last 40 of a race–75 strokes is what they were looking at–75 to 80 strokes for the last 750 and I said we'd bring it in there. And we didn't bring it in. We did not bring it in. We didn't go up in stroke until a lot later and … that's my recollection of not being real happy."

Both the varsity and freshman eights won bronze at the Sprints, with Northeastern and Harvard besting the frosh eight.

The JV won the petites.

While neither the crew nor the coach was remotely pleased with the result, all knew the varsity would have another shot at Sprints Champion Yale the next weekend. That's when SU would make its statement. But it would have to do that without varsity stroke Art Sibley, who was out of the boat with an injury.

Sibley had sat in the stroke seat for every race he'd rowed in at Syracuse, winning the IRA his freshman year and moving into the varsity as stroke after a very successful fall campaign. With Sibley out, fellow sophomore Gerry Henwood moved from bow to stroke, and Steve Anthony switched from the JV to the varsity. With a week to settle the new lineup, practices were intense and the crew was focused.

In 1978, the Packard Cup was rowed as a double-dual

140

meet with four crews racing. Yale faced off with Sprints petite-finals-winner Dartmouth in the morning while Syracuse and MIT raced off. The expectation was SU and Yale would meet in the afternoon final, but Dartmouth had other plans. Peter Gardner's Big Green shocked Yale in the opener, eliminating the chance for a rematch of the two Sprints-medalist crews. In the afternoon duel, SU edged the Big Green by just over half-a-length. While the rematch with Yale hadn't panned out, the weekend was a big success. With brimming confidence, the varsity dug into its workouts, preparing for the final race of the season.

That final race was supposed to be the IRA; however with the Orange winning the Varsity Challenge Cup, the season wasn't over after the IRA. With national championships under their belts, the varsity and freshman eights were bound for the United Kingdom.

Three members of the freshman crew were out; two man Charlie Feuer and four-oar Andy Groch for academic reasons, and Dave Pistacchio, their neighbor in the three seat headed home for work. They would be replaced by Jeff Braun in six, Steve Anthony in three, and Paul Dierkes would man the two oar. Bob Donabella coxswained the composite, or, as the oarsmen termed it, the "Compost Crew," with Jerry Jacobi remaining in the stroke seat, Steve Buergin at seven, Rick Ritter in five, future Olympic silver-medalist Tom Darling in four and Mark Bickford in bow.

For some of the athletes, this would be the second-consecutive summer spent in the UK, as Drew Harrison's '77 frosh eight had made the trip just twelve months earlier. This time, both boats would first race at the Nottingham course in two separate regattas on consecutive days. Both of the varsity's races would feature Bulgaria who had finished seventh at the 1977 World Championships, France, and the University of Washington. In the race for the Guinness Cup on Saturday, June 25th, SU came in fourth in what were described as "very rough conditions." The Orange crew was seven seconds behind Bulgaria, and 1.6 seconds behind second-place finisher UW.

Speaking to a reporter, Coach Sanford said, "We didn't row well … having only three practices hurt us. We're going to get a lot better. We're trying to beat Washington, they're reachable

… I think we can take 'em, in fact, I know we can. Washington, which got a week's work in here, had a full length on us at the thousand. We came back on them when we got into smoother water. That's encouraging. If we can get five or six more practices in before Henley, we'll be alright."

The Compost Crew was also fourth in the Saturday finals at Nottingham after winning their morning heat, but Sanford felt the oarsmen were hampered, in no small part, by their beautifully-crafted, but very heavy borrowed boat. While both crews gained valuable experience from their first race on European waters, their lack of practice had made for a less-than-optimal performance.

The third Syracuse crew entered on Sunday was the pair of Bob Devlin at stroke and Peter Henriques in bow; the duo came in second in their event, trailing the Washington entry.

For the varsity, things improved dramatically Sunday. SU defeated Washington, then deemed the "Best in the West." The Orange also closed the gap on the Bulgarians to less than a length, and the French, taking third overall. Apparently Sanford's comments after the Saturday race were prescient; according to an article in *The New York Times* datelined Nottingham, "Washington was never in the race, placing last of the four crews." As Syracuse was likely to see the East Europeans "up close and personal" on Friday in Henley, the improvement was good news indeed.

The Syracuse Compost Crew fared even better, winning the Senior A title and defeating Queens College, Belfast by a length with Yale's freshman eight another second back. This was no mean feat, as the Eli frosh had capped a terrific season with a win at the Eastern Sprints.

As Henley began, the varsity was awarded a bye in the premier eights event, the Grand Challenge Cup. With only five entries, the big boat would race the winner of the Bulgaria–Leander of Great Britain duel in the semifinals. This was markedly different from the Compost Crew's event, where 32 crews would compete for the Ladies' Challenge Plate for eights. Washington, winner of the event the previous year, would match up with Buzz Congram's Northeastern Huskies in the other semifinal.

June 29th, the first day at the Henley Regatta was quite enjoyable for the Compost Crew, entered in the second-tier event for eights, the Ladies' Challenge Plate. The combined JV / frosh eight defeated England's Newcastle University "easily," Henley-speak for at least five boat lengths. Despite the lack of competition, the Orange turned in the second-best time of the day among all eights in all events while racing in weather reminiscent of mid-March back home–a steady, cold rain. Their victory set up a match with Florida Institute of Technology, a fast Dad Vail crew that defeated Harvard's JV lightweight eight by almost three lengths in their "heat."

Fortuitously, the weather remained distinctly Syracusan for the match-up between SU and the Floridians. Off the starting line, SU was a deck back as FIT went off at a 39. Rowing at a 36 cadence, the Orange slowly but steadily reeled their opponents in, then moved in front by 1/3 of a length at the mile mark. From there, the heart appeared to go out of the Floridians as the margin continued to increase all the way to the finish. The final verdict was 3-and-1/2 lengths as the Orange oarsmen "sent up whoops of joy as they crossed the line." They'd made it to the quarterfinals, quite an accomplishment for a crew made up of freshmen and JV rowers competing in a newly-borrowed shell.

The quarter-final race saw the Composters defeating Isis Boat Club by 1-and-3/4 lengths. SU blew off the line at a 40, and had a "comfortable 2-and-1/2-length lead at the three-quarter-mile post." The ever-quotable cox Bob Donabella told a UPI reporter, "It was really easy, we gambled by borrowing Harvard's shell Friday because it was lighter, but it paid off today."

Things weren't so easy in the semis, where the Composters met, and lost to, Imperial College, London. The oarsmen could take some solace in the fact they were defeated by an Imperial College crew that went on to defeat Yale's varsity by 2/3 of a length in the finals.

Spares Bob Devlin and Peter Henriques raced in the Silver Goblets event for pairs at Henley. The narrowness of the course proved to be the duo's undoing as they hit an island just after the start and fell as much as ten lengths back before rallying mightily to close the final gap to their British competitors to just over two lengths.

In the Grand Challenge Cup semifinals, the Orange varsity

faced off against what was in reality the Bulgarian National Team, while Washington and Northeastern fought for the other finals slot in the other semifinal. SU couldn't hold off the Europeans, who won by 1-and-3/4 lengths. UW won its semi, using a blistering start rowed at a 44 stroke rating to build a length lead before the race was a quarter-mile old. Northeastern couldn't get it together, giving up an additional two lengths before the three-quarter-mile post.

In the final, the Bulgarians defeated UW, allowing the Syracuse varsity the same measure of solace as the Composters.

With the racing done, July was almost half over, allowing the oarsmen and coaches a mere six weeks before they'd meet again on campus. While the experience had been invaluable it had not come without cost.

Chapter 14
1979 – More IRA Medals

hree consecutive freshman eight national championships. A convincing win for Syracuse's varsity eight at the IRA. Two weeks in England racing international crews at Nottingham and Henley. A very strong recruiting class for freshman coach Drew Harrison, the return of most of the varsity eight and half of the bronze-medalist JV. All the pieces were in place for 1979 to be another championship year for the Orange, with expectations high for all crews. As the team brochure quoted Head Coach Bill Sanford, "They've all tasted victory and should be hungry for the title again."

1979 was going to be the year that cemented Syracuse Rowing's position among the elite programs in the nation. Bill Sanford had seen the program return to greatness after 58 years' absence from atop the IRA podium. Yet despite all the promise, the year after winning the IRAs would prove to be more than disappointing for the Orange. It wasn't just the failure to win the IRA, it was a sense that the entire season had been misspent.

All in all, the summer of 1978 had been productive on many levels. Racing two full eights at the Henley and Nottingham International Regatta had dramatically increased SU's reputation in the rowing community, a reputation that would help with recruiting efforts. On top of Drew Harrison's string of gold-medal-frosh eights, the daily mentions in the news generated increasing interest among experienced high school rowers. Sanford noted this in the preseason media kit, stating: "Because our program has done so well in recent years we keep attracting better athletes and this year's frosh group looks to be the strongest I've seen."

The multiple races for the varsity and a combined freshman / JV eight was "... like going to the Elite Eight in NCAA basketball, going up against teams that were really fast, more mature, and had a different approach. [The athletes from an Eastern Bloc country] were all in the army, mature and older– when one of their guys started talking to a couple SU guys, their coach yelled at him and he hurried back to his crew ..." Sanford recalled.

The pressure, the level of competition, and the reward of racing internationally raised expectations for the future.

But the season-extending trip to the UK had a downside as well. Sanford had a feeling towards the end that the guys had had just about enough racing and needed a break for a while. As campus came alive again in the fall and the team reassembled, there wasn't the same level of intensity in the boathouse that had been there the previous fall. It wasn't anything really noticeable, just a bit less energy. As Sanford recalled, "There was a motivational issue with some of those who had given all their life to crew, initially some folks wanted a break, yet they still came out and made an effort."

While the energy level may have dropped a little, the level of competition for seats in the top eight was higher than ever; anyone who wanted a seat in any SU varsity boat was going to have to work very, very hard. There were at least twelve athletes who could make the varsity; the five returning from the '78 IRA champion varsity, several from the '78 JV, and perhaps half of the '78 IRA champion freshman eight, all guys who had won at least one IRA gold. As the crews came off the water late in the fall for the last time, there were three full eights on the varsity and just as many freshmen heading indoors for winter training. The coaching staff had increased as well, with Graduate Assistant Jay Printzlau joining Sanford and Harrison. Printzlau, coming off a season where he had coached the Yale freshman lights to an Eastern Sprints Championship, would prove to be a valuable addition indeed, with his small boat crews contributing to a very solid team showing at the 1979 IRA.

That fall saw the first of what was to become many successful political campaigns for Sanford. The following spring, he entered the Onondaga County Legislature as a Republican from Salina, a second career that would last until his retirement in 2002 as Chairman, followed by a term in the state assembly. Sanford's government duties would necessitate some changes to practice schedules in the spring, as he spent time getting up to speed on county functions, learning the political ropes, and working on key legislative issues.

The winter of 1978–1979 saw the level of competition

indoors intensify. Sophomore Tom Darling set the bar in the early going, scoring well above 3,200 on the Gamut Erg–by far the highest on the team. Notice had been served to the upperclassmen; their seats in the varsity were far from guaranteed.

The racing season started with a first-ever trip to San Diego for the increasingly popular Crew Classic. The IRA championship had earned the crew an invitation, and two eights headed west to take on Harvard, Washington, California, 1978 Head of Charles-winner Brown, Northeastern, Wisconsin, Pennsylvania, Cornell and Navy. Although Syracuse had been touted by none other than Harry Parker as a legitimate contender for the championship, the varsity failed to make the finals, finishing fourth in the heats behind eventual winner Harvard–one of Parker's smallest crews averaging 6'2" and 185 pounds–California and Navy.

Back on the East Coast, the first race in the dual season was the annual Rutgers–Syracuse face-off. While the April 21st start date was a bit later than usual, the delay meant decent weather for the race on Onondaga. In the varsity, Art Sibley was in his usual stroke seat, facing Bob Donabella who had taken over for Ozzie Street. Gerry Henwood had moved to three from bow, with Captain Bill Purdy in seven. For the varsity, finishing more than a length of open water in front of the guests from New Jersey was more a meeting of expectations than great news. The JV, stroked by future U.S. National Team Lightweight Eight stroke Bill Bater finished a length back of Rutgers, with the freshmen crossing the line just a few seats ahead of the Rutgers first-years.

The next day, the crew made its way down to Cayuga Inlet to take on Yale. All three crews lost to Yale by considerable margins, with the closest finish–a length open–in the JV eight. SU's third varsity eight paired off with the Coast Guard Academy's JV and came back to campus with new shirts, courtesy of a two-length margin of victory.

There was some shuffling of lineups over the next few days of practice, as Sanford searched for the right mix while finding a substitute for Bill Purdy, who had an appointment with the U.S. National Team. With the short week of practice and travel on Friday to Annapolis to race for the Goes Trophy on the always-challenging Severn, it was a hectic time. Races were scheduled for early in the morning in an attempt to avoid boat traffic and potentially worsening weather, so the crews were at the boathouse just after dawn. Four crews were racing, and while the results weren't what the Syracuse fans wanted, things looked to be improving. Navy took the Goes Trophy by a few feet of open water over SU, with Cornell a couple of seconds back. The JV broke through, crossing the line just under a second before the Midshipmen and less than a length in front of the Big Red.

Drew Harrison's freshmen were in a dogfight all the way down the course, as conditions seemed to be getting sloppier. Navy won the event by a deck, with Cornell over a length behind second-place Syracuse. As none of the other crews had a third varsity eight and Pete Gaines had to move up to JV to replace Purdy's substitute, SU's 3V broke down into a four only to lose to Navy.

With four races under their belts, the eights were looking forward to returning home to compete for the Holding Trophy on May 4th. Vic Michalson's crew was beginning to hit its stride, and the race looked to be a good test for the Orange. The SU varsity was rowing a German rig with 5 and 4–Jeff Braun and Bill Purdy, back from his U.S. National Team duties–in a bucket on starboard. Sanford had shaken things up a bit, moving sophomore former-JV six-man Mark Bickford into the three seat while moving Bill Smuts down to the second eight to make room for Purdy.

The varsity race was not close; Brown won by more than ten seconds, with Vesper another length behind SU. Syracuse's JV and freshman eights had better results, with both crews winning by open water. The third varsity had taken off for Boston to race Harvard on Saturday and Northeastern on Sunday. Both races were within a couple of seconds but SU was on the losing end in both, with the Sunday race against NU tilting towards the Huskies when six-man Tom Weigartz shattered his blade on a floating object just after the start.

After the Sprints, the Orange headed back to Long Branch for IRA Camp, where the athletes would live in the boathouse except for a brief sojourn to Hanover to contest the Packard Cup on May 19th.

The trip would prove to be more of the same for the

varsity; it lost to Dartmouth by just over a length, with MIT disqualified for steering issues. The JV, frosh, and varsity four all were victorious in their races. Heading home, the bus stopped in Saratoga Springs for dinner. Evidently then-all-female Skidmore College's senior class was looking to celebrate its upcoming graduation, as the entire crew was invited to stay the evening as guests of the Skidmore ladies. Duty prevented any dallying, and the guys boarded the bus.

Back in Syracuse, there were a growing number of citizens who were less than enamored with the IRA Regatta. The event had become a rather large and boisterous party, with upwards of 15,000 "fans" taking the occasion to socialize on the banks of Onondaga Lake. While the partiers saw no problems, many of the locals didn't care for the noise, traffic, occasionally-inappropriate behavior, and general uproar that took place on IRA Saturday.

Nichols Supermarket owner Jim Hennigan was one of the Liverpool townsfolk who had grown disenchanted with the IRA. Speaking to a reporter for *The Herald-Journal*, Hennigan said: "It was a way of introducing people to Liverpool and Central New York ... it's just turned into a such a foolish beer blast ... [some of the regatta-goers] act like they've just been let out of Alcatraz." These issues may have been more perception than reality, as the police reported the previous year there were "only a few incidents, and they didn't amount to much."

It wasn't just the rowdiness that was turning some against the regatta; for several years the regatta's finances had been running in the red, leaving the Syracuse Regatta Association with a $5,300 debt to Onondaga County. With a revised parking plan including free nearby parking, the association hoped attendance would rebound from the low point the previous year.

The athletes at Long Branch were oblivious to the controversy surrounding the regatta; there were some big changes going on that were of more pressing interest. After the poor results of the last two races, Coach Bill Sanford decided to shuffle the lineup, and moved six-man John Shamlian to stroke and Art Sibley to four.

The IRAs began on the last day of May with heats for all seven crews on tap. Two freshman fours with would take to the line wearing orange, and grad assistant Jay Printzlau had a four with cox and pair with cox, both coming from the 3V that had enjoyed solid success in their races that spring. The four had been together since the Sprints and was determined to do better than their third-place finish at Quinsigamond. With seniors and former-IRA Champions Bob Devlin in stroke and Pete Gaines at three and juniors Tom Weigartz and Joe Paduda making up the bow pair, there was plenty of experience in the boat. There were nine boats in the four with cox competition, some comprised of lightweights from IRA schools, others boating the top four from the varsity eight, and the remainder breaking down their third varsity eights into small boats. In the first heat, racing was very tight until halfway through the third 500, when SU made its move with a power ten. Worcester PolyTech had been right with the Orange but couldn't respond. Syracuse pulled away from the field, finishing a very comfortable 12 seconds in front of the second place crew from Penn. With its spot in the grand finals assured, the crew was able to relax and watch the other fours race off for the remaining lane assignments.

Saturday's finals saw the SU four with lined up against Washington State, BU, WPI, Coast Guard, and Purdue. As the crews pulled into the stake boats they were facing almost directly into a headwind that had picked up significantly from the day before. Off the line, Devlin drove the rating up to a 42 for the first twenty, then kept it high for most of the first 500. Across the 500, SU was in front of second-place Washington State. The Orangemen were rowing a 38, looking to take advantage of what had been the strength of their race, a fast start. Truth be told, there had been a bit of miscommunication in the boat, and the settle didn't happen after the initial forty strokes.

Regardless, the lead held through the halfway point, when the size of the Washington State crew began to tell. Outweighing the Orange by 40 pounds a man, the Cougars began to pull away. SU tried to respond, using the same hard push midway through the third 500 that had crushed WPI. The move was hardly noticed by WSU, which continued to extend its lead. The combination of the lengthy start, high stroke rating through the first quarter of the race and stiff headwind proved to be too much for the Orange, while

150

the conditions were much to the westerners' liking. Washington State cruised to a comfortable victory with Syracuse winning the silver by open water over the Terriers of Boston University in third.

The pair with cox was rowed by seniors Pete Hausman and Dan Hanavan, both with a 1977 3V Sprints Championship to their credit. Their were seven other crews in their event, including what looked to be the top two guys from USC's varsity eight. Hanavan and Hausman rowed to a very comfortable second place in Thursday's heats, setting themselves up for a good race in Friday's reps. Rowing well within themselves, the men in the SU pair with cox "had swing and the rowing was effortless." They cruised into the finals, thereby ensuring every SU varsity crew would have a shot at the medals.

With Hausman stroking and Hanavan in bow, the pair were facing the same stiff headwind as the four with cox, but with two fewer oars to carry cox Jimmy Regan to the finish line. If the rowing was effortless in the reps, it was anything but in the first 500 of the finals as the crew came close to suffering the indignity of being passed by the officials' launches. Fortunately for the three Orangemen, this was going to be a long race and they'd have ample time to sort things out. That they did, smoothing things out in the second 500, and from there moving steadily up from fifth place into third. The result was ample proof of the depth of the program, and boded well for the eights.

Drew Harrison's freshman eight was saddled with the unenviable task of continuing the program's three-year reign atop the IRA podium, and the path was going to be anything but easy. The heat more resembled a final than a Thursday morning qualifier, with five of the six crews in the heat expected to be in the finals. Coach Harrison opined, "The heat is certainly stacked, without a shadow of a doubt, but it really doesn't matter to our approach. If we're to win, we have to take it away from other people–sometime." The crews his guys would have to "take it away from" in their heat were Northeastern, Cal, Cornell, Navy, and Brown.

The heat was a close-run thing, with the Huskies crossing the line in front of SU by less than a half-length. The other crews seemed disinterested in racing for the lone qualifying spot, with Cornell another six seconds back the closest of the also-rans. With the loss in the heats, Harrison's crew would face off with Dartmouth, Pennsylvania, California, and Brown in Friday morning's repechage.

Conditions Friday morning were distinctly unusual for Onondaga, with a stiff tailwind making for fast times. The freshmen won their rep, and would head to the line for a chance to win an unprecedented fourth-consecutive IRA championship. The competition was going to be fierce; although Wisconsin hadn't gotten on the water until April 18th, it had managed to post an impressive third-place finish at the Sprints behind the second-place Huskies from Northeastern. Given the late start for the Badgers and their result at the Sprints, they would almost certainly be among the medalists.

In the frosh finals, SU led off the line, and for almost the entire race, with the biggest gap at the thousand where the Orange crew had open water on Wisco. Towards the end of the third 500, Wisconsin started a charge that brought it even with Syracuse; unable to push through, Wisconsin found itself side-by-side with the Orange coming up to the finish line. For the last few strokes of the race, the leader was the last crew to take a stroke, both boats surging into and then out of the lead. The final margin was a fraction of a second, requiring the officials to review the finish line photo.

The streak had to send sometime, and it did in 1979. Wisco ended Coach Drew Harrison's IRA frosh championship string with a close win over the Orange, with Northeastern in third.

The SU JV eight, with Bill Bater at stroke and Jerry Jacobi at seven, would be facing off against four other crews at the IRA heats on May 31st with all but Brown being new competitors for the Orange. Northeastern, Wisco, and Long Beach were on the line for the early morning race. Northeastern won easily, as none of the other crews seemed interested in showing their cards, or wasting their legs, in the winner-take-all heat. Chances of making it into the grand finals via the reps were decidedly better, with two of the four entrants in each rep gaining spots. The stern pair were, in Sanford's opinion, key to the JV's chances of success, and "…such a great eight-seven combination, although neither was a big guy."

Racing in the first of the two reps, the Orange second boat won, followed by Dartmouth. Wisconsin and Cornell would join them in the finals along with Yale, winner of the other Thursday heat.

With the tailwind a thing of the past, the Jayvees would be facing a steady headwind. This would almost certainly hurt Yale's chances, as its entry in the second eight race was the Eli varsity lightweight eight. While the Eli had won their heat with ease, the longer, tougher slog in the grand finals would prove too much for the crew from New Haven. But before the race could start, Syracuse four-man Bill Smuts broke his oar and bent the rigger's top brace, necessitating a 20-minute delay while a replacement was found and brought out to the crew. When the race got underway, Syracuse led off the line, only to be overtaken by Wisconsin after the first 500 and then Northeastern around the halfway mark. With Cornell charging, Bater brought the rating up, the crew responded, and its effort was just enough to hold off the Big Red. The finals saw a repeat of the top three slots in Syracuse's Thursday heat, with Northeastern taking the gold by a second over Wisconsin and Syracuse six seconds back. SU's finishing sprint pushed it across the line a mere three-tenths of a second in front of Cornell, just enough to earn the JV from Long Branch the bronze.

Absent from the varsity entries were Yale and Harvard, both prepping for their annual four-miler on the Thames River in Connecticut. Cal and Washington also didn't send their varsity eights, although Cal's frosh eight had made the long trip eastward. Some thought this diminished the prestige of the IRA, making any victor's claim to be national champion hollow at best. "Some" did not include SU Coach Bill Sanford.

"There are probably three crews at this regatta who could beat [Eastern Sprint Champions] Yale, and that's taking nothing away from Yale," Sanford said, going on to discuss the Washington Huskies. "Usually they win their Western Sprints, come here and get their butts kicked. Of course, they don't want to come here." Sanford went on to say the crews that were at the

IRA were peaking for that race; the Sprints came too early in the season for the northern-domiciled universities to have enough water time to compete at their best.

The varsity lineup had coalesced for the IRA with Gregg Weinglass moving up from the 3V to cox the varsity. Facing Weinglass in the stroke seat was John Shamlian with Bill Purdy in seven, Mark Bickford in six and Jeff Braun in five, Art Sibley at four, Tom Darling in three, and Steve Buergin and Gerry Henwood rounding out the lineup. The top eight was looking at a five-boat heat that would include a rematch with Packard Cup winners Dartmouth, with Cornell, Brown, and Penn filling out the other lanes. Talking to a reporter about the loaded heat, Brown Coach Vic Michalson remarked "I suppose, based on the Sprints, you might say Dartmouth and Brown would be the favorites … and certainly, if we had our choice, we'd prefer another heat."

Among the crews that would compete for the Varsity Challenge Cup, Brown and Dartmouth were both considered solid contenders for gold, with Dartmouth the overwhelming pick to win it all in a pre-IRA Coaches Poll. In his third season as head coach, Fin Meislahn's Big Red crew was always tough, and a solid crew from a very deep Pennsylvania program could not be discounted. Although the Big Green was without Head Coach Pete Gardner, who was in Hanover with a heart condition, there was no doubt it was, as usual, getting faster as the season went on. Asked about the absence of Pete Gardner, Sanford joked "that's all they need, another reason to win." While Sanford may have been kidding, his Orange wanted to show the race on the Connecticut had been an aberration, and the changes in the lineup and work they'd done since the Sprints had added speed. As Sanford remembered years later, there was a "big change in boat speed from the Packard Cup up to IRAs, people settled into place and said, 'Okay, I am in this boat and we're going to make this boat go.'"

As with the JV race, the varsity's heat would qualify only the winner straight to the finals, with the others to a four-boat rep on Friday. The race turned into a duel between the Orange and Dartmouth's Big Green. Although the finish margin of one second was much closer than the Packard Cup result, Dartmouth still crossed the line in front. Brown, Cornell and Pennsylvania were all more than a length back, and few thought they had given it their best effort, deciding instead to take their chances in the reps.

The other heat saw Wisconsin win easily over MIT and BU, with Wisconsin coach Randy Jablonic noting, "To tell you the truth, I'm glad I wasn't in the other heat. There's no reason to tangle with the likes of Syracuse and Dartmouth more than you have to."

With Thursday's racing done, Syracuse was set for Friday's reps where it would battle Northeastern, Pennsylvania, and BU for the two slots still left for the grand finals. Unlike the heats, this was an easier route to the finals for the Orange, as Brown and Cornell were in the other rep. This time SU was victorious, finishing two-and-a-half seconds up on Northeastern in a blazing time of 5:49.2. NU wasn't coasting either, barely managing to edge Pennsylvania by one-tenth of a second for the final qualifying spot. The Brown-Cornell heat turned out to be much closer than expected, with less than a half-second–little more than a deck–separating first and third, and coincidentally a mere one-tenth of a second between Cornell and third-place MIT. While Brown may have decided to take its chances on what looked like an easier route to the grand finals, Bruno had to push very hard to even qualify on Friday.

Saturday's results would show if the strategy was a clever move or something else entirely.

The finals would feature rep-winner Brown, heat winners Wisconsin and Dartmouth and SU, Cornell and Northeastern. The headwind had remained steady throughout the day, and as Syracuse captain and seven-man Bill Purdy said, "You don't expect Brown. But when a headwind comes, they're there. They're a headwind crew: leg-oriented."

Evidently that close race in the reps hadn't adversely affected Bruno. Brown, sitting in last early in the grand final race powered through the field, finally catching and passing leader Wisconsin and winning by 1.4 seconds. Syracuse was three seats back of the Badgers. The racing was very, very close with just over a length separating first from fifth. While it wasn't what they wanted, the Orangemen were able to gain some measure of satisfaction, defeating Dartmouth by one-tenth of second for the final medal slot while also making up over eight seconds on

Brown from the Holding Trophy race.

Despite the failure to take home any gold, the five medals earned by SU's seven crews were a testament to the depth of the team and enough to put the Orange in second place overall for the regatta. It was also bittersweet for Sanford; while his crew hadn't been victorious, he was very happy for close friend and supporter Vic Michalson.

Reflecting on the season decades later, Sanford viewed the spring through the crystal clear lens afforded by hindsight. Dissecting decisions made at the time, he mused, "You look back, why didn't you change the lineup dramatically in the varsity, but I stayed with the winning guys [from the previous year's IRA championship crew] in their key seats, but in doing that [not making any changes we] were going to go just so fast, but just looking back I was going with what was proven, may have been as fast as any different lineup, who knows … when you start to lose earlier races, you lose a bit of confidence … that's not good in this sport."

The IRA was not the last of the racing for the 1979 Orange varsity. A week after the regatta, SU faced off with Penn AC for the privilege of representing the United States at the upcoming Pan Am Games. While Penn AC, with SU alumnus Dave Townsley, won, the margin was less than two seconds. It didn't make up for what had been a disappointing season, but it was proof there was a lot of speed in SU's varsity.

With six varsity oars manned by juniors and sophs, it looked like Syracuse would be back.

"A Pleasant Dilemma" was the title of the *1980 Crew Media Guide* referring to the ten oarsmen so close in ability that Sanford was still determining who would power the varsity eight. At the time the brochure was printed, the message was that despite the loss of Bill Purdy and John Shamlian from the '79 varsity eight, things were looking pretty good.

Sanford was expecting big things out of Tom Darling and Jerry Jacobi, there were several guys from a couple of IRA frosh championship crews along with the bow and stroke from the '78 varsity champion. That surfeit of talent, coupled with what the *Media Guide* described as a rebuilding period for most of the other EARC crews, a new and light Carbocraft shell, and newly-renovated indoor tanks at Archbold for the Orange foretold good things.

While the press release was positive, as press releases are supposed to be, a more accurate title may have been "more of the same." There had been twelve guys competing for varsity seats in 1979, a happy occurrence that had resulted in a bronze medal for the varsity at the IRA and a close second at the Pan Am Trials on Onondaga a week later. With most of the varsity eight returning plus the core of an IRA silver-medalist freshman eight, the material was there for another solid year.

The biggest change–besides the blue boat from Carbocraft–was the major renovation to the tanks. Funded by alumnus Hubert "Jock" Stratton, the SU Athletics Department, and SARA, the tanks now actually worked. More accurately, worked after a fashion. New motors had been added, the hydrodynamics improved with smoother returns, and the tanks themselves refurbished and repainted. The motors moved the water a bit quicker too, and the combination of all these improvements allowed the rowers to pick up the rating a few strokes-per-minute from the pre-renovation maximum of somewhere around 20 strokes-per-minute.

Fully half of the freshmen oarsmen that made it through fall and winter training were experienced, with the rest committed and tough as only those who made it through six months with

Drew Harrison could be.

There were ten guys competing for the top spots; overall the roster was noticeably thinner than in the past few years. There had been almost four full eights in 1978, but there were just two eights and a four on the water when racing started in 1980. Managed by Hugh Duffy and Doug Stone, the crew had only five oarsmen returning from the 1979 freshman program and five junior rowers on the squad. Given possible additional losses from attrition and injury, there was not much in reserve.

Adding to the uncertainty was the upcoming Olympics. Tom Darling, perhaps the most capable athlete on the team, was training for the U.S. National Team. He would be taking the season off to work out in Boston under the watchful eye of Harry Parker. This didn't sit too well with Coach Sanford, especially when Darling made the trip south for SU's Winter Camp.

The crew headed to Miami for winter training, rowing out of Key Biscayne on the same waters used for powerboat races. While the powerboats were thankfully absent, the conditions varied from very good to unrowable. At least twice the team had to substitute land training for water time, and other rows had to be cut short to avoid rough seas. That land training almost led to disaster, as Darling sprained an ankle while running stairs with the freshmen.

After several more weeks in the tanks and running the much-loved Peck Hill course, the oarsmen were looking forward to getting back in the boats. The weather gods had other plans. There was a bit of warming for a few days in late February, but a deep cold snap hit in early March with temperatures plunging to fifteen degrees below zero at night and barely breaking into double digits during the day for several days in a row. A few days of "normal" weather followed, only to see another cold snap hit in mid-month. Instead of returning to actual rowing early in March, on-again-off-again rowing resumed on the Seneca River in mid-March, with conditions improving enough for rowing every day at least two weeks later than normal.

Meanwhile, Darling was back with the squad. When the United States' Olympic boycott was announced a couple weeks into the semester, he had packed up and left Boston, enrolled in classes and rejoined the team. Darling remembers that he was welcomed back, although some members of the squad had been less than supportive when he announced he was going to take time off to train for the Olympics.

With just a few weeks back on the water, the coaches and crew had to prepare quickly for the higher stroke ratings and intensity of racing season. The racing started in mid-April in New Brunswick, New Jersey with the Orange taking on Navy and the Rutgers Scarlet Knights. In the varsity eights Navy proved to be the crew to beat, rowing a 5:50.6 to defeat SU by two lengths, with Rutgers an additional two lengths in back of the Orange. The Middies won the JV and frosh by similar margins, with Syracuse taking second place in each race.

Scarcely a week later, Coach Sanford's crews found themselves having a déjà vu, looking over at Navy on the starting line on the Cayuga Lake Inlet. Navy wasn't able to sweep the races, but it did capture the Goes Cup for varsity eights, improving the margin over SU to a full thirteen seconds. Cornell was a bit less than a length behind the Orange. Cornell won the JV with Navy six seconds in their wake; SU's JV was well behind, out of contention four lengths back of the Big Red. The freshman race wasn't much better, as Drew Harrison's oarsmen finished more than ten seconds back in third place.

All in all, the first two weeks had been pretty miserable affairs. Traditionally Syracuse was a slow starter, gaining speed as the season progressed. With the Holding Trophy, Packard Cup, Sprints and IRAs in the offing there would be plenty of opportunity to measure improvement against what was looking to be–contrary to the optimistic preseason press release–pretty stiff competition.

Interviewed for this book, Darling remembered there was tension between a couple of guys on the varsity and, perhaps in part due to the success in 1978, a bit of complacency as well.

After a week off, the Orange was once again on the road, headed to Providence and a matchup with former-SU freshman coach Vic Michalson's Brown crews. In fast conditions, likely an outbound tide, Drew Harrison's frosh eight crushed Bruno by some 28 seconds. That would be the sole victory for Syracuse, as Brown returned the favor in the varsity four event, defeated SU's

JV by two lengths, and edged out the Orange varsity by a mere four-tenths of a second–about a deck length. While the losses were tough, the tight finish in the varsity after some very close racing showed the top crew had plenty of fight.

The Sprints saw some very tough conditions with a stiff headwind resulting in very slow times. In what could only be described as a very disappointing regatta for SU, the Orange varsity and Jayvee both failed to make the grands; the varsity finishing fifth in the petites. Meanwhile the freshmen acquitted themselves well with a fifth-place finish, twelve seconds back of a very fast Harvard boat. Cornell was a further three lengths back of the Orange, a significant improvement for the SU frosh.

With finals week and the Sprints over, SU hosted the last dual race of the season on Onondaga Lake. In beautiful, very fast conditions, the Orange crews enjoyed a complete sweep of Dartmouth and MIT. The Varsity clobbered MIT by two lengths in 5:39, described as the "fastest 2000-meter clocking ever on Onondaga Lake" by SU's Sports Information Department. Dartmouth was a bit farther back. The Jayvees won by a length over Dartmouth, and Drew Harrison's freshmen doubled the gap in their race, this time over MIT with Dartmouth another two lengths back. Both of Harrison's frosh fours also won, racing in the A and B events.

In what would become an all-too-familiar event, lousy weather led to changes in the racing schedule for the IRA began as scheduled on Thursday, May 29th, and all was good until strong winds on Saturday forced postponement of the finals to Sunday. The varsity raced very well in the preliminaries, easily winning its race and thereby avoiding the reps on Friday. The JV did not fare nearly as well, placing fourth in its heat and by dint of finishing one second back of Cornell in Friday's rep, failed to qualify for the grand finals.

Drew Harrison's freshmen also failed to qualify Thursday with a finish two lengths back of Northeastern. They came roaring back on Friday, winning their rep by a length over Orange Coast College, who was not pressed in the least by a slow MIT crew.

Given the optimism reflected in the fall press guide, the IRA results were disappointing. In the finals on Sunday, rowed in

160

tough conditions with significant chop at the start, Rick Clothier's Midshipmen captured the Varsity Challenge Cup with SU 12 seconds back in sixth, well back of two crews the Orange had defeated in the heats. SU's JV entry finished fourth in the petites, ahead of MIT and ten seconds back of petite winner Navy. Orange Coast College, the only two-year program in the nation with a full rowing program, won the freshman eights, just edging out the Orange who would take silver for the second year in a row.

If the conditions on Sunday were tough for the eights, they were brutal for SU's two pairs and the two frosh fours. After qualifying for the petites with a second-place finish in their rep on Friday, the Orange pair without cox finished second with a time of 9:30.6, ample evidence of the stiff headwind and trying conditions. The pair with cox qualified via the petites, and was awarded lane six. The conditions were too much for the crew, which finished in fifth, almost a full minute back of Washington State in lane one.

Harrison had entered two freshman fours instead of cutting down to one for the regatta. With seventeen crews entered, only the crews that won their heat or rep would make the grand finals. SU's A boat won the petite final, with the B crew second in the third-level event.

As the oarsmen packed up to leave the boathouse, some to head home for the summer and others out into the "real world," there was a palpable sense of opportunity missed. Some time between early fall and the beginning of racing season, something had happened, or perhaps not happened, that had turned a pleasant dilemma into an unpleasant reality.

In retrospect, leadership and team unity were not what they needed to be. Talking about the year decades later, Tom Darling said, "There were [some] individuals who were all in and pushing themselves, but there was too much concern about making sure people were happy and not enough about pushing themselves to make a better team."

Darling and his fellow juniors would have a chance to make that better team in the fall.

161

Chapter 16
1981 – Bad Weather and an IRA Small Boat Gold Medal

Anew decade was beginning. With memories of the campus turmoil during the early seventies a distant memory, the women's crew at last achieving full varsity status and the last members of Drew Harrison's IRA champion eights entering their senior year, Syracuse rowing was once again among the nation's elite programs. The silver medal in the frosh eight at the 1980 IRAs was a disappointment, but Harrison had a very solid group coming in to put things right.

The returning sophomores were perhaps the people most disappointed in the silver medal, a result most other teams would have been delighted with. It was their job to bring the championship back to Long Branch, and the entire crew felt like they had missed out by not sprinting soon enough to overtake Orange Coast. Many of the guys from the first frosh also felt like they could legitimately contend for seats in the varsity. With three-year varsity stroke Art Sibley lost to graduation, Gordon Hull was a serious candidate for that seat. There were four seniors coming back to the varsity; cox Gregg Weinglass, Tom Darling, Mark Bickford, and Jerry Jacobi along with junior Ashton Richards. Sophomore Andy Hobbs was likely to occupy another slot, and other sophomores would compete for seats with senior Captain Rick Ritter, and classmates Brian Mahon and Jack Newby.

The fall saw the upperclassmen rowing primarily in fours as Sanford looked to see who was going to mesh well and who was able to move a boat. SU entered fours in several fall races, with mixed results.

Unlike past years, the team didn't head south for Winter Camp in January. They did make the trek for spring break, this time choosing Tampa as the location for eight days of intense practice. The river through the center of the city opened out onto Tampa Bay, providing miles of good water along with the great weather; the location on the campus of the University of Tampa was close and convenient. It also proved to be a bit of a travel challenge for some of the guys. A few rented a Winnebago and drove down together, arriving just a few hours late for practice and thereby earning the enmity of Coach Sanford. Unfortunately, that wasn't the only misfortune to confront the Orange in Florida; senior Captain Jerry Jacobi managed to run straight through a plate glass door in the cafeteria while screwing around, costing him a few practices and the coaches much agita.

While the water conditions were good for rowing, the then-common practice of through-hull sewage disposal employed by the numerous cruise ships and container ships sharing Tampa Bay with the crews made rowing on the Bay a noisome experience.

A final brush with Yale capped the week, and SU's crews were competitive. Despite the "challenges" of Spring Camp, there'd been lots of miles put on by the time Sanford, Harrison, et al. packed up to head north. Mahon, Newby, Hobbs, and Hull joined the returners from the 1980 varsity, making the crew one of the biggest Sanford had boated at an average weight of 193.

Before the actual racing season would begin, Sanford and Cornell coach Fin Meislahn arranged to get together for a scrimmage on Onondaga on April 10th. While it may have been a bit unusual for two programs as competitive as Syracuse and Cornell to meet a fortnight before their annual Cup race for a "brush"–an English term for a rowing scrimmage–Sanford was not pleased with the varsity's progress, telling a reporter "Things are not going as fast as I hoped … The lack of depth has taken away the pushing ingredient of recent years. Now the starters don't have to push to keep their seats …Without that incentive–last year I had three strong eights–people are going to have to be self-motivated."

The brush showed SU did have some work to do, as the papers reported only the first frosh won their practice race, with the two varsity eights and second frosh lost their contests to the Big Red. Fortunately, shirts were not on the line. Not yet.

To accommodate visiting crews, the racing season opened on Cayuga Lake, where the Orange's annual bell-ringer dual with Rutgers took place on April 18th. With temperatures around sixty degrees and a moderate headwind for the morning races, the eights split the events. Rutgers won both varsity eights by identical six-second margins, while Syracuse demolished the Scarlet Knight frosh in both the first and second freshman eights by 20-second-plus margins.

Yale was on tap for the afternoon of the 18th, but this time there were not to be any Orange oarsmen headed north with new betting shirts. Yale, deemed to be the fastest crew in the nation, swept SU, with only one race–the first frosh–decided by less than a length-and-a-half, and most by far more. While the results of opening day were certainly disappointing, it would become obvious in just a few weeks that these two teams were stiff competition indeed.

Things were a bit loose on the varsity squad, with at least one of the freshmen surprised about the fragmented, and somewhat undisciplined nature of the team. According to future Captain Peter Hilgartner, "They would have minor successes, go out and party and blow any progress." Although there was certainly a wealth of talent on the team, the dissension and lack of discipline may have been contributing to the lack of success.

The following Saturday saw the Goes Cup race return to Onondaga, albeit on a course shortened to accommodate inclement weather; winds were strong all day, with gusts over 20 miles-per-hour making the IRA course unrowable. Instead, the crews raced over 1740 meters in front of the Ten Eyck Boathouse, finishing at the John Glenn Boulevard bridge. Navy looked to be very strong, returning three-quarters of their IRA champion varsity eight, and adding future national tram members Gregg Montesi and Dan Lyons to the lineup. Knowing they had a battle on their hands, the Orange varsity started fast and was first as the crews entered the inlet. The lead was not to stick, as Cornell and Navy rowed through the Orange as they battled for the win, the Middies coming out on top. SU's JV was 5+ lengths–almost 20 seconds–out of first in their event. The first freshman eight race had Navy out to an early two-length lead, one that SU managed to reduce to a half-length by the end of the shortened course. Reversing the result from the brush two weeks before, the second frosh was the sole SU victor. Still, Sanford wasn't too displeased, telling a reporter "I think maybe we are starting to put some things together."

With Brown going through a bit of a down cycle, SU was

165

only too glad to host the Holding Trophy on Onondaga two weeks later. This time it was SU doing the sweeping as the varsity and freshmen won by a length open, and the JV by a bow ball, 6:58.1 to 6:58.2. The crews were beginning to show some speed, and with the Sprints two weeks away, it was none too soon.

The Sprints were, if not a booming success for the Orange, certainly a major improvement over earlier results. The three top eights all made the grand finals, with the varsity a mere three-tenths behind bronze-medalist Northeastern and within a length of winner Yale. A resurgent Rutgers was in second, just one second in front of the Orange varsity.

The JV made progress as well, crossing the line in fifth. While they were more than fifteen seconds behind winner Cornell, they'd made up considerable time on Navy and Rutgers. The same held true for the first freshman eight. Their fourth-place finish in the grands was less than a second back of third-place Northeastern, and six seconds in front of Yale.

The late-bloomers in Orange were once again beginning to round into form, just in time for the IRAs.

The academic year completed, the oarsmen once again moved into the boathouse for IRA Camp. While it wasn't exactly summer, temperatures were mostly in the upper fifties and lower sixties, perfect for the two-a-day practices that would continue until just before the IRAs. The benign weather provided a stark contrast to the tension in the varsity eight, tension that had been building for some time. Frustration with results and internal bickering led to a confrontation between two of the athletes, resulting in the departure of one from the team for the remainder of the IRAs.

The lineup shuffle moved Charlie Clark up into the varsity three seat from the JV, filling out a crew with Hull at stroke, Hobbs in six, Darling at five, Mahon at four, Rick Skomra in two, and Jerry Jacobi in bow. Senior Mark Bickford had been in and out of the lineup, but his chronically sore back was keeping him from performing at his best, and as a result Mark was in the second eight. The crew and coach would have a little less than three weeks to get things sorted out for the IRA, a process that would prove to be quite a challenge.

The first test of the new lineup came up quickly; the Orange were headed to Hanover to take on the MIT Engineers and Dartmouth Big Green at the Packard Cup. Racing on the course several miles upstream from the Dartmouth boathouse, the varsity and first freshman won their races with the JV taking second, two seconds behind Dartmouth. For the varsity, the margin was a length over Dartmouth and eighteen seconds over the Engineers; the frosh had a much easier time of it, defeating the Big Green by ten seconds and MIT by eighteen.

IRAs and Bad Weather

When they pulled back into Liverpool, there were just eleven days before opening day of the IRA Regatta. Fortunately, the next week saw excellent conditions for practice with light winds and temperatures mostly in the seventies right through the rest of IRA Camp. Those conditions would deteriorate dramatically, marking the second-consecutive year the regatta would be extended past Saturday, and the first-year races would be held on the following Monday. There was to be one more major change for SU before the first day of the Regatta. Sanford decided to break up the JV eight and enter two fours and a pair with. This would be the first time since 1974 that no Orange JV would take to the line at the IRA, but with the move of Clark to the varsity and the thin bench, this looked to be the best chance for the guys to medal.

As Thursday's heats began, the weather, which featured 25 m.p.h. crosswinds, caused major changes to the racing schedule, format, and venue. Crews for twelve races had launched before the officials called a fifteen-minute delay before putting the third heat of the first freshman eights on the water. That turned into a seven-hour rowing moratorium, with rowing finally back underway at 7:10 p.m.

For the varsity's Thursday heat, conditions were deemed tough but rowable, despite what were described in contemporaneous accounts as "20–25 m.p.h. quartering headwinds." The varsity took to the water in the "George Ninos," a very light Carbocraft shell that was state-of-the-art at the time.

While the blue boat was indeed light, it was also less forgiving with gunnels somewhat lower than most of the other shells headed to the starting line. With conditions getting choppier the further the crew ventured out onto the lake, the boat was becoming more of a liability than an advantage. By the time the crew pulled up to the stake boats, the water in the boat had risen enough to get some guys bailing while others did the maneuvering. After the start, water was coming in over the gunnels. Stroke Gordon Hull told a reporter "the conditions were so lousy we couldn't stay afloat. I knew after 20 strokes it was just a matter of time before we went down." By the 500-meter mark, there was so much water in the boat the race was all but over for SU. With 700 to go, cox Gregg Weinglass called a halt. As the boat sank beneath them, the crew abandoned ship, staying with their nemesis and awaiting rescue. The experience was humiliating, but they'd have another shot in the reps on Friday.

SU wasn't the only crew that foundered, as Wisconsin's four with also sank in their heat.

In what could only be described as a big surprise in the varsity eight heats, unheralded crews from Boston University and UCLA both won, with BU's winning time the fastest of the day at just over seven minutes showing just how much effect the winds had on racing. Navy, who had looked so strong earlier in the year, finished fourth in its heat.

While the weather for Friday morning's reps was great, the results–for SU fans–were not. With two crews advancing in their varsity eight rep, the Orange would have to contend with Rutgers, Cornell, and Navy. SU came off the line even with Rutgers and Cornell, but they just could not hold on, and by the thousand-meter mark, Navy had come through the Orange. By the finish line, SU had fallen back to fourth place, finishing two lengths behind second place Cornell and another half-boat back of rep winner and defending champion Navy.

Interviewed after the race, Sanford said: "…it's evident we've got to work on depth. It's depth that's carried us in the past. We're fooling ourselves. This was the first year we had no JV eight. That was the tip-off to no depth." Commenting on the varsity's race, he noted "we rowed short. The reason we had gotten faster [during the season] was because we'd lengthened out. We didn't do it this time. You can't go fast, short."

Coxswain Gregg Weinglass had a slightly different perspective: "Pain reflected the type of race it was ... a painful race as we watched the last spot in the finals slip away."

Harrison's freshman eight finished third in their heat, well behind Penn and Orange Coast. Continuing what seemed to be a trend, Drew's crew also encountered problems in the rep; for the frosh it was a crab followed by a jammed slide that cost them the lead. This gave Brown the only help they needed, and they slipped by the Orange to grab the lone qualifying spot. Despite their equipment problems, SU's time was a full four seconds faster than the winning time of the other rep, small consolation for the first Harrison crew ever to fail to make the finals.

Racing conditions took a dramatic turn for the worse on Saturday, with all finals postponed due to gusty winds out of the southwest averaging 18 m.p.h., hitting 26 in the early afternoon. With several miles of fetch allowing the waves to build to shoulder height, conditions on Onondaga were dangerous for small boats, let alone racing shells.

With the weather on Saturday precluding any racing, the finals were postponed to the following day in hopes conditions would improve enough for fair racing on Sunday. The first event, slated for 6:30 a.m., was pushed back to 10:30, yet still the weather gods ignored the pleas of coaches, officials, athletes and fans. By late Sunday, Regatta Director Clayton Chapman decided conditions had improved enough on the lake course to hold the grand finals for the three eights and four without cox. Some of the consolation races and the pairs would take place on a course beginning a few hundred meters out on the lake, enter the Seneca River Inlet at the breakwater, and finish past the Thruway bridge. But first, the officials had to get the big boats off, and figure out how to winnow the field for the consolation race to three crews, the maximum number that could race on the inlet. Alas, the delay meant several crews, including those from Yale, Dartmouth, the Coast Guard Academy, Virginia and St. John's would not be able to race as they had to return to campus.

For the Varsity Challenge Cup, it was to be another

big year for Fin Meislahn's Cornell crew. While they had been together in that lineup for a mere ten days, were rowing in a brand-new Schoenbrod shell–a replacement for a shell that had been wrecked in a trailer accident–and had to come through the reps, the Big Red was not to be denied. They defeated Navy by a full length, rowing a 5:57.3, with Northeastern earning the bronze just back of the Middies. Navy returned the favor in the JV eight, with Cornell taking the silver and Northeastern again in third.

By the start of the work week, the extreme northern end of the lake had calmed down sufficiently to allow racing, albeit in that modified format. The 2000-meter course was still unrowable, so the officials and coaches decided to start the races out on the lake, and race by the boathouse to finish at the far end of the boathouse straightaway. All well and good, but the change–deemed the only way to get any finals in, would only allow three crews to race at a time. Thus the officials had to resort to seeding the crews–after the heats, reps, and semis–to assign them to the "appropriate" three-boat race.

When all was said and done, the top three seeds would race off for the medals, with the next three–all finals qualifiers–racing for fourth through sixth places. The records don't record the feelings of the crews slotted into the "second level of the grand finals," but their disappointment must have been profound.

Racing Monday, SU's pair with cox won bronze, finishing third in the championship final behind winner Penn and Wisconsin. Their teammates in the varsity four without were sent to the grand petite, where the challenges of steering a non-buoyed course proved too much for the Orange and Northeastern, both of whom were disqualified for going out of lane, allowing Trinity to win the race.

By virtue of their time and placing in the heats, Harrison's freshmen were relegated to the petite final, where they defeated Wisco and Northeastern in what must have been a very disappointing seventh-place finish, and an end to a seven-year run of Syracuse IRA freshman eight medalist crews.

Syracuse's varsity four with was perhaps the only Orange crew besides the pair with to come away from the 1981 Regatta with anything other than bad memories and deep disappointment.

170

Comprised of top members of the JV eight, the four won their heat as did Washington State and Penn; SU's time of 8:13.5 looked more like the time for a slow pair with and was indicative of the tough conditions. While its time was the fastest of the day, that meant little at this year's regatta.

The other eleven crews raced off in the reps, where the winner of each would qualify for the grand finals. None of the reps were close, and Navy, Wisco, and Purdue were slated to fill the remaining lanes in the grand finals.

As a result, SU's Chris Colville found himself out on the lake on Sunday, preparing to cox his crew against Penn and Wisco, with the winner, and the fastest second-place crew in each of two heats headed to the championship race and the other three crews relegated to the petite. Colville, stroke Mark Bickford, three-oar Jim McKay, Captain Rick Ritter in two and Russ Johnson in bow finished less than a second behind Penn and well up on Wisco in a heat that turned out to be far faster than the other championship elimination race.

Small Boat Gold Medal

The championship race, held right at dusk, saw the Orange crossing the line with an open water lead over Penn, with Purdue about the same distance behind the Quakers.

With the victory, Bickford and Ritter won their second IRA gold medal, and SU had its second medal of the 79th IRA. Talking to a reporter, McKay said "… I think it meant something to the whole team to get this. When the eights went out [of the running for the championships] they started counting on us."

This was the 1981 IRA JV four with winning crew's line up:

Cox   Chris Colville
Stroke   Mark Bickford
No. 3   Jim McKay
No. 2   Rick Ritter
Bow   Russ Johnson

But the real news for the collegiate rowing community was the weather; for the second-straight year the IRAs had been postponed due to winds, leading *Post-Standard* columnist Arnie Burdick to opine "Onondaga's best chance for retention of the IRA is that no other site is knocking down the doors trying to woo it away."

Chapter 17

1982–1983 – Harrison Moves On

T he 1981 regatta was not only a weather-induced debacle but a financial disaster as well; the conditions kept fans away and resulted in a net loss of $20,000 for the IRA. Fortunately, profits from previous years were more than enough to offset the poor revenues, although a couple more bad years would be a big problem.

The fall program brought solid results for Syracuse, with a fourth in the four at the Head of the Charles and the eight coming in ninth behind winner Navy. SU also had a pair at the Charles which finished sixth.

Once again, Tampa would be the host for the annual spring break trip. While the good conditions resulted in more than 200 miles of rowing, frosh coach Drew Harrison spent even more time on the water. Evidently his outboard motor somehow fell off his launch while his crews were quite some distance from the boathouse.

Harrison paddled his powerless launch to a buoy about a mile offshore, tied up, and waited for rescue. With both of his crews tasked with reporting his location and distress to Sanford, he figured it wouldn't be too much of a wait. Something went amiss. The sun was going down, the weather was deteriorating and Sanford searched in the wrong location. Drew had to be rescued by a passing party boat.

Just two weeks after their return from the Sunshine State, the Orange had a test against Wayne State (Michigan), with the varsity and JV racing off in one heat after the frosh "race." This would be one of the last times Wayne State would take to the water, as the program was disbanded less than two years later. While the results weren't recorded, that may have been the last "win" for the Syracuse varsity for some time.

The 1982 season started with a loss to Rutgers in a race held at Princeton's Lake Carnegie. Chris Colville coxed the crew, with Rick Skomra at stroke, Joe Blade in seven, Gordon Hull at six, Tim Bristow at five, Andy Hobbs in four, Ashton Richards at three and Tom Lowe and Pete Hilgartner rounding out the bow pair.

The Goes Trophy was up next in Annapolis. Host Navy was particularly strong in '82 and showed it with its win in the marquee varsity eight event. Again the Orange did not come out on top in any of the races, taking second in the freshman and varsity events and third place in the JV eight.

The varsity's racing season continued with defeats at the hands of Brown, Cornell, Navy, Princeton and Yale, five of the top six finishers at the Sprints. The varsity broke the streak at long last at the Packard Cup, where they crossed the line in front of Dartmouth and MIT.

Except for Harrison's freshman eight, day one of the IRA was not a great one for Syracuse. The JV and varsity eights and freshman and varsity fours would have to do it the hard way–through the repechage races Friday. Fortunately, the frosh four won its rep by 1.2 seconds over Washington State, but the varsity four was relegated to the petites by virtue of their second-place finish behind Navy; with seventeen crews entered in the varsity four, only winners advanced.

The JV also qualified with a second-place finish in its rep, a second back of Northeastern. It went on to finish just out of the medals in fourth, a length back of bronze-winner Brown and three lengths behind the winners from Annapolis. The frosh four was never in contention, earning fifth place in the grand final, while the V4 dominated its petite final, winning by more than eight seconds.

In what would be Drew Harrison's last year at the helm, SU's freshman eight was joined by Princeton, Cal, Navy, Wisco, and Cornell in the 4 p.m. grand final. Cal won by less than a second over Navy, with Drew's crew just a second-and-a-half back in third. This would mark the eighth year of nine that SU's freshman eight medaled in the IRA, a streak perhaps unmatched by any program in any other event.

In the varsity eights, Thursday's heats were won by Princeton and Navy, with SU headed to the reps for a second shot at making the grand finals. Having to finish no worse than second, SU did just that. Rowing a 5:57, the Orange came in just behind defending IRA-Champion Cornell.

Speaking to a reporter at the IRA after the reps recalling the season, Bill Sanford said, "We were out of the frying pan and into the fire all the time. We've been racing the best crews all year and all we did was lose." With a slot in the grand finals assured, Sanford could then say, "Now it's finally paid off."

The varsity eight finals pitted SU and Cornell against the winners of Thursday's heats–Princeton and Navy, along with Brown and Boston University from the other rep. Navy had been dominating crews all season, and had qualified six of its seven boats for the grand finals in 1982. With three eights plus the frosh four in the grands, SU was showing once again that it was a late bloomer. The next day would show just how much progress the Orangemen had made since those bleak days in April. They'd be in lane six, well away from the shore and lane one that was thought to be shallow, and thus a bit slow, in the last 20 strokes of the course.

The grand final event was one of the closest in memory, with sixth-place BU just 6.1 seconds behind winner Cornell. With a third-place finish behind the Princeton Tigers, SU avenged its early season loss to fourth-place Navy, coming in a scant half of a second before the Middies.

The third-place finish at the regatta was worth more than a bronze for SU. Based on that strong finish, the new National Collegiate Rowing Championship invited Sanford's varsity to compete in the Cincinnati Regatta, where it would take on Pac 10-Champion California, Sprints-winner Yale, and IRA-winner Cornell.

The lineup changed due to bow oar Peter Hilgartner's injury; he'd pulled a chest muscle during the IRA. After trying twice to row through it, Hilgartner had been replaced by Jim McKay. McKay, who'd stroked the JV for three years and the four with cox to a gold medal in the most recent IRA, was known around the boathouse as a very good technician; Gordon Hull told a reporter you could … "put him in any boat, and he'll make it go."

The race was a four-boat final, with SU picked to bring up the rear in the battle of champions. Once again, the Orangemen were able to overachieve, taking third in front of Crew Classic and

PAC 10-Champion Cal. In fourth for most of the race, Syracuse's plan was for the oarsmen to row within themselves until the last 700 meters, then press hard to the finish. Unfortunately, conditions worsened appreciably just as they started their move as a strong sidewind hit the course. NCRC-Champion Yale finished a bit more than two lengths up on SU, with Cornell taking second by a couple of seats of open water.

1983

The fall of 1983 saw the departure of Drew Harrison, perhaps the most successful freshman crew coach at any program at any time. Harrison, already a legend at Syracuse and throughout the collegiate rowing world, accepted a split position coaching the University of British Columbia's women's team and the Canadian National Rowing Team. After nine years at Long Branch, a tenure that had seen eight medalist crews and an unprecedented three-consecutive national championships, Coach Drew was moving on. His decision was undoubtedly influenced by the work he had done with the U.S. National Lightweight Team, where he'd coached the eight and four, as well as world champion single sculler Scott Roop. That, and the relative youth of varsity coach Bill Sanford was enough to convince Harrison to accept the position in Vancouver, B.C.

Larry Laszlo from Liverpool High School took over the reins of the freshman crew.

In what may have been the earliest return to the water of any Syracuse crew in modern times, the shells hit the water on January 11th. That proved to be nothing more than a tease, as conditions changed quickly, returning the crew to indoor training. The cycle repeated itself several times, leading Sanford to characterize 1983's false spring as the worst he'd experienced.

The bronze medal at the IRA, and subsequent success in Cincinnati earned the varsity a trip to San Diego Crew Classic the following April. This time only the varsity and coach left the chilly environs of upstate New York for the sun, sand and gentle breezes of Mission Bay, California. With racing scheduled for April 2nd, this was the season opener for SU and most of the other teams in

San Diego for the Crew Classic. The field was about as tough as it could be; Yale, Cal, Washington and UCLA were among the crews competing for the Copley Cup for varsity eights. And with fewer than 20 days on the water before heading west, SU–along with neighbor Cornell–would be a bit behind the West Coast crews, at least in water time. Among the crews in Syracuse's heat, all but one were from climes much more accommodating; Washington, Stanford, UCLA, and the Florida Institute of Technology, one of the most consistently fast Dad Vail crews of that era. Even Yale, the sixth crew in the heat, had been on the water for almost six weeks.

The lineup had Tom Lowe at stroke, Tim Bristow in seven, Andy Hobbs at six and Peter Hilgartner in five, Rick Skomra at four, Charlie Clark was in the three seat with Mike Wodchis in two and David Belgrad at bow. Chris Colville was the coxswain.

Whether it was the short water time or something else, after the heats the Orange found themselves in the petite finals along with Cornell and several West Coast crews. In a very tight race, SU edged out the Anteaters of UC Irvine for first, with Cornell a half-length back in third. All in all, it was a decent start to the season with good competition and a chance to row in something other than wafflebottoms and heavy sweats.

The dual-race season opened with Rutgers and Yale on Onondaga Lake on April 17th. In the varsity eight, contested by SU and Rutgers, the Orange defeated Rutgers by 2-and-1/2 lengths. Yale won the JV contest by just under a length open over Syracuse, with Purdue another ten seconds back in third.

Midway through the month, SU was slotted in the tenth spot in the national rankings and Cornell in sixth. While top-ten rankings were pretty solid, the Orangemen would face some tough competition in Ithaca on April 23th. Ranked no. 1 in the nation in the Coaches Poll, Navy was deep, strong, and talented, and showed all three attributes in the Goes Cup. Speaking to a reporter before the race, Coach Sanford acknowledged the Midshipmen's status as favorite for the Cup, while also noting the tough conditions that had plagued the Orange and Cornell. Both crews had little water time in the week preceding the race, as snow storms and inclement weather had kept both crews indoors on most days. The ratings

177

proved their accuracy as Navy dominated the event, sweeping all three races it entered. More troubling, SU finished third in each race behind Cornell, although the gap for the varsity was a mere half-second. While the time gaps weren't overly large, it was clear the Orange had a long way to go.

Difficulties continued for the crew, with almost-record-heavy rains leading to high waters flooding up the apron and at times well into the boathouse. By early-May, the water had receded, but the 6+ inches of rain that fell in April had soaked the lower level of the Ten Eyck Boathouse, damaging boats as the water pushed some shells up against the racks just above them. Despite the inconvenience, practices were on schedule.

Syracuse had never been a big Sprints crew and 1983 was not going to be the year things changed. None of the eights made the grand finals, the varsity came in last in the petites, the JV took third, and the first freshman finished fifth. The heavyweight eight grand final was one for the ages, with Harvard rowing through Navy, then holding off a hard-charging Brown crew by a scant two-tenths of a second.

After the lackluster–at best–performance at the Sprints, Coach Bill Sanford and the varsity were anxious to get back on the starting line. Before SU faced Dartmouth on Onondaga, there was a major shakeup in the crew with six of eight oarsmen in different seats than they'd occupied in Worcester. Talking to a reporter, Sanford said, "We got beat up. We just stunk. So I beat them up pretty good. I was really disappointed in them, so I had to make some changes. I had to try something different."

Those changes were big indeed. Three seniors were moved out of the varsity eight, replaced by younger and bigger guys from the JV. Don Miller, Scott Kempton, and Jeff Meiselman moved up, and Andy Hobbs moved to port from starboard, taking over the six-seat. In all, only two guys were in the same seats before and after the shakeup, while the coxswain Marc-Antoine Lopez kept his seat.

At the Packard Cup, held in Hanover on May 21st, the new lineup took a while to settle down. Dartmouth led off the line and for the next 1,500 meters, but could not sustain the pace. With 500 to go the Orange pulled away smartly, finishing just under a length up on the Big Green in a race Coach Sanford described as the "best race of the year."

The JV won by more than 11 seconds, but the first frosh lost by the same margin. The second frosh came home with betting shirts after a one-length victory over the Big Green.

With its second-place finish behind Harvard at the Sprints, Brown's varsity was, according to *The Post-Standard's* Bob Snyder, an "overwhelming favorite to win" the 81st IRA. Coached by SU alum Steve Gladstone, the Bruins got 12-of-15 votes for top varsity eight in the annual IRA Coaches Poll despite boating two first-year rowers in the stroke and four seats. SU received seven points to Brown's sixty-three.

Things had changed a bit at the IRA Regatta. As more coaches and officials became aware of the shallow water at the end of the course near the shore, they had raised concerns about the effect of the shallow water on boat speed. Point in fact: shallow water tends to increase the friction on a hull as the bow wave bounces off the bottom, impeding the hull's progress as it passes. The officials decided to move the course farther out into the lake to alleviate the problem, making lane one, the closest to shore, some 200 feet out from the land.

The first day of the regatta saw decent conditions, although a strong headwind for the small boat races resulted in times that reached past eight minutes for some of the fours and almost nine minutes for the pair races. Despite the clement weather, Thursday was a pretty poor day for Syracuse. Of the six crews entered, only one (varsity four, second place) finished better than last or second to last in its heat, however Sanford reported "both the varsity and second varsity indicated they had better races than they showed today." His words would prove to be prophetic.

In contrast, Navy showed the depth of its program with a strong showing on Thursday, qualifying six crews directly into the finals.

Friday was more to SU fans' liking, as both varsity eights qualified for the grand finals with strong rows in the reps. After building a one-length lead on the field in the first 700 meters and maintaining a lead on the field for the first 1,500, the varsity finished in 6:01.4, less than a half-length down to Princeton after a strong sprint by the Tigers. The JVs won their heat by a mere half-second, gaining a measure of revenge over Princeton. On the calm waters that prevailed on Friday, their decision to row the Carbocraft looked like a smart move, as it handled the conditions beautifully.

SU's varsity four also qualified for the grand finals by virtue of its winning row in the reps. The frosh four didn't make it in, finishing fourth out of five in a heat with two to qualify. And most distressing to Syracuse fans, the freshman eight finished last in its four-boat rep. For the JV, the improvement from the poor performance in the heats was remarkable. The second boat captured the bronze medal behind winner Navy and second-place Princeton.

The varsity final was a two-boat race, with Brown and Navy fighting it out for the Varsity Challenge Cup. Syracuse held on to third for much of the race, but could not maintain the pace. As SU faded down the stretch, Buzz Congram's Northeastern Huskies managed to row through the Orange for the bronze. SU finished two lengths back of Brown, and comfortably in front of fifth place Penn and Princeton in sixth. The crew had exceeded everyone's expectations. After a dismal Thursday, the varsity's fourth-place finish and JV's bronze were a bit of redemption for the Orange.

While the races weren't affected by conditions this time around, the finances were. For the second year in a row, the IRA lost money. The overcast skies and cool temperatures kept attendance to 10,000 fans, fully four-thousand below the break-even point. With other sites–Camden, New Jersey and Lake Placid, New York–expressing interest in hosting the regatta, the stewards were looking for a five-year commitment from Syracuse.

Barely a month later, the SU rowing community was hit by devastating news. Rising sophomore and former-frosh-eight stroke David Godfrey died in his sleep while at home for the summer. Godfrey, a scholarship athlete from Connecticut's Simsbury High School, was going to be a strong candidate for the varsity eight in 1984. Instead, he was honored at a service in his hometown by Coach Sanford and more than a dozen of his teammates.

There was one more competition for Sanford that year–he would win his face-off against Democrat Jonathan Rosenthal and be re-elected to the Onondaga County Legislature in the fall.

Chapter 18
1983–1988 – Growing Pains
The Gary Jordan Years

In what was becoming a pattern, Jan Palchikoff's tenure as SU women's crew coach was to be rather brief; during the summer of 1982, she departed for a position with the United States Olympic Organizing Committee. Novice Coach Deb Quinn took over the head spot upon Palchikoff's departure with Beth Emery coming on board as the novice coach and Deborah Collum in the assistant coaching slot. Quinn would depart in three years, to be replaced by Gary Jordan.

Whether it was the new head coach, the payoff from successful recruiting, the product of two years of very good novice crews and / or other factors, 1983 would be the year the Orange women moved into contention with the top crews in the country. Their first race would be against Yale and Cornell in Derby. While SU did not win the varsity, it came in 1/3 of a length behind Yale, with the same margin over third-place Cornell. Coxed by Megan Waldron, Quinn's varsity had Margaret Gordon in the stroke seat, 5'7", 127-pound Colleen Waldron at 7, Kristine Jensen at 6 and Linda Zembsch at 5, Melissa Entwistle who later gained fame as plus-size supermodel Emme at 4, Kathryn Schaab at 3, with Sheila Roock–playfully called Shelly Rock by her teammates–and Nancy Newill in the bow pair.

The JV race wasn't as close, as SU's A and B boats finished 3rd and 4th, respectively. The novices weren't quite as successful as past editions; their third-place finish was ten seconds back of winner Yale.

The Orange Challenge Cup had long resided in Penn's trophy case; in the four-year history of the event, Pennsylvania had yet to lose. While the Quakers were sorely tested in the April 16, 1983-edition they managed to hold on to the Cup, if by the thinnest of margins. Quinn's SU varsity lost to Pennsylvania by a mere one-tenth of a second in a race on the Schuylkill with Northeastern well back of the Quakers and Orange women. This was a marked improvement from past years, as SU had never

183

before come within ten seconds of Penn. The JV race ran just a bit shorter than the varsity at about 1,200 meters. The location for this contest was likely just downstream of the Strawberry Mansion bridge, possibly due to fast currents and swirling waters around the bridge abutments, a common occurrence in April on the Schuylkill.

The lineups were juggled a bit for the next weekend's contest against the Terriers of Boston University, with Colleen Waldron and Nancy Newill swapping the seven seat and the bow seat. BU swept all three races on Onondaga, defeating the varsity by a half-length of open water and more decisive margins in the other two events.

While the outcome may have been far from what the Orange women wanted, they could later take consolation in the knowledge that BU's varsity was a very good crew; it went on to win the Sprints in May.

Quinn kept the varsity lineup static for the April 30th Rutgers race. The varsity again lost a nail-biter, finishing just four-tenths of a second behind the Scarlet Knights. The JV and novice crews were also unsuccessful in their races, both more than a length open behind Rutgers. With the cup racing season concluded, Quinn and her athletes had two weeks to prepare for the 1983 Sprints.

To help prepare and get just a bit more racing experience, the following Sunday the women traveled to Boston. In terms of wins, the trip was a success with SU taking three of the four events including the varsity race over MIT, in the novice race over MIT, and first and second places in the varsity four event. The Orange JV was well back of Harvard in the only race between the two programs.

The women's team had been carrying several more athletes than needed to fill the seats in three eights. While there had been enough for a second JV eight in the first race of the season, attrition had reduced the squad by just enough to prevent the team from boating four full eights. For the Sprints, Quinn moved Colleen Waldron and the stern three from the JV–Beth Clagett, Susan Church, and Pamela Carey–along with coxswain Eleanor Allen into a four. The four won bronze at the EAWRC

Championships on Lake Waramaug in Connecticut, the top finish for any SU crew.

Except for the novice eight's third-level final result, the other two eights ended up in the petite finals, with the varsity third and JV fourth. Three other SU novices teamed up with women from MIT to enter a second novice eight; their result was not recorded. Despite the abrupt departure of Palchikoff, the SU women's crew appeared to be in good hands. While the Sprints results were less than desired, the crews had shown a tenacity and toughness that seemed to bode well for the year ahead in terms of experience and depth.

The experience worked out. The depth did not.

1984's varsity crew included only fifteen upperclass-women, with just one junior and two sophomores on the roster. This was quite a decline from the prior year, when twenty-four names filled the books; more troubling was the drop off among last year's novices as only two of the nineteen stuck around for their second year. The novice squad was down in numbers as well, with only thirteen athletes rowing for grad assistant Christine Colello. While the varsity squad was small in numbers, it was not in stature with four women 6 feet or taller; the varsity line-up in the spring averaged 5'10" and was, according to Coach Quinn, one of the biggest in the conference. Two of the shorter members of that crew, Sue Church and Kathy Weber, were the senior captains.

Cornell was on the schedule for the season opener on April 7th, with the Orange victorious with a margin of nine seconds in the varsity race on Onondaga. Cornell exacted revenge in the other eights races as SU's lack of depth made itself felt. The SU second varsity finished behind two Cornell crews and the novices were five seconds back of the Big Red in their event. Apparently the JV and novice eights were low priority boats for Coach Quinn, as SU's JV four defeated two Cornell crews by open water. All in all, a decent beginning for the racing season, which would continue the next weekend in Boston.

With a three-foot loss in the 1983 Orange Challenge Cup, SU's varsity eight had all the motivation needed to bring the cup to Syracuse for the first time since the origin of the contest. It did so by a tight-but-not-nail-biting margin of two seconds over Penn, with Northeastern another five seconds back. There was no JV eight event, and Penn did not bring a JV four to Boston; SU's crew finished between two Husky crews. Quinn's novice crew won by a length over NU with Penn another six seconds back. Over the first twenty years of the Orange Challenge Cup, this was to be Syracuse's sole victory. Just two races into the season, the SU women's varsity had won both. The next weekend would be a stern test indeed, as 1983 Sprints-Champion Boston University would be the competition.

The race was on BU's home course, with Brown University also entered in the races. There were just two events on April 21st, varsity and novice eights. In what may have been a surprisingly easy race, the Syracuse varsity dominated, defeating BU by open water, with Brown another two lengths back in third. The Orange novices were outclassed by a wide margin, finishing over thirty seconds behind Boston and fifteen back of Brown.

After three varsity victories, Quinn opined that "the varsity is the best crew I've ever had ... they have the technique, the background to be champions." With the crew's size, power, and early season success, the coach was looking to a possible trip to Seattle for the National Championships in early June.

Just a few days later, Rutgers threw a rather large wrench into the nascent plan. Back on Onondaga for the last dual meet of the season the varsity suffered its first defeat of the season in a three-second loss. The JV eight won, while the novices lost to the Scarlet Knights.

The results at the Sprints were far from what was expected. After a poor heat including a major crab early in the race, the varsity found itself in the petite finals, finishing 11th overall. The novice eight fared even worse, winning the third-level finals finishing 13th. The best result, a fifth in the grand finals, was delivered by the varsity four, with Jane Clifford at stroke, Ann Czaja in three, Debby Knoblock at two, Claudia DeSimone in bow and Christine Casatelli at cox. Despite the lack of experience, the dual season had gone very well, but something had happened towards the end of the season, something that dropped the varsity from legitimate medal contender to barely hanging on in the petites.

For the six seniors in the varsity eight, the end of their SU rowing careers must have been disappointing indeed.

1984 would also mark the last year the women and men rowed different length races. Following the lead of rowing's international governing body and the International Olympic Committee, the collegiate women's race distance was increased from 1,500 to 2,000 meters in 1985.

1985

Quinn was back in the fall, with former Men's Crew rower Gary Jordan officially in as novice coach. Jordan had been coaching for a couple of years, but this was the first time he was officially listed as a coach by the University. Jordan had 20 women on the roster, including three upperclasswomen. While the novice and men's freshman crews were similar in composition, some women's novice crews included rookie rowers on their rosters while only true freshmen could race on frosh crews.

The racing schedule was rather limited, with only four races and the Women's Sprints set for the spring. The opening regatta saw the Orange varsity women defeating Ithaca College. The next weekend, Yale and Cornell proved to be far too much for the Orange as SU finished last in all but the second novice eight race, well out of contention in most events. The next weekend saw two different opponents but the same finish order as Northeastern and Penn dominated the event. SU was again far behind the competition.

Smith College delivered the same result later in the season albeit in a closer race, and the misery finally ended when Rutgers came to Syracuse's home course. The varsity lost badly, but the JV and novices crossed the line in front for the first time. The season ended in similar fashion at the Sprints. Only the second novice eight avoided a third-level final race; they won their petite. The varsity finished 14th overall.

When the season was over Coach Deb Quinn took her leave.

1986

Gary Jordan assumed the head coaching position for the 1985–1986 season, keeping it for the next three seasons. Jordan had been coaching the novices under Quinn since 1983. Prior to that he had rowed for two seasons at SU–graduating in 1977–and had coached the women's crew at UMass-Lowell.

Jordan's roster was a thin one, with only fourteen experienced rowers, ten of them sophomores and one a first-year. Senior Co-Captain Ann Czaja was out with an injury for the season, leaving fellow Co-Captain Claire Heinz as the only active senior on the team. Seventeen first-year rowers and three coxswains comprised Assistant Coach Margaret Gordon's novice squad.

Despite the low turnout for varsity, Jordan did not want to move any of Gordon's frosh up. According to the athletic department's *Crew Outlook*, Jordan said "There is too much pressure on the freshmen to step right in on the varsity level. The varsity is used to rowing a certain way and it is awfully hard to pick that up coming right in from high school or prep school."

Instead he'd rely on a mostly-sophomore crew with sophs Amanda Hock in bow, Beth Gummere in two, Vicki Kriemelman at three, and Sharon Cantor in the four seat. Juniors filled the engine room with Robin Clark at five and Angela McLellan in six. Heinz rowed seven and sophomore Kathy Schwingel sat in the stroke seat, while Tina Oliver coxed.

The 1986 racing season expanded to include Radcliffe and Dartmouth in a three-way race in late April; that was the only change to the schedule that included all the previous year's competitors. For the third year, the opening race saw the Ithaca Bombers on the line facing the Orange, and for the third year the Orange was victorious, cruising to a ten-length win on Onondaga over the new 2,000-meter distance. Ithaca took the novice race.

Gary Jordan and his charges made the short trip to Ithaca the following weekend for the Cornell-Yale Regatta. The varsity finished five lengths back of winner Cornell, while the novices came in second, well back of Yale but a half-length up on Cornell.

Conditions limited SU and Smith to a 1,500-meter

distance on Onondaga, where Smith won the varsity by 2/3 of a length and the novice race by a bit more. Jordan boated a JV for the day and it defeated Smith by open water.

The trip to Philadelphia for the Orange Challenge Cup was unsuccessful as both the novice and varsity crews finished behind Penn and Northeastern. The next weekend's racing was on Boston's Charles River, where the varsity was again far behind Radcliffe and Dartmouth. The novices turned in a good row, two lengths back of the 'Cliffies but 17 seconds in front of the Big Green.

Other than the opening day win over Ithaca, the best result was the crew's success against Rutgers where both the varsity and JV crews won; there was no novice crew competition.

In the days before the Sprints, Jordan was feeling more positive about his crew, telling SU's Sports Information Office, "We're having good practices, our best of the season. The varsity eight, four, and the freshmen are peaking at just the right time. The boat just has to row together."

But success in the final dual race and the improvements in practice did not presage success at the Sprints. The varsity did not qualify for the finals, finishing sixth in its heat. The novices made the petites, rowing to a sixth-place result.

The small roster, a very young crew, and a new coach had a tough season to be sure. However, they'd had a couple of wins and had seen just how good the best of the league was. The question facing the Syracuse Women's Crew members as they left for the summer was "Could they build on that success?"

1987

Sue Hartley joined Jordan as the novice coach in the fall. The team's roster was significantly larger, with a large number of returners welcoming the incoming first-years, thus enabling the coaches to boat five eights for some of the spring races. If not ebullient, Jordan was positive about his crew's changes, telling SU's reporter in a preseason prospectus that he would "be very surprised if we didn't do better this year than last year. The varsity is looking pretty good."

SU would be without several key members of the 1986 varsity; two were studying abroad, one was out with mononucleosis, and two decided against rowing in the spring.

Ithaca College welcomed SU to its home course on Cayuga Lake for the season-opening race. With a three-year-undefeated streak to protect, Jordan was leery of Ithaca's improvement over the 1986 season, telling a reporter "their novice team was good and beat us [in 1986]. I look for them to be more competitive than last year and I expect a close race." The varsity race was closer, with Syracuse crossing the line eleven seconds before the Bombers; the Orange also won the JV eight by a similar margin. Ithaca's novices continued to impress opponents, winning the first and third novice eight races, with SU taking the second novice eight.

Weather conditions in Derby precluded racing the following weekend, so the team returned to Syracuse, rescheduling the race for the day after the Orange Challenge Cup. With the Cup Regatta held in Boston, the change was relatively easy logistically for Jordan, et al.

Northeastern won the Orange Challenge Cup with Penn in second. SU was three lengths back; while likely not the result Jordan sought, it was a significant improvement over the prior year. Jordan's JV came in two lengths in front of Penn to win their race, and Hartley's second novices were also victorious. Syracuse's first novices and novice four were less successful, finishing last in their events. With the racing in Boston concluded, the Orange women loaded the shells for the three-hour drive to Derby.

Yale's women's varsity was fast becoming the team to beat in the mid-to-late eighties, and it showed why, defeating Cornell by open water and Syracuse by three lengths. Their lower boats were just as good, winning all but the second novice event, where Cornell took the race by a quarter-length. Syracuse brought up the rear in every event, with the second novice crew showing its mettle by finishing within a length of winner Cornell. All in all, a very tough weekend, with lots of hard racing against very good competition. There would be no respite, as next up on the calendar was an away race at Dartmouth against the Big Green and Radcliffe.

Alas the trip to Hanover did not mark a turn in the Orange's fortunes. The varsity lost a close contest to Dartmouth, crossing the line a half-length back with Radcliffe trailing. The rest of the crews suffered similar fates, as Syracuse failed to win any of five races.

Things got back on track the next weekend at home against Rutgers, with the Orange winning all but the novice four, including a four-tenths of a second win in the varsity event.

That was to be the end of the winning for the 1987 season. At the Sprints three weeks later, the varsity ended up in the third-level finals where it finished second. The other crews were in the petites, with the best finish a second place turned in by the varsity four.

1988

Jordan's third season in the head coach's launch was going to involve more hard work from his athletes. An SU Athletics Department press release read in part:

"Coach Gary Jordan is planning to institute some changes in the way the Syracuse University women's crew team operates in 1988 - - changes aimed at putting more 'Ws' in the win column for the Orange women. 'We're going to ask our rowers to work a lot harder this season,' Jordan said without any hesitation. 'I plan on looking for our people to make more of a commitment.'"

With only four seniors graduating in 1987, a schedule loaded with home races, trips to Florida and Oak Ridge, Tennessee, for warm-water rowing and a large pool of talent, Jordan was somewhat positive, although he couched any predictions in a caveat, saying, "If we get the stronger commitment I will ask of our rowers and they give back what's asked of them, we'll definitely win more races."

The '88 varsity had senior Tina Oliver at coxswain and Kathy Schwingel in the stroke seat, juniors Kim Jordan at 7 and Sue Drew at 6, senior Sharon Cantor at 5, sophomores Tracy Rude at 4 and Kristin Walker at 3, with senior Vicki Kriemelman at 2 and junior Shevaun Webster in bow.

They opened their season in what was becoming the

annual bell-ringer, a match with Ithaca College. Syracuse swept the Bombers in the contest on Onondaga on March 27th, with only the novice eight race close, a 1.8-second margin.

The next weekend saw the competitive level increase dramatically as perennial powers Cornell and Yale made the trip to Long Branch. Jordan's charges were overmatched, finishing last in each of the races and not competitive in any. The next weekend saw Penn and Northeastern on the line on the Onondaga course, but the results did not change. If anything, Syracuse's performance declined as the women were at least 30 seconds behind the winning crew in each of the four races.

The varsity continued to struggle the next weekend, coming in third by a margin of ten seconds behind MIT and Dartmouth. The JV finished second in its race in front of Dartmouth, while the first novice eight was second in that event. The JV finished out its season with a win over Rutgers in New Jersey; the other SU crews were not as successful.

Gary Jordan's last race as head coach of the Syracuse women's crew would be at the Eastern Sprints on Connecticut's Lake Waramaug. The varsity was the only crew to make the petites, where it finished sixth. The two novice crews both finished in third place in the third-level finals, while the JV withdrew from competition.

In spite of having some stellar athletes, after three years of the Jordan regime, it was evident the Syracuse women were not yet competitive in the EAWRC. Despite the promising beginning under Mark Lyvers, the program had stalled. Once again it was time for a change.

Jordan was out. His replacement was a woman whose mantra was hard work.

Chapter 19

1984 – Quite a Rebuilding Year

When the SU men returned to Long Branch for the fall season, they were facing what many generously called a rebuilding year.

According to press reports, Captain Peter Hilgartner "knew he wasn't going to be captain of the most talented crew in college rowing, so he set out to be captain of the most disciplined." That discipline would have to overcome not only a dearth of talent, but a dearth of athletes as well; only a dozen experienced rowers returned, with the best of the lot, Canadian Tim Bristow taking the year off to train at home for the National Team. Depth was such an issue that Sanford, interviewed at the IRA commented that he "… was actually wondering for a while if we would have a boat in the JV event at the IRA this year with all the injuries and sickness."

While the varsity might have been thin, the frosh were anything but. Freshman Coach Larry Laszlo had clearly done an exemplary job recruiting talent as he sought to return the Syracuse freshman crew to its usual place on the podium at the IRA. Three Canadians from Ridley College were on the team along with Pete Ayer and Steve Coutant, both of whom had international experience rowing for the U.S. Junior National Team where they had earned silver medals that summer. And for the first time, there would be two members of the Sanford family in the program. Shawn Sanford, a very experienced coxswain and freshman at SU, joined the team in the fall.

Once again the Orange would take on Rutgers and Yale in the first races of the season, taking on the Scarlet Knights in Princeton on Saturday, April 14th, before heading up to Derby to race Yale on Sunday. Laszlo's freshmen had no trouble in either dual race, contributing to a sweep of Rutgers on Saturday and defeating Yale in Derby the next day with the fastest time of any crew–a 5:37.6. For Coach Bill Sanford's guys, a convincing sweep of Rutgers–the JV by 4.6 seconds and the varsity by 5.4 seconds– made for a pleasant Saturday evening. Sunday's bus ride home wasn't quite as much fun, as the Eli defeated the Orange varsity by a half-length of open water and the JV by one length. The racing had been a good test for Syracuse, which would head home for three races on its home course, beginning with the annual Navy-Cornell-Syracuse race.

Talking with a reporter before the Goes Cup, Sanford lamented the lack of depth and relatively diminutive stature (average height of 6'2") of his crew, but remained hopeful, saying, "Our varsity boat is aggressive. They've got a take it to 'em approach." That approach would be tested in the annual three-way race with Cornell and Navy.

The wonders of upstate weather greeted the crews as they arrived at Long Branch on the morning of April 21st for the Goes Cup. Windy, cold conditions blew the crews off the lake course, pushing the races to the Seneca Inlet course. Even then the conditions were difficult, and described by Middies Coach Rick Clothier as "… the roughest water I've ever seen a race started in."

The conditions didn't prevent his guys from prevailing, as they dominated from the start. With a length lead at the 500, Navy increased its margin steadily from there to an 11-second gap over Cornell and five-plus lengths on the Orange at the finish line. The huge margin over SU came despite Sanford's last-minute shuffling of his lineup, a change designed to add more length to the crew's stroke. Hilgartner and seven-man Scott Kempton were moved back to six and five, with the former occupants of those seats, Jeff Meiselman and Bill Bragdon, taking the stern slots.

For the freshmen, the Goes Cup was more of the same–another win, and more shirts to add to the collection. Despite a far-less-than-perfect start, Syracuse crossed the line a full four lengths in front of Navy. Their teammates in the second frosh were also victorious, while the JV did not fare as well. The lack of depth on the junior varsity level showed in the JV's 16-second loss to winner Navy.

It was back to Onondaga for a four-way race the following Saturday. Boston University, the Coast Guard Academy, and Columbia were all in Syracuse in what was a one-time affair. The racing–except for the freshman eights–was very, very close. Fortunately for the local fans, SU came out on top in both varsity events, edging out BU by 1.1 seconds for the varsity and holding off the Coasties by 1.5 seconds in the JV. The freshmen took first over second place BU by a full ten seconds.

In the fifth race of the month, the Engineers of MIT took on the Orange the next day. With MIT's very small team, there was no JV race, while SU's varsity won by ten seconds and the frosh by six seconds.

At the Sprints, the frosh cruised through their heat, dominating just as they had in their dual races earlier in the season. But the finals proved to be a different race altogether with the crew well back of the medals.

According to Coach Larry Laszlo: "We didn't row well that day and we were complacent. We hadn't lost, hadn't even been pressured, up to that point."

The varsity rowed quite well in its heat, leading for the first three-quarters of the race before being passed by Harvard and Yale. While sounding somewhat pleased with the result, Sanford acknowledged his crew hadn't been at full strength, as Jeff Meiselman now occupying the three seat had been ailing the week before the Sprints. He was, according to Sanford, "a lot sicker at 1,500 [meters]."

The varsity went on to place second in the petite finals, as did the JV. With Harvard and Yale coming in fifth and fourth in the grand finals, it looked as if Coach Bill Sanford's guys might–just might–have a shot at the grand finals at the IRA. However, while the two Ivies would not be in Syracuse, Cal would. It remained to be seen if the discipline and hard work of the previous eight months would deliver the result Hilgartner and his teammates had been striving for.

For the SU men, there would be two more chances to test themselves before the IRA, the Packard Cup and a brush with Wisconsin. Against Dartmouth, the freshmen seemed to have regained a good bit of focus, defeating the Big Green by the unheard-of margin of six full lengths. The varsity won another squeaker, crossing the line 1.3 seconds in front of the Big Green, while the JV had just a touch more margin, winning in 5:53.7 to Dartmouth's 5:56.0. There was also a fours race, where SU's spares–novices all–raced the Dartmouth varsity and freshman fours. While the inexperienced Orangemen gave a good account of themselves in what was for most their first contest, they were two lengths back of the Big Green varsity four and just under a length behind the frosh.

The final dual race of the season was essentially a brush–a series of pieces between crews that was more of a tune-up, a chance to work out any last minute adjustments than an actual race. Wisconsin and Syracuse were slated to compete for the Jock Stratton Cup, three 1,000-meter pieces between each of the five crews entered in the IRA. In addition to the eights, the teams would compete in club fours and varsity pairs without, with two novices rowing in SU's entry. This would be the first year for the club fours, an entry allowing freshmen and upperclassmen to row in the same boat; the event replaced the pair with coxswain, which disappeared from the IRAs. SU "won" the varsity and freshman eights, while Wisco took the other races.

As the IRA began, it certainly looked as if SU's freshmen were back. They had been pushing the varsity every day in practice, occasionally defeating their elders in pieces, no small feat as the varsity had been steadily improving as events would convincingly demonstrate. With an undefeated record in dual races and an easy win in its heat at the Sprints–marred by a poor row in the finals– Larry Laszlo's crew was confident.

In the heats, Syracuse dominated from the start, rowing to a two-length victory over Princeton. The convincing, fastest-time-of-the-day win in the opening heat confirmed that the Orange would be a force to be reckoned with on Saturday. Of note, the SU time was not just the fastest among frosh crews, but among all crews racing in the heats. Certainly the variable conditions had much to do with the result, but that notwithstanding, it was evident that the young Orangemen were very fast indeed. Moreover, the deep experience of the men in the crew–only one rower, Dave Swenton, was a novice–coupled with the experience in the finals of the Sprints boded well. It was unlikely they'd be complacent this time around.

In addition to the eights, there was one other varsity crew wearing Orange at the 1984 IRA; a pair without cox that did quite well, finishing second in its heat and third in the rep to qualify for the grand finals where it finished fifth.

196

Saturday's IRA was a faint shadow of the same regatta a mere five years earlier. Attendance peaked at 3,500 for the day, a big drop from 1983's average of 10,000 fans and a far cry for the 20,000+ seen during the regatta's heyday. It may have been the first-ever complete ban on private alcohol; it was only available at beer stands for $1 per 16 oz. cup. Some blamed the windy conditions, which led to a postponement of the racing until late in the day, however others noted many of the "fans" attending in past years barely knew, or deigned to acknowledge, when a race passed by. Press reports earlier in the year quoted Bill Sanford citing comments by some rowing coaches concerned about the rowdy, beer-soaked crowds; Sanford told a reporter that other coaches were "more and more vocal about the fact they didn't think this was a real great atmosphere for a national championship event."

With Kevin O'Brien in the stroke seat, the frosh took to the water for the grand final. Conditions had improved dramatically, as the winds that had delayed the start of racing twice had dropped to a zephyr as dusk neared. The race turned into a two-boat affair, with Princeton, the crew SU had beaten by two lengths in the heats, pushing out to a half-length lead in the third 500. Syracuse couldn't respond, and the favored Orange were left with silver; Navy was 5.4 seconds off the pace in third. Laszlo, while disappointed, was philosophical about the results, commenting, "They set a pace we couldn't match. But I don't know if we could've gone any faster."

Coming off their razor-thin loss to Harvard at the Sprints, Steve Gladstone's Brown eight was the favorite to win the Varsity Challenge Cup. Navy had other ideas, and so did Cal's Golden Bears. Bruno ended up third in its heat behind the winners from Annapolis.

Hilgartner's leadership and the discipline of everyone on the team paid off at the IRA. Racing in the heats, the Orange varsity took second, just a deck behind Cornell, a result that would place it in the easier of the reps, avoiding Cal and Brown. While the margin was pretty much identical to Cornell's lead at the Goes Cup, there was a sense that Syracuse had a bit more speed. The rep was a three-crew affair, with Northeastern and Boston University also contending for the lone grand final slot. SU won, defeating the Huskies of Northeastern by a bit less than a length.

In what was supposed to be a rebuilding year the Orange varsity had made the finals of the IRA for the fifth time in six years. Talking about the race, and the captain, Sanford said, "These guys are real tight. Peter [Hilgartner] has been the influencer for that. I found out this year how important a strong captain is."

By 8 p.m., the water had turned to glass for the varsity eight grand final, a race packed with talent. Brown, second in the Sprints, was favored. Penn was right up there as well, and Navy also considered a threat. Then there were the California Golden Bears, Cornell and Syracuse. The Orangemen were not quite an afterthought, but certainly not considered in the same league with the other crews in the grand final. All that prognosticating was in the past, as the crews lined up just before sunset. With a clean start, Navy pushed its bow in front just past the 500-meter mark. Cal and Penn battled back, but Navy never backed down on the way to a one-length victory over Penn, with Cal in third. The Orange, given little chance to make the finals, came in a bow ball behind Cal in fourth, a very strong effort. One-tenth of a second out of the medals, SU was followed by Cornell with Brown bringing up the rear, a result termed "inexplicable" by Brown coach Steve Gladstone.

Navy's victory in the Varsity Challenge Cup along with its finish in three other grand finals earned the Middies the Ten Eyck Championship, a double win for the service academy's oarsmen.

For Syracuse the rebuilding year had been a success, and the future looked even better. With Bristow returning from his year away, a talented and experienced freshman crew, and five returners from the '84 varsity, Sanford was feeling pretty good about the next few campaigns, telling a reporter SU could definitely win its second IRA ever under his leadership in the next three years.

As the season ended, other crews started looking at Long Branch as an ideal spot for training. By mid-summer, the Canadian Olympic Team had relocated to Syracuse, seeking water similar to California's Lake Casitas, site of the upcoming 1984 Los Angeles Olympics. While the coaches were looking forward to the training, they also expressed surprise and dismay at reports that the boathouse might be demolished, wondering "Why tear it down when international teams want to come here ... the chief reason we are here is because this is a terrific rowing facility."

That terrific rowing facility would welcome back an SU crew with high expectations. Those expectations had been built by a crew that was determined, focused, and disciplined. If the next year's crews–comprised of more and more talented oarsmen–could maintain that focus, good things would happen.

Chapter 20
1985–1986 – Solid But Not Spectacular

If 1984's crew had been one of the smallest in terms of numbers in recent history, 1985 was just the opposite. Even after the usual attrition over the year, the Orangemen were still able to boat three eights, three fours, and two pairs at the '85 IRA. Compared to '84, the crew was deep indeed. The fall was to get busier for Coach Bill Sanford, as he was elected Republican Chairman for the Town of Salina in addition to representing the town in the Onondaga County Legislature.

Tim Bristow and Don Miller followed Hilgartner as the captains of the Orange. Bristow had first visited The Hill while still in high school, when he and current teammate Mike Wodchis drove south from Canada to visit American colleges. They had heard that some American schools actually gave rowing scholarships, and decided to visit Cornell and Syracuse to find out what their options might be. On campus in Ithaca, the two found no one to greet them and no workout to watch. But a few miles north, they walked into a Archbold Crew Room where, Bristow later recalled: "Everyone was working hard, the attitude was enthusiastic, the coach was interested. I decided then and there I wanted to go to Syracuse."

Now Bristow was back on campus, fresh off his year training with the Canadian National Team. He'd just missed making the eight as he was the last man cut from a crew that would go on to win gold at the 1984 Olympics in Los Angeles.

Rutgers would be the Orange's first opponent of the 1985 season–but only by a matter of hours. April 13th was opening day, and featured the dual Syracuse-Rutgers Regatta, followed by a three-way contest with Yale and Purdue. After a couple of years of very good crews, the Scarlet Knights were in a bit of a down cycle; they'd been swept the year before in the race at Princeton and the results of this year's contest on Onondaga were about the same. SU's Varsity won easily in a time of 6:40.1, nine seconds in front of Rutgers. The JV won by almost 14 seconds, but the frosh eight margin was just under a length in favor of Larry Laszlo's crew. Rutgers didn't have a second freshman eight, so Syracuse broke the frosh down into two fours, with the A crew winning by five seconds over Rutgers and the B crew ten seconds back of the Scarlet Knights.

After a couple of hours' break, the afternoon races headed to the line where conditions had deteriorated a bit since the morning races. The first two races went the way of Syracuse, as the second frosh defeated Yale by a time of 6:54 to 7:01.6 while the third varsity beat the Eli by a deck, 6:48.0 to 6:48.7. Yale came storming back in the first frosh eight, crushing SU by 18 seconds, with Purdue another 16 seconds behind the Orange. The second varsity race, while closer, kept the same finishing order with SU a length back of Yale while Purdue crossed the line a further 30 seconds back.

With Yale and Syracuse splitting the first four events, the seventh-ranked Bulldogs of Yale and guest Purdue headed to the line to take on Sanford's eighth-ranked Orange. The race was, according to Coach Bill Sanford; "one of the most satisfying in the last ten years ... we rowed on good water this morning against Rutgers, but it got a little choppy by the time we faced Yale." In a finish that likely shocked most of those watching, Yale was never a factor. Syracuse and Purdue battled for the win before Sanford's crew pulled out a one-length victory. Yale came in a length-and-a-half back of the Boilermakers.

This was an excellent start to the season for the varsity, and boded well for the next week's event–the Goes Trophy. The consistent strength of Navy's crew had kept the Goes Trophy in the Annapolis trophy case for several years. For 1985, the annual three-way contest would be held at Navy's course on the Severn River, where conditions combined to make for very fast times. Cornell gave the Middies a great race in all three eights, losing the varsity by four-tenths of a second, the JV by 1.4 seconds, and the frosh by 1.5 seconds. SU was well back in all but the frosh event, where Coach Laszlo's crew was five seconds behind Navy. Showing the depth of the program, Navy also placed first, second, and third in the varsity fours race, with SU two-tenths of a second back in fourth.

Back on the road for the next weekend's events, Syracuse's oarsmen headed to Boston for a double-header; the seventh-ranked Orange matched up with the tenth-ranked Terriers of Boston University on Saturday followed by MIT on Sunday. In a close race, the varsity took the measure of the Terriers, winning the Conlan Cup with a margin of 2.6 seconds while the JV won by a deck and the frosh by just under a length. The second frosh won in a laugher, while BU managed to avoid a sweep by taking the third varsity eights race. MIT, still in a bit of a down cycle, lost all races the next day except one—the second frosh, where the Engineers crossed the line a quarter-length before the Orange.

After five races in 15 days, Sanford and Laszlo had three full weeks of practice to get their athletes prepared for the Sprints. For upstate New York, the weather cooperated, with highs in the sixties and seventies for much of the time, little rain, and only a few windy days causing the crews to head north off the dock for the protected rowing on the Seneca River.

The Sprints would be a tough test for the ninth-ranked Orange varsity. After seeding, it was in a heat with third-ranked Princeton and no. 6 Brown. Princeton had beaten Cornell by a dozen seconds after Cornell had defeated SU by seven, while Brown was also strong. The field looked to be wide open, with perennial contender Harvard appearing to be on the rebound from a down year in 1984 and Brown looking especially tough after solid results in the early season including a win over the Crimson in a dual race. However, the Ivies would have to get past the reigning IRA-Champion Midshipmen. Navy was undefeated, returned three oarsmen from its '84 IRA championship crew, and the top seed for the second-consecutive year. The Crimson won every heavyweight final and two of the lights, to dominate not only Navy, but the entire Eastern rowing establishment.

Interviewed some time later, seven-man Bristow opined that the varsity had been inconsistent that spring, "'On' for the Yale race, then we weren't again for the Eastern Sprints." SU's varsity did not contend in the heats, finishing fourth, and going on to match that result in the petite finals, one spot below its seeding. The JV was third in its heat, and with two to qualify went on to the petites as well, where it finished last. The brightest spot of the day was the freshman eight's performance. After earning a slot in the championship finals with a second place—behind Yale by a quarter length–Laszlo's boys came in sixth overall.

For the first time in 48 years, the men's team would not be moving into the boathouse for IRA Camp. After a combined effort by SARA, Onondaga County, and the University to improve and upgrade the 1937 structure, housing inspectors found enough zoning, safety and housing code issues to keep the oarsmen from bunking in the boathouse. Instead they'd be driven to and from main campus, but take their meals at the Ten Eyck Boathouse.

There was another big change in store for the team; Annie Hall–mother of varsity bow oar Jim Haas–was in charge of meal planning. Ms. Hall, a professional food policy expert, had taken over nutritional duties, and the menu shifted rather dramatically. Bean sprouts, brown bread, potato-and-leek soup, shakes made with fresh fruit and brewer's yeast, and tahini spread were staple fare, but each athlete had a custom-designed menu. Hall had brought in a physician to assess each athlete's ability to tolerate and utilize dairy products, corn, wheat, bananas and eggs, among other foods. Hall's perspective was remarkably prescient as her views became much more widespread two decades later. That didn't make some of her recipes any more palatable; a reporter noted several rowers sought various ways to make her brewer's yeast shakes drinkable, and others vehemently protested the liver entrées.

The changed diet may have resonated with Bristow, who had been the last man cut from the Canadian eight that had gone on to win gold in Seoul's Olympic competition. After the camp, a nutritionist had told Bristow he'd made it that far in spite a diet that was "nutritionally deficient."

One proposed change would have had an even more dramatic impact. Steve Gladstone of Brown proposed returning the IRA to a three-mile event, an idea backed by Coach Sanford. The SU coach saw the longer race as one that would be a great contrast to the Sprints, required more rowing skill and strategy than the 2K, and could not be won by "just thrashing away at the water." Despite the backing of a few coaches, the idea never gained any traction.

Once again SU's final tune-up would see it facing off against Randy Jablonic's Wisconsin Badgers the Sunday before the IRA. Jabo's varsity eight came into the regatta with the top seed. That seemed to be well deserved. In a brush with Navy just the day before, Wisco had nipped the Middies. The margin against the Orange was larger; that plus the Badgers' bronze at the Sprints made it clear that Wisconsin, with an average height of 6'5", would be a major threat to any other crew seeking to climb to the top of the podium.

The coming trip to Henley put additional pressure on the Syracuse crew. Bristow noted "The alumni and Coach Sanford foresaw that this would be a year of tremendous opportunity and depth, an ideal year to go, only so far we haven't performed up to expectations."

For the IRA, the varsity lineup would be Russ Forbes at stroke, Tim Bristow in seven, Scott Kempton at six and Bill Duffield at five, Co-Captain Don Miller in four, with Pete Ayer in three, Bill Bragdon at two, and Jim Haas–he of the brewer's yeast–in bow; Tim McDermott sat in the coxswain's seat. Looking ahead to the IRA, Bristow said, "This weekend is kind of do-or-die for us. If we put together a good, mature race, we'll be right in there and a lot of people are going to be surprised by our speed." The strategy was to even-split the 500s, keeping the crew's focus in and on its own boat, "instead of worrying about the boat next to you."

That strategy didn't pan out in the heats, as SU finished 12 seconds down on heat winner Princeton, who had nipped Penn by less than a second to advance directly to the finals. Navy won the other heat in its quest to win the Varsity Challenge Cup yet again.

In what was becoming an all-too-familiar occurrence, high winds again caused a delay at the IRA, with Thursday's heats taking almost thirteen hours to complete after a seven-hour delay began just past noon. The delay on what JV cox Shawn Sanford called "Lake Ocean-daga" was especially frustrating as it came after excellent weather earlier in the week. The officials tried to get races off, but three crews swamped in the morning heats, making the decision an easy one. Despite the adverse weather conditions, all heats were completed by the end of the day. The final race saw Navy defeat Wisco by a quarter-length, exacting a measure of revenge for the favored Wisconsin varsity's narrow victory in the brush just a few days earlier. Princeton won the other heat.

The reps on Friday and Saturday were also affected by bad weather, and racing only got under way when officials decided to use the alternate course on the western side of Onondaga Lake. The Solvay shore would be the location of racing for all but the finals.

While the usual course was unrowable, the other side of the lake off the Solvay shore was deemed acceptable for racing. The Solvay course had been constructed several years earlier to give an alternate course for the regatta, the thinking being crosswinds from the west would be less problematic on that side of the lake. However, "constructed" may have been an overly generous characterization as there weren't lane markers, a situation that would make racing especially challenging for the blind–shells without a cox–boats. SU's four without cox actually collided with Penn's crew in their heat, an indicator of the challenge inherent in steering on an unmarked course.

Forecasters were calling for 30-mile-per-hour winds out of the south and thunderstorms for both days, following tough but rowable conditions for Thursday's heats. At least the officials deemed conditions rowable. Wisconsin's Randy Jablonic–no stranger to rough weather on Lake Mendota in Madison–had quite a bit to say, and none of it complimentary of the officials' decision to race: "That was the worst race I ever saw, weather-wise. There was swell, mixed with chop, mixed with wash from motorboats. It was the most intolerable conditions to qualify for a national championship that I can imagine. I felt it was a travesty being run like this."

For a while, Friday looked like a much better day, but that "while" only lasted for 40 minutes of racing as windy and rainy weather moved in rapidly. Fortunately for the Orange, three small boats–the frosh four, pair without, and four without all qualified for the grand finals. Regatta Director Clayton Chapman and his colleagues had to reshuffle schedules constantly; some races got off in the morning and early afternoon, but none of the eights raced that day. Saturday was no better, and the prevailing direction of the wind was constantly shifting with much of the day featuring a wind out of the south-southwest. This created a nasty cross-chop, even more difficult to handle than a headwind or a tailwind.

When racing finally resumed late on Saturday, the Orange varsity was in a four-boat rep, with two to qualify. The competition was Brown and Wisconsin; New Hampshire was also in the race but didn't look to be competitive. SU finished third, 1.1 seconds back of Wisco, a result that placed the Orange in the petites.

After all of the delays, the finals were scheduled to begin at 6:30 a.m. on Sunday, weather gods permitting. Fortunately, the weather early Sunday was as good as it had been bad for the preceding three days–no wind, no chop, a mirror finish greeting the early rising crews as they rowed out of Seneca Inlet and onto Onondaga Lake. The conditions may have been superb, but the racing was not for SU's varsity eight. It finished third in the petites, with only New Hampshire crossing the line after the Orange.

Sanford's second eight had placed third in its heat and missed a spot in the grand finals by less than a second in the reps held late on Saturday. Brown won its petite, with SU five seconds behind in second.

For the second year, SU's best shot at a medal looked to be the freshman eights. Larry Laszlo's frosh eight won its heat by a deck over Brown, thereby advancing directly to the grand finals along with fellow heat winners Wisconsin and Navy. Those three crews filled the medal stand for the frosh eight, with Wisco winning gold by a half-length over Navy and the Orange taking the bronze another half-length back of the Middies.

SU's top-performing crew at the 1985 IRA was the freshman four. After qualifying with a win in the reps on Friday, the Orangemen rowed to a silver medal in Sunday's finals just three-tenths of a second in front of third-place Navy. Navy had won its Thursday heat by defeating SU by a length making the Syracuse crew's silver all the sweeter.

SU also had an open four at the IRA comprised of freshman and varsity rowers. They finished fourth in the petites.

If ever there was a regatta that was going to be tough on blind boats–the 1985 IRA was it. The cross-chop conditions, changed race venue, and start-and-stop scheduling were doubly hard on crews without a cox to steer and keep all the details organized. After a second-place finish in the heats on Thursday,

SU's four without cox gained the finals with a second place in Friday's reps. Navy proved to be the class of the field, finishing more than a length of open water in front of runner-up Princeton. SU was just four seconds back of the Tigers, but in fifth place. Outside of Navy, the next five places all finished within 5.3 seconds, a very close race for coxless fours.

The deep SU squad also had two pairs at the IRA. They finished fourth and fifth in their heat, well back of winner Navy. The A pair made the finals with a second place in its rep, and finished sixth in the six-boat final. The B pair won its two-boat petite final held on the Seneca Inlet due to "wind conditions."

In the previous 82 years of the regatta, Princeton had never won the varsity eight at the IRA. Their performance earlier in the season and win in the heats had marked the Tigers, along with Brown, as most likely to win the Varsity Challenge Cup. But the Tigers had much more in mind than that one race. They had qualified six crews for grand finals, and most looked to be serious contenders for championship honors. In one of the most impressive performances by any team at the IRA, Princeton took four golds and two silvers on the way to winning the Ten Eyck Cup by a whopping 136 points over three-time Ten Eyck winner Navy.

The most precious of the Princeton golds was in the Varsity Challenge event. After trailing Navy for the first half of the final, Princeton pushed past Penn and Brown and rowed through the Middies in the third 500. The Tigers held on from there for a 2-and-1/2 second victory.

Princeton had two crews in the JV eights; its lightweight-Sprints-champion eight and the JV-heavies. The lights took gold and the heavies silver in that event.

Sanford took four crews to Henley that summer, including a four without to contest the Visitors' Challenge Cup, a four without for the Wyfold Challenge Cup, a four with for the Prince Philip Challenge Cup, and the varsity in the Ladies' Challenge Plate. The crews first headed to the Reading Town Regatta to get in a little competition before the big event in Oxfordshire. Racing the IRA-Champion Princeton Tigers, Sanford's varsity eight eked out a win by the narrowest of margins in both the heats and finals of the 1,000-meter senior eight race. In a three-boat race, the four with cox also was victorious.

The narrow course with big log booms along much of its length was much feared by blind boats. Georgetown's racing was over almost before it started due to a collision on the course. Fans, rowers, and coaches were undoubtedly relieved when the first trips down the course for the coxless Orange fours were successful as the Visitors' crew defeated Salisbury by over two lengths. The Wyfold four rowed to victory over Hereford Club, earning a race the next day against London RC, the top seed in that event. The eight lost in the first round of its event, the Ladies' Challenge Plate.

Friday saw two more crews knocked out, as the Visitors' four finished behind Trent Polytechnic of England and the four with was defeated by 1/3 of a length by Princeton. The last Syracuse crew racing at Henley was the Wyfold four. After beating top-seeded London in the quarter-finals, the Orangemen met their match in the semifinals, losing to Britain's Nautilus by a half-length.

1986

The following fall, the crew competed in the Head of the Charles as SARA, finishing 9th in the Club Eights, less than 16 seconds out of first, and 15th in the Championship Eights.

Just as the fall racing season was coming to a close, Bill Sanford found himself embroiled in a dispute involving his candidacy for re-election to the Country Legislature. A complaint had been filed alleging Sanford did not reside in Salina, the district he was representing in the legislature, however several maps conflicted as to the official location of the Long Branch Boathouse, the Sanford family residence.

Coach survived that kerfuffle, only to find himself immediately facing another–his political opponents alleged that by living in the county-owned and Syracuse University-leased boathouse–Sanford "appeared to be involved in a conflict of interest." Evidently the lease in force at that time specifically prohibited a County Legislator from benefiting from the lease.

That issue was also resolved in Sanford's favor, allowing him to return to his focus on rowing and legislating.

Spring racing began with the annual Rutgers race in New Jersey. The Orange varsity and JV were victorious by three and nine seconds respectively, but the freshman eight was clobbered, losing to the Scarlet Knights by 20 seconds. The following weekend was another road trip, with Sanford's charges racing Yale and Purdue on the Housatonic in Derby. Conditions were quick as the home team prevailed in the two upperclassmen's races. SU was two lengths back in second in the varsity event and almost ten seconds behind the Eli in the Jayvee. Purdue took the frosh race by six seconds over Yale; again SU was far behind, coming in 16+ seconds back in third.

In Ithaca, the annual race for the varsity's Goes Cup took place on April 19th. Navy prevailed by a half-length over Syracuse, with Cornell another five seconds behind the Orange. The Middies also won the JV and Frosh eights, with Cornell second in both. The frosh eight result was troubling, as SU finished 39 seconds–ten lengths–behind the two other crews. After the solid freshman results for the 1985 crew, the 1986 version looked positively anemic. With three races behind them, Laszlo's boys had yet to finish within five lengths of first place.

They'd get their chance the next weekend on the home waters of Onondaga Lake, as BU came to Syracuse for a Saturday race and MIT took to the line the following day. The Orange varsity won a nail-biter on Saturday, edging BU by a mere one-tenth of a second. BU returned the favor in the JV as they nipped Sanford's second boat by the same margin. For the frosh, the race was their most competitive to date with a losing margin of just under nine seconds.

MIT boated two crews on Sunday, and both lost to Syracuse by substantial margins. The freshman eight finally tasted victory with a convincing 30+ second margin over the Engineers; the varsity won by four lengths.

With the dual racing season all but complete, SU prepared for the May 18th Eastern Sprints with a three-week hiatus from racing. In Worcester, the varsity finished eighth overall with a second in the petite; the JV came in fourth in their petite on Lake

Quinsigamond. The official records do not contain a placing for the Orange freshman crew.

The IRA started late in 1986, with heats beginning Thursday, June 5th. The varsity found itself in the lone five-crew race with 1985 champion Princeton, perennial contender Navy, a very fast Penn crew and the Scarlet Knights of Rutgers. The race, billed as a tough heat indeed, lived up to that billing as the winning time was almost nine seconds faster than the next-fastest heat. Unfortunately, that time didn't belong to Syracuse; the Orange finished second behind Penn, three seconds up on the Midshipmen.

The varsity was in a different race entirely on Friday; an advantageous rep with two crews that had finished last in their respective heats and one that was second to last. Taking advantage of their good fortune, Sanford's top crew rowed to a six-second win, earning a lane in the grand finals.

The finals were a dogfight among the top three crews, as Brown, Penn, and Wisconsin battled their way down the course before Brown took the lead, winning by 1.6 seconds over Penn with Wisco just one-tenth of a second behind the Quakers. Navy took fourth, two-tenths of a second in front of the Orange, who where seven seconds slower than the winning Brown crew.

The 1986 IRAs were not kind to the Syracuse JV. A third place in its heat, no recorded time in the rep, and a last place in the petite finals–seven seconds behind a crew they'd beaten by six in the heats–marked a very tough ending to the season for Sanford's second eight.

The freshman crew was not in contention in its heat on Thursday, finishing ten seconds out of first place. A third in its heat put the Orange first-years in the petite finals, where they finished 12 seconds behind Dartmouth in fourth place.

SU's small boats were led by the four with cox. They would be racing for the Eric W. Will Trophy and begin with a five-boat heat on Thursday. The beginning was auspicious for the Orange, as a five-second margin of victory placed them directly into the finals. The winning time was more than ten seconds slower than the next slowest of the three heats, but the Orange hadn't been pressed. Whether the other heats were indeed much faster, or something happened between heats and finals, SU could do no better than fifth in the grand finals, well out of contention some eleven seconds back of winner Princeton.

The frosh four had a tough regatta as well, finishing last in its heat, fourth in the rep, and fourth in the petites, some eight seconds behind the winner.

There were two additional small boats–a pair without cox that was definitely in over its head–its times were more than thirty seconds back of the winners in each of its two races–and an open four that finished fifth in the grand final after a very close second in its rep. This crew's results were consistent across all three days, perhaps an indicator that the crews rowed up to their potential.

Chapter 21
1987–1988 – Back to Henley and into the Finals!

Orlando was on the schedule again for Winter Camp, with the athletes headed to Rollins College for a week of double-session steady-state rowing interspersed with dining events at the Rollins dining hall. While the camp wasn't overly intense, it was productive with lots of miles put in by all crews. They'd need the miles, as this season was looking to be a very tough one.

The schedule was tough: the crew's first test would be at the San Diego Crew Classic in early April; Brown had won the IRA the previous year; Navy was deep and had been IRA medalists for several years, Yale was on the schedule again and a resurgent Rutgers was on tap for an early season race.

While the competition would be strong, Syracuse's varsity wasn't giving anything away to anyone. SU would return stroke Richard McNamara along with fellow varsity returners and juniors Bob Price and Paul Wolfensburger, senior Captains Peter Ayer and Jay Greytok and classmates Steve Coutant and Allan Green as well as newcomer Paul Schmidt, its one international student from Germany. The varsity was confident and excited; everyone in the entire varsity eight–save their one international oarsman–had won medals at the IRA; juniors had won bronze as freshmen and seniors had won silver. And, they'd be headed back to San Diego for the Crew Classic in early April.

Larry Laszlo's freshman squad was a bit smaller than usual for the Orange. While six frosh tipped the scales at or over 200 pounds, there were ten oarsmen under 175 pounds and at least six under 6 feet. Whether the crew's impressive experience, including incomers from the United Kingdom, South Africa and Canada would more than overcome any size issues would be the key question.

To get to San Diego, they'd have to survive winter training. Bob Price recalled things were stepped up quite a bit in the winter of 1986–1987; the training load went up significantly, with the guys' longest erg pieces going from half an hour to a full hour. More stairs, longer runs, more sprints up Mt. Olympus, and hour-long steady-state tank pieces were other changes to the workout schedule. Partway through winter training varsity veteran Peter Ayer became ill. Ayer, a very talented and naturally skilled oarsman, would not get better until just before the team returned to the water. While the team was definitely more fit as a group, Ayer's inability to participate in much of winter training would certainly not help the crew's chances come racing season.

Regardless, when the team finished Spring Camp in Tennessee, Bob Price remembered the lineup was probably the most consistent, the best day in and day out in his three years in the varsity eight.

In March, there was a lot going through Bill Sanford's mind. The racing season was getting underway, and he was considering running for County Executive for Onondaga County. According to *Post-Standard* columnist Frank Brieaddy, Sanford would "probably have to give up the crew if he's elected County Executive."

Speaking to this, Sanford told Brieaddy, "I'm never going to be not a coach for very long." In preparation for the potential move, Sanford and his wife had bought a house near the lake, figuring there would be too much hay made of a County Executive living on county land in a building owned by the University. Sanford's efforts came to naught as he dropped out of the race late in the spring to back the eventual winner, Nicholas Pirro. Sanford's political career did advance as he was picked to become Chairman of the Onondaga County Legislature, a position he would hold for the next 14 years.

While the political intrigues were in play, the team was preparing for the upcoming racing season, which would begin in San Diego. The varsity oarsmen made the trip while their teammates stayed to train on Onondaga. They'd been very motivated throughout the winter to compete in San Diego, but the lack of water time showed–all too clearly. Syracuse failed to make the final, finishing third in the petites. Price recalled "we weren't ready to race." While the crew was fit and the boat was moving well, the first week in April was just a bit early for the always late-peaking Orange.

Price and company got back on track on Onondaga Lake

the following weekend, as the varsity edged Rutgers 5:51.2 to 5:52.4. The Scarlet Knights won the JV race by even less, 6:01.1 to 6:02.1 and the freshman eight by an almost identical margin. The guys in SU's varsity four defeated two Rutgers crews to earn shirts in a hotly-contested race.

The rest of the varsity's dual season didn't go as well, with narrow losses to Yale (1.4 seconds), at the Goes Cup (2.9 seconds to Navy) and to BU (0.3 seconds). It wasn't just one thing; at different times it seemed the varsity was just a bit overconfident, could have raced a little smarter, needed to work harder on the water to complement the rigorous winter indoor training, could have benefited from better coxing, or didn't respond well to the frequent changes in seating–the guys in the boat were the same, but they were moved around a good deal. The second boat had similar results–close–but not close enough.

The varsity's frustrating season was almost the polar opposite of the season Larry Laszlo's undersized but obviously talented freshmen were enjoying. The frosh were winning everything including the freshman eight at the Goes Cup, victories over Yale and Rutgers early in the season, and a beating of BU as well.

The 3V (racing mostly in fours) and second frosh were also winning more than their share, with victories over Navy, Columbia, and MIT (second frosh only).

In the final tune-up before the Sprints, SU took on MIT in Boston, and managed to sweep the Engineers in all five races.

Two weeks later, SU headed back to Massachusetts for the Eastern Sprints. Racing in the afternoon's petite finals, Sanford found Rutgers returning the favor as the Scarlet Knights bested his varsity by one-tenth of a second, pushing the Orange back into third in the petite. The JV was fifth in its petite, while the frosh finished just out of the medals in fourth in the grand final about five seconds back of winner Penn.

The Packard Cup was canceled in 1987. After 85 Dartmouth students were diagnosed with measles in mid-April, Dartmouth's crew was banned from participating in several races, even though no oarsmen contracted the disease. The crew was told it could race at the IRAs if no more students came down with measles, but when more cases were identified in late May, the New York State Health Department banned Dartmouth from the IRA.

Undeterred, two Dartmouth rowers paddled out to the start in hopes they'd be allowed to race. When they weren't, they headed back to the dock, and then proceeded to mingle with the crowd. As one rower told a reporter, the whole business was ridiculous, as no Dartmouth students, student-athletes, or fans were banned from Onondaga's shores, where they could have done real damage if they were contagious.

The short-lived Stratton Cup contested between Wisconsin and Syracuse, scheduled for the weekend before the IRA, was also canceled.

The National Collegiate Rowing Championship in Cincinnati had been in existence for five years and its success was causing some coaches to be "gravely concerned" about the future of the IRA. Given the travel cost, what some athletic directors saw as the IRA's duplication of the Eastern Sprints, and the NCRC's ability to pay top crews' travel expenses, the future of the IRA was the subject of some discussion. Several crews contemplated ditching the IRA in favor of the NCRCs.

Others, including SU alum and Brown Head Coach Steve Gladstone came down firmly in support of the IRA, calling it one of the two "major league races of the season." Chided by some for not keeping up with the times, the Syracuse Regatta Association had begun to raise money from local corporate sponsors, accumulating $22,000 by June of 1987. With memories of long delays and rough waters just now beginning to fade, the pressure from Cincinnati was just what the Syracuse Regatta Committee didn't need.

The crowds predicted for the IRA were also much smaller than in previous years. After the ban on all alcohol three years earlier, attendance had dropped to as few as 5,000 fans from 20,000–25,000 from previous years. That total ban had only lasted a year, with spectators now allowed to bring one six-pack of beer each into the Onondaga Lake Park.

As his crews prepared for the IRA, Sanford was faced by the fact that what used to be considered "fast" was no longer near "fast enough." In four of its five races leading up to the IRAs, the varsity had rowed sub-six minutes, a time that a decade earlier would have resulted in four wins rather than 1987's 2-and-3 record. Interviewed before the IRA, Cornell coach Fin Meislahn said his 1981 and 1982 IRA champions wouldn't win this year's regatta, and may not even qualify for the grand final. He went on to opine that some of the crews that would fail to make the finals actually were good enough to win the championship.

Thursday's heats saw the Syracuse varsity matched up against Brown and Wisconsin, a tough draw as the Bruins were considered the overall favorite after winning the Eastern Sprints in early May, with Wisco seen as one of the few crews capable of upsetting Brown. The results were as expected–SU in third behind winner Brown and the second-place Badgers. None of the other five SU crews qualified Thursday, so all would row in the reps. In contrast, Randy Jablonic's Badgers won four heats with three more finishing second or third.

What was described by Coach Bill Sanford as "as fast as we could go today" was not fast enough for the varsity, as it was beaten by Navy in the reps, an outcome that put SU in the petite finals. Although the margin was 1.2 seconds at the line, for about 1,800 meters Syracuse was, if not in command of the race, at least even or slightly better. Navy's late push was just enough to make the difference. Years later Bob Price recalled, the crew "battled stroke-for-stroke down the course, bow ball-to-bow ball, probably the most intense race I ever had at SU." As a measure of just how hard that battle was, Navy finished well back in the grand finals.

After the reps, Frosh Coach Laszlo had a four and eight in the finals, joined by SU's varsity pair without which consisted of Joe Kieffer and Pete Liefeld. The JV eight failed to make the grand finals.

The frosh four returned SU to the medal stand with its silver medal row in the grand finals, which presaged another medal-winning performance by the crew's classmates in the eight. Laszlo's eight won bronze, ceding just a half-length to winner Penn and a mere three-tenths of a second to silver-medalist Wisconsin. Future SARA President Kieffer and teammate Liefeld weren't as fortunate in their grand, as they finished sixth.

Despite dismay at losing to Navy in the reps, there was plenty of fight left in the Orange varsity and it was out for revenge. The crew won the petite final by just over a second, defeating a talented BU crew that had not only had edged SU earlier in the year, but was the only boat to beat Brown that season. Rutgers was a full length back of Syracuse.

Brown's grand final win was not only its second-consecutive Varsity Challenge Cup, but came in convincing fashion. Just across the thousand-meter mark, 153-pound stroke Mike Tuchen and crew took only 200 meters to move a length on Wisco on its way to an open water victory.

While the competition was indeed getting faster, it was evident there was a lot of talent coming up to the Syracuse varsity in the fall. The key would be keeping those soon-to-be-sophomores on the team and integrating them quickly with the returning athletes. Bob Price recalled the mood at the end of the IRA was, "kind of excited." The varsity's petite-finals win coupled with the bronze in the frosh eight boded well for the Orange in 1988. The team would be looking to make the next season all that '87 was supposed to be.

That task would be in addition to Coach Sanford's newly expanded duties as Chairman of the County Legislature.

1988

If 1987 was frustrating, 1988 was going to be a payback year. The solid performance from the '87 freshmen combined with a core group of talented and tough upperclassmen promised better things for the Orange. With 1988 also slated to be a Henley year, there was a bit more pressure on the crews than normal to perform, as they'd have to be pretty competitive to earn their trip. Sanford was confident, saying, "The additional depth will cause better intrasquad competition and in turn cause more speed. I expect that not only will the varsity boat have much more speed than this past year's boat, but that the depth also will show up at the second and third varsity levels."

While crews were definitely getting faster, recruiting was still a bit in the dark ages, with many crews relying on walk-ons, actually complete newcomers to the sport, to fill out their freshman crews. Writing in *The Post-Standard* the day before the 1988 IRA Regatta began, reporter Jeff Thoreson described the process used by Northeastern Freshman Coach Gary Caldwell to identify incoming freshmen with potential–one based on assessing potential rowers' height and apparent athleticism. Thoreson opined that a rowing coach's ability to find novices, teach them to row, and get them to mesh with others in a shell as distinctly different from football and basketball coaches, who could rely on past performance in their chosen sport, rather than forecast how a complete novice might someday be able to perform.

With that being said, 1988 was a bit of a different season. Navy, which had enjoyed several years of very solid results, looked to be in a bit of a down year; its varsity failed to make the finals of the Sprints. So did Wisconsin, silver medalists in the 1987 IRA. And the Orange crews were going to get a lot of racing in before the big regattas, beginning with a win at the Augusta Invitational Regatta April 2nd in Georgia. The early start would likely help assimilate the four sophomores from Laszlo's medal-winning '87 frosh eight that had earned seats in the top shell. Dirk Stribrny was in bow, Don Smith at three and Jeff Pesot at four, with Allan Green at five. They were joined by three seniors; Co-Captain Richard McNamara at stroke, Paul Wolfensburger at seven, and Co-Captain Bob Price in the crucial six seat. The only juniors in the boat were Paul Schmidt at two and Robert Heinstein in the coxswain's seat.

Before the season started, Wolfensberger, an electrical engineering major, learned he had won a Fulbright Scholarship to attend graduate school in Germany the following year. Wolfensberger would be researching optical circuitry at Karlsruhe University; as his father and roommate (and teammate) Paul Schmidt were both German he viewed academic work there as "a natural choice."

The varsity would get its first test against pretty solid competition at the Augusta Invitational the first weekend in April. The results were quite encouraging; SU defeated Rutgers by open water, with the Scarlet Knights trailed by Cornell, the Bulgarian National Team, and Princeton. Rutgers would turn the tables on the varsity two Saturdays later, winning by a length on the Raritan River. The Orange JV, 3V, and first frosh won their races, with the second frosh race going Rutgers' way.

Sunday would be no day of rest for Syracuse. All five crews had races on Yale's home course on the Housatonic River in Connecticut. The varsity took the Eli by two seconds and the 3V won by a half-length of open water. Yale's Jayvees were victorious, and Brown (Bruno only entered freshman crews) won both freshman races with SU well back in third in both.

Sanford saw the win in Georgia as a key to the crew's success, telling a reporter, "That sort of set the stage, when you have a crew that has a bunch of youngsters. It gives that enthusiasm. I think that's the reason we've had the season we've had."

Each crew has its own personality, its own racing strategy. For the 1988 varsity, it was dictated by the crew's tendency to start slow, trust the cadence and conditioning, and relax through the body of the race. That was embedded in Rob Heinstein's approach to coxing a race, where he worked constantly on getting his athletes to relax and stay loose.

For the first time in twenty-nine years, the Goes Cup would head to Long Branch for a year.

That strategy was proving to be a winning one; the varsity's 1.1 second victory over Navy on the Severn River showed the young crew could battle with the best of them. SU was third in the JV and frosh races with Cornell taking the JV and Navy the freshman eight (more than 5 lengths in front of Syracuse).

Back home on the Onondaga Lake course a week later Boston University won every race but one–the varsity. Orange Co-Captain McNamara's crew followed the same race plan to a solid win with BU five seconds back. While the "top of the ticket" was having a very solid season, the lower boats were not. None of the other races were close, continuing a troubling trend.

The second Sunday race of the season saw the lower boats join the varsity in the winning column, thanks to MIT. The Engineers' closest finish was four seconds back, with the varsity and Jayvee deficits 12 seconds and the 3V twice that.

Next up, the annual trip to Lake Quinsigamond for the Eastern Sprints. The only finishes recorded were for the top three crews and they were solid if not spectacular. The JV and frosh won their petite finals for the best result since 1981 for both crews. The conditions for the freshman eight race, won in a time of 7:04.4 were particularly challenging, described as "very, very windy, very slow times" by Sanford.

The varsity did them one better, making the finals to finish sixth in a race wind-delayed by almost 3 hours. While that was also the varsity's best result in 7 years, two crews defeated by the Orange earlier in the season–Yale and Princeton–finished second and fourth respectively.

The young Orange varsity had compiled a 4-and-1 record in dual regattas, including the first-ever win over Yale, plus a sixth-place finish in the grand finals at the Sprints on May 15th. Fellow Sprints finalists Northeastern, Princeton, and Brown were also in the IRA; Yale and Harvard, second and first at the Sprints respectively, had not yet made the IRA a part of their racing schedule. Two man Paul Schmidt was confident, promising SU would make the final, citing a combination of senior leadership and better technique from the sophomores. Talking before the race, Schmidt noted, "Our finish is really strong this year. We know how to relax in the first thousand meters and still be with the pack. Then we have more power in the last 1,000 meters."

The draw was pretty good to SU as none of the other Sprints finalists was in its heat. The Orange lined up Thursday with BU, Cornell, and Wisconsin for the coveted "win-and-in" awarded to the first boat across the line in the heats. Wisco, silver medalists in 1987, proved to be just a bit faster than Syracuse, nabbing first place. SU was off the line at a 38 cadence in an effort to hang with Wisconsin in the early going. Despite the high rating, the Badgers opened up a slight lead right around the halfway point and were able to hold it to the finish line. Sanford noted the crew "had to pay an early price for rating high ... we didn't have the kick I thought (we would at the end). Heinstein thought his guys were also pretty nervous before the race. From the impression I got from the guys, they felt it was the first race of the season ... we know we can go faster."

SU headed to the reps, where the varsity would take on Rutgers and Columbia in what looked like very fast conditions.

Heinstein's crew wasn't tested, yet rowed a 5:49.5, good enough for second-fastest time of the day behind Cornell's record-setting 5:45.5. There had been a bit of a shift, or perhaps progression in Heinstein's approach to coxing the race. While earlier in the season he had been more relaxed and calm, the IRAs had the varsity cox pushing his crew more, demanding more from individuals and getting more aggressive in tone. There was a good deal of pressure on the crew, and perhaps Heinstein was feeling it as much as anyone.

SU had crews in all of the events but one, the varsity four with cox. The pair without cox suffered through a "Did Not Finish" in their final-only event. The four without cox was deemed to look the strongest of any Orange crew headed to the finals. According to stroke Joe Kieffer, the power twenty at mid-race sealed the heat win for the Orange, "After we took that twenty, we started to move. Usually that's the point when you're tired, you start to pick up the second wind." The win ensured Kieffer, Perry Navab, Colin Goodale, and Joe Barnes could take Friday off, watch their competitors race off in the reps, and get ready for their grand final on Saturday. The Orangemen finished with a silver, just a half-second back of the Middies. The headwind may well have worked to the advantage of a Navy crew that was about fifteen pounds heavier per man.

For the freshmen, the last practice before Thursday's heats was a chance for a little shenanigans. A 20-pound carp somehow found its way into freshman Coach Larry Laszlo's chase boat. Discussing the incident with a reporter, Laszlo said, "This is a good sign, it means they're relaxed and working well together."

Unfortunately, the frosh eight's performance in the heats was rather lackluster, as it finished fifth, a bit more than five seconds back of heat winner Penn. Laszlo's frosh four had a better day with a second-place performance. The four qualified for the grand finals and finished sixth, some 22 seconds out of first. The eight was fifth in its petite final.

SU's JV also qualified for the grand final, finishing sixth.

Meanwhile, other crews also had designs on the Varsity Challenge Cup. After taking third at the Sprints behind Harvard and Yale, Buzz Congram looked to have his Northeastern varsity at peak form. The Huskies won their heat in a blazing fast 5:46, despite a sluggish start and pretty poor first 500. To get the crew moving after the first 500 the cox asked them to "do it for Charlie," the Northeastern boatman who had been killed earlier that week. Charlie Smith was the only person killed in an auto accident as he and about a dozen NU oarsmen were driving to Syracuse just two days before the heats. In tribute, the Husky varsity named its boat for him.

The aptly-named Husky crew, which averaged 6'2" and 194 pounds, rowed a 36 cadence–a pretty high rating for the time–the entire course before raising the rating in the last twenty to hold off a charge from second-place Brown. Despite finishing less then a length behind NU in 6:16.6 to the Huskies' 6:14.0, SU was fourth, out of the medals by less than a second. Co-Captain Bob Price recalled his crew had been in third after the first 500, and then they "made our move at 1,000 and wanted to pull away from the pack with 500 to go. It just didn't gel the way we wanted ... but as a varsity oarsman, this is the best I've finished."

Sanford had asked his crew to make its move in the third 500, then raise the cadence two strokes-per-minute every ten strokes for the last 500. With a seven miles-per-hour headwind blowing down the course, the crew managed to get to a 37 stroke rating but no higher. Still, Bill Sanford did not sound overly disappointed about the performance, saying, "We may not have been able to go any faster ... the crews that beat us out there were the fastest crews we've ever raced."

Brown may not have been varsity champs, but the Bruins won both of the other eight-oared events and the varsity four with cox. For Syracuse, this had been the best overall IRA in years, as the crew had made the grand finals in five of the seven events it entered.

After the regatta, Sanford had strong words for the frosh crew. Disappointed with the petite-final result, and perhaps thinking of the headwind conditions that prevailed in the varsity eight and four without finals, he attributed the difference between the Orange and the frosh eight gold-medalist crew from Wisconsin to depth and strength, saying, "I've challenged the freshmen. I want them to work out heavily with weights ... I've got to get more strength from below. I have to have a youth movement."

But before he could worry about the next collegiate season, Sanford would have to prepare his crews for Henley. The varsity was entered in the Grand Challenge Cup, and two fours with cox entered in the Prince Philip Challenge Cup.

One four with cox, entered as Syracuse Chargers, raced on opening day, June 30th, with the verdict being easily, over the competition, St. Paul's School of Concord, New Hampshire.

In the quarterfinals, the eight readily disposed of UCLA, winning by a margin of three lengths. Sanford was effusive in his praise for the crew, calling it his "best ever." Watching the crewmen before the race, their confidence came across. Speaking of the crew's relaxed attitude, Sanford said, "When I saw [it], I said, 'This is over.' We really went out of there like a rocket ... the peaking process was paying off." That was the good news. The not-so-good news was the opponent in the next round, the British National Team. And with 14-to-1 odds against, few thought Syracuse would give the Brits much of a battle. SU was the last American crew in the Grand Challenge event, as Northeastern had been defeated in its quarterfinal match by the national team from Hungary.

The second four with cox's path was less exciting; much less. Rowing against the SU crew entered as the Syracuse Chargers, it won in a headwind-slowed time of 8:22, and would face a Northeastern crew in the semifinal.

SU's unlikely march to the semifinal round of both races caught the attention of many Americans at Henley. On opening day, there were forty-two US crews at the Henley; now there were four, and two were from Syracuse. Speaking to a reporter, Sanford said, "Everybody from the United States is behind us. There's got to be 3,000 ... 4,000, maybe more ... flags are flying."

For the varsity, the final race came in the semis, as it lost to the British National Team rowing as Leander and London University by 3-and-1/2 lengths. After the Brits had pushed out to a two-length lead around the halfway mark, Syracuse rallied back and cut into the lead. The Orange couldn't sustain the effort, and the British crew pulled away for the win. Leander and London went on to win the Grand Challenge Cup by the closest of margins over the Australian National Team.

The four with rowed a very strong race against Northeastern, winning by just 3/4 of a length and earning a spot in the finals of the Prince Philip Challenge Cup. The finals were a different story, as the SU oarsmen were no match for the Vancouver Rowing Club a.k.a. Canadian Olympic Team, losing by a verdict of easily. The Orangemen had nothing to be ashamed of, as the Vancouverites had been together for some time, winning the World University Games the year before, and were slated to represent Canada in the Olympics.

Overall, the season had been a very good one. While the IRA results had not been what any Orange fan wanted, except perhaps for those closely following the four without cox, the stellar results at Henley and the youth of the varsity eight boded well for the future.

Chapter 22
The Chris Lang Years

C hris Lang assumed the women's head coaching position during the summer of 1988 as Gary Jordan's tenure came to an end after the season.

An athlete at Oregon State University, Lang had been a coach at the University of Washington and then handled Oregon State's novice program for a year. Lang, who would hold the position longer than any other coach so far, was joined by Elizabeth Powell, the new assistant women's crew coach. Powell had three years of experience coaching novices at Mount Holyoke and Tufts.

Reflecting back on her early days with the program, Lang remembered her goals as making the program competitive, increasing expectations and increasing the crews' performance. There was good support from SU Athletics Director Jake Crouthamel and Doris Soladay, Associate Director of Athletics, as well as the rest of the administration. What there was not was a close relationship with the men's team. While Coach Bill Sanford was supportive, a "separateness" existed between the programs that was markedly different from Lang's experience with West Coast crews.

The tension between the programs at the boathouse was palpable, manifested in ill-advised pranks and occasional taunting. However, away from Long Branch the athletes from the two programs often socialized together on weekends, and several dated each other with at least one relationship leading to a marriage.

For Lang, there was another difference between East Coast and West Coast women's crew; instead of one or two fast crews as was the case out west, there were a lot of fast boats in the East, and "day in and day out, they were all very fast."

But that was to come. Under Jordan, the toughest workout was "Blue Collar Monday," a series of three pieces of 20, 15, and 10 minutes with a few minutes' rest in between. Chris Lang believed in hard work–and lots of it, and the SU women were in for a bit of a shock. Thinking back, three-year varsity stroke Tracy

Rude Smith recalled that was far from the toughest workout under the new coach. In fact, it was pretty standard stuff with Lang, and "it was a real shock to have to work really hard all of a sudden." The volume was dramatically more than they'd been used to.

Lang was also less personable, less warm than Jordan. Some athletes were rubbed the wrong way by her demeanor, but Lang's workouts definitely increased the crews' fitness.

For spring break in 1989, the women traveled to Tennessee for a week of practice in the warm southern sunshine. Talking to a *Daily Orange* reporter after the trip, Lang was quoted as saying, "I demand a lot from my rowers. If I told them in the beginning of the day what was planned they wouldn't think they could do it."

The women agreed. Co-Captain Cami Engler remarked, "It was harder than I thought it would be. Coach pushes us until we make it." Senior Shevaun Webster echoed Engler, saying, "What I got out of the training session was exhaustion." Despite the heavy workload, the women sounded enthusiastic about Lang. Engler again said, "She has turned this team around. The difference is, when we go out on the water now, we know more of what we are expected to do and what we have to do. I think there's going to be a surprise factor, we're obviously stronger. I thing we're going to scare some teams."

Lang thought so as well; saying, "I'd like us to finish in the top six at the Eastern Sprints this year. In four-years' time I want them to be of national caliber and put some rowers in the Olympics."

The season began with an end-of-March race at the Augusta Invitational. It was an auspicious beginning for the Orange women, as they won the varsity event thereby setting the stage for what looked to be a strong season. To open the dual meet season the Syracuse women would take on neighbor Ithaca College on the road for the first of four consecutive away races. The varsity, which included Engler, Co-Captain Kim Jordan, junior stroke oar and future U.S. National Team rower and U.S. Olympian Tracy Rude, and senior Pam Langmaid made quick work of the Bombers, winning by 32 seconds. Their teammates continued the domination, with all four SU eights victorious, the closest race decided by a margin of 14 seconds.

While Division II competitor Ithaca College was a pushover, the women rowed the race as if they were up against Yale, starting fast and increasing their margin throughout the 2,000 meters. The following weekend, they didn't have to imagine lining up with the Eli–the women were on the Housatonic in Derby to test themselves against Yale and Cornell.

The crew was looking to stay close, to be competitive with these two elite programs. "Earning respect," was the way Engler put it. To prepare, Lang worked the women hard. Engler described the week as, "She's been beating us into the ground. She knows what type of effort it will take to be competitive in this meet."

Lang's women were not very competitive, finishing last in all four events. In the varsity, Cornell topped Yale by a half-second, with SU another 14 seconds to the rear.

Things didn't get any easier the following week as Syracuse hit the road for the third weekend in a row, with Philadelphia the destination for the 1989 Orange Challenge Cup. Penn and Northeastern would be their opponents. With just one victory in the seven-year history of the Cup the SU women were focused on bringing it back to Long Branch. The previous year, the varsity had been in the thick of the race until the final 500 meters, when Penn had pulled away. Now, after another tough week of practice, the Orange women were ready to take on top-ten Penn–loser to Yale by five seconds earlier that season–and an unknown quantity in Northeastern.

While the result–a 1.4-second loss to winner Penn–wasn't exactly what Syracuse wanted, it was a confidence booster nonetheless as third-place Northeastern was more than five lengths back of the Orange. The JV and second novice eights had identical second-place-by-a-length finishes, while the first novice eight was not competitive.

The fourth road trip was a long one, as SU traveled to Hanover, New Hampshire, to race Dartmouth and top-ranked Radcliffe. Despite the crew's string of defeats, it had moved up to 11th in national polls and looked to improve on that standing as the ranking would be used to seed the crews for the upcoming Eastern Sprints. Speaking to a *Daily Orange* reporter, Tracy Rude said:

"Dartmouth ranked us below them after we had beaten them in a spring race in Tennessee." Lang knew the challenge was tough, stating her varsity's goal was "beating Dartmouth and going after Harvard [Radcliffe]."

The upperclass boats succeeded, both finishing second to Radcliffe and well up on Dartmouth. The varsity was ten seconds back of Radcliffe and seventeen seconds in front of the Big Green; the JV was second by a length with Dartmouth another two lengths back. This was especially sweet as Dartmouth Coach Chuck Nagle had insisted that SU come to his course, as he would not travel outside the Ivy League to race the Orange. The Syracuse novice crews both finished last, well out of contention.

The last dual meet was a welcome one as Rutgers came up to Onondaga on April 29, 1989. SU swept the Scarlet Knights, winning each race easily and regaining the Orange Plus Cup.

Three weeks later, the Syracuse women were at the Eastern Sprints, looking to improve on their no. 11 seeding. That they did, the varsity finishing third in the petites, seven seconds back of a much-improved Penn crew and just a second behind New Hampshire. The JV was second in its petite and the 2nd novice placed fourth, also in the petites. The first novice crew finished second, but well back in the third-level finals.

While the varsity had not made the grand finals, it was a top-ten finish and both an improvement on prior years and a base to build on for the future. For the second-consecutive year, Tracy Rude's teammates named her the recipient of the Lucille Verhulst Award–as most valuable athlete–while sophomore Katie Connolly of Liverpool was invited to the Olympic Development Camp in Lake Placid.

Led by Rude and fellow Co-Captain Sue Meiselman (Jeff's sister), the Orange women opened the 1990 racing season the same way they did in 1989, with a win down south. This time around, SU won the Augusta Invitational Regatta at the end of March, defeating Wisconsin by eight seconds with Mount Holyoke and Trinity College also in the race. Rude attributed the win to the team's off-season conditioning, telling *The Daily Orange*, "Our crew worked hard on endurance over the winter. We definitely had that over the other crews." The win brought out another side of Coach Lang, one the athletes hadn't seen much of, with Tracy continuing, "Chris usually keeps to herself, but she was very pleased with our performance."

The crew continued its dominance against Ithaca College, with the novices and JV squaring off against the Bombers in Syracuse. The lower boats didn't lose a race, with the JV defeating Ithaca's varsity by a half-length of open water to round out a pretty solid weekend.

With defending national champion Cornell next on the schedule, the crew traveled to Ithaca on Saturday, April 7th. Yale joined the upstate neighbors, and split the wins with Cornell. The Orange tied with Cornell for second in the varsity race, six seconds behind the Eli. SU was not competitive in the other races. Nonetheless, this was a major step up for Lang's women, who had made Cornell the focus on their winter training. The motivation was evidently inspired by an intemperate remark on the part of a Cornell coxswain, who was overheard telling a teammate that Syracuse was pretty good this year, so Cornell was going to have to do a power 10 to get through SU instead of walking through like they usually do. Rude's reaction was telling; she was quoted in *The Daily Orange* saying, "We're out for blood."

Another intemperate remark or perhaps the overconfidence it projected may have played a part in the next day's race against BU. Interviewed by a *Daily Orange* reporter, Syracuse junior Gina Vincent was quoted as saying, "We are going to kill BU. We are going to blow them out of the water."

That did not happen.

Instead, the Terriers were the ones doing the winning, defeating Vincent and her varsity teammates by open water in a 1,500-meter race on the Seneca River. That capped off a sweep by BU, and the once-confident Orange needed to quickly regroup if it was going to win the Orange Challenge Cup, a goal that had so far eluded the seniors. Once again Northeastern and Penn would be the competition, and once again SU would come up just a bit short. Going in to the race, the focus was on Penn with both Lang's and senior Kristin Walker's comments identifying the Quakers as the key.

SU accomplished part of its objective, beating Penn by

three seconds. But Northeastern, perhaps enjoying the opportunity to race on its home waters, came in first, a length up on the Orange. Lang was a bit taken aback, saying: "We were a little surprised. We all got out to a quick start, but Northeastern was about a half-boat length ahead after 750 meters. Every time we tried to make a move after that Northeastern would counter." The Orange was second in the JV and first novice eights, and third in the second novice event.

Back in Boston the next weekend, the varsity dropped a close race to Dartmouth, finishing just a deck back of the Big Green. The JV won its race by seven seconds, while the novice eights were not competitive in their events. The results were better in the last dual meet of the season on New Jersey's Raritan River, as all crews but the first novice won their races with Rutgers, the varsity capturing the Orange Plus Cup.

With the dual meet season behind them, Lang and the athletes had two weeks to prepare for the Eastern Sprints. In what was not terribly different from their results just a year earlier, the varsity was fourth in the petite, the JV won the petite finals, the first novice eight was second in the third-level finals and second novice finished fifth in its petite finals. What was perhaps more troubling was the varsity's defeat at the hands of Wisconsin, a crew it had handled easily in Augusta.

1990 marked SU women's first appearance at the National Collegiate Rowing Championships, held in Madison, Wisconsin with the finals on June 3rd. SU's varsity eight made the final, finishing sixth out of the eight crews entered in the race. Cornell, a crew that had clearly improved over the season, won the bronze while Wisconsin was four seconds up on SU in fifth place. Despite–or perhaps because of–the hard work in the winter and over the spring, the Syracuse women had started out well, but faded down the stretch as other crews got faster. For the next season, they'd have to do it without Tracy Rude, a key member of the squad for four years, now moving on to graduation and the U.S. National Team.

While some athletes thought the workload was too much, leading to overtraining, others didn't. Interviewed for this book, Jen Sacheck opined that some of the athletes didn't have a great work ethic. She recalled practices where the last piece or two on the schedule would be called off when some of the athletes said they were too tired. Sacheck wasn't sure that other teams weren't actually doing more work. If anything, it may have been Lang's inability to connect with the athletes, despite her efforts to do so.

Rude headed to Vesper to row in a pair, and that's when things took off for her. The fitness she'd developed gave her a solid base, and the technical improvements brought about by the Vesper coaches helped her move rapidly up through the list of candidates for the U.S. National Team, making the squad for the first of three times that summer.

In a way, the experience at SU had helped her; in an interview Rude said, "I could not leave rowing and let that [her senior year at Syracuse] be the end." That determination earned Rude a silver in the eight at the World Championships later that summer as well as fifth-place finish in the straight four. In 1991, she was back, this time stroking the pair at the World Championships. In 1992, Rude held down the all-important six seat in the United States' women's eight that came in sixth at the 1992 Barcelona Olympic Games.

Early in 1991, the University's budget process generated serious stress among the non-revenue teams' athletes and coaches. Chancellor Kenneth Shaw and the Board of Trustees were looking at the 19 non-revenue sports for about $3.7 million in savings, and one option was for the Athletics Department to come up with its own scholarship funds. Lang and Bill Sanford thought SU Athletics Director Jake Crouthamel, long a supporter of the rowing programs, would come through for both teams. In Lang's view, the eight scholarships she spread among forty-five athletes was more than balanced out by the tuition and other fees paid by the rest of the athletes. With each athlete not on scholarship paying almost $20,000 to attend SU, Lang thought she had a good case. In the end, the program avoided serious cuts. The large number of women on the team may also have been a factor in the continued existence of the program, as Title IX was becoming more of an issue as schools struggled to meet the various tests and metrics used to assess compliance, or progress towards compliance.

The 1991 season saw twenty-six athletes on the team,

losing only two members of the 1990 squad to graduation or other interests. The women were again working very hard, with Lang emphasizing upper-body power, an area she evidently viewed as a deficiency to be addressed over the winter. Unfortunately, the results did not appear to be altered significantly by the change in focus. The varsity eight won two races all year–against Ithaca College and Rutgers–although the crew was just a length back of Radcliffe in a contest in mid-April and finished sixth at the San Diego Crew Classic in the varsity grand finals.

Switching to an emphasis on technique and leg strength for the 1992 season, Lang continued to work her women very hard throughout the winter and into the racing season. If anything, the results–an 0-and-7 record for the varsity, and only three wins for any boat all year including two from the novice crews against Ithaca–got even worse. In some of the races, the crews just weren't competitive at any level. As the results continued to disappoint onlookers, the workload, if anything, increased. By the end of the season, things had improved slightly, with all four crews making the petite finals where only one–the JV at second place–did not finish last in the petites.

While the 1992 season may have been a disappointment, Molly Tibbetts Scannell had nothing but great memories of her time on the novice crew. She says, it was "so fun, I just loved it, the novice coach [Lisa Glenn] was great, she wanted everyone to have fun, yet take it seriously as well. She made me want to work hard."

Scannell also recalled any tensions that had existed between the women and men had largely disappeared by the time she donned orange. The freshmen on both teams seemed to get along well, many were friends and there were a couple of dating relationships as well. In fact, she remembered the teams as supportive of each other and close enough that she knew everyone on the men's team her senior year.

The women's results did not improve in 1993, with the varsity again winless, and the only three victories of any kind in novice events. In many regattas, the Orange finished behind the rest of the crews.

Lang was named leader of US Women's Rowing for the

1993 World University Games, held in Buffalo in mid-summer. Several of her SU athletes were on the team along with fellow up-staters from Cornell, demonstrating the high level of talent resident in both programs.

Kris Sanford, the daughter of SU men's coach Bill Sanford, joined the SU women's coaching staff in the fall of 1994. Lang and Sanford had known each other in Washington and Sanford had experience with U.S. Rowing.

The 1994 season entered the final stretch with mixed results; a 3-and-4 record for the varsity including defeats of Ithaca and Rutgers and an impressive victory in the Georgetown Invitational. Looking to the IRA, then a relatively new event for women, Lang told a reporter, "We're as fit as any crew. We've lost because we've made mental errors." With just eight crews entered in the varsity, the Syracuse women finished sixth. The JV and second novice eights mirrored that result, with the first novices fourth.

Chris Lang's penultimate season closely resembled the previous few, with wins against Ithaca and Rutgers and convincing losses to the cream of the women's rowing programs. Results at the Eastern Sprints and IRA consisted of finishes in the petite or third-level finals.

Lang's final season began in the fall of 1995, with highly-touted recruit Rachel Treadwell of Grosse Ile, Michigan, joining the squad for the fall season. Treadwell had medaled in two events at the prior summer's National Championships, and would be joining a crew that had seemingly become stuck in a pattern of winning against lesser crews while remaining well out of contention in races against upper-level teams.

For the 1996 season, the novices continued to win on occasion but the upperclass crews were not able to break through to higher level successes, remaining consistently uncompetitive when racing the likes of Dartmouth, Yale, Cornell, and Northeastern.

Then, the wheels fell off at the 1996 Eastern Sprints.

The weather the week before the Eastern Sprints was a harsh reminder of the worst of Syracuse's winter–cold, damp, with wind and snow towards the end of the week. Complicating plans, the seniors' graduation conflicted with the Sprints in 1996, a scheduling problem that arose every few years as the weekends coincided.

As the varsity headed out to warm up for the first race, the women were swathed in layers of clothes to ward off the wind-blown snow and spray. Just as they lined up to begin their race, a delay was called. For the next half-hour, the crews sat at the line, getting wetter, colder, and more miserable by the minute. Finally, the start was called, and the race was on.

For Captain Molly Tibbetts Scannell, it was the worst race she'd ever been in. The crew, she recalls, was "out of sync and raced horribly ... we had an extraordinarily bad race." That poor performance relegated Syracuse to the third-level finals, the dreaded "trucks."

This was a new experience for the varsity. None of the women on the eight had ever raced in a third-level final. This wasn't what they'd been training for, what they'd endured years of practice and great personal sacrifice for. For at least one of the non-seniors on the crew, it was too much; she refused to race. As the women gathered to discuss the situation, they talked back and forth about what to do. The conditions were still miserable, but it wasn't any worse then they'd experienced multiple times back in Syracuse. The crew was divided on whether to race or not. Some tried to defend their right to row, to bring the boat together; others were ambivalent or concerned about racing as a broken unit, one without mental cohesion.

At some point, Coach Chris Lang joined the group, visibly angry. She told the women that the decision was theirs. Remembering the day, Scannell said, "As the captain it was my job to bring the unit together. I needed help from my coach. I just remember feeling very sad, this was my last race ever with these people and we have one more shot to do this, and there's no support here to say 'get over it, grow up, let's do it.'"

Ultimately, the crew did not race.

With the NCAA taking a more active interest in women's rowing, Lang was one of seven appointed to a committee charged with setting up a championship for women's rowing early in 1996. This would mark one of her last achievements at Syracuse as it was her final season coaching the women's crew.

With the benefit of 20-years' hindsight, Lang attributed the women's lack of performance during her tenure to a multitude of factors including difficult weather, late winters and ice into March; personality conflicts both within the team and between herself and the team which, as a relatively new coach, she had yet to develop the right skills to address; the new challenge of recruiting; and differences in perspective on what was needed to be a top-performing crew.

Despite the challenges, Lang "would not trade that experience" for anything. Now working as a police officer in Seattle, Washington, Lang is very active in rowing, heading up officiating at the NCAA Championships and other National Championship Regattas.

Lang would not be around to coach the Syracuse women in the upcoming NCAA women's championships. As the 1996 edition of the Syracuse women's crew racing season came to a close, the program once again clearly needed a change.

Lang exited and without having to search very far, SU Athletics Director Jake Crouthamel picked a familiar name to succeed her.

Chapter 23
"The Fastest Crew I've Ever Had"

Larry Laszlo's recruiting efforts for the men's frosh paid off big-time in the fall of 1986 as fourteen experienced oarsmen joined the team. They would go on to become what Bill Sanford described as one of, if not the, best of his crews ever. They would really make their presence felt in their junior year, a "presence" notable as much for their non-rowing antics as their performance in the boat.

Reflecting on the Class of '90, Coach Bill Sanford characterized his relationship with the guys as "... a love fest–it was like a marriage because we fought all the time because of the crazy stuff and the antics that these guys would do. It was my wildest crew I ever had as far as off the water. I didn't even know about these Saturday night things when they would buy that special–100 wings and 3 quarts of beer or whatever the heck it was ... and they would be legendary for doing that and yet they worked so darn hard."

Two athletes who were not part of Laszlo's recruiting class came to rowing from lacrosse midway through their college careers and contributed to SU's successes in 1989. The first "competition" of the 1989 season occurred at the oldest indoor erg event, the hallowed "CRASH-B Sprints," held at Harvard's Boathouse in February. Senior John Rademacher finished fourth among all college men, the 6'8", 223-pound converted lacrosse player happy to break up the Harvard "cartel," as the Crimson filled out the rest of the top five spots. Rademacher had played sparingly for SU's excellent lacrosse team his first two years on The Hill, switching to rowing as a junior because he "wasn't fast enough on his feet." He began the spring in the second-boat's engine room, while fellow senior and former-lacrosse-player Dan McClimans started out in the two seat in the varsity.

Rademacher and his teammates headed to Tennessee in March where Oak Ridge would be the site of Spring Camp for the sixth-consecutive year. While the racing competition at the end of the week was not close to EARC standards, Sanford preferred the Volunteer State as a training site to Florida, telling a *Daily*

239

Orange reporter, "There are so many other things to do in Florida that I didn't have the control of off the water, while in Oak Ridge there is nothing else to do." The training conditions in Oak Ridge were also optimal, Sanford continues, "It is one of the finest water facilities that there is because they have flat water almost all the time."

After Spring Camp and end-of-the-week Augusta Invitational Regatta, Sanford was enthusiastic about the crew's chances in the upcoming season. Again speaking to a *Daily Orange* reporter, he opined, "I'm looking at a boat this year that could develop to be faster than last year's crew, and if they do, then we are going to go all the way this year." The first "official" race of the season was the traditional Rutgers contest. Orange won the varsity rather easily, finishing six seconds in front of Rutgers with Temple and Dartmouth trailing.

Two weeks later, Rutgers had gotten quite a bit faster. Racing over 1,850 meters on the Seneca River, SU won the Ten Eyck Cup by just 1.3 seconds. The next weekend was another home race, with Yale taking the varsity by a three-quarter-length margin.

Grad student and German national Paul Schmidt stroked a very talented varsity at the Goes Cup with future Lightweight National Team member Allan Green at 7, Jeff Pesot at 6, future World Champion (in eights) and U.S. Olympic Single Sculler Don Smith at 5, future Pan Am Team rower Chris Ludden at 4, Rick Horn at 3, McClimans in the 2 seat, and Captain Dick Stribrny in bow; Robert Heinstein coxed. Despite the loaded lineup, eighth-ranked SU was picked to finish third behind the seventh-ranked Big Red and sixth-ranked Navy. Cayuga's waters were the site of the Goes Cup in 1989, and while the racing was close, the rankings held as SU's varsity placed third, 4.6 seconds behind winner Navy and 2.4 seconds behind Cornell.

With two losses following the opening wins, Sanford and crew packed up for Boston. First on the schedule was a Saturday, April 29th race, against BU's Terriers on the Charles River. Heinstein's crew finished five seconds up on BU and doubled its margin the next day against the MIT Engineers. The JV, also victorious that day, was coxed by Jay Rhodes and stroked by Colin

Goodale, with Scott Baltazar in 6, Mike Van Maarseveen in 5. Pat Young and Bill Sheehan were in 4 and 3, and Chris Smith and Joe Barnes rounded out the lineup in the bow pair.

With two weeks to go before the Sprints, Sanford's tenth-ranked crew was looking to surprise the competition in Worcester. That it did.

While the varsity had been slowly improving, it was not getting fast enough soon enough for six-man Pesot. A *Post-Standard* article at the time noted that Schmidt, while technically proficient, was tough to follow as his stroke was shorter than the other rowers'. In an interview, Pesot said he had been badgering Coach Bill Sanford to move him into the stroke seat, and the coach finally did about ten days before leaving for Worcester. Sanford has a somewhat different recollection. According to Sanford, "He came up to me one day and says 'Coach, when are you going to cut the bullshit and put me in the stroke seat?' So I said to him 'do you think you're ready?' and he gives me the look and so the next day he was in the stroke seat and we took off."

The boat seemed to gel after the switch. Whether it was the lineup move, the crew's "chip on the shoulder" attitude born of frustration with the results to date, or just the crew coming into its own, the Orange crew showed it belonged among the elite, finishing fourth in the grand finals behind winner Harvard, second-place Wisco, and a length back of bronze-medalist Penn. Trailing behind the Orange were 1988 IRA champion and top-seeded Northeastern and, in a measure of revenge for the Goes Cup loss, Navy was 2/3 of a length behind the Orange at the finish.

Notably, Pesot et al., had been in the lead through the first 1,250 meters, despite their position in the outside lane. Even more notably, they were the only crew rowing in that lane that finished higher than last place that day.

The Packard Cup lineup had Pesot in stroke with Schmidt in the two seat for the varsity. With weather conditions precluding any racing on Onondaga, the Big Green and Orange raced off in a best-time-out-of-three 1,000-meter pieces on the inlet, won by SU by a length in a time of 2:40.7 to Dartmouth's 2:44.9. The boat was coming together, the final tune-up was done, and it soon be regatta time.

While Syracuse's varsity performance at the Sprints showed the crew could row with anyone, Sanford classified his crew as a "dark horse" for the IRA championship. Thursday's heat would immediately test the Orangemen, as they'd drawn Wisconsin, a pre-race favorite. After a fast start and strong push at the thousand-meter mark the Orange was just a half-deck behind the Badgers. The first thousand was a dogfight, as Wisconsin coach Randy Jablonic described his crew's effort as "Like pulling teeth to get out on them … they weren't going to give up anything." Even though SU varsity's time was solid, the row was not. Wisconsin was able to pull away in the second half of the race, coming in a length up on Syracuse. Despite rowing the second-fastest time of the day in Thursday's heats, the Syracuse varsity eight found itself in the reps on Friday in a must-win race against some very tough crews.

"We were rowing a little unsettled, a little rushed. Usually our crew is like that. In our first race we're a little shaky. Then in the second race we're more relaxed," was coxswain Rob Heinstein's take on the heat. Pesot agreed, acknowledging that he and the rest of the crew rowed short for much of the race, a mistake they'd remedy by being relaxed for the reps.

Navy, Syracuse, BU, and Princeton were all going to be fighting for the lone qualifying spot.

In contrast to the varsity's tough second-place finish in the heats, the other four crews wearing Syracuse colors performed poorly, with none finishing higher than fourth.

Once again the weather gods were not smiling on Onondaga, as high winds forced a delay of almost nine hours for the varsity reps. Despite the rough conditions, SU and Navy battled all the way down the course, with the Orange once again rowing the second-fastest time of the day–by 14 seconds. And again, the fastest time of the day belonged to the boat in the lane next to them. After the Navy cox pulled out a cow bell, and rang it for all he was worth midway through the third 500 meters, Navy eked out a deck-length win over a somewhat-distracted Orange eight but only after a furious back-and-forth last 700 meters. A very talented, very tough Syracuse crew that had placed fourth at the Sprints, found itself in the petites where they finished second, just 0.9 behind Brown, for eighth overall.

Unfortunately the lower boats were not nearly as competitive, with the best finish from the freshman eight being a second in the petites. The JV was fourth in the petites, while the varsity four with was sixth in their petite final and the open four second in a three-boat petite.

Despite the less-than-desired showing from the hometown team, the crowd for the finals was bigger than expected, with 7,400 fans on the banks of Onondaga during the regatta on a bright, sunny day with light breezes. The crowd size may have again been influenced by the county's decision to allow race-goers to bring one six pack of beer per person into the park. The high attendance and associated entrance fees, along with funds from corporate sponsors including the Adolph Coors Co., made the financial picture bright indeed for the IRA in Syracuse.

While the crowd and regatta organizers may have been pleased with the results, Syracuse's athletes were anything but. With a summer to stew over a season that came down to a half-second shortcoming, the new seniors would be on a mission come fall.

1990

Four seniors–Pesot, Stribrny, Don Smith, and future U.S. National Team sculler Allan Green returned to anchor the Orange varsity for the 1990 campaign. Along with fellow seniors "Englishman" Colin Goodale–JV stroke for the 1989 campaign– and Steve Locke–who had rowed as a freshman, and returned to the team after a two-year hiatus–and junior Chris Ludden, the upperclassmen would comprise the most talented crew to row out of Long Branch in many a year.

For the third-consecutive year, fall racing began with the "Head of the Erie," a 2-and–3/4-mile head race from the mouth of the Erie Canal past the boathouse, around Klein Island, and back in front of the boathouse. The race had become a staple of the upstate early fall rowing season, and Sanford tirelessly promoted the event to the press and competing programs alike.

In one of the program's more painful and troubling

episodes, in early November, two hundred women showed up to protest what was described as a graphic, sexist party invitation to an event hosted by the men's rowing team. Responding to the protest, Captain Dirk Stribrny told a reporter that members of the team would attend a sensitivity seminar, and apologized. The article went on to paraphrase Women's Coach Chris Lang, saying: "Perceived friction between the men's and women's teams–which is often marked by name calling is difficult to understand for those not connected to the teams."

The 1990 season began inauspiciously with a first-ever loss at the Augusta Regatta on the Savannah River. The Orange finished a full five seconds behind winner Princeton to capture second place. For a crew that had such high expectations, this was tough to swallow, made doubly so by the grins on the faces of the Tigers as they accepted the Syracuse varsity's betting shirts.

A week later things had improved quite a bit as the varsity, a heavy crew rowing in a midweight shell–collected an official–if misleading, sixth-place finish in the grands of the Copley Cup at the San Diego Crew Classic. The finish some 30 seconds back of first would have been troubling if not for a broken oarlock suffered by the Orange early in the race. After lodging a successful protest, SU finished fourth in a re-row behind Harvard, UCLA and Navy. That protest was later overturned, making the initial result the official one. All of that said, given the crew's lack of water time, the distance, and SU's tradition of gaining significant speed in late April and into May, the result was encouraging indeed.

Mid-April races built on the success on the West Coast. In a long road trip, the Orange first defeated Yale in New Haven by a half-length, followed by an eleven-second win over Rutgers at the Ten Eyck Cup races in New Jersey. If there was a race that solidified the crew, it was the Goes Cup in 1990.

Bill Sanford's crew got a measure of revenge for the Crew Classic loss to Navy at the Goes Cup, a race into a headwind so stiff that it required an effort from the crew Pesot described as "unreal." The distance was shortened to 1,850 meters and held from the inlet down the Seneca River past the boathouse. Navy jumped out to an initial lead, one which it held until Syracuse pulled even with just 200 meters to go. The Orange kept its momentum going, edging into the lead in the race's final few strokes. The photo finish had SU just two-tenths of a second in front of the Midshipmen, with Cornell another nine seconds back.

When the latest college poll came out later that week with Syracuse ranked fourth nationally, Pesot was nonplussed, telling *Post-Standard* columnist Frank Brieaddy "We didn't get any respect. [SU] and Brown (ranked third) should be switched."

Interviewed by Brieaddy in late April Sanford was ebullient. "I think it's the fastest crew that I've coached. They're turning in times now that we usually turn in for the IRAs." The crew's three early-season wins and no losses after the San Diego Crew Classic had the coach thinking of a return to the top of the IRA podium.

First he'd have to get by BU, a team coached by none other than SU alum and former-U.S. National Team member Tom Darling. Darling was miffed at Sanford's characterization of the 1990 edition as Sanford's "fastest crew ever," reminding his former coach that he'd rowed on a very fast gold-medalist frosh crew, and the 1978 IRA champion varsity crew was no slouch either. Darling also had the benefit of having memorized all of Sanford's pep talks, and told the reporter he would "employ the Sanford Symphony in five movements" to get his Terriers ready to take on the Orange.

Despite Darling's undoubtedly eloquent rendition of the Sanford Symphony, his Terriers finished five seconds behind Sanford's crew.

The Orange was back on the Seneca River race course the next day, defeating MIT by 13 seconds in a 2,000-meter race.

With the exception of the Augusta Invitational and the equipment problem at the Crew Classic, the season had been all it was supposed to be. Next up were the Eastern Sprints, where Syracuse would see how it fared on the big stage.

If anything, the varsity was overconfident. The crew's success to date, and a heat where the toughest competition looked to be BU, a crew it had handled with relative ease just a fortnight earlier had the crew thinking about the finals instead of racing to qualify. Darling's Terriers took advantage of the lapse, squeaking into the grand finals just ahead of Syracuse.

The Sprints were a disappointment for the Orange to be sure. A ninth-place finish, with crews the varsity had defeated earlier in the season turning the tables on the four-seed Orange varsity was almost the direct opposite of the result a year earlier, when the then-tenth-ranked Orange finished fourth in the grand finals.

The Packard Cup had been held by Syracuse for a decade, and the 1990 race would see that domination continue. The varsity defeated Dartmouth by a quarter-length open in a time of 5:40.9 to Dartmouth's 5:45.6.

Back at the Ten Eyck Boathouse, senior Steve Locke was concerned that the recently renovated facilities weren't conducive to team unity. In an effort to promote more togetherness, he removed the stalls around the toilets, telling his teammates that the "team that sits together, wins together." As much as some of the guys would have liked a bit more privacy, Locke made it clear that anyone attempting to rebuild the walls would have to deal with him.

And so the open concept facilities remained that way through the end of IRA Camp.

The first day's IRA heats didn't see any quick trips to the finals for Syracuse, as all six crews finished out of first. In Friday's reps, the frosh four missed qualifying by two seconds, losing to Brown. The varsity four with cox brought up the rear in its rep, while the open four, coxed by first-year Jennifer Sanford, won theirs by a comfortable 7 seconds over second-place Navy after being down by a length to the Midshipmen early in the race. It was Sanford's first race, as she'd been drafted when the 3V was broken down into two fours with and her dad needed a cox for the open four.

The freshman eight missed qualifying by a hair, with just one-tenth of a second separating them from Northeastern. The Syracuse crew's time would have won the other rep by open water.

The varsity would get a chance in the heats to see if Pesot's post-Goes Cup opinion of his crew's position over Brown was realistic. Late on Thursday–the answer was–almost. Once again, weather conditions on Onondaga were poor, with a stiff wind making the course choppy all the way to the finish. After leading the race through most of the last 500 meters, the Orange varsity hit a particularly troublesome wave within the last hundred meters and almost came to a standstill. Despite the conditions, Syracuse finished a mere four-tenths of a second back of Bruno, forcing the Orange into the Friday reps.

The times in all the heats were a bit strange; Northeastern was third in SU's heat, nine seconds back of the Orange, having previously defeated SU at the Sprints. The fourth and fifth place crews in heat two were forty seconds back of the winner as well. And Princeton, winner of the Augusta Invitational, was dead last in its heat. The Tigers would go on to finish last in their rep and 14th overall.

In Syracuse's rep, the pressure was on the crew that had been undefeated in dual and tri meets. Six-man Chris Ludden told a reporter, referring to Temple, Columbia and MIT, says, "The other crews had nothing to lose. We had everything to lose. It got us motivated." Pesot agreed, saying the rep helped the crew recover from what had been a brutally hard heat, letting the athletes work sore muscles just enough to get them ready for the finals.

The crew didn't leave anything to chance in the Friday rep, charging out to a full length lead over Temple at the 500 before coxswain John Parella called the rating down, the crew settling in to row into the final. The final margin was just under a length. In the other rep, Tom Darling's Terriers came in one second back of Cornell. The win put Syracuse into the grand final with Cornell, Navy, Brown, Sprints silver-medalist Wisconsin, and defending champion Pennsylvania. BU would head to the petite finals.

The grand final race was delayed for more than an hour, as winds gusting to 20 miles-per-hour roiled the waters of Onondaga. Just past 6 p.m., they died down to a zephyr, and a few minutes later the water was almost perfectly calm for the start of the race.

Syracuse led off the line and held that margin until the thousand-meter mark. Wisconsin took over at that point, and with the Orange paying perhaps a bit too much attention to the Badgers, a fast-charging Penn crew looking to repeat as IRA champions snuck by for second place just before the finish line. With the bronze, Bill Sanford was not disappointed. He told a reporter, "They were out there in dream conditions. I just can't believe the quality of all those six crews. Our kids were right there with them."

The open four finished just out of the medals in fourth, while the JV was third in their petite and the frosh eight second in the petite as well. The varsity four won their petite; the frosh four was sixth in theirs.

And once again, the crowd had exceeded expectations, with 7,200 fans on hand for the Saturday finals to watch, as a few undoubtedly did, SU return to the podium.

The season was not over quite yet. The next weekend, SU was in Cincinnati's East Lake Park to take on Harvard, Wisconsin, UCLA and Washington. The Orange finished fourth, two lengths back of winner Wisconsin and in front of UCLA.

Four years earlier, Freshman Coach Larry Laszlo had brought fourteen talented, experienced and tough oarsmen onto campus. Now that class was leaving campus, along with Laszlo.

Like Larry Laszlo, the new freshman coach would be a local guy.

Chapter 24
1991–1998 – Hitting Bottom

"It seems to me that the years at the end of the Bill Sanford era are commonly viewed in a negative light by alumni who were not on the team during that time, which I tend to attribute to the fact that our performances in the Sprints and IRAs were disappointing. This is a fair criticism in the sense that a crew is rightly judged by its results, but to me it overlooks what I found to be a lack of focus and intensity that existed at the time many of us joined the team. The relatively slow boats and ensuing losses during this era were obviously the responsibility of the guys pulling on the oars, but the culture at the time was a factor."

– Jamie Bettini '99

Bill Sanford brought in his older brother Paul, who had been a successful coach at Liverpool High School, as a second assistant coach along with Larry Laszlo. That lasted a season before Laszlo ended his ten-year run with SU, taking the job as head coach for Jacksonville University in the summer of 1992.

Paul Sanford became the frosh coach and held the job for the rest of the decade.

The 1990s passed as a blur of names and faces, practices and races. There was the occasional cause for celebration but mostly the Orange crews slipped into the middle of the pack at best.

Looking back on those years Bill Sanford shakes his head. "I remember that we were having difficulty with cohesiveness in the crew program. There were all these things that were happening that would tear the team apart. They were off the water. You had cliques–stupid stuff that would happen. I can't remember the players now. In the middle '90s it seemed like things were deteriorating there a little bit. I don't know if it was leadership. Whatever it was it just wasn't right."

Sanford was heavily involved in running the Onondaga County Legislature as Chairman and critics groused that there was nobody who could do that job effectively and coach crew successfully. On the other hand some pointed out that without SU's administration being aware of Sanford's political clout it might have jettisoned the men's program as it would dump wrestling and swimming.

His friend and former-assistant-coach Gary MacLachlan had become Commissioner of Parks for Onondaga County, and then Regional Parks Director for New York State. "I can't pinpoint the time but clearly I wondered to myself," MacLachlan says years later. "Because at that time I'm working with him not only as a County Legislator but then as Chairman of the Legislature and saw what he was doing with that kind of workload ... and I'm paying attention to the team's records and I'm asking myself anyway 'how in the hell can he do both of these things proficiently?' And I don't remember ever leading any charge to get rid of him but in my heart I'm saying you've got to choose one over the other."

MacLachlan continues: "I don't know where that would lead with me other than–sure. It crossed my mind. I had no idea who would do better or how or whether people would support it but definitely because of my friendship with Bill I wanted it to be his idea."

It was not Sanford's idea. Not then or now.

"I can't sit here and say that I felt that that was the cause of that five-year period of time but I can sit here and say that you know it may have been a part of the problem because I wasn't sitting in that office at the University twenty-four hours a day. As problems came to me I would deal with them–take the time to deal with then I'd get them solved. At the same time if I look back at it could I have prevented some of that from being there if I had been in that office all morning because I was spending a good four hours a day at that legislature.

"Sometimes we'd have the morning practices and I'd go down to the legislature at 9 and get out at lunch hour and I'd go to the crew so then on the first Monday of every month I was there we would have the morning practice and then I wasn't at the University all day because I'd have the [legislature] meeting.

"I've thought about it but I can't bring myself to say it was a major cause of that but yet it might have contributed, being honest about the things but I can't bring myself to say it because I don't believe it. I don't believe it would have been much different with some of the people I was dealing with at that time–the people we brought in just didn't ... we didn't work ... it didn't work and that's too bad. So I guess that period was a stressful time."

A Stressful Time with Few Wins On the Water

Dartmouth won the Packard Cup in 1991 after Syracuse had dominated that competition over the previous decade. The Big Green would hold onto the cup for the next 15 years.

After winning the Goes Trophy in 1990 the Orange came in third for the next six years before edging Navy by a second in a terrific race in 1997 with Cornell well behind.

The Temple Owls became an Orange nemesis, beating SU regularly in competition among Big East schools and at times SU also found itself behind Georgetown, Rutgers and once even Miami in 1994.

There were occasional wins over Boston University for the Conlan Cup and Rutgers for the Ten Eyck Cup but more often SU was on the losing end of those competitions.

Syracuse crews found themselves regularly in the third-level finals at the Eastern Sprints and the IRA.

"We had a period of time where we got some bad advice on some recruits–some of them turned out to be pretty tough to get through to because they were doing it their way or the highway," the coach says. "There was one particular school in Philadelphia we had a series of guys we had a series of problems–good recruits on paper and not so good when it came to team stuff."

The toms-toms beat on the internet with e-mails circulating calling for Sanford to step aside or be dumped. The coach was well aware of the noise.

"I remember that. I remember the strain and the stress of not only of not winning but having to deal with those everyday problems–the strain and the stress of satisfying some alumni ... so it was a difficult period of time and I say probably the most ... since the first two or three years."

251

The Loss of the IRA Regatta

The end of an era came in 1995–the end of Syracuse being the home of the IRA Regatta and thus the end of Syracuse University serving as the host team. The tradition died in a torrent of rain and wind that was one last body blow to something that once had been enormously important to the area. The truth is that when it ended the general reaction in the Syracuse area was a shrug.

"You Gotta Regatta," is what they used to say every June in Syracuse.

The Intercollegiate Rowing Association Regatta was recognized by almost everyone who mattered as the National Championship of collegiate rowing–everyone, that is, except Harvard and Yale–and after decades in Poughkeepsie and two years in Marietta, Ohio, it came to Onondaga Lake in 1952 and it stayed there. In the early days the crews lined up side-by-side across the lake for a winner-take-all three-mile race and it remained that way until 1967.

Larry Kimball became Sports Information Director at SU that year and found that part of his job was handling publicity and media relations for the IRA. He remembers that year mostly because of the weather.

"We had a couple of shells that swamped and then there's lightning and you're already rowing so you can't really say you can't be out there rowing, you've got to wait until the thunderstorm's over. So the first year–it was my first and last IRA under the old format–but it was that thunder and lightning storm."

It was a one-day event then–a freshman eight two-miler–and JV and varsity eight three-milers. They'd be scheduled early on Saturday afternoon but sometimes there'd be so much wind the races would have to wait until near sundown, or even the next day. And, as Kimball says, if the crews were already on the water when the weather turned ugly there wasn't much choice but to row.

In the Olympic year 1968 the format was changed to 2,000-meter sprints and small boats were added, meaning three-days of heats and repechages leading up to finals and a greater chance for delays and difficulties. Kimball's job also included

252

making the schedule. "I remember one year we finished the regatta on Monday morning rowing like at 6, 6:30 in the morning because of weather," he says. "We'd spent all day Sunday on the water just waiting, waiting, waiting and the wind just never died down." The finals had been scheduled for Saturday.

But the event was popular and the truth is that many of the thousands of people who lined the eastern shore of the race course paid little if any attention to what was happening on the water. It was–to put it bluntly–a beer and alcohol fest. "I think by the time we got into the '70s it really comes back to the weather the time of year and good spring early summer weather where a bunch of young people could get together," Kimball says. "And in those days we used to allow traffic in the park from both ends, and you used to have sheriff's people who would direct traffic."

Traffic became a problem, and in the 1980s it was a problem that belonged to the new Onondaga County Commissioner of Parks. Gary MacLachlan who'd been captain of the SU crew and later served as freshman coach, had worked his way up the parks administration hierarchy. He remembers the situations well.

"I'm responsible for this park and we're meeting for a month in advance of the race with 50 New York State Police and sheriffs and patrol dogs and ambulance people because there was 15,000 drunk people on the shore of the lake and there were motorcycles on fire and car accidents and destruction of the park and literally ten-percent of the people watching the race."

It had become a community problem, MacLachlan says. "We were trying to cut back on the drunkenness and make it more of a sporting event–or bring it back to being a sporting event– or a spectator sporting event anyway. I mean the guys were still rowing their ass off on the lake but who cared?" He cut back on alcohol being allowed in the park and limited vehicular access.

Things calmed down but the crowds shrank significantly.

"The park is much better for it," MacLachlan says.

There also were issues with coaches having control of where their teams were housed and fed during the regatta. Before it became a three-day event with 40 to 50 schools involved, all the teams bunked in dormitories at the New York State Fairgrounds and were fed there, as was the SU squad although its members slept in the boathouse. With the explosion in numbers of competitors there was not enough room at the fairgrounds and many teams wound up staying in SU dormitories.

"The coaches started complaining about the cost of coming to Syracuse," Kimball says, "and if they took the University housing they'd complain about the price and they'd complain about the cost of meals–why can't we do this on our own? Well … you can't have them half doing it one way and half doing it another way."

In the spring of 1993 the weather in Syracuse was so bad and there was so much flooding that the regatta was moved to the Cooper River in Camden, New Jersey. It came back to Syracuse in 1994, but the writing was on the wall. The IRA moved its regatta to Camden the next year, for good.

Kimball was not surprised. "The county parks people really–it was an event that they tolerated the last ten years maybe but it was one of those they almost wished it would just go away."

MacLachlan does not concede that. But he does say this, "The thing that lingers in the back of my mind is–here is a Commissioner of Parks who was an oarsman and a crew coach and a member of the board of the Syracuse Regatta Association–I basically put myself in a difficult moral position of having to say 'It ain't right. It ain't right.' And I don't know how Camden funds it. I don't know what kind of crowds they get. I don't know what the drinking deal is there. But at the same time the community culture moved on and you don't see events like that any place in Onondaga County anymore."

Dead Last at the IRA

Most of the men involved in the spring 1998 season are reluctant to discuss it and those who will are cautious, concerned about stirring up bad memories.

"A coach's ability to produce wins requires one-hundred-percent 'buy in' from every member of the team, but unfortunately Coach Bill did not always have this during my four years," Jamie Bettini wrote fifteen years later.

"Only in retrospect can I see how difficult it must have

254

been to deal with the task of managing the dynamics of a team on which decisions / philosophy were not only questioned, but at times rejected. It was clear that everyone wanted to win, but there were sometimes differing ideas on how to best achieve success."

There was a competition between the JV and varsity that spring that went back to the previous fall, when the crews battled daily in practice and the JV wound up coming in second in its race at the Head of the Charles.

The Syracuse squad trained in Tampa over spring break that year and finished the week off at the President's Cup Regatta on the Hillsborough River. Michigan State edged the SU varsity eight and the only Syracuse crew to come in first that day was the second frosh.

Back home on Onondaga Lake, the varsity eight lost to Boston University by open water to start the season. But the rest of the Syracuse crews were winners, the JV by less than a length.

The varsity broke through on Lake Carnegie two weeks later to take the Ten Eyck Cup from Rutgers and the JV won again.

Then, rowing on the Severn, the JV showed some serious strength, coming from a length back to edge Navy with Cornell well behind. The freshman eight also won, but the varsity eight was last.

"The JV was doing very well," Coach Sanford says. "They had won the Goes Cup in a come-from-behind race which was fantastic. I recognized that there was some synergy going together in that JV."

SU's second boat took the Georgetown Invitational and with it the de facto Big East title while the varsity finished behind Temple and Georgetown.

In Hanover the JV beat Dartmouth easily while the Big Green took the V8s and the Packard Cup.

The JV went to the Eastern Sprints still unbeaten–the Florida race didn't count–but missed the grand final when Boston U's Terriers got revenge by rowing through SU in the morning heat. In the petite final the Orange finished third behind Yale and Navy, beating Rutgers, Northeastern and Cornell.

The varsity eight wound up in the third-level final winning a three-boat race over Rutgers and MIT. While the JV's ninth place overall was not spectacular, Sanford had a dilemma to deal with.

"The varsity was going along and they were improving in slow increments just like the JV was, but of course the JV doesn't have to go as fast in competition as the varsity," the coach recalls. "So what happened is that all my career I had put my fastest boat in the varsity and I was going to do that. And the JV had become faster than the varsity. But the second thing was that the JV wasn't fast enough to be a varsity."

He decided to take two of the strongest oarsmen from what had been the varsity eight and mix them with six of the JV guys. But the JV guys would not go for it.

"And so after about a week of trying and getting nowhere and having these two great guys in the varsity be rejected I sat them down and said 'OK you know this is the situation.' And they said 'we want to row together as a unit' so I gave them the boat back and they got it together," Sanford remembers.

"That sounds about right," says Paris Daskalakis, who was in the JV that season. "It just didn't work out, from what I remember and to be honest I don't even think it was a week. It seems like it might have been a practice or two to see what happens and it just didn't work."

Jamie Bettini says he doesn't remember Coach Sanford giving the guys who had been the varsity eight the word that they would now be the JV.

"Maybe I've put it out of my mind," he says. But, prodded, he concedes, "It seemed to me that the mentality of the JV boat was to make the JV go fast as opposed to allowing Syracuse to put the fastest eight guys together regardless of what that combination might have been."

They went to the Cooper River with what had been the JV rowing as the varsity and the former first boat now competing at the JV level. In theory that crew should have done well against lesser competition.

"These two guys that I moved up had felt disenfranchised and so they weren't as good … and had they maintained the speed that they'd had as the varsity before I tried to shake it up they'd have been pretty much up there in the ranks in the JV race," Sanford says.

But they weren't. They finished fifth in the petite final. And the fastest SU crew?

"The JV rowing as the varsity eight is ready to spit nickels. I mean they are ready to go and they get down in the heats at the IRA and they row a very, very fine race and they get killed–they get slaughtered," Sanford says. "In the boat they looked at reality and it hurt them psychologically big time and the next race was worse and the last race was worse."

It was a two-boat fourth-level final and the winner was Grand Valley State by a length.

"We felt awful," Daskalakis recalls. "In going into the championship season we were hoping to medal possibly at the IRA as the JV. Being aware of the anniversary–in '78 they won the national championship–then 20 years later coming in dead last was not something we were proud of. It still stings today. It still stings today."

Sanford describes it this way, "A tough time and a low, low, low time in the history of crew at Syracuse" and says he thought about retiring then. It was the worst he'd felt since his very early years. Sanford continues, "But then there are so many IRAs in so many years that I can tell you that for a month I agonized over the finish–whether we finished seventh, ninth, eleventh or in the finals or whatever I agonized because of the fact that we hadn't done as well as I thought we should have done."

As if the height of irony the coach had already arranged for Syracuse to compete at Henley that summer. So the athletes stayed and eventually headed across the Atlantic where the SU eight beat Dartmouth at the Reading Regatta but then lost to the Big Green in a rematch in the opening race on the Thames.

The second SU boat also went out in its first Henley matchup.

Bill Sanford came home to his apartment in the Ten Eyck Boathouse and knew he would carry on. He was not going to go out on the bottom.

In spite of the difficulties, or perhaps because of them, the men on the squad–the classes of 1998 and '99–bonded as closely as any in the history of Syracuse crew–gathering at each other's weddings and staying close in the years that followed. Much of the credit goes to Jason Premo, a third-boater from Cicero-North Syracuse High School who in 2008 became the youngest President of the Syracuse Alumni Rowing Association at the age of 31. At this writing they remain close and as a group have been among the most generous contributors to the SU Men's Crew Endowment fund.

"At the time I wouldn't have said that going through the challenges that we were–I wouldn't have thought that was going to be a good thing in the end in terms of the friendship that we all have," Jamie Bettini says. "But to the extent that it brought us all together I guess it was a good thing outside of crew."

"I know, speaking with other oarsmen from other schools who have had successful programs, they say they are not as close as we are as a group," Paris Daskalakis says. "Not just one or two people, a small clique, but most of the whole. So maybe that experience brought us together. I don't think it could be that one season. I would say the four years together."

For those whose SU careers did not finish that spring things would get a little better.

Chapter 25
1996–1999 – The Kris Sanford Era Begins

None of Bill and Nancy Sanford's three daughters rowed for Syracuse University. Their oldest daughter Shawn coxed the men's team. Jennifer, the youngest daughter started as a cox but outgrew it and became manager of the men's team. Eventually she became head coach of women's rowing at the University of Connecticut.

The middle daughter Kristen grew up in the boathouse with her sisters but never planned to row at all. She was a varsity swimmer at Liverpool High School in the seventh grade but when a bunch of her friends decided to row she joined in. They were coached by her "Uncle Paul" Sanford and his pal "Dicky the Dog" Hirsh.

She wanted go to Cornell but didn't have the grades so was about to settle for rowing at Syracuse when the University of Washington and Coach Bob Ernst came calling. He'd met her when she was on the U.S. Junior National Team.

Kris Sanford was 16, graduating from high school early–midway through the school year–and did not know much about Washington. "I'm like, 'cowboys and Indians, Washington? Like the West Coast?' I knew nothing."

Ernst sent a video and Sanford got a quick understanding of how good the Huskies' program was. "Two weeks later I was on a plane."

She stroked a national champion freshman crew but the Huskies missed out on a title her sophomore year. It was the first time in seven years. Sanford's junior and senior years, the Huskies returned to glory.

Some said she should try to compete for the U.S. National Team.

"I knew I was not going to continue rowing," she says. "It was always a struggle. I was just done. I was ready to stop."

The girl who had grown up around rowing figured she was done with it and came home to Syracuse to work for Marty Yenawine in his "I'm Smart" program which was a service to provide people who'd had too much to drink a way home without driving. Yenawine was well known and connected in the Syracuse area, and Sanford says he was a wonderful mentor.

But when a chance came to go to Indiana as director for the Indianapolis Rowing Club, she jumped. The club became the Indianapolis Rowing Center and with Sanford as Executive Director it grew from 50 members to 500. She became Regional Technical Director for U.S. Rowing and in 1993 worked as Race Director for the World Championships.

Then came another chance to go back to Syracuse and this time stay in the sport she loved. "Chris Lang called and said 'I have this position [freshman coach]. Do you want to come home?' And it was a no-brainer."

Kris Sanford says she didn't come home to Syracuse to supplant Chris Lang. She came to work with her. "I was friends with Chris. I was coming home because I wanted to be at home and I thought it would be fun to work with Chris. But it soon became apparent that it wasn't going to be fun."

Their approaches to coaching were very different. Sanford says Lang pushed her athletes too hard. "The coaching technique was awful. Instead of trying to build up confidence or training correctly I think that she just tried to make them tough. I just remember the practices and going 'they were done an hour ago and now we're just going to have injuries.'"

Sanford says she always had Lang's back, even when athletes came to her to complain about the head coach. But when Lang was gone and Athletics Director Jake Crouthamel gave Sanford the reins, she went about making changes.

In Indianapolis, Sanford had struck up a relationship with Craig Milburn, who was then at Butler University. When she left for SU he came along as volunteer coach. And when she rose to become head coach, she didn't have to look far to find an assistant. Milburn got the spot. They married in 1999.

There was some talent on the squad in the fall of 1996. Working with some of the athletes Lang had, and the novices she had coached to some success, Sanford found ways to get the crews back to performing well. "Just build people up instead of breaking them down," she says.

"They were good athletes. I just worked on the whole confidence thing. How you carry yourself on race day. How you make sacrifices to be able to enjoy the benefits of those sacrifices.

"We trained hard. We had a lot of rules; a lot of rules. That was hard on some people. People still talk about how if you weren't ten minutes early for practice you were late. It was a little bit of tough love and it was building confidence."

In 1997 the NCAA held its first National Championship for women's rowing. Early in the season it didn't look as if Syracuse was going to be involved. But after struggling in dual races, the Orange women's varsity eight came up strong in the Eastern Sprints, finishing fifth and earning an invitation to Lake Natoma in Sacramento, California.

"The season didn't get us there," Sanford says. "It was the Sprints finish and the progression up to it."

In Sacramento the Orange women lined up in an opening heat with then-powerful Massachusetts, Virginia, Oregon State, Northeastern and Georgetown. The Minutewomen won the Friday heat with the best time of the day–6:29.2–and SU's crew was last, just half-a-beat behind Georgetown. The Orange did not get out of the repechage and into the semifinals, having to watch on Sunday as Sanford's alma mater Washington won the championship over UMass.

Sanford has pretty much put it out of her mind. "It wasn't a good finish–I don't remember how it went. I want to say that maybe we finished in the third level some place. But I don't remember."

The seniors graduated and performance slipped a bit in 1998 and 1999. There would be no invitations to the NCAAs.

"We were losing races by 20 seconds, by 30 seconds," Sanford says. "How do you build confidence on that? 'At least it wasn't 30 like last week.' That's hard."

Katie Modolo remembers. In the spring of 1998 she became the first freshman to row in an SU varsity boat. "At our first race we were blown out of the water. I can remember getting off the water, hugging my dad, and saying, 'What the hell did I do coming here [to SU]?' I wasn't used to losing, and it really sucked. But I saw Kris building a team year after year with strong recruits and the tides started turning. She was building her team and by my senior year there wasn't a more dedicated or loyal rower in the bunch than I."

By her fourth season Sanford had boatloads of her own recruits and talented walk-ons on board and they were ready to compete at a higher level.

Chapter 26
1999–2002 – The End of the Bill Sanford Era

"My four years as a Syracuse Oarsman were some of the best of my life, and I am proud to have been part of a tradition that is currently thriving."

– Jamie Bettini '99

In the fall of 1998 the task of Coach Sanford and his returning team members was to get off the bottom and back on the path to being competitive with the other crews in the league. The effort in the fall and winter training plainly led to better results in the spring of 1999. While the Orange crews did not rise to the upper half of the IRA, the varsity did return to winning.

SU clobbered Boston University for the Conlan Cup and gave highly-rated Brown a fight on the Seekonk, losing by less than half-a-length. The Bruins later finished fourth at the IRA behind three record-breaking crews: Cal, Princeton and Wisconsin.

The Orange came from behind to beat Rutgers, winning in the last five strokes by less than a second. SU was second behind Temple at the Big East's and Dartmouth continued its streak in the Packard Cup.

But Sanford's men pulled–literally–a big upset, taking back the Goes Trophy over Cornell and Navy. "My recollection of that race is just really, really, really close all the way down the race course and us just never giving up," Jamie Bettini says.

Syracuse crews did not get back into the higher levels at the Sprints or the IRA that year, but they were done finishing at the bottom. "So while we definitely did not succeed by the yardsticks of Sprints and IRA finishes, we did row our hearts out–or balls off to borrow from our favorite acronym–every time we took to the water," Bettini says.

Chris Ludden, a Liverpool guy who'd rowed in some of Bill Sanford's best boats in the early '90s, came back from coaching in Oak Ridge, Tennessee that spring, as a second assistant coach. He would replace Paul Sanford coaching the frosh in the fall.

Spring 2000

With Adam Jackson and Josh Stratton as captains, the Orangemen faced the usual suspects in the spring of 2000. Opening the season at home on April Fools' Day, the varsity eight took care of Boston University by a length. It was a clear, sunny day with the temperature in the 40s and flat water. The frosh and second frosh both beat the Terrier pups, but BU's JV prevented an Orange sweep with a win by a couple of lengths of open water.

As had become habit, Brown showed up the next day and Bruno just hammered Sanford's lads. Brown's varsity eight broke the Syracuse course record, covering the 2,000 meters in 5:46.2. Conditions were pristine with the temperature in the upper 40s, no wind and a surface SU Assistant Coach Chris Ludden described as "glass." Syracuse rowed a respectable 6:03 but the Brown win would have been described at Henley as "easily." Brown's JV also clobbered SU and the Bruin cubs won by open water.

The Orange varsity got a win twelve days later, taking Rutgers by a couple of lengths on a Friday afternoon. Rowing into a bit of a headwind on New Brunswick's Raritan River, Sanford's men swept Coach Steve Wagner's Scarlet Knights, also winning the JV and freshman eight races by open water.

Rutgers' frosh were highly touted and then first-year coach Chris Ludden says his crew caught the Scarlet Knights by surprise. "You should have seen the looks on their faces," he says. "And the coach's."

It was Syracuse's turn to host the Goes Trophy race but except for Ludden's frosh, it was not the Orange's turn to win. Navy took the Big Red by two seconds in the varsity eights, with SU open water back. Cornell returned the favor in the JV with the Orange again trailing.

SU's freshmen won a humdinger of a race, besting the Navy Plebes by two seconds, with Cornell's frosh another second back.

The second frosh won also–beating Cornell by a length with Navy way behind.

Three weeks later the Syracuse armada headed to Hanover where the currents on the Connecticut River were so fast that the races were rowed as 6:00 minutes against the current instead of 2,000 meters. The water was flat and the Big Green maintained their Packard Cup dominance over the Orange, winning by 1/3 of a length open. The Orange had grabbed a lead at the start but Dartmouth pulled even about 1:30 into the race and at 3:00–the halfway point–had a lead it would not surrender.

SU also took a two-seat lead early in the JV race but Dartmouth rowed past to win by 3/4 of a length open.

The Orange frosh won again, grabbing the lead off the start and then leaving Dartmouth behind in the last 1:30 to win by a couple of lengths of open water.

The frosh included a deep group of experienced oarsmen, featuring U.S. Junior National Team member Kevin Klein, plus a couple of big, strong walk-ons, Steve Boselli and Kevin Boyle.

"That was my best freshman team," Chris Ludden recalls. "The chemistry was there."

At the Eastern Sprints, the Orange frosh again had the best finishes. Ludden's first eight was third behind Princeton and Northeastern in the morning heat, then won the petite final by a length over Cornell. The second frosh were second in the morning heat behind Cornell then came in fourth in the grand final following Wisconsin, Rutgers and Cornell, two crews they had beaten earlier in the season. Nobody was taking the Orange cubs for granted at that point.

The JV struggled as it had most of the season, finishing fourth in the morning and last in the petite final in the afternoon. Sanford's varsity suffered the same fate, trailing Penn, Yale, Columbia, Cornell and Navy in the petites.

Brown edged Princeton for the Eastern Sprints varsity eight title.

Preparing for the IRA, Sanford decided not to compete with a JV eight, instead boating a four with cox and a four without. The V4 with wound up fourth in the petite final and the four without was second in the third-level final.

The varsity eight was never close to the upper level, finishing 5th in its heat (last), and 4th (again last) in the repechage. But the Orange won its semifinal contest over Stanford, then finished second to Oregon State in the third-level final doing its strongest racing on Friday and Saturday.

That ridiculously speedy Brown varsity eight finished second at the IRA, open water behind an even more ridiculously fast Cal crew.

The Orange freshman eight ran up against two fast crews in the opening heat, trailing California and Oregon State. In the repechage the Orange rowed into the upper-level semis by taking second behind Cornell. But Ludden's lads were fourth in the semi, consigning them to the petite final where they lined up one more time against the Big Red and Rutgers.

The Scarlet Knights again got the best of it, with the Orange exacting a bit of revenge on Cornell, which was third.

Ludden's frosh four made the grand finals where they finished fifth.

A dozen rising sophomore oarsmen and a couple of coxes who had won some races were set to move up the varsity. The Orange fortunes looked reasonably bright for the next year.

Fall 2000

Filling the men's rowing ranks with Forestry College students had not been an option for some time but there still were walk-ons who joined the recruits, young men who'd competed in other sports at the secondary school level but were not about to continue their high school sport in college. Many who tried out for crew soon discovered it required more discipline and dedication than they cared for and they dropped out. Those who stayed often turned out to be influential even if they never made it into a first eight. One such walk-on is Adlai Hurt who tells of how he wound up a member of the team that transitioned from Bill Sanford to Dave Reischman.

"During freshman fall orientation in 2000, I was leaving the Schine Student Center trying to catch a shuttle to my dorm. Naturally, my mother struck up a conversation with another mother. Turns out, this lady and her daughter were from New Jersey and the daughter was recruited to be a member of the SU women's varsity rowing team. Being from Iowa, I had never seen the sport in person, but somehow I was aware of it. The rivers in

266

Iowa, I thought, were a mile wide and a foot deep and thus must be unable to handle rowing.

"As we grew impatient for the next shuttle, my mother and I headed to the quad and a large information tent. While we were meandering around, a woman at one of the tables noticed my height and pointed across the quad at a gentleman standing next to a shell in slings. She told me that the crew team always looks for tall incoming freshman and that this group had been looking at me from across the quad. Now being encouraged by this stranger and my mother to walk over to the shell I simply wanted to leave and walk back to my dorm. I was a mediocre high school athlete, having earned only one varsity letter–in the 110-meter high hurdles–after my senior year. And what good is a high school varsity letter if you can't even wear a letterman's jacket? I knew I wasn't collegiate athlete material nor did I have any desire to participate in anything other than recreational leagues. The path to my dorm, however, went directly past the boat."

Hurt continues: "While walking by the boat one of the people quickly wrapped up a conversation and stopped me. It was Chris Ludden, freshman crew coach. He handed me a flyer about an informational meeting and encouraged me to try the sport. Eventually, I made it to my dorm. As it turns out, one of my floor-mates Nick Alexander had also received a flyer. So Nick Alexander and I went to the informational meeting for novice rowers. Quickly these informational meetings turned into time on the water with spoon oars. Of the approximately fifty novice freshman that fall, only two remained by the 2004 IRA–Nick Alexander and myself."

2001 – Spring Season

Captained by senior Josh Stratton and junior Matt Heumann the Orange opened the 2001 spring season in Boston against the Terriers of BU. The varsity eight was a sizable group with Karl Sudar stroking, Andy Berster at seven, Stratton at six and Heumann at five. Future Olympian Chris Liwski was at four, Jay Abbott at three, Jason Bourcier at two and Kevin Boyle in bow. Eric Miller was the cox and the Orange took BU by a couple of lengths of open water on the Charles River. The Orange also took the JV and freshman four races but the first frosh trailed BU and Harvard which joined in for the frosh competition only and was first.

There was no time to bask in the win as once again Syracuse packed up and headed for Providence to take on Brown the next morning. The results were not pretty. The Bruins swept Syracuse, winning a very quick varsity eight race by three lengths open. Brown roared down the Seekonk in 5:31.1 to SU's 5:44.0. Bruno also took the first and second frosh and the third varsity and JV, with SU's second boat getting the closest to a Brown crew, five seconds behind.

The Orange welcomed Rutgers for the Syracuse home opener and won by a baseball score as reported by *SUAthletics. com*. "The Syracuse University men's varsity eight retained the Ten Eyck Cup Friday by defeating Rutgers, 2-0, on the Onondaga Lake Outlet. It was the fifth time in as many years that SU won the trophy."

What the 2-0 score meant was that the crews raced twice over 1,000 meters and Syracuse won both. Winds were high out on the lake so the coaches agreed to race on the inlet, in a best-of-three race format.

The third race was not necessary.

Sanford's JV also took two in a row but Rutgers returned the favor in the varsity fours and both first and second freshman eights, taking the Orange two straight in each.

The Goes Trophy competition was held on the Severn that spring and Cornell took the cup home with an open water win over Sanford's varsity eight. Navy was well back of the Orange who also came in second to the Big Red in the JV and trailed in the varsity four and freshman eight races.

SU took four of five races at the Georgetown Invitational but not the big one.

The Orange was second, more than a length behind the Temple Owls. SU won the JV and freshman eights and the third varsity and freshman fours.

At the Eastern Sprints, the Orange JV and third varsities made the grand finals but the V8 did not, winding up fourth in the petite. The frosh were sixth in the petite. Princeton took Harvard by a length in the varsity eight grand final.

Dartmouth held onto the Packard Cup with a length-open win over the Orange varsity on Onondaga Lake. Syracuse took the other three races, with the Orange cubs coming from behind to take the Big Green frosh.

The Orange men were bunked in now at the boathouse rowing twice a day to get set for the IRA. In between practice sessions, Adlai Hurt recalls the crew men passed the time with another competition–foosball. "Guys would pair up and over the course of IRA Camp there would be a foosball championship–complete with a bracket–seeding and a series of best-of-three final."

On the water they looked for a way to get into the competitive upper levels at the IRA. For the varsity eight, it was not to be.

The JV wound up in the petite final and finished fifth, losing by six-tenths of a second to the Dartmouth crew it had beaten a couple of weeks earlier. Northeastern won it with Yale and Oregon State next.

The freshman four with cox was fifth in the petites and the varsity four without was sixth. The varsity pair without manned by sophs Andy Johnson and Adam Stivala won the third-level final.

The varsity eight wound up in a Big East-loaded third-level final and once again lost to its nemesis Temple, this time by a length open. The Orange finished 14th overall.

Fall 2001

What happened to the world early in the fall of Bill Sanford's final year as head coach has a far greater impact on everyone's life than anything having to do with crew.

Adlai Hurt '04, recalls it this way: "On the morning of September 11, 2001 we had a morning practice on the lake. Under Coach Bill this probably would have been a 6:00 or 6:30 a.m. shove. As I remember, it was calm with a lot of blue sky and a few wispy clouds. It was a normal day. Yet, while we were on the water four planes were being hijacked by terrorists before being flown into the Twin Towers, Pentagon, and crashed in rural Pennsylvania. I remember hearing initial reports on the radio while driving by downtown Syracuse on my way back to campus. It was so strange to hear the initial reports of a plane hitting the first tower. I thought some small propeller plane might have gotten disoriented, had a mechanical failure, or got lost in fog."

Hurt continues: "I made it back to DellPlain Hall and showered there before heading to Haven to grab breakfast before a 10 a.m. class. When I entered the dining hall I could see the small TVs anchored from the ceiling along the windows. It looked like there was breaking news about a coal power plant. I grabbed breakfast and saw a former-novice walk-on who had since left the team, Roger Samuels. As I approached Roger to sit with him I realized what was being shown on TV. We just sat there watching. I went to my 10 a.m. class, but all we did was watch the breaking news coverage. At my 12:30 class we did not watch the news, but we talked about the events of that morning.

"Jump to the next day's practice, which I think was a 4 o'clock afternoon shove. Coach Bill gathered the varsity squad in the upstairs of the boathouse. He said a few words about the attacks. I don't remember anyone crying, but I think some guys were still in shock, but there was nothing for us to do but hit the water and practice."

Winds of Change, Wounds of Workout

In the winter of 2002, Bill Sanford ran for, and won, the New York State Assembly seat in a special election after long-time Assemblyman Michael Bragman resigned. Sanford told *The Orange Oar* that his main focus would remain on coaching the Syracuse crew. "Albany will have to suffer," he said.

Sanford left his position as Chairman of the County Legislature, began his duties in Albany on February 25th and set up a schedule of heading for the capital after Monday morning practice and returning in time for Wednesday's workout. Freshman Coach Chris Ludden and assistant Mike D'Eredita would hold the fort while Sanford was gone.

He said he planned to retire as crew coach at the end of the season.

It turned out that the coach also had to fight through injury.

"During the spring break training trip to Miami in 2002, Coach Bill was in the launch with Mike D'Eredita," Adlai Hurt recalls. "We had just turned back for our long row back to the UM dock when all of a sudden the launch stopped. Coach Bill who was standing went head over heels. Mike had run aground on a hidden sand bar. Thank goodness Coach Bill did not break anything. He had a massive deep purple bruise on one leg and may have been in a walking boot the rest of the trip."

Spring 2002

The Orange team that trained through that winter had size and experience. Among the group were two cousins from Sarasota, Florida, Andy Berster and Chris Liwski. Liwski would go on to make the U.S. Olympic Team as a spare. Liwski's older brother Matt also had rowed for Syracuse.

Sanford's final varsity eight opened the 2002 season on a typical winter day in Syracuse even though technically it was the third day of spring.

It was twenty-seven degrees with a 10–15 mile-per-hour tailwind and the Orange and the Brown Bears lined up to race just after the snow stopped. Maybe it was the tailwind. Maybe it was just that the crews wanted to get off the water. Probably it was some of both, but they flew down the course, with Brown finishing in 5:33.3 and Sanford's men in 5:38.6.

It was the closest race of the day as Bruno swept the SU crews again, getting Paul Cooke's tenure as Brown head coach off to a solid start.

It was a headwind a week later. The opponent was Boston University and the Orange varsity eight outfought the Terriers by half-a-second to win the Conlan Cup. Senior Eric Miller was the coxswain with Berster stroking backed by Kevin Klein, Matt Heumann, Liwski, Steve Boselli, Andrew Wright, John Merzig and Jason Bourcier. They crossed the line in 6:13.6 to BU's 6:14.1.

The SU JV also won but Chris Ludden's two freshman

eights fell to BU.

The Orange went to New Jersey after a week off and the varsity held onto the Ten Eyck Cup for the sixth-straight year by defeating Rutgers by two lengths open. But the other Syracuse crews lost to the Scarlet Knights; the JV by half-a-length and the freshman eight and four easily.

Cornell was host for the Goes Trophy race and took Navy by open water in the varsity eights, with Syracuse another half-length back. The order was the same in the JV race but Navy won the freshman 2K with relative ease.

The Orange frosh were in third, out of shouting distance.

The third varsity took second place behind Cornell.

JV cox Peter Romano got tossed into the water at the Georgetown Invitational, a fate varsity cox Eric Miller would have loved to have suffered. The Orange second eight won its final over Temple by less than a second with the Hoyas third. But it was the Owls again in a bang-bang-bang varsity eight final, edging Georgetown by a single second.

This time SU was third another 1.3 seconds back.

The varsity four won its final but the frosh continued to struggle, finishing third, open water behind Boston College and Georgetown.

Dartmouth continued its domination of Syracuse in the Packard Cup race in Hanover, clobbering the Orange varsity by three lengths open.

It was the 12th-straight win for Dartmouth and a sweep for the Big Green that included walloping both the Orange JV and freshmen.

Sanford shook up his varsity eight a bit before the Eastern Sprints, moving John Merzig into the stroke with Andrew Wright at seven. Matt Heumann was at six, Chris Liwski at five, Steve Boselli at four, Kevin Klein at three, Andy Berster at two and Jason Bourcier remaining in bow. The results were not significantly different.

The varsity was fourth in the morning heat and then sixth in the petite final.

The JV, also fourth in the morning, was fifth in the afternoon.

The frosh managed to get past MIT for second in the third-level final.

It was the last race for the freshmen, who did not bring an eight to the IRA. Not only had the crew not won a race; it had never come close. "We rowed a four," Coach Chris Ludden recalls. "We only had maybe seven or eight guys left and we just knew it wouldn't be any kind of an experience."

Ludden remembers the events of 9/11 having a terrible psychological effect on a couple of oarsmen–one in particular. "He kind of snapped ... and brought his roommate down with him. The team couldn't recover when we lost a couple of good guys. It was too much to handle."

Only four members the Class of '05 stuck it out the next year: cox Mike Wzontek and oarsmen Justin Burgess, Sergei Bourlatski and Andrew Cooley.

SARA scheduled its annual meeting at the IRA and alums turned out in fairly strong numbers. Shirts had been made up to honor Sanford and many a toast was raised to the retiring coach, but the finishes on the water were not what he might have hoped for in completing his career.

The JV got to the petite finals and finished sixth–12th overall–with a time of 5:59.60. Dartmouth, Oregon State, Michigan, Pennsylvania and Drexel finished ahead of SU in the petite.

The Syracuse varsity four with cox was third in its third-level finals race. The men's open four with coxswain finished sixth in the third-level finals.

And SU's varsity eight finished second in the fourth-level finals with a time of 5:49.61. Marietta won the race with a time of 5:47.42.

Sanford's final crew was 20th overall.

At that same IRA, a crew full of walk-ons that rowed out of a tin shed on the bank of the Willamette River was finishing in the grand finals with a young coach who'd been quietly making his mark against Washington, California and Stanford.

For the first time since 1967 Syracuse University was looking for a new head coach of men's crew.

This time the answer would not lie in SU's own back

273

yard.

Scott Sanford

Just a few days after Bill Sanford's last IRA, his brother and former teammate Scott Sanford died at his home in the Poughkeepsie area after an illness. He was 60. Scott Sanford had made a name for himself as a rowing coach and school principal and had been head coach at Marist College for nine years. "Scott's loss is one that will be felt by everyone within the Marist community," said Marist Director of Athletics Tim Murray. "He was someone who had a tremendous amount of passion for not only rowing, but for education and teaching those who rowed for him."

It also was a loss felt deeply by the Syracuse rowing community.

Syracuse Alumni Rowing Association

Thousands of athletes would come and go through the Syracuse University Crew program over the second half of the 20th century and into the 21st. But starting in 1953 there has been one constant–the Syracuse Alumni Rowing Association. SARA's members were the older, sometimes much older guys who'd show up at the boathouse, especially during IRA Camp to swap stories and memories with one another and to tell the young men then in the boats how much it meant to be a member of the Syracuse Crew. Sometimes they'd even share a meal of dry toast and tea back when that was a staple of training table.

Crew alums Doctors Tom Kerr and Bruce Chamberlain formed SARA partly over dissatisfaction with Coach Gus Erickson's performance as head coach.

The group's pressure helped force Erickson out and bring in Loren Schoel from Cornell to take the Orange to glory in the late 1950s. Schoel survived until 1967 when less successful times and pressure from team members forced him out.

When Bill Sanford took over the IRA was still in Syracuse and SARA was holding its annual meetings to do business and elect officers at the Onondaga Yacht Club during IRA week. It was never an organization with deep pockets–although some of its key members were well-off–but the organization and its members did provide funding for new shells and trips to Henley and spearheaded the renovation of the Ten Eyck Boathouse in 1988, which SU and Onondaga County funded.

Most of the board members lived in the greater-Syracuse area.

SARA board meetings during the year were held in the boathouse and the group was generally seen as coach-friendly, which of course meant Bill Sanford-friendly. Stalwarts included long-time Treasurer Charlie Roberts, Joe Peter, Bill Hider and Sandy Pisani. Alumni who were not Sanford-friendly generally were not involved in SARA.

Barry Weiss '83 served four years as SARA President.

"Up to the early 1990s, crew was an Eastern college sport and then evolved into a national sport and as the sport changed, so did the way we communicate," Weiss says. "The Board of Directors was made up of individuals who lived in Central New York. I recognized that we could not survive on this model. [We needed to] broaden the board for a better geographic, and class distribution. With more alumni getting involved and as e-mail became a popular way to communicate, the fortunes of the men's program declined."

As Sanford's crews slipped in the early 1990s the drums of discontent began to beat on the new medium of e-mail and the complaints grew louder with each successive disappointing season.

There were calls for Bill Sanford to step down or be fired.

Weiss was one of Sanford's strongest supporters. He had started on the crew as a coxswain but soon outgrew the role and became team manager. He is as close to Sanford as any team member has been, having run his campaigns for political office after graduation and started his own career in county government with a hand up from Sanford, then chair of the county legislature.

"I did have a few conversations with Bill about the drumbeats for change among the alumni and one of the suggestions was to use the internet and e-mail to communicate through coach's reports to the constituents around the county," Weiss says. "Since Dave Reischman still uses the same concept, I guess it was the right method, but the work and results on the water did not meet the level of expectation."

Weiss was not happy with the complaints, not only because he felt they were unfair but because in his view they were coming from alums who had done nothing to help the program over the years.

Weiss issued a challenge: "Get involved or shut up."

A goodly number rose to the challenge, among them Rick Holland, Tom Darling, Austin Curwen, Ted Kakas, and Bill Purdy, all of whom lived outside of Central New York. There were more. Holland was elected SARA President and the others became Directors, joining alums such as Barry Weiss, Bob Donabella and Treasurer Colin Goodale.

They spruced up the SARA newsletter, which Holland titled *"The Orange Oar"* and began organizing events to support the crews in their races in Boston, Philadelphia and Washington, D.C., as well as at the Eastern Sprints and the IRA Regatta in Camden.

When Sanford announced his retirement in 2002, SARA was given a spot on the search committee for his replacement and Darling brought his expertise and contacts into the mix, while keeping his agreed-upon silence when it came to candidates being considered.

The search brought Oregon State Head Coach Dave Reischman who, after his hiring was greeted in an informal session at Joe Peter's house and told, in essence: "We don't have a lot of money to give you but we're here to help any way we can."

SARA also made a renewed effort to involve women in the group and to support the women's program, something that had been tried in the early '90s with little success.

This time, alumnae including Tracy Rude Smith, Lynne Della Pelle Pascale, Martha Mogish Rowe, Kristin Bidwell and Sheila Roock, joined as SARA Directors.

In 2010, Smith became SARA's first female President.

Through the years there's been discussion of folding SARA into the SU Varsity Club or putting it under the umbrella of

276

the athletics department. SARA has remained fiercely independent and dedicated to the support of SU Rowing.

Chapter 27
2000–2005 – Salad Days

While her father was wrapping up his Syracuse Crew career with less-than-stellar teams in the early 2000s, Kris Sanford's teams were hitting new heights. The varsity eight made the NCAAs three-consecutive years and in 2001 reached the grand finals.

She says it was done with the right athletes and the right attitude. "We had Katie Modolo, Alicea Kochis, Jillian Kott," Sanford recalls. She names Rachael Kirchoff, Libby Graves and others. "It was a group of people that they were all good athletes. It just worked."

Some, such as Kott, Modolo and Graves were experienced and highly sought after. Others, such as Kochis and Kirchoff, whose father had rowed for Syracuse, were walk-ons. Modolo was a driving force.

"She was like the bull in the china shop," Sanford recalls. "She upped the expectations. You need people on the team who will kick people's butts if they're not doing what they're supposed to do and that was Katie. She wasn't used to losing and we were losing."

Modolo calls Sanford innovative and intuitive. "Kris just always had a knack for knowing what the best approach was for reaching me and others on the team who were driven by different motivators. I'm not someone who does well with being yelled at. I need to know the person or coach I'm talking to understands my perspective. She knew this about me and always tailored the countless 'you're intimidating' talks she had with me about how I carried myself on the team. This intuitiveness also benefited many of us as she drove us to new levels of success."

Spring 2000

The Orange women opened the season on April 1st in Boston against a very tough Terriers crew and the Miami Hurricanes. The sun was bright, the temperature in the 50s and the headwind strong. The V8 wound up in second, a length open behind BU and less than a length in front of Miami. The only Syracuse win came in the varsity four.

The next weekend with flat water and no wind on Onondaga Lake, it was Yale taking the measure of SU's V8 by just over a length, but Cornell trailed in third. No Syracuse crew won its race.

The Orange stayed home a week later and lost again, this time to Northeastern and Penn in a strong quartering tailwind.

The V4 got the only win for Syracuse.

They went back to Boston where the conditions were so awful in the Charles River basin that the course was moved upstream between the Boston University bridge and the Weeks Footbridge and rowed as a head race, single file. Radcliffe swept the competition, taking California by a length in the V8 with SU a couple of lengths farther back and Dartmouth trailing.

Four weeks. No wins for the eights.

Kris Sanford's varsity eights got off the schneid in Washington, D.C. at the Georgetown Invitational for Big East crews, winning both the varsity and 2V events.

Back home again on flat water, the V8 took UMass and Villanova with relative ease and the Orange had some momentum heading into the Eastern Sprints.

The Sprints petite final was tight. Northeastern crossed the line first, with SU 2/3 of a length back in second and just a tick ahead of third place Dartmouth in a photo finish. Wisconsin was fourth, less than a length behind the Big Green.

The eighth-place finish overall got Syracuse varsity eight back to the NCAAs.

The Orange women were third in their opening heat behind top-seed Brown and California. The repechage brought a second-place finish a length behind Radcliffe and a trip to the semis. Fifth place there meant the petite final and Sanford's crew wound up third (9th overall) behind Boston University and Michigan State, beating Northeastern, Ohio State and Radcliffe.

The Orange women had improved through the racing season and finished strong.

Fall and Winter

Sanford added strength to her squad in the fall of 2000, bringing in two rowers from the Netherlands–Helen Tanger and Froukje Wegman. The connection was made through a Dutch friend Sanford and Craig Milburn had worked with in Indianapolis. Milburn went to the Netherlands, took a look and brought the two rowers back.

"When we first arrived Kris told us which days we would have practice," Tanger says. "And I still remember her saying, 'Leave campus at 5:30.' So I thought 5:30 p.m. is a normal time for practice, not bad at all–in the Netherlands I was used to practice in the evenings. Then she said 'A.M.' And my jaw dropped an inch or two. I do not like getting up early in the mornings, so that was a BIG thing for me. But of course Kris told me to 'suck it up' and that's what I did, and after a while I got used to it. On Sundays I could sleep in, and would wake up at 8:30!"

"The Netherlands was known for their nice skilled rowing but not knowing how to pull on the oar," Sanford says. "So they came over here and we taught them how to pull on the oar."

SU took first place that fall at the Stonehurst Invitational in Rochester and the Head of the Schuylkill in Philadelphia, then there was a fifth-place finish at the Head of the Charles. "With the addition of competition among teammates during practices, we improved in leaps and bounds," Sanford said then. "This fall was the best season we've ever had."

Practices mixed hard work with a bit of goofiness. Helen Tanger tells this story: "I remember one day we were in the V8 rowing together with the JV8 and we would let [the boat] run, and had a little competition which boat could remain in balance with the blades not touching the water. Both eights were good at it, and the minutes passed and passed. We all started giggling, really trying not to touch the water with our blades and trying to break concentration for the JV8, because we always wanted to win. We won that competition with the JV, but then we still did not want to touch the water with our blades."

Tanger continues, "So Kris finally made things really difficult for us and started circling our boat with the launch to make wakes. I don't remember how long we just sat there with the blades of the water, but it was loooong–maybe 15 minutes?–good times!"

The Orange women spent a lot of time running stairs in the Carrier Dome that winter as well as long workouts on the ergometers. *SUathletics.com* reported: "Sanford said that the flu and nagging colds plagued the women this winter, but most are eager to begin practicing on water again." They got on the water in Miami in double sessions and finished up with a scrimmage against Miami, Navy and Duke.

Going into the spring *Sports Illustrated for Women* put out a Top-10 list of women's crews and SU was not listed. "We have the ability to be fast, but anything can happen," Sanford said, reluctant to predict her team's future. "On paper we should be the fastest we have ever been."

Spring 2001

The Orange women faced a jam-packed schedule in the spring of 2001 and the varsity eight rowed through the competition without a stumble. They opened on the Indian Creek River in Miami at the end of spring training with a pair of races.

SU's V8 clobbered Central Florida in a 2K race in the morning, then came back in the afternoon and walked away from Miami and Navy in another 2K.

The morning races were a near sweep for Syracuse, with the 2V8, V4 and novice eight winning easily. The novice four lost to North Carolina.

It was tougher for the other Orange crews in the afternoon with only the novice eight joining the V8 in winning.

The other boats trailed Navy in their races.

Two weeks later Kris Sanford's squad went to the Charles River in Boston and swept BU, Texas and Duke in the V8 and 2V8. But the V8 race was one of the closest of the season as the Orange women edged the Terriers by only about half-a-length.

The V4A boat beat Duke with the V4B in third place.

The women went to Ithaca next and the V8 took 10th-ranked Yale by open water, with no. 19 Cornell trailing. The

Orange varsity eight was paced by All-American stroke Jillian Kott.

The course at Cornell involves negotiating several angles and rowing under a couple of bridges.

"We had the outside of the turn and therefore started the race with a few seats ahead," Alicea Kochis remembers. "Kris prepared us even if we're going into the turn ahead, expect Yale to be right there by the end of it. Our crew attacked that turn to limit their advantage and came out with the same margin, a half length ahead. I just remember the Yale coxswain yelling, 'We are Yale. We are Yale,' as we pushed ahead. That was the first time we ever beat Yale. And that was when we knew we were fast."

By now the Orange women were ranked sixth in the nation. The top eight looked strong but the lack of depth was showing in the lower boats. SU did not enter a second varsity eight that day and none of the fours or the novice eight managed to win.

Somehow the varsity eight slipped to no. 7 in the poll the next week but went to Philadelphia and stayed unbeaten, taking no. 20 Penn by more than a length open, with Northeastern trailing. It was the first Orange Challenge Cup win for SU since 1984.

This time the 2V and V4B also won, with the V4A second behind Northeastern.

The varsity edged back up to no. 6 and prepared for another fight in Boston, this time against no. 7 Radcliffe and Dartmouth. Weather put the start off from morning until almost dusk. Kochis says she was rowing "a little blurry" after having an abscessed tooth lanced. "I remember being behind going into the last 500 and thinking 'how are we a length down, this feels fast?' Then our coxswain, Heather DiLoreto, called the sprint and we started taking seats–literally a seat a stroke. We ended up walking through Radcliffe and winning by a length."

Katie Modolo recalls more specifics including that they'd gone 1,000 meters in awful conditions when the race was stopped and taken back to the start line. "[Kris] knew we were a bit all over the place with adrenaline. She gave us a few pointers and told us we had proven in our work that we can beat Radcliffe. I believed her. Everyone else must have, too. We started the race again, and again were down at the 1,000-meter mark. Then the greatest third 500 of my life took place and we pulled even with Radcliffe, who we then broke in the last 500. It was incredible. I had gone from a varsity boat in the spring of my freshman year that didn't beat a single crew, let alone win a race, to being part of a crew of women who believed in Kris and all of our training, and beat Radcliffe–something I'm not sure any SU women's crew had ever done before. Talk about igniting a fire for the rest of the spring!"

Dartmouth was well back. Once again the V8 was the only Orange winner, with the 2V8 and V4 finishing second to Radcliffe and the novice eight way back in third in its race.

The Orange women rolled on, taking the first Big East Rowing Challenge title in the varsity eights over Rutgers and Notre Dame and the second varsity over Notre Dame and Rutgers. But the lower boats struggled again in the competition in Worcester. The V4 was second to West Virginia and the novice eight and four did not make the top three.

Still, Syracuse won the Big East title on aggregate points and her fellow coaches voted Kris Sanford as Big East Coach of the Year.

The Orange women finally got their first and only home race of the season–the Orange Plus Cup on May 5th and the varsity shrugged off choppy conditions to beat up on UMass and Villanova.

Both varsity fours and the freshman eight also won, but the 2V8 trailed UMass and Villanova romped over the novice four.

It was the final home race for the only two seniors in the first boat, Meredith Kyle, who rowed bow and Kate Modolo in the seven seat.

Here's one more story from Katie Modolo about Kris Sanford's ability to connect with her charges: "Kris once pulled me from seven seat my senior year during a training practice in Melbourne. I'm sure I was being pissy about how the workout was going or something. Instead of telling me to get my head out of my rear in front of all the boats and my crew mates, she pulled me into the coach boat and we drove off so that we weren't within ear shot of the team. We settled our differences and she drove me back to my seat, but not before giving me a Krispy Kreme donut and telling me to make it look like we just wanted to have a donut together. I know, it sounds odd, but she really did know how to reach each of her rowers differently. She just got me."

Eastern Sprints

Sanford's varsity eight went to Camden for the Eastern Sprints unbeaten and ranked sixth in the nation. Racing on the Cooper River, the varsity eight would finally taste defeat but also would show that it belonged with the best women's crews in the country.

The Orange won the qualifying heat and marched right to the grand final where it would have to face the only two Eastern crews ranked higher in the national poll, no. 1 Brown and no. 3 Princeton. The order of ranking turned out to be the order of finish with Brown first in 6:38.4 and Princeton just getting across ahead of SU, 6:41.4 to 6:41.8.

There was no doubt about an NCAA bid for the SU varsity eight. But a team bid seemed unlikely, with the 2V8 winding up third in the petite final and the V4 winning its petite.

The varsity 4B boat made the grand final and finished fifth. The novice eight wound up in the third level and the novice four in the petites.

Two days later the bids went out. The varsity eight had an at-large bid, its third in the five-year history of the NCAA rowing event.

For the rest of the squad the 2001 season was over.

Overall depth brought team bids to Boston University and Radcliffe, two crews the Orange varsity eight had beaten.

NCAAs

Preparing for the NCAAs, the squad picked three captains for the next season. Libby Graves would serve a second year as captain with her fellow rising seniors Rachael Kirchoff and coxswain Heather DiLoreto joining her.

They raced on Lake Lanier in Gainesville, Georgia, and Sanford's varsity eight, now ranked fifth in the nation, moved right to the semifinals with a second-place finish behind Michigan in the opening heat.

DiLoreto was the coxswain, junior Jillian Kott stroked, senior Captain Katie Modolo at seven, then juniors Libby Graves, Rachael Kirchoff, Alicea Kochis, Helen Tanger and Froukje Wegman and senior Meredith Kyle in bow.

The semifinal competition brought a third-place finish, just over a length behind Washington and, again, a hair behind Princeton. For the first time Syracuse had made the grand final.

Southern Cal won the other semi, upsetting Brown and Michigan but all three went to the grand finals.

The Orange eight was never in it for a story book ending in the grands. Washington took Brown by just over a second, with SU back in sixth, 15 seconds behind. Still it was the best finish ever for an SU women's crew and Kris Sanford had no complaints. "I can't express how proud I am of this team. As a coach they've been my dream team," she said. "Of course we would have liked to have rowed a better race today, but I'm proud of the way my team competed. This type of history-making season is one that we will build on for next year and the year after."

For good measure at the NCAAs, SU's alternates, Shannon Mercurio and Seana Miller won the spares race by a nine-second margin.

It had been the most successful season ever for an SU women's rowing team.

Sanford was named Mid-Atlantic Region Coach of the Year by the Collegiate Rowing Coaches Association (CRCA).

Orange women rowers Jillian Kott and Katie Modolo were First-Team Mid-Atlantic selections, while Alicea Kochis and Froukje Wegman were named to the Second-Team Mid-Atlantic selections.

The CRCA named Kott a First-Team All-America for the second year in a row and voted Modolo to Second-Team All-America honors.

Modolo and Meredith Kyle graduated and Tanger and

Wegman returned to the Netherlands to compete for their national team. Both made the Dutch first boat that summer.

"I only worked with Kris for one year," Tanger says. "But what a year it was. I honestly think it has shaped my rowing career and helped me achieve the goals which at that moment I did not even realize I had. The work ethic that Kris herself has, and which she expects from the team is something I still benefit from in my everyday working life."

Sanford still had five of her first-boaters coming back.

Fall 2001

The SU women's varsity eight started an ambitious fall season October 14th with a second-place finish behind Radcliffe at the Stonehurst Invitational in Rochester. Adding the time from the morning three-mile head race to three times the finish time of the afternoon 1,500-meter sprint, SU posted a championship time of 33:12.43, 22 seconds behind Radcliffe's 32.51.31.

The 2V eight was 12th and the V4A won its competition, with Cornell second.

In Boston, on October 21st, the Orange women's V8 was 11th at the Head of the Charles. The U.S. Rowing National Team was first with Princeton second.

A week later later Sanford's armada rowed at the Head of the Schuylkill in Philadelphia, coming up with four second-place finishes. The V8 trailed Penn's time by five seconds.

The squad split for competition on Sunday, November 11th with the varsity in Charlottesville, Virginia for the Ravenna Romp and the novices in New Jersey at the Belly of the Carnegie. The V8 was fifth behind Ohio State, Clemson and a pair of Virginia Crews with the Orange a split second behind Clemson and the Virginia B boat in the fight for third place.

Meanwhile, three Orange eights raced on Lake Carnegie, finishing eighth, 14th and 18th.

Princeton's A and B boats finished one-two, with Radcliffe third.

Winter Training

While there is a lot of hard work involved, winter and spring trips to warm climates are also a nice break from the harsh Syracuse weather and the grueling workouts in the tanks and on the ergometers.

But a little creativity combined with fitness testing also helps. In the fourth annual edition of the event, the men's crew and women's rowing teams competed in an individual triathlon and a combined team triathlon on Saturday, February 3rd. The triathlon was established to give both programs a chance to work and compete together.

"It brings the men's and women's teams together to compete in something that is both challenging and rewarding as well," Kris Sanford told *SUAthletics.com*.

The teams are made up of a varsity male and female, a freshman male and a novice female. Times were recorded for individuals and as teams.

The women ran 25 flights of stairs on the upper level of the Carrier Dome, then ran to the Flanagan Gym, got on the erg and pulled for 8,000 meters, then ran across the way to the Archbold Gymnasium pool for the final leg of the triathlon–a 500-yard swim. The men ran 30 flights of stairs, rowed 10,000 meters on the ergometer and also swam 500 yards in the pool.

Chris Liwski won the men's individual event and Jillian Kott won the women's individual event. The winning team was made up of Liwski, women's team Tri-Captain Rachael Kirchoff, Nick Alexander and Diana Stevens.

Spring 2002

Heading into the 2002 spring season the Eastern College Athletic Conference honored Kris Sanford as its Coach of the Year for 2001 based on her team's performance, the most successful ever by an SU women's rowing team.

"The Syracuse women's program has made consistent progress and come of age under Coach Sanford's tutelage," said Gary Caldwell, ECAC Director of Rowing. "I'm sure this is only the first of many for her."

"Some of the best coaches in the country are in the Sprints League, so being recognized by those coaches means a lot to me," the coach told *SUAthletics.com*.

Sanford was looking for her team to do as well or better in the upcoming season.

The Orange opened at the end of Spring Camp in Florida, sweeping races against the University of Miami and Central Florida at Creek Lake on Friday, March 15th.

Back home, the varsity eight stayed undefeated, beating Boston University and Clemson on Saturday, March 30th, on Onondaga Lake. The Orange women took the Terriers by a couple of lengths open, with the Tigers another length back.

Senior Erin Gallagher coxed the top eight with Jillian Kott at stroke, then Shannon Mercurio, Alicea Kochis, Rachael Kirchoff, Libby Graves, Kelly McGrorey, Nicole Garofalo and Bonnie Chapman.

The 2V8 also won.

Losses

Kris Sanford's varsity eight was rated seventh in the nation the next weekend as the team went to Connecticut to take on fifth-ranked Yale and Cornell on the Housatonic River. The V8 hadn't lost a dual race in nearly two years so the Orange women went in expecting to win.

They came home with a loss.

Then-six-seat Alicea Kochis wrote afterwards, "… when we entered the last part of the race only six seats down on Yale, I still thought we'd win. It wasn't until i heard a victorious yelp from the lane next to us that I knew we had lost."

"Hopefully this loss will spark a stronger desire and determination to win," she wrote. "Obviously no one wants to lose but we can use this loss as a stepping-stone. At the end of the season, I'd like to say this was a turning point."

It didn't turn out that way. The team went to Boston next, with Kochis now in the stroke seat and Jillian Kott back at two. But the weather and conditions were awful and the Orange varsity eight struggled, trailing way behind no. 19 Northeastern and Penn.

The SU novice eight did manage a win and the rest of the races were called off.

Back home on Onondaga the next weekend, the now 12th-ranked Orange took on no. 10 Radcliffe and the 'Cliffies had the better of it, sweeping the Orange fleet.

SU's varsity eight was open water back, with Dartmouth in third, well behind.

Sanford's squad prepared for the trip to Worcester to defend the Big East title no other team had ever won.

Wins

Notre Dame was starting to come on but the Orange women still led the Big East in 2002 and they showed it, winning every race but the varsity fours which was second to Notre Dame. Kott was back in the stroke seat and the universe was again was in proper alignment. The V8 took the Fighting Irish by open water, while the 2V8 edged Notre Dame by a deck.

Sanford was named Big East Coach of the Year again.

Villanova and UMass came to Onondaga for the SU seniors' final home race on May 4th and the Orange crews swept the Wildcats and Minutewomen.

It was, in effect, a warm-up for the EAWRC Sprints.

How Sanford's squad performed in Camden would determine whether it would get a third-straight invitation to the NCAAs.

The Sprints and a Team Bid

The varsity eight came into the Sprints ranked 10th in the nation and advanced to the grand final, finishing fifth behind some of the powerhouse women's crews in America. Brown, Yale and Radcliffe were one-two-three in the race.

The 2V8 and the V4 both wound up in the petite finals where each finished second. The 2V8 lost by less than a second to Columbia and the V4 trailed Brown. That was good enough.

When the bids came out for the NCAAs, Syracuse had its

first team invitation. Kris Sanford's crews would get to compete on Eagle Creek Reservoir in Indianapolis.

Again there was no Cinderella story for Syracuse at the NCAA Championships, but Sanford's crews did not turn into pumpkins either. All three boats wound up in the petite finals with the V8 fifth, a length open behind winning Yale but fighting for second to the finish. The contest wound up like this: 1) Yale 6:39.99, 2) Southern California 6:43.71, 3) Michigan 6:44.31, 4) Virginia 6:44.87, 5) Syracuse 6:45.73, 6) Harvard (Radcliffe) 6:47.46.

There was at least a small victory in getting by the 'Cliffies at last.

The 2V8 finished sixth in the petite and the V4 was fifth in its petite final.

The Orange squad finished 12th overall–quite an accomplishment. SU rowing careers had come to an end for more than a boatload of seniors. From the V8, Jillian Kott, Libby Graves, Alicea Kochis, Rachael Kirchoff, and coxswain Erin Gallagher were done. So were 2V8 members Jordan Brophy-Hilton, Odette Mitchell-Servilio and Christine Getzler.

Kott was named First-Team All-America for the third-straight year. She and Gallagher were named First-Team CRCA all Mid-Atlantic Region and Kochis and Kirchoff made the Second-Team. And let's not forget work in the classroom, Kott, Graves and Kirchoff were Mid-Atlantic Region National Scholar-Athlete Award winners for the third-straight year.

Staying among the top women's rowing teams was going to be tough.

Struggle and Personal Loss

What the rest of the world did not know in those years is what Kris Sanford and her husband Craig Milburn were going through personally. Kris had been pregnant in the spring of 2001 when the team went to Lake Lanier to race in the NCAAs. The team arrived on Monday. On Tuesday she miscarried at the team hotel. "Craig had to leave to get the team to the race," she says.

"I had five miscarriages, all on the road with the team

over the next few years. That probably was where the breakdown [in the program's success] started. The team was always great," she said. Her athletes knew the situation.

Fall – Winter 2002–2003

Sanford went into the fall of 2002 with only three women returning from her NCAA varsity eight and Kelly McGrorey, Nicole Garofalo and Bonnie Chapman had been the bow three. Coxswain through four oar had graduated and the second varsity had not been especially strong in the spring. Chapman stayed in bow but Garofolo and McGrorey moved up to stroke-seven. Chapman and Garofolo were now seniors.

McGrorey, who had cracked a veteran eight as a freshman was now a soph. There was another sophomore in the five seat who would turn out to be pretty good. She was a walk-on named Anna Goodale.

SU had made a habit of finishing second behind Radcliffe at the Stonehurst Invitational and the V8 did it again that fall, then finished 20th at the Head of the Charles. A brief fall season wrapped up in Philadelphia as the varsity eight won the championship eight competition at the Head of the Schuylkill against less-than-stellar competition.

Lehigh tied SU for the fastest time and West Virginia was third.

The time off the water in winter brought the usual. "Heavy indoor training, which includes a lot of erg work, cross training and lifting weights," Tri-Captain Leslie Wolf told *SUAthletics. com*. Winter Camp in Melbourne, Florida also brought a bug that went through the team. "Rowers had to sit out practice and were throwing up," Wolf said. She managed to escape the misery.

It was back to Florida for spring break, this time to Miami where the week-long training included double sessions each day, emphasizing shorter, intense rowing pieces along with race strategy, *SUAthletics.com* reported. There was no competition against other schools.

Spring 2003

The spring season got off to a good start on March 29th with a sweep of Boston University on the Charles River. It was windy and the varsity and 2V8 races were close but Sanford sounded happy even though wind and waves led to cancellation of the V4 race. "It was a great day because we swept all the races," she said. In the process SU won the inaugural Kittell Cup, donated by former-SU-rower Kristin Bidwell '90, and named for SU's Associate Director of Athletics Janet Kittell.

Kittell was Jake Crouthamel's right hand and Sanford says she had a huge imprint on the women's rowing program. "She fought for us tooth and nail. She made our team feel like they were wanted and needed by the Athletics Department."

It was tougher competition at home the next weekend and the Orange women finished third behind Cornell and Yale. They stayed at home and rebounded the next week, winning the Orange Challenge Cup over Penn and Northeastern. In Hanover, Sanford's V8 beat Dartmouth, but finished just over length behind Radcliffe.

The coach called it "a good showing."

Racing on Lake Quinsigamond in Worcester, the Orange V8 continued its hold on the Big East Championship as well as taking the team title. Notre Dame was second in the varsity eights, but open water back.

The Orange moved up to number 15 in the national rankings.

Home again, SU swept UMass and Villanova and kept the Orange Plus Trophy.

Eastern Sprints

The Eastern Sprints were held on the Cooper River in Camden and Kris Sanford's varsity eight fought through to the grand final. Radcliffe was the winner and the Orange eight was more than 30 seconds back. The finish was not strong enough to get the team into the NCAAs for a fourth-straight year.

The other Orange boats finished in the petite finals with

the exception of the novice four, which was second to Brown in the grand finals.

Nicole Garofalo and Anna Goodale made the CRCA Division I Mid-Atlantic All-Region First-Team, and Kelly McGrorey and Leslie Wolf were named to the Second-Team. Goodale, McGrorey and Wolf were further recognized as 2003 CRCA Division I National Scholar-Athletes.

Soon after, Goodale was named First-Team All-America. She had another two years to row for SU before she would go on to succeed at a much higher level.

Fall 2003

The fall of 2003 saw the Orange women's varsity eight finish second at the Stonehurst Regatta, sixth out of thirty-nine crews at the Princeton Chase and seventh out of sixteen in a West Coast trip to the Head of the Lake in Seattle. The novices went to the Belly of the Carnegie as had become habit in those years.

There was no ducking the top teams in the spring and in 2004 the 17th-ranked Orange varsity eight lost the opener at home to no. 16 Boston University by open water. The Terriers swept every race but the varsity four B event. A week later the Orange V8 came in third in Ithaca behind a resurgent Cornell crew and Yale.

Four days later it was announced that Kris Sanford would not coach the Orange women on the water for the rest of the season because she was on pregnancy leave. Her husband and Assistant Coach Craig Milburn took over as interim head varsity coach working with the varsity and junior varsity eights. His father-in-law, former-SU Men's Head Coach Bill Sanford would fill in as a volunteer coach and Kris Sanford would "continue to be involved as much as possible, including reviewing video and making practice decisions." She planned to return as head coach in the fall for the 2004–2005 season.

That weekend, SU beat Penn and Northeastern.

A trip to Boston brought a second-place finish behind Radcliffe and ahead of Dartmouth for both the varsity eight and the 2V8. Then it was off to Worcester for the Big East Challenge which SU had never lost.

Big East – Changes At The Top!

The Fighting Irish of Notre Dame had been steadily improving, getting closer and closer to Syracuse crews with each passing year. 2004 would turn out to be the first time Notre Dame got over the top and the Irish would then hold the team title for as long as Big East rowing continued to exist.

It wasn't really close. Notre Dame won the varsity eight grand final by a length open. Syracuse edged third-place Miami by half-a-length. Notre Dame swept the grand finals and Miami's overall finishes put the Hurricanes in second place, with the Orange in third.

On May 1st, the SU V8 stumbled badly at home in the Orange Challenge Cup race. UMass bolted off the line and grabbed the lead with the Orange second and Villanova third. SU tried to overhaul the Minutewomen in the second-thousand meters but they would have none of it, besting SU by open water.

The EAWRC Sprints held out hope for the 19th-ranked Orange to get back to the NCAAs but both the first and second eights finished fourth in the petite finals and Syracuse's season was over.

Anna Goodale was named Second Team All-America and invited to the U.S. Pre-Elite Camp. She made CRCA Mid-Atlantic Region First-Team and Kelly McGrorey made Second-Team. Goodale and sophomore Catherine "Cat" Henny earned the CRCA National Scholar-Athlete Award—Goodale for the second-straight year.

The Milburns had a healthy son. They named him Aiden.

Change at the Top

Nancy Cantor took over as Chancellor in the summer of 2004, coming from the University of Illinois. It was soon evident that she wanted to choose her own Athletics Director. Jake Crouthamel had survived 27 years in the job—but in November came word that he would retire.

On December 17th, Cantor introduced Daryl Gross, Ph. D., as the new SU Director of Athletics. Gross came from the University of Southern California where he had been Senior Associate Athletics Director. One of the first things he did was to dump head football coach Paul Pasqualoni. It would not be the last coaching change in the Gross administration, but the women's rowing program had some time.

2005

Kris Sanford had some solid athletes on her squad in the fall of 2004 but what she did not have was a lot of depth. The varsity eight finished in its traditional second place at the Stonehurst Invitational and a creditable 13th at the Head of the Charles. A 16th place finish at the Princeton Chase however was nothing to get excited about.

The women doubled up on visits to Melbourne, Florida that winter, spending both breaks in training there and scrimmaging in March against the University of Connecticut crews coached by Kris Sanford's sister Jennifer.

"We have athletic talent," Sanford told *SUAthletics.com*. "We need to put it together. We have a smaller team this year, so we can't afford injuries. But, that also means that everyone on the team has a definite place and will be expected to contribute."

The Orange opened the regular season in Boston and the varsity eight took the Kittell Cup in a terrific race against BU by a margin of less than a second. The crews went back and forth over the last 500 meters on the Charles and the Orange women got their oars in the water last. "It just showed that we were really gutsy and had a lot of heart and that is what is going to win it for us at the Big East Championship in a month," Sanford said.

There were other races before, however, and the first one took the Orange to Derby to take on no. 2 Yale and the Big Red of Cornell. Sanford's no. 18 V8 gave the Eli a fight but lost by just over a length, finishing well ahead of Cornell.

"Our goal for last weekend was to win," SU Senior Captain Anna Goodale said. "We raced a great race and came within four seconds of Yale. Although it was not a win, I feel it was a success.

I think that we came away from the race with confidence, but we realize that we have more work to do and are not satisfied."

The Orange 2V8 and 4V were third, underlining the lack of depth.

Back to Boston they went, this time to take on Northeastern and Penn for the Orange Challenge Cup with UMass also joining in. The Orange V8 had edged up to a no. 15 ranking. The V8 won but the second varsity eight and varsity four finished third, beating only UMass.

The team returned home to take on fifth-ranked Radcliffe and Dartmouth. It was a chance for the SU varsity eight to show what it had against a very good crew. Instead it got hammered. The 'Cliffies won by more than two lengths open over the Orange V8 which in turn clobbered the Big Green. Radcliffe won every race except the novice eight which went to Dartmouth.

"I think all of our crews raced really hard and put in the effort, but it obviously was not enough," Sanford said. "We will do everything we can to turn it around and get it right."

Big East

For the first time the Big East Challenge was now the official Big East Championship. Notre Dame had broken the Orange stranglehold on the Big East Challenge the year before and while the Irish kept the team title for the next decade, the Orange got the varsity eight championship back one more time in 2005.

SU had won its morning heat and Notre Dame followed suit.

Then the weather got really ugly. In a rainy, windy final on Lake Quinsigamond, the SU eight covered the 2,000 meters in 8:05.18.

Notre Dame was more than three-lengths open behind.

The Syracuse second varsity eight had won its morning heat but wound up inundated with water in the final and the Orange hopes sank with the shell.

The other Syracuse crews struggled so much that the Orange wound up fifth in the team standings behind the Irish,

Boston College, Rutgers and Connecticut.

Villanova and UMass came to Syracuse and took their medicine in the Orange Plus Cup as the Orange swept. It was a bit of payback for SU to UMass, which had pulled off the upset the year before. The races were moved up from Saturday morning to Friday evening because of predicted bad weather but the results were as expected.

The varsity eight went off to the Eastern Sprints with a no. 17 ranking, again hoping at least for the V8 to get back to the NCAAs for the first time in three years with a strong showing in Camden.

"The next two weeks will determine a lot, with final exams and graduations," Sanford said. "How we do at Eastern Sprints will depend on how each person handles everything in the next two weeks."

It turned out to be a strong showing indeed. Sanford's V8 finished 2/3 of a length behind Yale in the morning heat to move into the grand final, where the Orange edged out BU for 5th. While the crew was well behind Yale, Princeton, Brown and Radcliffe, the performance was enough to get the top Orange boat an at-large invitation to the NCAAs in Sacramento.

Makiko Muraoka coxed the boat with four-year first-boater Kelly McGrorey at stroke. Then it was Jaime Doerr, Anna Goodale, Cat Henny, Allison Doodeman, Katie Schneider, Carolyn Taylor and Shawna O'Brien in bow.

They were up against it right away, opening in a heat that included top-ranked Cal, no. 8 Stanford, no. 13 Washington and no. 14 Michigan State. SU finished fifth, meaning it had to be in the top three in the repechage to even make the semifinals. The Orange women finished seventh and wound up in the consolation race where they finished last behind Michigan State, Wisconsin and UCLA. Whatever they'd found at the Sprints, they were not able to find it again on Lake Natoma.

Goodale was back on the First-Team All-America list as a senior and McGrorey was selected as Second-Team All-America. Both were All-Region First-Team members and Goodale was named a CRCA National Scholar-Athlete for the third-straight year. She was not close to being through competing.

That summer, Goodale made the U.S. Rowing eight that would compete in the World Championships in Japan. The Americans led the first half of the race but were passed by Australia, Romania and the Netherlands, and finished in fourth place. In that Dutch eight was former-Orange rower Helen Tanger.

Tanger and Goodale had never met, but had heard a lot about each other. "I knew that Anna made the US 8+ from the SU website," Tanger told *SUAthletics.com*. "I checked which seat she was in so I would recognize her." They met and compared notes once the final was over.

Kris Sanford had boated some powerful crews and developed impressive athletes in the early years of the new century.

2005 turned out to be the last hurrah.

Chapter 28
2003–2005 – The Reischman Era: Beginnings

The Syracuse Alumni Rowing Association had a seat on the search committee that would recommend a successor for Bill Sanford in the summer of 2002.

SU's Athletics Director Jake Crouthamel had agreed to that, but like everyone else on the committee, Tom Darling was sworn to secrecy. It is possible that a close look would have detected a smile on the three-time Olympian's face. It turned out that there were several strong applicants and when the choice was announced there were many more smiles from SU Crew backers. Impressed by the miles of rowable water and the opportunity to bring a traditional program back to prominence, Dave Reischman had agreed to come east and take on the challenge.

"Dave is the real deal," Darling said. "He has all the attributes I would associate with a great coach–commitment, motivation, technical know-how and physiological expertise."

Reischman likes to call himself "a dumb farm boy from western Washington." He did grow up on a farm in Silvana, north of Seattle.

The "dumb" part is hooey. He graduated from Gonzaga University summa cum laude with a degree in computer science.

He'd rowed on a club team at Gonzaga then interned under Harry Parker at Harvard and coached the freshmen at Florida Institute of Technology, before returning to his alma mater. There he took the Gonzaga rowing program to varsity status, and qualified a crew for the IRA. He moved to Oregon State, and working without scholarships, brought his crews to the top level at the IRA.

Now he was ready to move up again.

A New Sheriff

Dave Reischman started the fall of 2002 with about thirty men on his varsity squad. By winter he had eighteen remaining. "A few of the guys quit on their own for good reasons," the new coach said then, "but the bulk of it was what I would call 'growing

301

pains.' Anytime you do a 180-degree philosophical change you are going to lose guys that were comfortable in the old system and unable to change to fit the new."

Coxswain Peter Romano recalls an early fall afternoon when at the end of practice the varsity crews bustled down the canal, swinging around slow moving or sitting high school crews to beat them to the docks. Once ashore, the new coach called Romano and fellow cox Mike Wzontek aside.

"He began a four or five minute tirade about the rules of the water, the respect of other crews, and the safety of everyone involved," Romano says.

"He went on and on–and rightfully so–about how we should never be going around crews it if involves the 'wrong' side of the river, and how even though the coast was clear it wasn't worth risking the lives of the oarsmen and the costly boats and oars that we were in control of. I knew then that Dave was going to be more of a stickler for the rules, a guy who wanted to do it right, and even though at the time I wasn't too pleased with the verbal lashing, in the end it was just the kind of structure that Syracuse Crew needed."

Reischman made it very clear very quickly that he had certain expectations for his squad members. "Most of the 'cuts' were due to lack of physical fitness or conduct not appropriate to a Syracuse oarsman," he said. What misbehavior there had been he kept within the squad. And while he would have liked greater numbers, the eighteen he had left were the kind of men he wanted. "I feel like we have eighteen guys that are committed to turning this program around and willing to do the work necessary."

"I remember that Dave was set on changing the mentality of the team, and it took some hard lessons to do so," oarsman Justin Burgess says.

"In our first meeting as a team, he set some pretty clear guidelines and expectations regarding out-of-practice activities and wanted us, as a team, to pride ourselves on academics. In my first personal meeting with Dave, I was told that I had two numbers, my erg score and my weight, and one of them needed to come down. It was up to me, and he said it jokingly, but Dave was serious about every athlete reaching his absolute maximum potential."

Training in Pairs

"If there was one thing that the crew did when I got here really well was that they were aggressive almost to the exclusion of everything else," Reischman recalls. "And I thought what they were lacking was more of an elite level feel for the boat–feel for the water, feel for how a boat moves. I think at some point they would sacrifice feel for the boat and moving together in the name of being aggressive."

Reischman often put his oarsmen in pairs during fall training and kept his coxswains in the launch, observing and learning.

"Pairs don't lie," Reischman says. "Pairs are the great truth teller of our sport along with singles. When you're in an eight all it feels to you is that you're being aggressive and it feels to you like you're moving a boat and when there are seven other idiots around you it's easy to think it's someone else and it's harder to feel exactly what effect your motions are having. If you're in a pair there's a fifty-percent chance it's you."

There's nowhere to hide in a pair without cox and sometimes, the coach says, what an oarsman could be hiding from was himself. He tells the story of an oarsman with a solid erg score, who found himself trailing the pack during practice pieces, no matter who his partner was.

"One of the coxswains said 'coach, why aren't you coaching him?' And I said 'because he isn't ready to be coached yet … because he doesn't think he's the problem yet. And when he realizes he is the problem he's going to come to me and ask me to coach him. And it's my job to show him that he is the problem.' So when the coxswain said 'well, how long's that going to take?' I said 'two-and-a-half-weeks.' So I just kept switching his partners. Every pair he was in was off the back. Two weeks later he comes into my office and says 'OK, I get it. What do I need to do?' I could have coached him 'til I was blue in the face in an eight. He never would have understood that he was the problem."

Some got the lesson faster than others did that there's

more to it than pulling hard.

"Dave's attitude towards moving the boat," Burgess says, "was that you should be exhausted at the end of a race not from pulling hard (maybe also from pulling hard) but from maintaining a rhythm that made the most use of all eight athletes' motions in a coordinated, fluid motion."

The new coach took his crews to the Head of the Charles where the eight finished thirty-third of forty-two and also to the Princeton Chase where the eight was eleventh out of twenty-two and the four finished seventh of twenty-five.

It would take three seasons for Reischman's varsity eight to get a win, but change already was evident.

Working with The Sanfords

Part of his agreement in coming to Syracuse was that Reischman would work with Kris Sanford and the women's rowing program. He was happy to do that and the coaches seemed to hit it off. Sanford and her husband Craig moved into the boathouse apartment where she had grown up and Reischman said he preferred it that way.

In the class races at the end of the fall season there was competition among eights with four men and four women rowing together. It didn't hurt that Sanford's team had just come off another spring that ended in the NCAAs and was among the top women's programs.

The new men's coach made sure to keep his predecessor involved too and Bill Sanford was very happy to be included. Sanford and his wife Nancy had moved into a house on a bluff overlooking the lake, about a mile from the boathouse. He would ride along with Reischman in practice, taking in what was new, comparing notes and giving advice when it was asked, which was with some regularity. In the spring he'd relay the stroke-by-stroke account of races from a launch to announcer John Nicholson, who would pass the information on over the public address system at the Ten Eyck Boathouse. Reischman's team dedicated a new shell to the longtime coach toward the end of the season.

Another commitment Reischman had made to then-

Athletics Director Jake Crouthamel was that he would keep Bill Sanford's Assistant Coach Chris Ludden for at least a year. He remained as freshman coach and recruiter.

"We're not going to consistently get to the grand final at the varsity level if our frosh are finishing in the third and fourth level finals," Reischman said that fall. "Coach Ludden and I have been working hard at the recruiting business and we are in contact with a lot of talented athletes–both academically and athletically. Our current frosh class is definitely a work in progress. Not a lot of size but we'll see if we can turn them into fighters."

Winter Training

Once off the water and indoors, Reischman turned to working his oarsmen into shape. "This fall we spent a lot of time changing our technique and we didn't spend a lot of time on fitness," the coach said. "That has officially changed as we move indoors–IT IS TIME TO GET IN SHAPE. You can tell the crew guys around campus … they tend to be moving very slowly when going up stairs."

"Dave introduced what I'd call 'educated training' on land," says Adlai Hurt, then a junior. "He introduced the team to the heart rate monitor. Now, instead of maintaining certain splits on the erg, you were expected to maintain a certain heart rate. For example, steady-state pieces should stay between 150–160 beats-per-minute. More anaerobic workouts would be 160–180 or max. heart rate."

After grueling sessions on the ergs, the crews got on the water in Melbourne, Florida, over winter break and in Miami during spring break, preparing for the season opener in Boston. Reischman pronounced himself pleased with improvements in the team's fitness through winter training.

"For the race, we're focusing on coming down the course with rhythm," he said. "Our emphasis is on the middle 1,000 meters and trying to row aggressively."

Spring

The coach settled on Kevin Klein as his varsity stroke to open the season. Matt O'Neill was at 7, Will Russo at 6, Andrew Wright at 5, Justin Burgess at 4, Sergei Bourlatski at 3, Mike Horvath at 2, and Pat Mahardy was in bow. Mike Wzontek was the cox.

On March 28th Reischman's varsity eight came tantalizingly close to winning its first race. The 15th-ranked Orange took on Boston University's 19th-ranked Terriers on the Charles River and lost by half-a-second.

SU led off the start but 500 meters in Reischman knew his crew was in trouble. "After 1,000 we shortened up. We got choppy." BU caught up with 800 to go but the coach was encouraged by the fact that the Terriers were not able to pull away. "With 500 we take it up to 37-1/2–38 and it got shorter and choppier and when you've got no rhythm you've got to try something and we threw everything we had at them."

The JV did get a half-length win for the new coach, rowing through the Terriers to win from behind. "They rowed sort of like I envisioned a Syracuse crew rowing," Reischman said. "We just sort of steadily came back even and came through and I thought rowed a great race."

Adlai Hurt stroked the JV backed by Matt Costigan, Steve Boselli, Kevin Boyle, Andrew Weisberg, Nick Alexander, Andrew Cooley, and Matt Brocks. Peter Romano was the cox.

Chris Ludden's freshmen got clobbered.

The next day the squad was up at 4:30 to race Brown in the rain on the Seekonk River in Providence. Bruno swept–the varsity by about a length open, the JV by several lengths–and the frosh by several more.

Still Reischman was happier with his varsity's performance than the day before. The crew stayed with the eighth-ranked Bruins in a tailwind for the first 500 meters and never gave up water in bunches. "We kept fighting hard," he said. "They [Brown] had to fight for every seat they got."

That would turn out to be the end of a series of regular season races against Brown. For years the Bruins often had rested at home while SU took on BU in Boston the day before the Sunday race in Providence, or traveled to Central New York and relaxed while the Orange and Terriers battled on Saturday, then beat up SU on Sunday.

Brown Coach "Paul Cooke and I tried to move the race to later in the year and the main reason for that was that I didn't want to race in March," Reischman says. "Not in Syracuse, Providence, or anywhere else. March is the time for selection and making the transition to race-pace-type workouts. Racing in March shortens the amount of time you have for this and often leads to issues later in the season. Paul and I looked at a lot of options but couldn't find a spot in the schedule that both of us were comfortable with."

In the 1960s and '70s SU and Brown had competed annually for the Holding Trophy, but Bill Sanford says that stopped when SU alum Steve Gladstone was Brown's head coach. He says Gladstone cited budget constraints and an administration desire to row against more Ivy League opponents, specifically Dartmouth.

When the races resumed, it seems, the trophy was not involved. By the early 2000s, "No one had seen it for a couple of years," Reischman says. "A few years after that last race I found out as I was cleaning out the attic back in a corner in a box buried under a bunch of other stuff. I cleaned it up and gave it to Brown as the winner of the last race."

The Orange had two weeks to prepare for the home opener against Rutgers but it was the Scarlet Knights who took the Ten Eyck Cup in the varsity race by more than a length of open water. "We were disappointed," Reischman said. "I don't think they rowed poorly but the lineups aren't figured out yet."

Kevin Klein and Matt O'Neill were still stroke and seven, but Andrew Wright was now six and Will Russo bucketed with Bryan Goody at five-four. Mike Horvath was at three, Bourlatski was at two and Chip Gibson in bow. Peter Romano moved up from JV to cox the varsity.

The JV got another win easily and Chris Ludden's frosh picked up a victory by a couple of lengths open.

Navy and Cornell came in for the Goes Trophy races a week later and while the varsity eight turned out to be a tremendous fight on that cold, rainy morning, the Orange crew was not in it.

The races were rowed on the old IRA course out on Onondaga Lake and the seventh-ranked Midshipmen took the no. 5 Big Red by about half-a-length with now 20th-ranked Syracuse more than ten seconds back.

Cornell won the JV and freshman races with SU in third in both.

Reischman had done some major rearranging in his varsity eight for this one with Wzontek back in as cox, Pat Mahardy at stroke, backed by Chip Gibson, Goody, Russo, Boselli, Boyle, Wright and O'Neill.

The Orange crews had a month to get set for the Eastern Sprints. This time the varsity lineup would stay the same.

Ludden Moves On

On May 2nd, it was announced that Chris Ludden would be leaving as assistant coach after the season to pursue a career in secondary education. In Worcester, his freshman eight was fourth in the morning heat, behind Harvard, Cornell and Northeastern. In the petite final the Orange frosh faded to fifth, behind Northeastern, Penn, BU and Navy.

The JV also wound up in the petite after a third-place finish in the morning. Northeastern's Huskies edged Syracuse by a deck to win the petite.

Reischman's varsity was last in the morning heat, a whisker behind BU and that dropped the Orange to the third-level final. The Orange won that one over Georgetown, Columbia and MIT.

Packard Cup and IRA – Not Yet

SARA set up a Weekend of Champions for the middle of May, welcoming back members of the 1959 Pan Am Games Crew and the 1978 IRA champions, among others. They'd witness the efforts of a team that aspired to that kind of success but was not yet close to it.

Dartmouth continued its winning streak in the Packard Cup with a length open win over the Orange. The Big Green won the JV race by a length but Ludden's freshmen walloped the Dartmouth frosh by a couple of lengths open.

At the IRA in Camden the Orange crews struggled. The freshmen were fifth in their heat and third in their rep. A fourth-place finish in the lower division semifinal meant they did not get to race on Saturday.

The JV suffered the same fate. After coming in third in its heat, the second boat was last in the repechage and fourth in the semi.

As for the varsity eight, it was fourth in the heat and last in the rep. In the semifinal the Orange just missed escaping the bottom rung. The battle for third place–and the final spot in the third-level final–came down to a photo finish as Princeton, Syracuse and Marist all crossed the line within three-tenths of a second of each other. The Tigers finished in 5:51.58, SU's time was 5:51.77, and Marist finished in 5:51.83.

On Saturday, Tony Johnson's Georgetown crew took the fourth-level final by half-a-length over SU, with Marist third.

Reischman's first season at Syracuse was over. Now he needed a new assistant coach and some fresh horses.

Fall 2003

Canada has been a source of important athletes for Syracuse rowing over the years and Canada is where Reischman went to find his new freshman coach. Phil Marshall had been coaching at Upper Canada College, a private boys' school in Toronto as well as the Brockville Rowing Club where he helped prepare rowers for the Canadian Regatta Summer Circuit. The junior men's eight he worked with won the title at the 2002 Canadian Henley.

"Phil came from a long rowing background in Canada," Reischman says. "He understood the sport. He understood boat moving on the level that it needed to be. Phil was a fun guy to row for and could connect with the kids and certainly with that crew he connected and that was a fun crew to watch race."

"That Crew" was the Class of '07–Will Aramony, Jimmy Bader, Dave Barone, Mike Beck, Jon Flynn, J.P. Geise, Tim Mambort, Matt Morrow, Tim Munz, Andrew Ross, Brett Russo,

Justin Stangel and coxswain Chad Taylor. They came with solid credentials. Five of them were in the U.S. Rowing Junior National Team Camp that summer.

Reischman signed them over some strong recruiting competition.

"I think a lot of people bought into what we were selling which was looking for kids that were interested in doing stuff that hadn't clearly been done in a long time," the coach recalls, "looking for kids who had sort of that frontiersperson spirit about them and were determined to be agents of change. I think we surprised a lot of people when we landed a couple of those guys and after you get your first one or two–Justin Stangel was the first, Matt Morrow was the second–two guys that did a lot of great work in the stern pair over those years and those guys were legit–the other pieces just fell into place for that recruiting class after that."

Spring 2004

Reischman had some horses on the varsity but they were still learning. Dan O'Shaughnessy had arrived as a transfer from Northeastern and while the plan had been to hold him out for a year, Dan O' decided he didn't want to wait. "When I saw these guys and watched them erg and thought 'Omigod I can't miss this!' Chip Gibson, Bryan Goody, that whole class of guys … ."

But the varsity eight continued to struggle, opening the season by losing at home to BU by half-a-length, then to Rutgers by a length in New Brunswick. A powerful Navy team won the Goes Trophy easily over Cornell and the Orange varsity was far back at Annapolis. "I don't think the varsity showed up to race today," Reischman said afterward. "And it's my job to get them ready to race so I take responsibility."

A week later Reischman called the home race against 15th-ranked Temple "one of our best races of the year." It was still a loss by a length open, although SU did beat Georgetown for second.

Orange boats took three of four races in Hanover two weeks after that, but it was Dartmouth winning the varsity eights and winning the Packard Cup for the 14th-straight year.

Phil Marshall's freshmen meanwhile had taken the Orange spotlight. They barely got past BU in the opener but the steamrollered an undermanned Rutgers squad, beat Navy and Cornell by open water and walloped Georgetown and Dartmouth to go undefeated into the Eastern Sprints.

Hurdles are not just for track athletes.

Things did not go as planned for the six-seed Orange frosh on Lake Quinsigamond. They fell just short of the grand final, coming in fourth in the morning heat, then slipped to last in the petite. It turned out that stroke Matt Morrow had a medical issue. His season was over.

The JV was third in the petite finals and the varsity eight wound up in the third-level final, which it won.

"The Sprints were a bit of a disaster for us," Reischman recalls. "We had to sprint like crazy not to finish last and barely beat an MIT crew that was having an off year.

"And we went home and did a lot of fours' work, a lot of seat-racing work—again tried to demonstrate to some people that we had to change what we were doing and in that process we came up with an new lineup."

Marshall shuffled the freshman lineup also, moving Stangel into the stroke seat and while the boat was strong, the Orange fell short of the IRA grand final, finishing second in the petite by rowing through Navy in the last few strokes of the race.

The JV was fifth in the petite and the varsity eight got to the third-level final, where it finished third—15th overall of twenty-four crews.

While those finishes wouldn't look impressive in years to follow, they were a significant improvement over the recent previous years, so much so that the inaugural Clayton Chapman Trophy for "most improved at the IRA" went to the Orange squad.

"We at Syracuse don't aspire to the 3rd-level finals," Reischman said afterward. "But these guys raced hard and wore the uniform well. This was definitely our best racing of the year."

At the Senior Banquet in April, he had praised the Class of '04—Nick Alexander, Kevin Boyle, Matt Brocks, Chip Gibson, Bryan Goody, Adlai Hurt, and Andrew Wright—saying, "You guys are the start of it and I will make sure you are not forgotten."

Years later he would tell this story about the 2004 IRA: "In both the semifinal and the final we were back a little early, and we were able to come through some crews in the second thousand and that's a sign that you're starting to understand rhythm and you're starting to understand how to race the full 2K distance. There were times in the first two years that we would be in the race at the 1,000 and then we would fall off pace in the second thousand."

Explaining the success, Reischman continues: "I can't remember if it was after the semi or after the final–Chip Gibson coming up to me and very emotionally telling me that that was the first time in the four years of rowing that he actually passed somebody in a rowing race; that he actually in the second thousand moved past other crews. So, that was a key turning point that was the first time that I saw a rhythm."

Fall 2004

Chancellor Cantor had announced SU Athletics Director Jake Crouthamel's retirement in November. While the retirement would not be official until the following June, Crouthamel was gone from his office soon after the announcement.

Crouthamel had pronounced himself a supporter of rowing, citing fraternity brothers who were on the crew at Dartmouth when he played football there. He'd given SARA a spot on the search committee that identified Reischman as the man to replace Bill Sanford in the fall of 2002. He had shown up for home races, many times standing on the boathouse balcony, smoking the ever-present cigarette. Now he would be gone and by the end of the year, Daryl Gross would arrive from USC to take over.

Recruiting had not been as successful for the Class of '08 as it had been for the previous years. Reischman and Marshall were in the hunt for some highly-coveted athletes but did not land them. There would still be gems among the group that did sign on with the Orange. And Marshall upgraded the search for walk-ons, running a physical education class that brought in forty men willing to give rowing a go. Marshall said he'd identified seventeen oarsmen and three coxswains to join the four experienced rowers on the team.

On the varsity squad, freshman stroke Matt Morrow was back and building strength during the fall season, while sophomore Jimmy Bader and Dan O'Shaughnessy put in stints in the stroke seat.

The Class of '07 already was having an impact, with six sophomores in the varsity eight for the Princeton Chase, including Morrow in bow. The crews had not done badly there or at the Head of the Charles, but the coach said, "It drives me absolutely nuts that Cornell and Navy have two boats that beat us."

Winter – Changes in Equipment and Approach

Indoor training was done in improved facilities that winter. SARA dedicated the new "Bill Compson Erg Room" in the Flanagan Gym with its 50 new ergometers. And the tanks in the "Jock Stratton Crew Room" got a long-needed overhaul. "We've redone the guts of the tank from oarlock to oarlock," Reischman said. During winter break the big, old, noisy motors in the giant orange boxes were replaced with new, quieter, more efficient motors.

Looking back years later, Reischman said he'd made some mistakes in approach in his first two years at Syracuse. "We were trying to adapt our program we had at Oregon State and we were on the water year round and I think we got–the first year I ran a very similar program and I thought we'll just do some of our water stuff on land–on the ergometers and that will be fine and I think that first year we got to February 1st and the guys were fried. The intensity level was too much."

"The second year we made it to the middle of February before I thought 'man, these guys are cooked.'" Now with the refurbished tanks and the new erg room, the coaches found ways to change things up and get better results.

Reischman remembers "me and Phil Marshall sitting down with a jigsaw and an old set of oars and trying different shapes and changing the size of the slot in the middle of the oar and trying different length oars to get a load that felt right in the tanks. So out of that we had another tool in our bag to teach technique and we could avoid sitting on the erg day after bloody day and staring at a number.

"Whenever we're in this room we can mix it up. So we not only had an effective teaching tool, we had an effective training tool.

"The third year we made it through the winter and I felt like we were eager the whole time, and were making improvements the whole time instead of reaching those points where we were mentally tired and burned out and the tank I think was the first step in that.

"The next evolution was 'OK, we can get body positioning. We can get blade work and make improvements over Christmas on those over winter training so that to the point where we went back on the water we were better in those areas–what's the part we were missing out of that? A sense of rowing together, a sense of rhythm.'

"And that's where we really started experimenting with the slider configurations that we use so that whenever we were in Flanagan, again, we got off the stationary erg. We got on the sliders. We practiced team rowing and how to move together. We'd practice movement skills.

"You learn push timing on the sliders. You learn rhythm on the sliders. And it takes the 'distraction of the oar' out of the way. To get good push timing in a boat you don't focus on the oar. That's one of the biggest mistakes in rowing. And this came as a younger coach of seeing crews and seeing a blade that's late and looking at the guys and saying, 'catch timing is off,' and they would look at me quizzically and say, 'No, it feels pretty good.' And there were other times when I would look at a crew and the blade work would be right on and I'd say, 'yeah the catch timing is great' and the guys would look at me and say, 'It feels bad.' And the problem is that, is the blade work important to catch timing, yes, but not as important as having eight guys pushing on the foot stretcher at the same time. So you can put your weight on the foot stretcher and push and if your blade's not in it's going to have a greater effect on the feel of the boat than the blade timing. That's what the sliders taught us. It got rid of the distraction of the blade and taught us how to feel for the push timing which is the most important part of the catch timing.

"So I felt we now had a program and a system that could keep us mentally engaged through the winter and not hit these stagnant points like 'oh, no! We are sitting on a stationary erg rowing by ourselves again.' We needed to keep them engaged and make them feel that they were continuing doing something other than suffering for those weeks. And adding those two components I think were huge to being able to do that to keep us mentally fresher for when we got back on the water."

The team went to Florida for winter break and again in March and returned looking to move up to the next level in collegiate crew. Five seniors and seven juniors were on the varsity roster along with the dozen in the sophomore class.

Spring 2005

Perhaps the most important individual in that group was Dan O'Shaughnessy, the Canadian transfer from Northeastern. Reischman characterized him as "an agent of change. He gave the guys some character. He was a voice from within the ranks that said 'we can do this.'"

O'Shaughnessy had rowed for the Canadian Junior National Team, won gold at the Canadian Henley and after graduating from SU would go on to row for Cambridge and win "The Boat Race" over Oxford.

The sophomores were a "Super Class," then-junior Dan O'Shaughnessy recalls. "They'd even beaten the varsity in a couple of pieces as frosh, so they came up with a lot of confidence. But they were young and they didn't know what it was going to take to be a varsity level kind of guy."

The season did not start, to quote Coach Al McGuire, as "seashells and balloons." The sophomore-laden varsity lost its opener on the Charles by a length to a highly-regarded Boston University eight.

O'Shaughnessy and senior Andrew Cooley were the only non-sophs in the boat. BU swept every race but the second frosh.

SU was to take on Rutgers at home next, but weather in

Syracuse forced moving it to Princeton, where the 19th-ranked Scarlet Knights took the 16th-ranked Orange by a length. SU's JV and frosh were winners.

SU trailed Navy and Cornell for the Goes Trophy in Ithaca. The JV and second frosh were third while the first frosh were disqualified.

Then, on April 24th the Orange varsity eight finally got a win for Coach Dave and did it by a length of open water on the Schuylkill River. Temple got the oars in last to edge Georgetown for second, but it was the Orange collecting the shirts.

The JV also won but the freshmen were half-a-second back of Georgetown.

Back home, two weeks later the Orange varsity was two lengths open behind Dartmouth, although the JV and freshman eights won.

At the Eastern Sprints the varsity was fourth in the third-level finals; the JV 3rd in the petite finals, and the frosh won their third-level finals. The second frosh made the grand finals and finished fourth.

In Camden, the V8 was up a spot from the year before, taking second in the IRA 3rd level behind Cornell–14th overall; the JV was 6th in the petite finals, and the frosh 5th in the third-level finals.

The freshman four came in second in the third-level finals.

Reischman had a single varsity eight win to show for his first three years–but there was more to it.

"Those guys did what I call the 'hard miles,'" the coach recalls. "They were putting in a lot of work and not seeing much reward on the race course. Change, on the level we were trying to do it, is very hard. I think it is easy to think that the effort wasn't there because of our lack of success. That wasn't the case. After every race we would talk about staying the course. About how it was the nature of our sport to test your perseverance to make sure you were worthy. I suspect the guys were tired of hearing me say, 'good things come to those who keep working hard.' We talked a lot about how easy it is in life to start pointing fingers in these situations and about how the harder choice is to stay accountable for your own contributions. I am eternally grateful that those guys stuck it out. The result of their efforts was that by the time those three years were done we had a culture and a program that was the foundation for the successful years to come."

A year later the varsity would not lose a single cup race and would vault into the Top-10.

Chapter 29
2006–2009 – The Orange Returns to the Upper Level!

T he Orange squad picked up another major player in the fall of 2005 when Bartosz Szczyrba transferred in from Dowling College.

Reischman was always looking for game changers and the junior from Poznan, Poland was just that.

Fellow transfer Dan O'Shaughnessy tells it this way, "He had so much belief in himself and everybody around him. He just thought you were going to win. He was really contagious and he was with a group of talented guys."

Those talented guys were now juniors. O'Shaughnessy, having been granted a third year of eligibility at SU, was co-captain along with Tyler Page. "The Super Class had matured a lot," O'Shaughnessy says. "They now understood that we have to put the work in to actually be really good. This was just different from the beginning–more a sense of mission–enjoying the belief."

Fall Results

With O'Shaughnessy stroking and Szczyrba at seven, the varsity eight came in 4th at the Stonehurst Invitational, 14th at the Head of the Charles, then third at the Princeton Chase. Matt Morrow was again on the sidelines.

After the racing on Lake Carnegie, Page, who rowed in bow, told *SUAthletics.com*: "This race was a good chance for us to see a lot of the other programs and it was a good opportunity to see where we are at relative to the other programs. We had some troubles at the first two races but we took it all in stride and have been racing faster and faster each race."

"Reischman, though pleased with his team's results at the Princeton Chase, told his team that this is a great start but must carry this momentum into the spring season," *SUAthletics.com* reported.

"I thought we raced hard today and accomplished what

319

we've been working towards," he said. "I emphasized to the guys after the race that it's fall racing, it's like the preseason, we showed that we are on track and now it's up to us to keep working and use this to carry us into the spring."

Winter Training

The squad had newly refurbished tanks to work in that winter and there was plenty of work done there and on the ergs. The team went to Miami for winter break and did a lot of rowing in fours which Reischman said helped him start to get a good feel for who would be in which eight once the season began.

There would be another training trip to Florida over spring break.

Co-Captains Tyler Page and Dan O'Shaughnessy answered questions for SARA Directors who took a break from their annual meeting in late January to visit the Bill Compson Erg Room during a workout. Both said team spirit and attitude were high. "We can't wait to get on the water," O'Shaughnessy said. "Everyone is pushing everyone else hard."

"We just need to keep working hard," Page said.

Reischman described his own attitude as "cautious optimism." "I've got a great squad this year," he said. "They've got a lot of commitment. They make it fun for us as coaches." As he spoke, more than three eights worth of varsity oarsmen were blasting away on the ergs. That was the assigned workout. Reischman said oarsmen are doing additional work on their own.

"Their motto is 'friends don't let friends erg alone,'" he said.

Spring Season 2006

Coaches voting in the preseason poll did not see the Orange varsity as a boat full of world beaters. They ranked the crew 16th nationally.

The season started in miserable conditions in New Brunswick, New Jersey and Reischman's varsity trounced Rutgers by several lengths open to win the Ten Eyck Cup for the first time in four years. Morrow was back in the stroke seat, with Stangel at seven, Szczyrba at six, O'Shaughnessy at five, Dave Barone at four, Tim Mambort at three, Terry Wilkin at two, and Ryan Armstrong in bow.

"Morrow didn't row that fall," O'Shaughnessy recalls. "And he was like a maestro in the stroke seat. When he moved back everyone was so much more comfortable. You can really lay on it in the five seat. There was a lot less confusion and questioning. Everyone seemed to know what we were doing."

The JV also won easily but the freshmen trailed.

"At Rutgers we were rowing in the apocalypse," O'Shaughnessy says. "We started behind and soon enough were miles ahead, thinking 'Holy s**t! This is good.' Everybody was doing their bit and from there it felt great. It just built on itself. At the Goes Cup we lined up again. I remember being halfway through the race–we dusted Cornell and Navy. Not in a million years would they expect to be behind Syracuse. Their wheels fell off like they used to fall off for us. We just kept going."

Racing at home, the now 14th-ranked Orange beat no. 8 Navy by nearly three lengths of open water, with no. 13 Cornell another couple of lengths behind. It was the first Goes Trophy win for Syracuse since 1999.

The JV and 3V also won with the freshmen second behind Cornell.

After the racing the team and alumni grouped in front of the boathouse to honor Dr. Bruce Chamberlain for his service to SU rowing. The 86-year-old co-founder of SARA beamed as family members christened a new shell named for him. There's no doubt that "The Doc" was honored but he was at least equally pleased with the turnaround in the SU crews' fortunes.

"I've been waiting a long time for results like these," he said.

The Orange jumped to no. 9 in the U.S. Rowing Coaches Poll and headed for Boston, where the varsity knocked off no. 10 BU by a length, with no. 19 Columbia trailing. That broke a three-year BU streak in the Conlan Cup competition. The JV was second to BU and the frosh finished third.

SU's varsity crept up to no. 8 in the poll and went to

Philadelphia, where the crews swept Temple and Virginia.

Reischman's men had one more cup streak to break. Dartmouth had taken the Packard Cup fifteen years in a row. In getting it back at last, Syracuse made it look easy. The varsity race on the Connecticut River in Hanover saw the Orange finish in 5:46.3 to the Big Green's 6:10.6. The JV and 3V both beat Dartmouth's JV and the frosh completed the sweep.

Syracuse's varsity eight was going into the Eastern Sprints unbeaten. The Orange carried a no. 8 national ranking and a six-seed at the Sprints–theoretically favored to make the grand finals.

Heartbreak was ahead.

Split Seconds

"If you're undefeated and you're not number one, you haven't arranged your schedule right," a smiling but serious Reischman said before the Sprints. The Orange had not faced any of the teams ranked above it. That was about to change.

The morning heat in Worcester pitted Syracuse's varsity against the top-seed Princeton, then no. 1 in the nation and seven-seed Yale, ranked tenth in the Coaches Poll. Say "bang, bang, bang" as fast as you can and you probably can't say it as fast as the finish was. SU came within four-tenths of a second of Princeton. But Yale came within two-tenths of a second. No. 1 and top-seed Princeton finished at 5:59.547, no. 10 Yale at 5:59.782, no. 8 Syracuse at 5:59.971.

"If you watched that race how could you be disappointed in the effort the guys put into it?" Reischman asked afterward. "It was the best effort of the season and that is all you can ask for as a coach."

The varsity went out and took the petite final in the afternoon, beating Cornell and Navy again in the process.

The JV eight was third in the morning heat and third in the petite finals, in a tight race with BU and Cornell. With a last-place finish in the morning, the freshmen fell to the third level, which they won over Dartmouth, MIT and Columbia.

Having just missed the grand final at the Sprints, the varsity set its sights on the top level at the IRA where the competition would be even tougher with Washington and Cal joining in.

"These guys are not afraid to race anybody," Reischman said during IRA Camp. "They don't care who it is. They just want to race."

"We had a really good IRA Camp," O'Shaughnessy says. "The ones I'd been at before were pretty loose. On this one I think people knew we had a shot. Guys were more serious about what they did outside of practice."

Storms had been rolling though the Camden area in the days before the IRA and SU lined up next to Princeton and Yale again in the first qualifying heat on the swollen Cooper River. Bartosz Szczyrba had been moved into the stroke seat, to give Matt Morrow a bit of a break after stroking all year. Princeton and Yale battled stroke-for-stroke to qualify and SU trailed in third. That afternoon Morrow returned to the stroke seat and the Orange won the repechage, getting into the A / B semifinals for the first time in the twenty-first century.

"Matt had the magic touch," Dan O'Shaughnessy says.

Overnight storms led to even higher water greeting the crews on Friday and the Orange lined up with Yale, California, Harvard, Northeastern and Penn in the first semifinal. Somewhere around 900–850 meters to go, with SU in third, leading Northeastern by a couple of seats and Harvard by seven or eight, the "Dr. Bruce Baker"–named for Bruce Baker '59–crashed into what Co-Captain O'Shaughnessy described as a huge pile of weeds–floating debris in lane five.

"The boat was going as well as it could," Reischman recalled several years later. "We had 3/4 of a length on Harvard and Northeastern had just taken a move to get within two seats. Coxswain Chad Taylor told Morrow it was time to respond and said he saw the stroke grinning from ear to ear. The boat jumped for the first three strokes." And then, "The guys felt like they hit a truck," Reischman said. As Taylor fought to get the debris out of the rudder, Northeastern and Harvard rolled by within ten strokes. Harvard wound up edging Northeastern for the third qualifying spot to join Yale and Cal in the grand finals. Syracuse recovered to finish fifth over Penn. Then SU protested because of the obstruction.

The Orange wanted a spot in a seventh lane for the grand final.

"They said it's an outdoor sport," O'Shaughnessy recalls. "It stops being an outdoor sport when you clean Harvard's lane but you don't have time to clean Syracuse's lane. We won the protest but then Northeastern protested."

The protest went into the night because having finished ahead of Syracuse in the semifinal, Northeastern argued that letting the Orange in and keeping the Huskies out would be unfair. The proposed settlement was to have Northeastern and Syracuse race at dawn for the seventh grand final spot.

"When I got back to the hotel I got the guys together and I said 'this is what's been decided,'" Reischman says. "And I could see that their eyes kind of went down. And Dan O'Shaughnessy spoke for the crew and said, 'Coach, we've been talking this over and there's nothing anybody in this crew wants more than to row in a grand final. But people are going to question it. If we make the grand final–if we beat Northeastern and we make it in–the winner is going to be in no shape to race a grand final and the loser is going to go into the petite and have no legs left to do anything. We don't want this program's first grand final in a long time to have an asterisk next to it. So … we would rather give those people in the grand final a tip of our hats and take our medicine and say, you know what it was bad luck that we hit those weeds and we're going to go race our butts off in that petite. We want it to be honorable and … we just don't think back-dooring our way into a grand final is the way we want to do it.'"

"It's one of those moments when, as a coach you realize these guys get it," Reischman reflects. "These guys understand what it's about. And so we called Northeastern and said, 'thanks very much.' We called the race committee and said 'we're going to decline. We are going to race in the petite.'"

On Saturday the freshmen raced in the third-level final and finished third. The varsity four did the same.

The JV made the petite and finished a half-length or so behind Cornell and California, in third.

In the varsity eight petite finals, the three crews that just missed the grand final battled for seventh place. The Orange led at the halfway point but Northeastern and Wisconsin slipped past. Syracuse fought back and got through the Badgers in the last ten strokes, but came up just short of the Huskies. The petite finals' times looked like this: Northeastern 5:43.61, Syracuse 5:45.41, Wisconsin 5:45.91. Cornell, Navy and Penn finished behind.

"There's nobody in this sport that I respect more than Harry Parker," Reischman says. "And there's nobody that has done more for my coaching career than Harry Parker. And that was the only time in 26 years that I thought I had him 'dead to rights.'"

"On top of that you have a group of guys that had given me everything that year and had bought into what we were doing and this was the big payoff. Would we have beaten Harvard or Northeastern straight up in that semi? I don't know, to be perfectly honest with you. I know the strength of that crew all year long was the second thousand; had been their ability to be closers. So I sure would have liked to see it play out."

The Syracuse varsity eight that had been ranked 16th in the preseason poll, finished eighth. Dan O'Shaughnessy's collegiate career was over, along with those of varsity two-man Terry Wilkin, JV-stroke Adam Conrad and Co-Captain Tyler Page. The Super Class of 2007 had one more chance.

2007

Now the members of Dave Reischman's first highly-touted class of recruits were seniors. The program plainly was at a much higher level than when the coach has arrived. But they missed the IRA grand final through a stroke of bad fortune. This was the last chance to prove this class belonged among the elite of men's collegiate rowing.

O'Shaughnessy was gone, graduated and off to row for Cambridge.

The fall racing season opened October 9th in Rochester with what was now called the Head of the Genesee Regatta and the Orange showed it had some speed, although not quite as much as Brown.

The event included a morning 5,000-meter race and for

the top-dozen finishers, an afternoon 1,500-meter dual race. The Orange varsity eight was second in the morning, three seconds behind Bruno.

Going against each other in the afternoon, Brown covered the sprint distance about eight seconds faster than Reischman's V8 did and when times were multiplied and added by the regatta's formula, Brown had won the overall event in 26:56.98 to SU's 27:25.09. Syracuse's second eight was sixth in the same competition and the third boat was seventh, just 18 seconds behind.

Bartosz Szczyrba stroked the first eight, with Justin Stangel at 7, Marko Trnavcevic at 6, Martin Etem at 5, Jimmy Bader at 4, Tim Mambort at 3, Matt Morrow at 2 and Ryan Armstrong in bow. Chad Taylor coxed.

Thirteen days later at the Head of the Charles, the Orange V8 was 12th, sixth among collegiate crews.

Miserable weather greeted the crews on Lake Carnegie for the Princeton Chase the following weekend. Princeton wound up chasing Yale with the Orange varsity eight in third, and the fours racing was canceled because of the poor conditions.

The fall season wrapped up with the Syracuse Invitational, a head race finishing in front of the Syracuse Boathouse. Racing in fours, the Orange 4A boat finished second to Cornell.

"We had a really breakout season last year," Reischman said afterwards. "We had an undefeated cup season and bring back six members of that varsity eight. We have a sophomore and a transfer student who have really proved themselves and could be a part of that boat. The other teams in our league really haven't lost much from last year, so it should be an exciting season."

Winter

The Orange men trained hard through the winter, wrapping up with a spring break training trip to Columbia, South Carolina. Reischman said conditions there "were the best we have seen in the five years I have been here. I think we had a ripple, and I mean slight ripple, on the water twice in twelve practices."

The crews and coaches took advantage of it, Reischman

recalls. "After about three days of getting the feel for the water back we pretty much used the rest of the week for seat racing with a couple of recovery rows in between so no one accused the coaching staff of cruel and unusual punishment. We made a lot of good technical changes over the winter by alternating between the ergs, sliders, and tank. The guys seem to have a more uniform rhythm and we seem to be able to get in decent rows even though we are changing lineups daily, or several times in a practice as the case may be."

Back in Syracuse the team found the ice melting off the Seneca River but the water was high, and that brought with it the usual problems including the stray tree limb and an occasional ice floe. Everybody hoped for higher temperatures.

SU backers had probably hoped for a higher preseason ranking but the U.S. Rowing Coaches Poll had Reischman's men just outside the Top-10 at no. 11. The coach and his team were not concerned.

"When you have confidence in yourself and your boatmates–that they are doing everything they can to make the boat go fast–all the other worries just sort of disappear," Reischman said.

Spring

After scrimmaging against a tough Yale squad the Orange opened the spring season at home against Rutgers and swept the Scarlet Knights who had lost numbers when it was announced that their program was no longer going to be a varsity sport.

Matt Morrow was back in the stroke seat with Bartosz Szczyrba, who handled those duties in the fall, at six where he belonged.

The first big test came on the Severn River early on a Friday morning and the Orange varsity passed it. SU rowed through Cornell in the last 250 meters of the Goes Trophy race, with Navy trailing. Navy wound up being awarded second after a protest that the Big Red had encroached on its lane, but the race plainly was between Syracuse and Cornell. With that 250 meters left, four-man Dave Barone said afterward, "It was like 'it's time to go right now' and we did!" It was the first time since 1959 that the Orange had won the Goes Trophy two years in a row.

Reischman warned afterward that Cornell would be better as the season wore on and the Orange surely would see the Big Red again. For now, Syracuse rose to no. 9 in the U.S. Rowing Coaches Poll and headed for New York, where the varsity out-rowed Columbia's Lions with BU behind. Once again Syracuse headed for the Eastern Sprints unbeaten and the 6th-seeded Orange were determined not to miss the grand final this time.

Sprints

Chad Taylor was still the V8 cox and most of the oarsmen were seniors: Morrow stroking, Justin Stangel at 7, Szczyrba at 6, Dave Barone at 4, J.P. Geise at 3, and Jimmy Bader at 2. The only non-seniors to break into the boat were Martin Etem at 5 and Ryan Armstrong in bow.

While Morrow had set the pace since their freshman year, it was Stangel who was the horse now.

"Matt was a rhythm guy," Reischman says, "a fierce racer–needed a backup. Stangel is a very willing backup. Stangel is going to go in a race. He's an incredibly talented racer."

The big man from Wisconsin was never a guy to give in to pain. It turned out he'd been having pain since about two weeks before the Sprints.

Reischman says he and trainer Brad Pike kept close watch on Stangel and limited his workouts leading up the Sprints. "The pain that Justin presented to me at the time didn't sound like a rib injury," Reischman says.

"Brad and I were pretty good at predicting these things or so we thought."

When the crews lined up that Sunday morning in Worcester, Stangel was in his usual spot, ready to give it everything. He certainly did.

Three strokes in, Stangel heard a pop. But he kept pulling as did the rest of the eight and while the Orange men could not catch top-seed Harvard, they were second, qualifying at last for the grand final.

To do it they beat the Big Red of Cornell by less than a second.

"Chad Taylor comes up to me afterwards," Reischman recalls, "and says 'something's wrong with Justin.' I walk over to Justin and I'm like 'What's wrong?' 'Nothing.' I said, 'Justin, I can tell that something's wrong' and Justin said 'Coach, there's no way you're taking me out for this final.'"

Stangel iced himself in the hours between the heat and the final and then wrapped his rib cage in an ace bandage and declared himself "good to go." But as the team warmed up, a referee's boat accidentally cut off the Orange crew and Chad Taylor ordered the oarsmen to hold water. The coxswain later told the coach he could see the blood drain out of Stangel's face. The pain was excruciating. Still the crew went off and finished last in the final. It was not a good race for other reasons, the coach says.

Back home a day later, X-rays confirmed that Stangel had broken two ribs. In the world of "couldas, shouldas and wouldas" Reischman says he should have held Stangel out before the Sprints.

"I made a mistake. It was a bad decision. The mistake was–and I haven't made that mistake since … if it's ribs we fix them." Stangel's senior season was over. The crew's season was not.

Reischman shuffled the boat and the varsity managed to get by Dartmouth before going into IRA Camp. When the Orange squad headed for Camden the first eight looked like this: Chad Taylor at cox–Matt Morrow, Andrew Ross, Bartosz Szczyrba, Martin Etem, Marko Trnavcevic, J.P. Geise, Dave Barone and Ryan Armstrong.

The Orange had the nine-seed which meant an opening heat on Thursday morning against the top-seed Washington and eight-seed Brown. SU did not pull the upset, finishing third, and when Oregon State crossed half-a-length ahead of SU in the afternoon rep, the SU crew wound up in the lower half semifinals.

The frosh eight also wound up in the lower semis, but the JV jumped right to the upper semis with a second place behind top-seed Wisconsin in the opening heat.

On Friday, SU's open four and varsity four without cox

won repechages and moved to the Saturday grand finals.

But the JV was fourth, once slot short of the grands and headed for the petites.

The frosh and varsity eights got into the third-level finals; the frosh taking second in their semi and the varsity third, behind Virginia and BU.

Saturday

The Syracuse alumni eight won the masters championship on Saturday morning, edging Cornell with Brown, Navy and a couple of Penn eights behind.

Other than that, the bright spot for Syracuse on Saturday was a third-place finish by the varsity four without cox, behind Navy and Hobart. Mike Beck stroked it, backed by Mike Bagnall, Ryan Knapp and Bill Della Giustina. The Syracuse open four was sixth in the grands.

The JV was third in the petite final behind the Harvard B boat and Penn.

The freshman eight was fourth in the third-level final.

And for the varsity eight, the season that had started with such great hopes ended with a fifth-place finish in the third-level finals. In a race that had all six crews fighting all the way down the course, Boston University took Navy by 2/3 of a length, with Virginia in third, half-a-second behind, Georgetown a couple of seats back in fourth, SU not even a deck back in fifth and Penn another hair behind in sixth.

"These seniors put their put their heart and soul into the program," Reischman said then. "It's not how any of us wanted it to end."

Typically, Reischman was still putting a lot of the blame on himself in an interview five years later. "You think back on things as a coach and it was on me. In those three weeks we couldn't find the rhythm. It might be psychological more than anything else to lose a guy–like Stangel–that is the heart and soul of a boat as anybody, but we couldn't find a combination that generated the same rhythm that we needed."

Henley

Reischman took two crews to Henley that summer–the first time under his leadership that SU had gone. During the training period, the Orange went to Boston and worked with Harry Parker's Harvard crew for four days. "I thought both boats came away from that trip with some nice rhythm and the ability to do it under the pressure of racing," Reischman said afterward.

Each won its opening race and then was defeated in the next round. The first boat lost to Brown, the second to West England. "The guys raced hard all the way down the race course," Reischman said. Stangel had not healed enough to race there. Perhaps ironically, he would get his chance the following year as he went off to row and advance his education at Oxford. A couple of other varsity oarsmen missed the trip because of commitments to summer internships, so the first eight was a combination of varsity and JV and the second was a combination of JV and third-boat guys.

"I think Henley was a great learning experience, particularly for me," Reischman said that summer. "I'd been over there to watch the racing once but this was the first time I had taken my own crew."

"I hope we get the chance to go again," the coach said then.

Fall 2007

Phil Marshall ended his stint as freshman coach after the 2007 season and returned to coaching in Canada. He'd shepherded that graduating class to success as freshmen and seen them go all the way through. "Trying to be a freshman coach in our league at a place like Syracuse I think has a high turnout rate," Reischman reflects. "I think that the amount of effort that you need to put in recruiting, into shaping young men is very high and when you're putting in 80 hours a week I think it grinds on you after a while."

Dave Weiss–an assistant who had coached the frosh at George Washington University–was chosen to take over the coaching slot.

The departure of the Class of '07 left SU with just two oarsmen who'd been in the varsity eight that spring: Martin Etem and Ryan Armstrong. So–rebuilding?

"I don't believe in rebuilding years," Reischman said that summer. "The job is always the same–take a group of athletes and make them go as fast as you can."

To do that, he put his oarsmen into pairs and they rowed a lot of miles working on technique and boat moving. He'd set the lineups just a couple of days ahead of the regattas they entered.

The Orange competed at the Princeton Chase, the Syracuse Invitational and the Foot of the Charles and while the results were not stellar, the coach seemed unconcerned. "The goal was to really enjoy racing hard and not get too caught up in the lineups or where we were finishing."

"I know this group is working hard," the coach said. "As hard as any group I have ever had."

Spring 2008

The schedule was stepped up a bit in the spring of 2008. To start things off, Reischman took his varsity eight to face the big boys at the San Diego Invitational and big boys they were. The Orange eight was in a qualifying heat with defending IRA-Champion Washington, Harvard and Stanford, as well as Oregon State, UC San Diego and Colgate. SU took fourth, about a length behind third-place Stanford and well behind winning Washington and second-place Harvard.

The Orange then went out and won the petite final by about a length over Oregon State.

Coming back east, Syracuse went to the George Washington Invitational and came home with the Oliver T. Carr Bowl for the highest men's point total. The only SU boat to suffer a loss was the second freshman eight. In the process the varsity held onto the Ten Eyck Trophy by beating Rutgers in the morning heat.

The Orange beat Cornell and Navy for the Goes Trophy for the third-straight year, something no SU crew had done before. This time the race was in Ithaca and the crew that got it done

332

consisted of coxswain Jamie Hubbell, Ryan Armstrong at stroke, Ryan Patton at 7, Martin Etem at 6, Brian Azeff at 5, Tyson Bry at 4, Mike Bagnall at 3, John Combs at 2, and Dan Lombardi in bow. Armstrong, Combs and Lombardi were the only seniors in the boat. The frosh also won with Navy second.

The JV finished second to the Big Red as did the second frosh.

A week later racing at home the now eleventh-ranked Orange varsity lost to seventh-ranked Columbia by a little over a length. SU held onto the Conlan Cup by beating Boston University. SU's JV and two freshman boats were winners.

In Hanover the varsity made it three Packard Cups in a row over Dartmouth and the Syracuse crews swept the Big Green.

The freshmen were Syracuse's top finishers at the Eastern Sprints, making the grand final with a second-place finish behind Harvard in the morning heat. In the afternoon they finished sixth. Athletes who would be key to SU's success in the next three years were in that crew: Kenny Marfilius was cox and Mike Gennaro stroke. The Berry twins—Dan and Vince—were at seven and five with Dan Turner between them at six. The bow four included Matt Hopek at four, Kyle Daugherty at three, Chip Keyes at two and Julian Morrison in bow.

The JV was third in the morning heat, then won the petite final over Yale, Navy, Georgetown, Columbia and Boston U.

For the varsity eight, morning disappointment led to a poor finish in the afternoon. The Orange could not catch Brown and Columbia in the heat, then wound up fourth in the petite behind Navy, Harvard and Cornell.

During IRA Camp, Reischman made some changes, moving Azeff up to seven and putting Clai White in at five and Mike McHarris at four.

The IRA

The Orange freshman eight had the best showing for SU at the IRA and the fact that it was fourth in the petite final—a 10th-place finish overall—indicates that it was a disappointing year for the rejuvenated faithful.

The freshman four was second in the third-level finals and the JV fifth in the third-level finals.

As for the varsity, it finished in the lower half of the field. SU was fifth in its opening heat, then lost the repechage to Princeton by open water. Once in the semis the varsity performed to its no. 13 ranking and won the third-level finals by a bow ball over Oregon State. While the cup racing season once again had turned out quite satisfactorily from a fan standpoint, the crew was not doing what the coach set out to do—its best at the Eastern Sprints and the IRA.

The freshmen who would move to varsity in the fall included four Philadelphia guys: coxswain Kenny Marfilius, stroke Mike Gennaro, Vince and Dan Berry, plus Canadian Dan Turner. All would become regulars in the first eight for the next three years.

Only Gennaro was an "A-recruit," Reischman says. But the coaches had learned to find guys who were good fits for the squad. "We got the best athletes we could but we had to develop them. From freshman to senior year [we] had to take B-level athletes and coach the living daylights out of them to get them ready by their junior year."

These guys would be pretty good even as sophomores. Then they would get better.

Fall 2008

There was one man Reischman identified as key going into the next school year. As a sophomore, Martin Etem, the California surfer-turned-oarsman had broken into the senior-dominated varsity eight and held down the five seat. He was now a senior and the coach expected the squad to follow Etem's lead.

The Syracuse men opened the 2008 fall season at the Princeton Chase with the varsity eight set like this: Etem stroked with Dan Berry at 7, Mike Gennaro at 6, Vince Berry at 5, Dan Turner at 4, Mike Bagnall at 3, Clai White at 2, and Brian Azeff in bow. Jamie Hubbell was the cox and the Orange placed fifth with a time of 13:27.083. Yale won the race in 13:17.595.

Kenny Marfilius coxed the JV that day and the crew

finished 26th.

The V8 broke into two boats for the fours competition and finished third and sixth.

"I think the results in the both the eights and fours says we are on track," Reischman said afterward. "It serves notice that we finished fifth and were only seconds seconds behind the winner. Our eight boat had a good day and our 4A and 4B boats also raced well. We need to spend a little more time on our second varsity squad to see what they are all about."

Racing against less daunting competition at home in the Syracuse Invitational, the Orange four of Etem, Gennaro and the Berry brothers, with Marfilius coxing won the "A Flight" in a romp over Cornell. The freshman eight also won its race easily, with the Big Red second.

The same four did it again in Boston on November 22nd, this time in much faster company. The Orange A crew won the Foot of the Charles with Harvard A in second place less than two seconds behind.

Syracuse's 4B boat was ninth, with Jamie Hubbell coxing and Dan Turner at stroke, backed by Brian Azeff, Clai White and Ryan Patton.

Syracuse's freshman eight was fifth out of nineteen crews.

Reischman is never willing to make much of fall results, but allowed that "it was a good day and not just for our V4A boat, but for all our boats. We continued to show improvement and raced hard in tough conditions."

A Crew of Distinction

That fall, thirty years after winning the IRA, Bill Sanford and his 1978 varsity eight became the first team winners of SU's Letterwinner of Distinction. Coming to Manley Fieldhouse for the ceremony, the eight oarsmen, coxswain and two coaches, Bill Sanford and Drew Harrison were all together again for the first time since that summer. Stroke Art Sibley, Bill Reid, Tom Evancie, Bill Purdy, Dave Townsley, John Shamlian, Andy Mogish, Jr., Gerry Henwood and cox Ozzie Street were all on hand.

"270 years of living that have gone on since we won the

335

IRA and we're all here together," Gerry Henwood said. "That's saying something that we're all here as a team, able to come back together and be healthy and be here."

"It's as if our friendships were renewed after being away from each other for a week–a bunch of great, great guys," Street added. "Solid citizens, great parents and mothers and fathers and it's wonderful, wonderful to see them again."

The reunited championship crew went out for a row together and looked sharp, still. And when it was over they threw Ozzie Street into the water. He came out smiling.

Winter

Dave Reischman's crew headed for the tanks and the ergs as winter closed in, dealing with first semester finals before heading for Florida over winter break and then South Carolina for spring break. The spring season would begin and end in California and some people in the collegiate rowing world were not thrilled about the ending spot.

The IRA had decided to head west every four years and the 2009 championship races were to be held on Lake Natoma in Sacramento.

For the first time crews would have to reach a certain performance level to get an IRA invitation–it was no longer a given for SU or anyone else that an invitation would come.

And among other changes was the elimination of most of the small boat competition.

Orange alumni squawked, with former-SARA President Rick Holland putting it this way, "It strikes me that these moves will: 1–reduce the opportunity for students to participate in a full season of rowing, 2–have negligible effect on increasing the visibility and popularity of the sport, and 3–drive up cost to travel to the vast majority of athletes to get to the regatta's destination du jour; all in the name of allowing the IRA to operate more like national championship events for other sports."

But team members expressed support. "Most of the rowers and their families are excited about this move," said Ryan Knapp '08. "A chance to go to California is a big opportunity which most student athletes hold in high regard. This is a good move for the sport and will strengthen our program."

Coach Reischman ended the discussion. "As well as the traditional format of the IRA has served the sport over the past three decades or so [since small boats were added], rowing is trying hard to adapt to an ever-changing collegiate environment. It's important that rowing does not relearn the lesson of the dinosaur–if you don't adapt to a changing environment you become extinct."

He and his team set about earning an invitation to Sacramento.

Spring 2009

Both Reischman and Captain Martin Etem called the spring of 2009 "A Season of Belief." Etem had been using his experience with top crewmen at the summer 2008 Under-23 Camp to motivate himself and the rest of the team with the belief that SU could row with anybody.

"I learned through seat racing, through being with those guys that you have to believe no matter what size you are, what team you're on, no matter what you want you've got to believe that you can be there, that you deserve to be there," Etem told *The Orange Oar* in January. "You've got to believe in yourself and the guys around you. I believe that will promote a harder work ethic and you'll be able to go a lot further and be in the dog fight."

The Syracuse varsity eight began the season ranked 13th in the U.S. Rowing Coaches Poll and headed for San Diego and the Crew Classic against some of the top collegiate teams in the country. The crew turned out to look a lot like the two fours that had done so well in the fall. Kenny Marfilius was cox facing Mike Gennaro at stroke. Then it was Vince Berry, Martin Etem, Dan Berry, Dan Turner, Brian Azeff, Tyson Bry and Ryan Patton in bow.

They were fourth in the morning heat behind Washington, Harvard and Brown with a length between Bruno and the Orange.

"Equal parts disappointment and encouragement about the race," Head Coach Dave Reischman said. "We are disappointed that we did not make the grand final, but when you finish a length off the second and third-ranked crews in our league, it's a good marker as to where we are and where we need to be."

The Orange then went out and won the petite final, taking Yale by a length, with Oregon State, Michigan and Purdue behind.

The performance in San Diego moved SU into the no. 10 spot in the Coaches Poll.

Syracuse's three-year winning streak in the Goes Trophy race ended at home on April 18th with a four-second loss to Cornell. Navy finished well behind the Orange. The loss also snapped Syracuse's three-year undefeated cup race streak and marked SU's first loss in a cup race since it lost the Packard Cup to Dartmouth on May 8, 2005.

The Orange JV took the Big Red and the Midshipmen but that was the only win for SU. The frosh and third varsity were second to Cornell and the second frosh trailed Cornell and Navy.

Having fallen to no. 10 in the poll, the V8 got back to winning a week later, knocking off no. 7 Columbia and no. 11 Boston University on the Charles River in Boston. The Orange crossed 2/3 of a length ahead of the Terriers with the Lions a couple of lengths farther back.

The win over BU gave SU the Conlan Cup for the fourth-straight year.

"I think Cornell was kind enough last week to show us some of our shortcomings and we did a good job of refocusing and working on those," Reischman said. "We got out to about a two-seat lead in the first 500 and extended that to about a four-seat advantage at the thousand. BU threw two good pushes at us, but we did not panic and were able to handle both."

The freshman eight and varsity four also won but BU prevented an Orange sweep with an open water win in the JV race. SU was second.

Eastern Sprints

BU got back at the Orange varsity in the morning heats at the Eastern Sprints. Wisconsin, BU and Syracuse tore down the 2,000 meters on Lake Quinsigamond with two spots available in the grand final.

The Badgers crossed first in 5:48.022, followed by the Terriers in 5:48.10, and then the Orange in 5:48.312. Reischman's crew was .29 seconds from winning the heat, but consigned to the petites.

That turned out to be another bang-bang final with a revitalized Columbia crew taking the Orange by a bow ball.

"I saw a lot of good things today," Reischman said. "The guys were disappointed to not make the final, but I can't fault their effort as they all raced very well. I think we just let the morning race results linger too long."

The JV and freshman eights also wound up in the petites with the frosh winning theirs and the JV taking second in its race.

The third varsity eight made the grand final and finished fifth.

The Orange varsity came home ranked no. 11 and a week later swept Dartmouth, securing the Packard Cup for the fourth-straight year. The Big Green was ranked no. 14 but SU led from the start and won by several lengths open.

The JV and third varsity cruised past Dartmouth's eights and the frosh completed the sweep with the closest race of the day, still an open water win. After a floating start in rough water, the two boats stayed close until Syracuse finally took control. And while Dartmouth challenged the Orange down the final stretch, SU's freshman eight won in 6:32.9 to the Big Green's 6:36.4.

Another two weeks of practice and it was off to Sacramento.

IRA 2009

With a good-sized group of West Coast SU alums looking on, Harvard and Brown fought at the front of SU's Thursday morning heat and both qualified for the semis, leaving the Orange having to win the afternoon repechage to make the upper-level semifinal. That's exactly what the crew did, taking Oregon State by open water.

The Orange would have to get past Washington, Stanford or Brown on Friday to make the grand final and that didn't happen.

Washington won the semi with Stanford two seconds back. Brown took third, a length ahead of the Orange, who did out-row Cornell and Northeastern. So it would be the petites for SU.

The Orange JV also came in third in its heat and because of the smaller number of entries had to wait until Friday for the rep. When it came, BU and SU fought side-by-side through the first 1,500 meters only to have the Terriers get away in the last 500, qualifying for the grand final by open water. The Syracuse second boat also would race in the petite final, as would the frosh, who were third in their opening heat and second to Wisconsin in the Friday repechage.

Syracuse's open four with cox got to the grand final with a second-place finish in its rep.

Saturday

The Syracuse alumni eight started Saturday off right, winning the masters race easily over Cornell, Stanford, Gonzaga and Cal.

The SU open four got past Princeton in the last 500 to come in fifth in the grand final. The frosh eight fought the Tiger cubs all the way down the course, but Princeton never gave up its early lead and SU's freshmen were second in the petite final by half-a-second.

The petite final for the second varsity eights was the most exciting finish of the day on Lake Natoma. Stanford edged out off the start with Cornell second and the Orange right behind with 500 meters gone. By the halfway point SU had gotten ahead of the Big Red and trailed Stanford by a second. With 500 to go SU had cut the lead to half-a-second. And when the crews crossed the finish line, the naked eye could discern no difference between them.

The finish line camera could discern the difference, however, and it showed: Syracuse finished in a time of 6:02.118 with Stanford barely back at 6:02.122.

Per the photo, Syracuse won by a bow ball.

Boston University's varsity eight had continued its banner year after the early loss to Syracuse, and capped it with a third-place finish in the semi on Friday, edging out five-seed Wisconsin by two-fifths of a second. When the Badgers lined for the petite at noon on Saturday, they were not going to be beaten again.

Five crews were tightly bunched after 500 meters, with Columbia and Cornell dead even, Northeastern just behind, then Wisconsin and Syracuse. Only Dartmouth had fallen back. The Badgers powered through to take a lead over Cornell at 1,000 meters and the Orange came along, now just a second behind the Big Red. With 500 left, Wisco had open water and Cornell in second had maybe a deck on SU.

The Orange blasted through in the last 500 and while Wisconsin was an open water winner, Syracuse took second by a length over the Big Red. Northeastern, Dartmouth and Columbia followed.

It was the best SU finish in the V8s since 2006 when the crew had its heart broken by weeds in the rudder. The Syracuse crews had finished above their seeds.

The SU careers were over for six-man and Captain Martin Etem and five-man Marko Trnavcevic, but the rest of the V8 would return along with five of the JV oars and a boatload of strong freshmen moving up to varsity.

"I thought it was a great day," Reischman said. "Good racing across the board. All of our crews finished eighth or better, which is a great finish for us. I am pleased with the racing and the effort and hopefully we can use this as a springboard to a few grand finals in the near future."

His words turned out to be prophetic.

Chapter 30
2006–2010 – Years of Struggle

K ris Sanford's husband Craig Milburn stepped aside as assistant coach after the 2005 season and was succeeded by Sarah Cannon who came from an assistant job at Connecticut College. Cannon had been captain of the rowing team at Bates College in Maine, graduating in 2000.

The opening race of the fall of 2005 did not look like a good omen for the Orange women. They finished fifth in the varsity eight behind Western Ontario, Williams, Colgate and Radcliffe. The V4A boat finished in third while the V4B boat placed in fourth. The V8B crew finished 19th.

The next race was at the Head of the Charles where SU's V8 was 25th out of forty-six crews. Looking for something positive to say, *SUAthletics.com* reported "Out of the five Big East crews that competed in the Championship Eights, SU placed the highest. Rutgers (18:14.248) finished the closest in 27th. Georgetown (18:18.292) placed 29th, Connecticut finished 40th (19:00.450), and West Virginia (19:06.271) placed 42nd to round out the Big East competitors."

That wasn't saying much. The next weekend the V8 had a 19th-place finish at the Princeton Chase. Tina Campagna was the coxswain with Jaime Doerr stroking, Cat Henny at seven, then Lindsay Lentini, Karlyn Downing, Casey Irving, Ally Doodeman, Ruth Frantz and Erica Mahon. Sanford had changed out her coxswain and six, three, two and bow oars.

Orange varsity fours took the top two spots in the Syracuse Fall Race but the strongest competition was from UConn and the University of Buffalo.

The fall wrap-up came all the way across the country at the Head of the Lake Regatta on the waters where Kris Sanford had rowed so successfully in college–Lake Washington in Seattle. This time the V8 consisted of cox Erin Cunningham, Jaime Doerr still at stroke, Erica Mahon, Lindsay Lentini, Cat Henny, Ruth Frantz, Karlyn Downing, Ineke DeSimone and Ally Doodeman. The order of finish was Washington State, Yale, Washington, UCLA, Stanford, Oregon State, Victoria, Duke, British Columbia,

Gonzaga, and then Syracuse. The Orange finished two seconds behind Gonzaga and a full minute behind the winning-Huskies' time in the three-mile race.

It was time for winter training and the Orange squad had a lot of work to do.

Turkey Trot, Christmas Wrapping and a Texas Trip

The women's team got out into the community in between the ergometer and tank training that late fall and winter. The athletes ran in costumes in a 3-1/2-mile Turkey Trot on November 28th and wrapped Christmas presents at the Carousel Center to raise money for Home for the Bereaved, the National Council for Negro Women, and Vera House.

Kris Sanford decided to go for a change of pace from the years in Florida and winter break training had the SU women in the capital of Texas, rowing in Austin in eights, fours, and pairs with mixed lineups as well as ranked boats. A blue and orange race wrapped it up on the last day with the crew captained by Katie Schneider taking the honors.

Back indoors the coach interviewed her team Captain Ineke DeSimone for *SUAthletics.com* and she sounded upbeat. "The team's attitude has stayed positive," DeSimone said. "People have not settled in to a routine, they continue to work hard and improve, which has made this winter training seem very short.

"For spring break training, the goal is to apply all the hard work we have done over the fall and the winter to racing on the water. This trip is the last time we have to fully focus on our rowing and training before we get in to our spring racing season and we intend on taking full advantage of it," she added.

Off they went to Melbourne, Florida, for a spring training trip that ended with a third-place finish in the Governor's Cup Regatta behind Central Florida and Columbia.

Spring 2006

The Orange came home to Syracuse but soon was off to the West Coast again, this time racing in the Windermere Classic in Redwood Shores, California. The V8 had three races over two days and lost them all, to Oregon State, no. 15 Stanford and no. 10 Washington, each time by open water. The second varsity eight fared no better, losing to Stanford, Washington and Boston University.

Heavy rain and strong headwinds greeted the Orange, Yale and Cornell on April Fools' Day in Syracuse. *SUAthletics. com* described the conditions as "harsh throughout the morning." Weather led to some course adjustments and delays and when they got going it was no. 4 Yale that handled the conditions best, as the Bulldog V8 rowed away from the Orange and Big Red. They fought back and forth throughout the race but Cornell wound up second by more than a length.

Syracuse's best showing was a second place behind Yale in the 2V8.

A week later the Orange hosted Alumnae Weekend, honoring plus-size supermodel and author Emme and U.S. Olympian Tracy Rude Smith as part of the gathering. The guests on the water were Northeastern and Penn in the Orange Challenge Cup and while Penn did not spoil the SU party, the Huskies took four of five races with the SU varsity eight way behind in second and only the Orange novice eight getting a win.

They headed for Hanover next to take on Radcliffe and Dartmouth and the V8 came home with another third-place finish. No. 19 Dartmouth pulled off the upset over no. 8 Radcliffe but SU was not within shouting distance.

The second varsity managed a second-place finish between a pair of Radcliffe crews. The Big Green trailed.

At that point the varsity eight lined up this way: Erin Cunningham in the coxswain's seat, Cat Henny now the stroke with Casey Irving at seven. Then Ally Doodeman, Katie Schneider, Lindsay Lentini, Ineke DeSimone, Karlyn Downing and Andrea Mueller.

The V8 was rearranged again before the Big East Championships. Tina Campagna was back in the V8 cox seat and while Cat Henny was still the stroke, Schneider moved up to seven, swapping with Irving who went to the five-seat. Likewise, Mueller moved to three and DeSimone to the bow.

Notre Dame asserted itself that year as the top V8 and the top squad in the league and would stay there from 2006 on. Louisville was second in the varsity eights and team standings and the Orange finished third.

There was a glimmer of hope in the Eastern Sprints but it died out quickly with both the V8 and the 2V8 finishing second in the petite finals.

Senior Cat Henny and junior Katie Schneider were both named to the CRCA Mid-Atlantic All-Region First-Team. Sophomore Allison Doodeman was selected to the Second-Team. Doodeman was the first Orange sophomore to be recognized by the CRCA since 2003 when Anna Goodale and Leslie Wolf were both named to All-Region Teams.

Henny, Mueller and Karlyn Downing were named National Scholar-Athletes.

2007–2010

The next four years saw the Syracuse women's crews slip out of contention with the top collegiate rowing programs. The Orange women won the Kittell Cup from BU in 2007 and 2010 and the Orange Challenge Cup from Penn and Northeastern in 2009, but other than that it was mostly losses, sometimes by large margins to Yale and Cornell, Radcliffe and Dartmouth, Penn and Northeastern and BU. Notre Dame dominated the Big East with Louisville also moving ahead of the Orange. Each spring season ended at the Eastern Sprints with the Orange V8 and 2V8 in the petite finals with no chance for an NCAA bid.

Sanford tried a variety of approaches including stricter standards for the athletes keeping in shape over the summer and integrating Pilates and yoga into their training. The coach says there were some athletes who caused problems. "We were getting into a more and more entitled group," she says. "And that was our fault. We recruited them."

"You start every year and you think it's going to be different," she reflects. "I think I was pretty unhappy in the position watching these other teams get the stuff [scholarships and assistant coaches] that they're allowed to get."

There were flashes of hope. In 2007 Sanford's team had its best overall finish ever in the Sprints, sixth place, but that was done on the success of the lower boats. The coach seemed to see a good sign there, telling *SUAthletics.com*: "The majority of our team is freshmen and sophomores and that shows a lot for the future of our program. It shows we are going in the right direction and this speed will show in the higher boats next season."

Senior Katie Schneider was named a First-Team Regional All-America for the second year in a row, while fellow senior Karlyn Downing was again recognized as a CRCA National Scholar-Athlete.

That summer Assistant Coach Sarah Cannon left for a position at the University of Virginia and was replaced by a member of Sanford's top teams, Alicea Kochis. "Her experience as an athlete here at Syracuse included being part of the group that brought the team from being mediocre to being one of the best crews in the country in 2001," Sanford said then. "She knows firsthand what it takes to reach the top and will be instrumental in helping to direct the team toward the same success that she saw while rowing here."

The predictions of good things to come in the 2008 season turned out not to come true. The only teams the V8 beat during the dual season were Boston College, Gonzaga and Texas. The varsity and JV eights both finished fourth in the Sprints petite finals.

Allison Doodeman, now a senior, was named to the CRCA All-America Second-Team and Regional First-Team, while freshman Natalie Mastracci earned CRCA Mid-Atlantic Region Second-Team honors.

Both rowed for the Canadian Under-23 Team that summer.

The biggest success for SU rowers that summer came for alumnae Anna Goodale and Helen Tanger. Goodale's USA eight won gold in Beijing and Tanger's Dutch crew got the silver medals.

In 2009, a second-place finish behind Yale but ahead of Cornell in the Cayuga Cup race was cause for optimism. "Even though we did not beat Yale, today was a good day for Syracuse rowing," said senior V8 coxswain Kate Todd. "We rowed a hard, fast, gutsy race and accomplished our goal. We will take the momentum from this weekend into our race with Penn and Northeastern next Saturday."

Sure enough, SU got the Orange Cup at home. "We had a really good start and walked through our competition during the first 500 meters," said senior stroke Liz Henwood, whose father Gerry was in the SU Men's 1978 IRA Champion V8. "They tried to make a move in the middle of the race and we were able to hold them by starting our sprint early. Our race plan was to win and we followed that plan very well."

But the Big East Championships brought a fourth-place finish for the V8 behind Notre Dame, Louisville and Georgetown and the Sprints saw the Orange women in the petites. The novice eight did win the Big East grand final and was sixth at the Sprints.

Kochis was named the CRCA Mid-Atlantic Region Assistant Coach of the Year.

Senior Liz Henwood and sophomore Natalie Mastracci were named to the CRCA Mid-Atlantic All-Region team. Henwood earned First-Team accolades, while Mastracci was named to the Second-Team for the second-consecutive year.

Mastracci won gold and silver medals competing in the Canada Games that summer. Sophomore rower Rachael Ogundiran was invited to train at the Women's National Pre-Elite Camp.

The 2010 spring season got off to a good start with a V8 win over BU on a bone-chilling day at home. The Orange went to Ithaca next, looking to beat Cornell and give highly-rated Yale a fight. Instead it was Yale and Cornell fighting to the finish, with Yale first and Syracuse far back. That took the starch out of SU which lost to Gonzaga in Ithaca the next day and just managed to edge Buffalo by a length.

Losses to Northeastern and Penn and Radcliffe and Dartmouth followed before the squad headed west to the site of Kris Sanford's glory years as a rower, Lake Washington. The Windermere Cup event was a festival for Huskies fans who crowded the edge of the course in yachts on the water and by the thousands on the shore.

Washington took the SU women's and men's varsity eights without difficulty, while both Orange boats finished second ahead of Oxford.

The women's 2V8 was third behind Washington and Western Washington.

Back on the right coast it was another third-place finish in the Big East and more petite finals at the Sprints.

Coach Kris Moves On

It is an understatement to say that Kris Sanford's relationship with Athletics Director Daryl Gross was never what it had been with Jake Crouthamel and that was okay as long as team was winning. But as the losses and margins of loss piled up the writing seemed to be on the wall.

Sanford says she told Gross in her first meeting with him that family would always be her first priority. She says she and her husband Craig decided then that Craig would get out of coaching right away. She hung in there.

Asked soon after the 2010 season whether she was going to retire, Sanford told *The Orange Oar* that was not her plan. But she said if she did leave it might be good for the program because she expected that Gross would give her successor the second assistant coach she'd wanted for a long time.

On June 10th it was announced that she indeed was retiring and would pursue a new career as a nurse.

Looking back, she says she had made a plan. She'd always wanted to become a nurse and so when it was announced that she was leaving the program the plan for nursing school was in place.

"I don't think I could have made the team any faster because Daryl was never going to give me anything, and he told me that," Sanford says.

"He was not going to increase my budget. He was not going to give me another coach. He was not going to give us anything that would make us equal to the other programs because he didn't feel like I was the right person. That's athletics. That's just the way it is."

The new head coach turned out to be Justin Moore. And Kris Sanford's prediction came true.

Chapter 31
2010–2011 – Into the Grands

It was a short fall racing season for the Orange men in 2009, the entire schedule consisting of the Princeton Chase and the Syracuse Invitational.

The varsity eight had Kenny Marfilius coxing with Mike Gennaro, Dan and Vince Berry and Dan Turner in the stern four. They also made up the V4A boat. The bow four in the eight and in the V4B boat were Nemanja Bogdanovic, Ryan Patton, Tyson Bry and Kynan Reelick with Isaac Budmen at cox.

Princeton won both events with the Syracuse men's varsity eight finishing sixth on Lake Carnegie with a time of 13:30.115, while SU's second varsity eight placed 25th with a time of 14:19.719. The Orange varsity 4A finished second with the varsity 4B coming in thirty-first.

Plainly there was a big gap between the stern four and the bow four.

Racing at home in the Syracuse Invitational on Halloween, the Syracuse A boat finished first, with three Cornell fours following before the Syracuse B boat in fifth. The Syracuse C boat was another two places back.

The freshman eight was second behind Cornell.

Pan Am Games Gold Medal Crew

The highlight of the fall was the return to Long Branch of the gold-medal-winning crew from the 1959 Pan Am Games. The seven surviving oarsmen and cox Jerry Winkelstein were inducted into the Syracuse Rowing Hall of Fame on a chilly but sunny day in a ceremony at the Ten Eyck Boathouse.

Winkelstein, stroke Charlie Mills, captain and seven-man Jim Kries, Nelson Miller, Ed Montesi, Tom Rouen, Bob Schoel and Jim Edmonds were there. Commodore Lou Buhrmaster was honored along with backup coxswain Charlie Roberts who joined them at his teammates' insistence.

They remembered Mike Larsen who died in Idaho in 2001.

"He was a great guy," said Chuck Levy '60, who filled in at four when they went out on the water before the ceremony. He adds, "A great guy to row with and great guy to have as a friend."

And they remembered The Bear–Coach Loren Schoel. "My father would be very, very proud," two-man Bob Schoel told the crowd.

"I cut my teeth in rowing listening to stories about Loren Schoel and the '59 Pan Am Crew," said SU Head Coach Dave Reischman, who got coaching from Nelson Miller in college. "To finally get to meet these guys and see them in action and to see the joy and the camaraderie that they still obviously have with being together, it means a lot to our program to have these guys around."

And Reischman remembered something Nelson Miller had told him in his third week of rowing at Gonzaga. "Rowing is a disease," he said. "And you'll never get rid of it."

Nobody seemed the worse for that.

Winter Training: Trials and Tribulation But No Excuses

The men's squad went through some trials during the fall and winter, including illness that cost some practice time and a winter break training trip to Louisiana that had a strong upside but also led Reischman to compare to "The Seven Plagues of Egypt."

It started with the crew trailer sliding off an icy Thruway and wrecking a good chunk of SU's shell stock. It continued with mud, ice and a downpour in Louisiana plus the theft of boat motors and oarsmen's shoes and climaxed with leaking and thus unusable tanks back in Archbold Gymnasium.

"It's kind of fun to tell that story and play the 'woe is me card' but nobody in our program is playing that card," Reischman said. "We've got a pretty resilient group of guys."

About $200,000-worth of shells were destroyed or damaged and while insurance covered most of the loss, the team had to make some adjustments, with more training in eights than Reischman had planned, rather than in smaller boats. "The rowing aspect of it was really good," he said. "It was a great camp. We definitely plan on going back. It was a positive experience."

For spring break they went to Columbia, South Carolina.

"The varsity boat will be a majority of juniors and sophomores–that's the strength of our program," Reischman told the SARA Directors at their annual meeting. "It's a group that is understated about it but pretty keen to go fast. There's a lot of erging and rowing left to prove who deserves the seats."

At that annual meeting, with very little fanfare–although she was presented with a pink gavel as a gag–Tracy Smith became the first woman elected President of SARA. The vote for the former Olympian was unanimous.

Spring 2010 – A Grand Finish

Without a single home race, the spring of 2010 was an up and down season for the Orange competing in what was SU's most ambitious schedule in more than a decade. It finished on the highest note in a long time.

SU's varsity eight opened the season by returning to San Diego and this time made the grand final, finishing third behind California and Brown. The U.S. Rowing Coaches Poll ranked SU 5th, its highest spot ever.

Now juniors, Kenny Marfilius and Mike Gennaro still occupied the cox and stroke seats, but big Chris Lutz, a sophomore moved in at seven. Dan Turner and Vince Berry held in the engine room at six and five. Then it was Tyson Bry, Mike Dietrick, Ryan Patton and Dan Berry in bow.

The Orange crew was riding high. But three weeks later the Goes Trophy stayed with Cornell in a photo finish on rough water at Annapolis.

Reischman's men recovered and held on to the Conlan Cup with a win over BU and Columbia in Pelham, New York, and then headed west again for their biggest challenge yet–top-ranked Washington.

An estimated 40,000 spectators watched from the shore and aboard pleasure craft as the Huskies defeated the Orange by more than a length open, but SU managed to out-row an Oxford eight that had come across the pond and the continent to take part. UW's junior varsity eight also won the Erickson Cascade Cup with a time of 5:42.4, finishing eight seconds ahead of Syracuse and twenty-seven seconds ahead of Oregon State.

"It was a good day," Reischman said afterward. "I think we did some of our best racing of the year so far. It's tough to say that when you lose, but Washington is the top-ranked crew in the country for a reason. Both crews executed the way we wanted to in a crazy environment you don't see anywhere else in collegiate rowing."

In Worcester–where the Orange was expected to make the grand final of the Eastern Sprints–the varsity was third in the morning heat, behind a flying 12-seed Dartmouth crew and top-seed Brown.

Disappointed at the loss, SU was edged out by Cornell in the petite final.

"I thought we gave the petite away," Reischman says, reflecting. "I thought that our disappointment carried over into the petite. And that hangover from that sort of lasted through the Dartmouth race the next week."

The Big Green came out flying again on the Connecticut River and instead of revenge the Orange tasted defeat again, ending its Packard Cup streak.

"We were trying to race a power-based 35-1/2 to 36 and Dartmouth rowed 38," the SU coach says. "I just sort of got the sense that we needed a change."

During IRA Camp they shortened the oars "a little bit" and started rowing at 38 to match Dartmouth. "To do that we had to change the lineup I thought," Reischman says. "I thought we had to get Vince Berry closer to the stern." He also put in a bucket and moved Ryan Patton to the bow.

In By a Whisker

They went to the Cooper River as the IRA ten-seed and battled through to the semis where they lined up against top-seeds Washington and California, 9-seed Columbia, 11-seed Northeastern and 15-seed Boston University.

The Huskies and Golden Bears ran away from the pack and the Orange got out into third place, seemingly cruising to the third and last spot to make the grand final. But in the far outside lane, the Terriers were coming.

Senior three-man Tyson Bry said the cox shouted a warning to stroke Mike Gennaro. "With about 400 meters to go Kenny just goes 'Mike, BU!' We all take a glance over and they're cruising, like, son, they're sprinting coming through us. We just bump it up a couple beats and try to hang on."

When the two crews crossed the finish line even the public address announcer thought the Terriers had done it. "We were all heads down, smacking the oars on the water and they were celebrating and throwing water in the air," Bry said.

But Powerhouse Timing told a different story. Syracuse finished in 5:40.111. BU had finished just two-hundredths of a second back at 5:40.131.

Reischman had raced along the shore on his bike and couldn't tell with the naked eye who'd won.

"I sprinted ahead on my bike to be right on the line. BU was surging right as the bows were about at the line. At the line of buoys BU was ahead. If I had to bet I thought BU maybe had got us. I thought, 'I am so tired of giving the speech about near misses.'"

But as he got to the staging area he was greeted with congratulations. "I ran into the Cornell coaches and then Wisconsin Coach Chris Clark. And the only thing I could think of was 'about frickin' time.'"

"We got to the shore and I think it was like the Wisco coach was holding up 'three' to us and Coach Reischman came onto the dock and pounds his chest when he realized that we actually got it," Bry said.

For the first time since 1990, an SU men's crew was in the IRA grand final.

With a large contingent of SU alums cheering them on including most of the crew that had just missed in 2007, the varsity went after it again in the grand final but didn't have enough to pull off another surprise. As California upset Washington for the title, and Cornell out-dueled Harvard for third place, the Orange finished a length behind Brown, winding up sixth.

"It was tough," senior bowman Ryan Patton said afterward. "We took our shot. From the minute he dropped the

355

flag we went physically all out as far as we could."

"It's not the result you want," junior stroke Mike Gennaro added. "You always want to win but given the last three weeks, I think we showed a lot of character."

As for Coach Dave Reischman, "I told them I was proud of them. It's been a rough couple of weeks I think in people's minds and I think in that process they learned to really trust each other."

The Jayvee won the IRA petites, knocking off Princeton, Northeastern and Yale which had been seeded ahead of them. The varsity four was third in the petites and only the 11th-seeded frosh did not perform to their ranking, slipping to the third-level finals which they then won.

Summer – Change And An Awful Accident

That summer Assistant Coach Dave Weiss left quietly. Reischman replaced him with Shawn Bagnall, who had rowed for Washington State and coached there and at Reischman's alma mater, Gonzaga, where he'd earned a master's degree. "It was obvious from the beginning when we talked on the phone this was the person I was looking for," Reischman told *The Orange Oar*. "This is a person that has a similar ethic as I do. This is a person that has a passion for recruiting, which we need. It's about having athletes. So it was pretty obvious choice in my mind."

It was a bicycle ride in Belarus that nearly led to disaster. While coaching a U.S. Team, Reischman crashed, suffering multiple injuries that included shattering one arm. He flew back to the States for surgery. Some people might have expected a coach who was that badly hurt to sit out the year and recuperate.

Anybody who knew Dave Reischman knew better.

"I think as head of the program, the guys come into an important year and they know their coach is banged up and they want to know if you're OK," he said not long afterwards. "So I think you adopt an attitude that 'this isn't going to slow me down one bit. You'd better keep up.' It's sort of my approach to things anyway."

He didn't miss a day and didn't talk much about his

injuries after that.

2011 – The Weight of Expectations

Only four members of the varsity and JV eights were seniors in the spring of 2010: Ryan Patton and Tyson Bry from the varsity and Clai White and Peter Kruse from the JV. With a ton of experienced and successful oarsmen and coxes returning, the Orange appeared set for a regular place among the top-level crews.

As fall practice began, Reischman spoke about the weight of expectations.

"You can pat yourself on the back and think, 'well we made the finals,' a task increasingly harder to do. But I think you can have one of two responses to that: you can get satisfied and have the 'we have arrived syndrome' and think because you've got so many oarsmen coming back that it will be easy to do the same thing. And the answer is our league is really, really tough as the racing at the IRA showed out. I mean we got to the final by point-zero-two seconds and everybody at the time I think was like, 'Oh that must have been the easier semi.' And then BU goes and wins the petite, so clearly it was a pretty tough semi. I think these guys have done a great job of ... I told them when they left at the IRA, I said 'I'll know the first time I see you in the fall how you're going to approach this year.' And the guys have come back fit. We have a few guys who have some weight control issues and they've already got the weight under control and they're in fighting shape that way, so we'll see.

"To have a successful year you need a lot of things to go your way. You need to be injury free. You need to catch some luck along the way and I think that we've got some challenges. The challenges this year are going to be greater. Maybe people think they owe you one or two from last year. But again the goal is the Sprints and the IRA. We haven't cracked the Sprints, not yet. That's a major focus of what we're trying to do and then to go back to the IRA and see if we can't have another good regatta from heat to finals."

Autumn Racing / Winter Training

Fall racing opened at the Head of the Charles with the Syracuse eight finishing 16th out of thirty-five crews.

SU crews finished well at the Princeton Chase, with an Orange eight taking second and the top varsity four winning its race.

The Orange V4 was first at the Syracuse Invitational in a field that included Cornell crews.

At the Foot of the Charles the V4 was third, the 2V4 was eighth and the freshman eight took fourth.

Reischman has never been willing to make much of fall results but did concede this: "We have had a useful fall racing season—the challenge for us is to keep moving forward for the next three months while we are training indoors."

And indoors they went to the tanks and the ergs with a couple of southern trips over winter break and spring break, emerging with the seniors Mike Gennaro and Vince Berry as co-captains.

A week before Christmas, Reischman was honored at the Joy of Sculling Coaching Conference as University Men's Coach of the Year for leading the crew to its sixth-place-IRA finish. SU's new women's coach Justin Moore won College Women's Coach of the Year award for his sixth Division III title at Williams College.

Spring 2011

Syracuse headed for Princeton and scrimmages with the Tigers and Georgetown Hoyas, carrying a no. 7 ranking in the preseason U.S. Rowing Coaches Poll. SU crews trailed the fourth-ranked Tigers and defeated the no. 18 Hoyas in a series of races with various lineups.

SU had slipped to no. 12 a couple of weeks later when the season officially opened on the frigid Cayuga Lake Inlet against no. 9 Cornell and no. 13 Navy. It was the Orange crew getting the best of it, taking the Big Red by just about a length, with the Middies behind.

Orange crews were second in the rest of the day's races.

SU took the Goes Trophy back home but everybody knew they'd see the Big Red again. And again.

But first they would see the Boston University Terriers again and this time Syracuse would not get to keep the Conlan Cup. BU came to Onondaga Lake still smarting from the loss by an eyelash at the IRA. The Terriers were ranked 6th, Columbia 12th and Syracuse has moved up to no. 8. The race was moved up to Friday afternoon because of high winds expected on Saturday but the conditions were still miserable–so miserable that the freshman race was shortened to 1,000 meters–and BU's varsity eight simply handled those conditions better, by about half-a-length. Columbia was open water behind.

The Orange had led early but BU went through at about the halfway point and just held on in the sprint. The Terriers' stroke Todd Sukolsky punched the air in triumph. A cry of frustration rang out from the Syracuse shell.

"We came out on the short end," sophomore bowman Tyler Toporowksi said. "But we're looking forward to seeing them again soon."

"My guys are pretty fired up right now," Reischman said. "We've got three weeks. We're looking forward to the challenge."

That challenge would be the Eastern Sprints.

The Sprints

There is a thought among some Orange alums ... OK, more than a few ... that Lake Quinsigamond is not a place where good things happen. No SU varsity eight ever has won the grand final of the Eastern Sprints and while the 2007 crew made the grand final, Justin Stangel broke his ribs doing it and he and the Orange paid the price for the rest of the season. This time it would be different. While Reischman's V8 didn't win, it did make the grand final and finished fifth. And the JV got in as well, finishing third, giving top-seed Harvard a fight in both the morning heat and the final.

"Getting two crews into the grand final was our plan coming into Eastern Sprints," Reischman said. "The varsity eight had a great race and was beaten by faster crews," Reischman said. "The second varsity eight should be very proud; taking home a medal is a great accomplishment. All of our crews raced up to their level."

The V4 won its race and the frosh were 10th overall–fourth in the petite final.

A week later, rowing at home, Syracuse took the Packard Cup back from Dartmouth with the varsity winning by a length and the JV, V4 and freshman eight completing the sweep.

Ranked seventh in the Coaches Poll, SU took the weight of those high expectations to the Cooper River. And disappointment.

IRA – Return of the Big Red

After the win at Ithaca everybody knew Syracuse and Cornell would face off again and when they did at Worcester the Orange won again. That would change at the IRA.

The varsity was fifth in the opening heat, which Washington won over Brown and Princeton. Cornell finished ahead of the Orange but both faced off in the afternoon repechage. This time the Big Red was first and the Orange squeaked into the semifinals with a third-place finish.

"The rep was 'the tough rep,'" Reischman says. "We were on the wrong side of the course. We finished third and qualified through."

On Friday Syracuse faced the "big boys"–Washington and California–plus right: Cornell, Navy and BU again. This one was for a trip to the grands. And this time it was those pesky Terriers getting through along with Washington and Cal. SU was fifth. Cornell was fourth.

For the fourth time in three days the Orange varsity eight lined up against Cornell in the petite final on Saturday and for the fourth time Cornell came out ahead, winning the race. Stanford slipped in for second and SU was third.

It was an even more heartbreaking IRA for the Syracuse JV. The second boat came into the event seeded fifth but missed the final spot in the third-level finals in the semi by .596 seconds. The crew ahead of SU? Cornell.

The Orange JV also wound up third in the petite–ninth overall.

The V4 was sixth in the petite and the frosh third in the third-level final.

"Doing well at the IRA for all but the two or three crews at the top is about getting on a roll and getting the right draw and the right lane at the right time," Reischman said afterward in an e-mail to SU crew supporters. "I thought we raced hard all weekend but just couldn't seem to get the break we needed to get over the hump. That is boat racing though and you take the good with the bad."

Still, characteristically he was still putting much of the blame on himself in an interview more than a year later.

"I know that we gave everything we had on the water but we never had that one race at the 2011 IRA that we felt we had the type of rhythm that we had the previous two weeks. And I hold myself responsible for that."

And now the Class of '11 with its seven first-boaters was done.

Summer

That summer Reischman got the second assistant coach position he'd wanted for so long and he filled it with Brad Hemmerly. Hemmerly had succeeded Justin Moore at Williams College when Moore left to become head coach of the SU women's team. All Hemmerly did was coach the Williams women to their seventh national championship.

Chapter 32

2011–2012 – "What Do We Have To Do To Get Better?"

T he fall season began and ended in Boston, appropriately enough at the Head of the Charles and the Foot of the Charles.

With Kenny Marfilius having graduated, senior Isaac Budmen moved up to cox the varsity eight. Four of his classmates Aidan Barrett, Chris Bickford, Mike Dietrick and Chris Lutz manned the oars along with juniors Brendan Murphy and Mason Leasure and sophomores Jake Martens and Mac Zink.

Syracuse placed 18th out of thirty-four crews in the men's championship eights race at the Head of the Charles, crossing the finish line with a time of 15:03.27.

Reischman took a positive approach. "I thought we executed well," he said. "We rowed with the kind of rhythm we expected to. We need to work to on our fitness, but this is where the crew is right now. The guys know they have to take advantage of every opportunity to get faster and they are up for that challenge."

Afterward, Reischman says, the team asked him what they had to do to get faster. That question became a theme.

At the Princeton Chase the SU varsity eight was sixth out of 33 boats and the JV 12th with times of 13:26.73 and 13:48.10, respectively. Princeton's Tigers won in 13:09.23. Cornell was second in 13:16.7 and Navy finished third in 13:18.82.

In the men's fours race, the 4B boat posted SU's highest finish of the day, taking fifth–with a time of 14:58.75–with the 4A boat in seventh place competing against forty other crews.

Again, the coach sounded positive. "I thought in the eights we made some good progress," Reischman said. "Cornell was a boat we had our eye on. They were 20 seconds ahead of us last week and only 10 this week, so that was good. To be ready for the spring we still have work to do, but the crews we will be competing against are within our sights."

"The fours are always interesting," Reischman said. "Today was our first fours race. Over the next couple of weeks we'll continue to tweak our fastest lineups to create some separation between those groups."

Home for the Syracuse Invitational on November 5th, Reischman put Budmen, Leasure, Lutz, Bickford and Toporowski in the 4A boat and Matt Cosmann, Barrett, Zink, Dietrick and Martens into the 4B boat. The B boat won with the A boat in second. Perhaps the best part was that both Orange boats finished ahead of Cornell's, who were in third and fourth.

"I did not see the finish, but I saw the results and was obviously pleased," said Reischman, who was out at the start line for the head racing.

The Hall for Coach Bill

When the racing was over it was former-Head Coach Bill Sanford's time to shine. The man who'd spent most of his life rowing and coaching for SU was inducted into the Syracuse Rowing Hall of Fame.

"I truly am humbled and I also am very, very blessed to have the experience of life that I've had that was all around rowing," Bill Sanford said to the applause of more than two-hundred present and past members of SU Crews.

Following the ceremony at the James A. Ten Eyck Memorial Boathouse there was a banquet that night and it too was packed with family, friends and alumni paying tribute to the coach.

This is what it says on his Hall of Fame plaque:

Oarsman, Captain, Coach. Bill Sanford defines an era that stretches nearly half a century in the history of Syracuse University Crew.

A Syracuse man in every way–a native son who walked on to the squad as a freshman, rose to lead it as a senior, became Freshman Coach, then Varsity Coach for 35 years. His tenure includes the 1978 IRA Championship. More importantly, his instruction, concern and often his personal assistance helped his athletes on their way to successful lives in a myriad of ways.

Bill Sanford has three daughters and hundreds of sons.

The Passing of The Doc

The joy of Sanford's Hall of Fame induction was tempered by what had happened three days earlier.

One of the most loyal and enthusiastic supporters of Syracuse Crew, Dr. Bruce Chamberlain, had died at Iroquois Nursing Home.

He was 91.

Chamberlain had co-founded the Syracuse Alumni Rowing Association with Dr. Tom Kerr and had been actively involved, coming to practice and home races until failing eyesight and lessened mobility kept him from riding in the launch in his final year. Still he followed the fortunes of the crews avidly through conversations with fellow alums and Coach Reischman as well as *The Orange Oar* and was overjoyed to see Syracuse back among the top competitors.

The DeWitt Community Church was packed for his funeral and afterward family and close friends got together at his favorite restaurant in Fayetteville.

As darkness came, standing in front of the building you could see municipal fireworks going off in the sky–a brilliant display.

Coincidence? It seemed as if they surely were in celebration of the life of The Doc.

Fall Finish at the Foot – Not Fulfilling

The Orange crew wrapped up the fall on a bit of a down note. The top Orange four finished eleventh at the Foot of the Charles in a race contested over a 2.3-mile stretch of water between Harvard's Newell Boathouse and MIT's Pierce Boathouse. The SU A boat was about 30 seconds behind winning Harvard. SU's second, third and fourth varsity four entries placed 15th, 20th, and 30th, respectively.

Harvard also won the freshman eight race, with the SU cubs in fifth–the best Orange showing of the day.

"As a team we weren't very satisfied with the racing," Reischman said, finally sounding less than sunny. "I talked with the guys afterward and they were disappointed. They're determined to have a strong winter training season to improve the results by spring."

Winter – Better

Training between the racing seasons included a winter break trip to Florida and a spring break in Clemson, South Carolina again.

While Coach Reischman had been less than thrilled with the squad's performance during the fall season, he seemed encouraged by progress during winter training.

"We had four or five seniors hit personal records on their March 2K test by 4 or 5 seconds and that is significant and represents a lot of hard work," Reischman said. "This group was led by Chris Lutz who tied the school record at 5:49.6. The record he tied belonged to teammate Nemanja Bogdanovic, who was out with an injury when we tested."

The Orange opened the spring by scrimmaging Princeton and Georgeown in New Jersey; losing to Princeton and beating Georgetown.

SU's varsity eight headed into the official season ranked 14th in the U.S. Rowing Coaches Poll with Georgetown right behind at no. 15 and Princeton at no. 4.

Goes Trophy

Reischman's V8 lineup had Isaac Budmen coxing, Aidan Barrett at stroke, then Mike Dietrick, Chris Bickford, Chris Lutz, Kynan Reelick, Mac Zink, Mason Leasure, and Jake Martens.

The Orange opened at home in the Goes Trophy race but it was Navy who went home with the trophy. The water was calm, the temperature in the 50s and while it was close the Middies crossed the line first, 2/3 of a length ahead of Cornell with the Orange another 2/3 of a length back.

SU's JV was second to Navy and both freshman eights were third in their races.

Conlan Cup

SU's varsity was ranked no. 13 heading for Boston and the Conlan Cup race against no. 12 BU with no. 14 Columbia thrown in. In yet another in a series of nail-biters against the Terriers, Syracuse took it by just over a second, with Columbia back in third.

"I thought the guys did a nice job learning from last week," Reischman said. "This week we got out to the early lead, BU came back and made it a one-seat boat race through the middle thousand and we kept our composure and executed the final 500 better than last week."

The JV, with former 3V stroke James Olson stroking, also won a tight one, with BU in second and the two frosh eights each took second in their races.

Sprints

Kynan Reelick went out before the Eastern Sprints and the coach bumped Mason Leasure up to the four seat and moved JV stroke James Olson up to two in the V8. Otherwise the crew was intact.

Syracuse had the eight seed and a no. 11 national ranking heading into Worcester and the Orange varsity stepped right up to the challenge, getting revenge for the Goes Trophy loss against five-seed and no. 7-ranked Cornell in the morning heat, rowing past the Big Red in the last 500 meters. While SU did not catch Brown, the two seed, it came in second to the Big Red's third and secured a spot in the grand final.

The Orange did not get back at Navy in the grand, finishing sixth behind the Middies, who were fifth. Brown won it all, followed by Harvard, Wisconsin and Princeton.

But once again the Orange had qualified for the IRA.

The JV won the petite final and the frosh were fifth in their petite.

Packard Cup

His team "showed up at the boathouse on Monday," Reischman says, "and said 'what can we do to get faster?'"

Looking at tape, Reischman saw Wisconsin, Navy, Princeton and the Orange bunched within a length at the Sprints finish, and Wisconsin had a slight lane advantage because of the wind.

"I thought maybe we could make some changes that would get us a half-length and the rest would be up to the guys."

SU's varsity went to Hanover ranked no. 8 the next weekend and the Orange crews swept the Big Green. But it wasn't easy.

After no. 15 Dartmouth led the first 800 meters of the race, the Orange came on strong in the third 500 meters, taking the lead and holding it for the duration, winning by less than a length.

"It was a nice gut-check win for us," Coach Dave Reischman said. "I think we came in a little tired and did a good job of grinding through it and getting the win."

The Orange second varsity eight took a 13-second, open-water victory over the Big Green. The V4 won by about a length and Coach Shawn Bagnall's freshman eight edged the Big Green frosh at the line in a time of 5:41.15, just a one-quarter of a second ahead of Dartmouth's 5:41.40.

IRA

Sitting in his office in the Crew Room in the basement of Archbold Gymnasium months later, Dave Reischman says there was reason for hope heading for the Cooper River in 2012.

"We get to the IRA and again I was starting to think we had a shot maybe if things went our way. If we got the right lane and the right draw at the right time it would go our way."

The draw for the eight-seed Orange in the Thursday morning heat included two-seed Brown, five-seed Wisconsin, plus Yale, Penn and Gonzaga.

Rowing in a crosswind, SU finished two lengths behind Bruno and just over a length behind the Badgers, meaning the

Orange would have to race in the afternoon repechage for a spot in the upper-level semifinal.

Reischman recalls Captain Chris Lutz calling the team out afterwards, saying the crew could have gone harder after Wisconsin in the second 500 meters. "And Chris has street cred," the coach said.

All season long the Orange crew had thrived in headwinds. Tailwinds–not so much. Reischman and the athletes worked on that between the Eastern Sprints and the IRA. "We played with a heavier load in tailwind–I'd put a little more load on the oars. We were getting better at tailwinds.

"People think that in tailwinds you have to be technically proficient. I don't think that's true. I think what you have to do in tailwinds is catch the speed of the boat at the catch you have to be quick enough on the turn to connect to the water. That's why tailwinds are crazy races and strange things happen in a tailwind."

The wind turned from cross- to cross-tail before the repechage and the Orange lined up against California, Stanford, Yale, Northeastern and Drexel, racing for three spots in the upper-level semifinal. Cal jumped out early and led throughout. Syracuse was fourth early, but got through Yale and Stanford to finish second, a half-a-length off the Golden Bears.

Yale was a deck behind the Orange for the third spot.

"It was a tailwind so we survived sort of our worst conditions," Reischman recalls. "But I still thought, OK we're racing well, we were close to Cal, we beat some good crews, if the wind is right in the semi we've got a shot."

On Friday, it was a headwind. They went back and changed the oars.

"But it was a cross-headwind and we were on the wrong side of the course. I didn't think we had a shot in hell I'll admit that straight up be honest. I was watching the races and nobody was doing well from lanes five and six."

"DIETRICK, I'M ON SILVERA!!!!! KEEP WALKING!!!!!"

Reischman says there are two things he almost always

369

tells his crews when conditions are rough. One he says in any conditions: "Fellas, I've got some good news for you. We drew the fastest lane on the race course." It is often an egregious lie and everybody knows it. That's the point.

The other, saved for rough weather is, "It's nothing other than good old fashioned Syracuse racing weather."

On that Friday, Reischman recalls that when he told the lie about getting the fastest lane, one oarsman piped up, "Damn straight."

And the coach told his crew this: "How we're going to be judged is by our effort. If we don't make it through this race it's not going to be because we didn't lay everything on the line.

"In the third 500 we're going to have a lot of excuses– wrong day, wrong lane, rough water we're going to make a decision and when we make the decision it's got to be all in.

"When we go we've got to go without reservation. We've got to be all in, we've got to commit to it and go and we can't look back. We can't go halfway and decide that no we made the wrong choice. If we make that choice to go, we go."

"Dave loves developing men who know how to handle adversity and he prides himself on his ability and this program's ability to handle anything that can be thrown at it, seven-man Mike Dietrick says. "This team is not afraid of adversity and we know how to deal with it because that is how Dave teaches us to live.

"Adversity was the name of the game on Friday. After we shoved to start the warm-up, the cox box had a glitch and our warm-up was cut from thirty-five minutes down to under twenty minutes because Isaac Budmen had to hunt down a new cox box for us to use during the race. One was lent to us by Topher Bordeau, the head coach at Dartmouth. It was much appreciated."

Evidently nobody was rattled. "We got this," they told the coach. They lined up against Brown, Harvard, Princeton, Cornell and Penn.

Brown and Harvard rowed away early leaving it a fight among the Orange, Tigers, Big Red and Quakers for the last grand final spot.

Soon enough Cornell and Penn fell back.

370

Mike Dietrick takes the story from there. "There was nothing pretty or sharp about our rowing. Approximately 6:20 of slapping around and grinding it out. Princeton at one point had upwards of four seats on us as we crossed into the second half of the race.

"Isaac had been calling for a huge change of speed as we crossed the thousand in the prior two races and we knew we needed a big change in hull speed to beat the Tigers. Isaac made the 'Decision Call' as we crossed the thousand and all nine of us decided to go. Like I said, it wasn't pretty, but we put the blades in the water and pulled. We kept grinding it out for the last thousand, lifting rate every 20–30 strokes, finally ending up above 40 for the better part of the second half of the race. We slowly ate back into Princeton's lead.

"I'll never forget Isaac's call as we came into the last 500. Ian Silvera has been stroking the Princeton 1V for the past three years and everyone in my boat knew who he was and where he was sitting. As we started to take the lead from Princeton, Isaac yelled at the top of his lungs, 'DIETRICK, I'M ON SILVERA!!!!! KEEP WALKING!!!!!' I'll never forget that. Syracuse hadn't beaten Princeton in a very long time and doing so in the face of adversity and crappy weather was the perfect way to make it to the grands. I know Dave was proud!"

Reischman chokes up just a little as he remembers that race. "The guys got it done."

They would not come up short this time. "Not on our watch."

Grand Final

Back at the dock the coach greeted his crew.

"I, of course, am ready to do backflips. I can't believe that from lane five on the wrong side of a cross-headwind that we just made the grand final of the IRA. I'm ready to jump out of my shoes and I pull up to the dock and the guys are calm.

"We talked about the race and they said it was just basically guts, it was a slugfest it wasn't our most clever rowing and someone said what do we need to do to get better?"

371

They had one more race to row. And a chance to do something no Syracuse varsity eight had done since 1978.

Saturday, June 2, 2012

The Saturday morning masters' race was a disappointment for the Syracuse alumni eight, finishing a second-and-a-half behind Cornell. Penn and Northeastern were well back.

The Orange open four was fourth in the petite final. The freshman eight won the third-level final over Stanford, Penn, Drexel, Gonzaga and George Washington. The JV was fourth in the petite final.

For the second time in three years, Reischman's varsity eight was up there with the big boys: Washington, Brown, Harvard, California along with Syracuse's fellow upstart, Boston University.

After the semifinal on Friday the coach had pulled his crew together and asked them how they wanted to approach the grand final.

"Mike Dietrick and Chris Lutz spoke up and they were in the boat their sophomore year that made the final and they said, 'Coach, when we were in the final in our sophomore year it felt like we were just happy to be there and we got there and we didn't have much left and we kind of limped home in sixth place. Not this year. We're not going to do that this year. We don't care what happens. We're probably not going to win it but we're not finishing sixth.'

"And they had right from the second they hit the dock ... they were happy to make the grand but they were racing in the final and the thought was we had to execute. We were in lane six it was a straight tail it was about as fast a tailwind as you can and we had struggled in tailwinds but ... we're better.

"They said the first 250 was bad but the last 1,750 was as good as they raced and rowed all year long. We were able to get out on BU in the third 500 we knew that Cal would be fast off the line and at some point they would start coming back to us was our guess. Whoever the fourth place crew realized they were out of the medals we were hoping to take advantage of that discouragement. We got control of BU in the third 500. Cal was the crew that started to fall off the pace and we made some inroads on them but obviously didn't quite get it."

Washington was first, then Brown and Harvard right behind.

The Orange finished fifth, a length back of Cal and 2/3 of a length ahead of BU. It was the best since the Jeff Pesot-stroked crew took bronze in 1990.

Senior Leadership

"We did the exact opposite of 2011," senior Captain Chris Lutz reflects.

"We went in with the attitude we deserve whatever position we deserve depending on the work we put in throughout the year and depending on where we are at in our capabilities and didn't expect anything more or less. I think that that particular boat would have been happy with however we placed as long as we raced with the same mindset as we did. We knew what we needed to do but we simply just raced how we would have in practice.

"We didn't change anything. We didn't have to. This is the difference between 2011, we thought we needed to change something in that race but we really didn't and last year has proved that. In 2011 we practiced and raced completely different. We would show up to race day and think we needed to pull something out of our ass to hang with the guys we were racing but that wasn't the idea. This past IRAs seemed to be my most intelligent racing.

"We looked at racing as just another chance to improve on a 2K piece. We didn't expect anything more or less. We had nerves, no doubt in that, but we controlled them by understanding that we were going to do the best we could dependent upon the work we have put in and we would be happy with what results come out of it ... and if we weren't happy with the results it would have been that we were unhappy with the amount of work that we put in previous to that race not the amount of work we put in during the race."

"For this group of guys the IRA was a microcosm of the

season," Coach Dave Reischman says. "Take it race by race. Get better each race so that we have our best race on the last day and that's what the guys did.

"[They were] very composed, very poised, not rattled by anything. Lost to Princeton [in the spring scrimmages]–Monday morning–what do we need to do to get faster? Make the grand final at the Sprints–Monday morning, what do we need to do to get faster? Qualify for the grand final at the IRA–what do we need to do to get faster? There was some great, great senior leadership.

"Dietrick and Lutz certainly. Aidan Barrett in the stroke seat. Dietrich and Bickford were walk-ons. James Olson was nobody's idea of a collegiate oarsman when he came here. [He came into the boat when Reelick went out] and they didn't miss a beat–maybe got a little faster.

"Isaac–just an unbelievable job of staying calm. Poise under pressure.

"Everybody had something to work on. For Isaac, the guys felt that junior year when races were tight he would get a little bit out of control. The proof's in the pudding. Your feet are to the fire at the IRA and Isaac's running the ship and the guys are responding. You could look at every guy in the boat and say that they needed to change this, and they did. They needed to do this, and they did.

"It was just one of those years where all nine guys in the boat were on the same page and really committed to making changes and going as fast as they possibly can. We didn't once all year talk about making a grand final that I can recall. The guys probably did. And purposely. The year before it was the focus all year–grands, maybe making a medal. The guys put a lot of pressure on themselves. And I think we were able to keep the expectations off this crew. And they just went out and rowed, enjoyed it and had fun doing it."

Senior oar Dietrick gets the last word. "We had a lot of success this year, but not enough praise can be given to Dave. Not only for this year, but for the past ten years that he's been at this program. He has a very clear understanding of who he is and how he wants his program to be run. He constantly challenges his guys to be better students, better rowers and better people.

In my graduation speech the night before Eastern Sprints, I said something along the lines that Dave in many respects knows us all better than we know ourselves. He has hundreds of sons from all over the world and we are all far better individuals for having spent time in his program. He's an excellent teacher and one hell of a role model."

Another great group of seniors moved on and Reischman set about filling their seats.

In an interview for this book, Bill Sanford talked about "WHEN, Dave wins an IRA"–as if to say he expects it. Does Dave Reischman? The stars will have to align.

J ustin Moore's Williams College crews owned Division III women's rowing. They'd won the NCAA championship five years in a row from 2006 through 2010 in addition to a 2002 title. Moore also had coached the U.S. Junior National Team. He was ready for a move up and SU Director of Athletics Daryl Gross was ready to bring him in to join his highly-touted group of head coaches in what used to be called minor sports.

"There could not be a more perfect fit than to have Justin Moore join our amazing coaching staff," Gross said in a statement released by *SUAthletics.com* in late July. Moore was off coaching the U.S. Junior National team at the time.

Gross gave Moore the second assistant coach Kris Sanford had wished for. Moore kept Alicea Kochis and the institutional knowledge she'd gained rowing for SU and then coaching the returning members of the squad. He added Andrea Buch who'd most recently been an assistant at Louisville and the head coach for the U.S. Rowing Junior National Team Development Camp in New London, Connecticut. She had rowed for and captained a University of Kansas squad which was ranked in the Top-25.

They set to work.

New Standards

Moore knew a little about fitness, having coached all those national championship teams and he had competed in five Ironman triathlons himself. He was about to find out the fitness levels of the young women he would now be coaching for Syracuse; the ones who stayed, anyhow. They were going to have to make a change.

"Right now it's a very exciting time to be on this team," he told *The Orange Oar* that fall, "because the women want to make this change but they're not sure whether or not they have the stuff to do it and we're just going to go one step at a time."

He said a lot of luck and hard work could get them the Big

East title back come springtime. Getting back to the NCAAs that soon simply wasn't realistic.

On September 11th, the team members were tested for fitness. Moore assessed the results like this: "From a numbers standpoint the assessment was entirely pedestrian. I don't think any of us–coaches or athletes–were surprised by this result. We knew the conditioning was not where it needed to be. This was confirmed. So now we have the starting point.

"What was pleasing to see was the women's willingness to compete in a positive manner, and support one another throughout the process. In other words, we have the spirit of a championship squad. There were no excuses for poor performances, and several women displayed some serious courage in what I term 'outstanding failures.' We also had several women display good 'athletic maturity' in the pacing and toughness."

As is so often the case when a coach of long standing is replaced, there was an air of "a new sheriff in town."

"Truthfully, what Justin came in and said during his opening meeting was no different than what Kris said," Assistant Coach Alicea Kochis says. "It just had a different effect with him being new. And he was able to make cuts and hold standards that Kris couldn't enforce in her final years."

They worked through the winter and the athletes who were left after two trips south and long hours indoors were pretty much those who had bought into Moore's training regimen.

Spring Results

The varsity eight had some talent with Allison Todd at cox, facing stroke Macey Miller, backed by Carmen Failla, Emma Karpowicz, Maggie McCrudden, Chelsea MacPherson, Rebecca Soja, Tiffany Macon and Miranda Williams in bow.

They did not have a home race that spring although Boston's Charles River might have seemed like a home course. They raced there four times but the closest the V8 ever got to winning was a length behind BU in the opener.

Other opponents included Penn, Northeastern, Radcliffe, Dartmouth, Minnesota and Louisville. They also lost to Yale and

Cornell in Connecticut.

"This year, we have had to work a great deal on responding to adversity and demonstrating the quality of character we admire when we have not achieved what we set out to do," Moore said after losing the Orange Challenge Cup to Penn, with Northeastern second. "If we are to be successful, we must persevere and continue to believe in ourselves."

The last race in Boston could have been a reason to believe. While trailing Minnesota and Louisville, the Orange did get back at BU, taking the Terriers by open water in the V8 and a heartbeat in the 2V8.

But the V8 finished fifth at the Big East and fourth in the petite final–10th overall–at the Eastern Sprints. The 2V8 and V4 were fifth in their petites. Moore found some sunshine in the Sprints result as his V8 finished ahead of Rutgers and Georgetown, which it had trailed at the Big East Regatta.

"Today ... showed the tremendous amount of progress throughout the season," he said. "We are not satisfied, but clearly understand we have made progress and are motivated for the 2011–2012 season."

In May he announced his first SU recruiting class; ten women including one from Canada, one from New Zealand and two from Australia.

Fall 2011

In the fall came word that Syracuse was going to join the Atlantic Coast Conference (ACC). Notre Dame and Louisville would also be coming along. For the Orange women that would mean competing against powers such as Virginia and Clemson as well as the Big East Champion Fighting Irish, an Orange nemesis. But not until the spring of 2014. First the Orange, Irish and Cardinals would have to finish their commitments to the Big East.

Moore was thrilled but the ACC was still a couple of years away. Now there was fall competition and he was looking for improvement over his first year.

The squad started well at the Head of the Genesee with the varsity eight coming in second to Cornell and the SU fours taking the top two spots against lesser competition.

The V8 was eleventh at the Princeton Chase. Three Virginia eights were among the ten crews ahead of the Orange.

An SU 4 with cox won the Syracuse Invitational over two Cornell crews. The Orange women's B boat was fourth.

"It was the first win in my tenure, the first time we ever came out as the no. 1 crew in the varsity women's four," Moore said. "That was a testament to how hard the women in that boat worked."

SU 4s came in third and fourth at the Foot of the Charles behind Radcliffe and Brown. There was less than one second difference between the Orange women's A and B fours and it was the B boat made up of Allison Todd, Carmen Failla, Anna Kaszycki, Maggie McCrudden, and Rose Aschebrock that had the faster time, just a beat behind second-place Brown.

A shot at the Big East title and maybe the NCAA Championships seemed more realistic than they had a year earlier heading into winter training.

Spring 2012

The Orange opened the 2012 season at the end of Spring Camp in South Carolina with the varsity eight coming in third behind a Top-20 Clemson team and Indiana which finished in a dead heat.

SU was ahead of Iowa, Boston University, Purdue and Marist.

Back home on a frigid opener Saturday morning SU took on BU in a morning race with the winner to face the winner of Cornell and Rutgers later in the day. The Orange crew was looking for an early showdown with the Big Red which had dominated the rivalry for several years. But the Terriers had other ideas and rowed through SU in the second thousand for a 2/3-of-a-length victory. Cornell dispatched Rutgers easily and did the same with BU in the final race. Syracuse had to settle for whipping Rutgers in the consolation match.

The Orange women rowed without their head coach that day.

Moore was with his daughter Mackenzie, who'd been diagnosed with cancer. He kept up with the racing on his cell phone as Kochis and Buch handled things at the boathouse and on the water.

"It continues to be impossible for me to describe the feeling one has when you hear the words, 'your daughter has cancer,'" Moore said later in an e-mail to *The Orange Oar*. "Late March and early April were a blur of hospitals, diagnostic tests and communication with loved ones and the Syracuse community. Missing the BU-Cornell-Rutgers race was extremely difficult, but also very necessary. Assistant Coaches Kochis and Buch did an amazing job of continuing to keep the team focused and each training session and race productive."

Mackenzie Moore went home with her family soon after the hospital stay and continued the fight.

The Orange were home again the next week but trailed again, this time to Penn and Northeastern. Sophomore stroke Maggie McCrudden found a reason for optimism. "Our sprint was stronger than last week," she said. "Our goal is the Big East and we have a lot of time for that."

They went to Boston and finished third again to Radcliffe and Dartmouth but it was close; just a length behind the Big Green and another half-length behind Radcliffe. This time the Orange crew was not just an "also-rowed."

The Orange almost caught Notre Dame in a double-dual in Indianapolis–finishing six-tenths of a second behind the 15th-ranked Fighting Irish in the grand final. Moore pointed out later that Notre Dame had just come back from competing on the West Coast so might have been a bit worn out. The proof would come at the Big East Championships the next week.

The Orange V8 consisted of Allison Todd at coxswain, McCrudden, Anna Kaszycki, Miranda Williams, Emma Basher, Rebecca Soja, Tiffany Macon, Caroline Habjan and Emma Karpowicz. Only Todd, Macon and Karpowicz were seniors. The rest were frosh and sophomores.

Big East

The Orange got a win in Camden, but it was not in the varsity eights. The V4 with–coxswain Kristina Herb, Amy Ludovici, Ashley Marsh, Laura Adams and Gina Biascochea–finished in 7:29.9, beating second-place Notre Dame by 1.5 seconds. It was the first SU win of any kind at the Big East Championships in three years.

But the Fighting Irish once again had just enough to hold off the Orange V8, winning by less than a length in 6:31.7. Notre Dame again was the team champion and SU was second.

No longer competing in the Eastern Sprints, SU's best chance for an NCAA bid was a strong showing in the Big East Championships. It turned out that getting close to the Irish was enough to move SU's varsity into the Top-20 in the CRCA poll but not enough to bring an invitation from the NCAA. Still, it was the first Top-20 ranking since 2005, the last time SU had made the NCAAs.

"We all knew we were improving as a team and gaining a tremendous amount of speed, but it is really rewarding when the coaches around the country recognize it," Moore said. "This is an accomplishment that the seniors who are leaving the program can feel deeply satisfied about."

Moore brought in eight new freshmen in his second recruiting class but the best news for the coach was that six of his eight rowers in the V8 for were scheduled to return. The Big East boat had featured freshmen Emma Basher and Anna Kaszycki, sophomores Maggie McCrudden, Rebecca Soja and Miranda Williams and redshirt-junior Carmen Failla.

After two years at the helm he seemed to have the Orange on the doorstep.

In 2013, the men's varsity eight slid back into the third level at the IRA, finishing 16th overall after a season in which it did not win a race and was fifth in the petite final at the Eastern Sprints. There was a lot of talent among the now varsity-eligible frosh but not enough experience at the college level and evidently not enough buy-in to what it takes. The JV eight was fourth in the petites at the IRA.

The Orange women hung on tenterhooks at the end of the season hoping for an at-large bid to the NCAAs but it did not come and they finished the season at their final Big East regatta coming in second to Notre Dame once again in the V8s and third in the team standings.

The Orange women wound up ranked 19th in the Coaches Poll.

In February, former Coach Kris Sanford was honored before an SU men's basketball game at the Carrier Dome with the dedication of a shell named for her. SU Director of Athletics Daryl Gross stood with his arm around her for photos.

After the season Assistant Coach Andrea Buch moved on to work for Pocock in Seattle and Justin Moore brought in Jim Lister who'd been coaching the previous 10 years at Duke, most recently as the Blue Devils' associate head coach and recruiting coordinator.

In the summer Reischman's Assistant Coaches Shawn Bagnall and Brad Hemmerly moved on and were replaced by former-SU-oarsman Justin Stangel and Jason Cottingham. Stangel had been coaching the SU women while Alicea Kochis was on maternity leave. Cottingham had been a volunteer assistant for the men's lightweight varsity at Dartmouth since 2010. Hemmerly became head coach of women's rowing at Marietta. Bagnall became head coach of lightweight rowing at Navy.

There was strong interest in Coach Reischman from outside of Syracuse but the SU Athletics Department gave him several reasons to stay including more athletic scholarships for his team.

On June 25th the man who was Harvard Crew, Harry Parker died after a two-year fight against cancer. He was 77. Dave Reischman is one of the many crewmen and coaches Parker mentored through the years.

Nancy Cantor left Syracuse in the fall and was replaced as chancellor by Kent Syverud who had been dean of the law school at Washington University in St. Louis.

Joe Kieffer completed his term as SARA President in January of 2014 and Lynne Della Pelle Pascale became the second woman to lead SARA.

As so the story of rowing at Syracuse University continues with no finish line in sight!

Previous Page
1978 – IRA Varsity Eight Champion SU Men's Head Coach Bill Sanford enjoys some bubbly courtesy of Dave Townsley and John Shamlian

Facing Page
SU Alum and Olympic gold medalist Anna Goodale shines at the Ten Eyck Boathouse

1960s – "The Bear" – SU Head Coach Loren Schoel

1960s – SU Freshman Coach Vic "Mike" Michalson

1960s – Racing shell dedication

1960s – Men's Crew at Spring Camp, Coach Vic "Mike" Michalson, Head Coach Loren Schoel

1960s – IRA Race Day at The Ten Eyck Boathouse, MIT in foreground, Navy to the rear

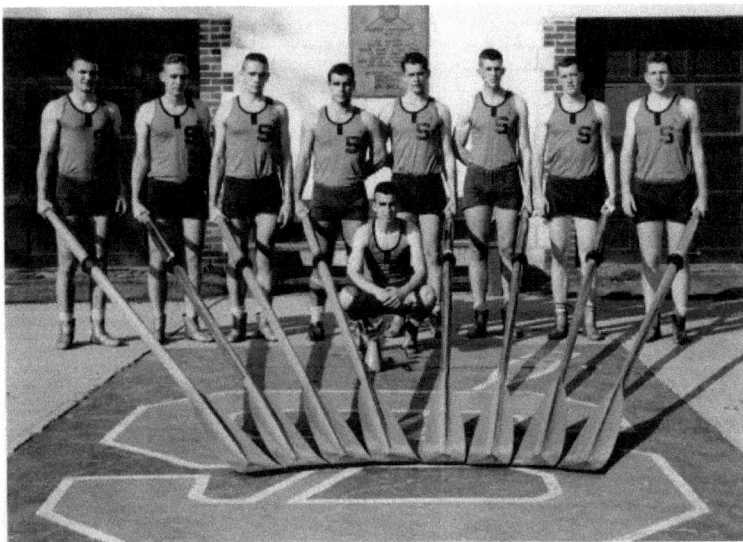

1962 – SU Men's Varsity – L to R: Dan Hogan, Walter Barber, Ted Kakas, Steve Gladstone, Donald DIck, Gary Gardner, Giles van der Bogert, David Norris, cox Dick Hersh

1960s – IRA Regatta dinner

1960s – "The Bear" at work in The Bear with son Bob and Vic Michalson

1960s – Working out in the tanks

1964 – IRA crowd from the grandstand

1964 – IRA JV heat

1964 – SU Varsity
L to R: Ted Kakas, David Norris, Giles van der Bogert, Donald Dick, Dan Hogan, Tom Prindiville, Bob Whyte, Bill Rossell, cox John Reed

1965 – SU Freshman Crew

L to R: Harrison, Clark, Estoff, Yochum, Hartwell, Nicholson, Sprague, Meyen, cox Bell

1966 – SU Varsity

L to R: Doug Kraai, Norm Magers, James Gulnac, Gary MacLachlan, Walter Okenica, Drew Harrison, Robert Whyte, Ned Kerr, cox Pat Nalbone

1967 – SU Varsity

L to R: stroke Barry Singer, Steve Rogers, Roy Sea, Gary MacLachlan, Drew Harrison, John Campbell, Doug Kraai, Ned Kerr, cox Pat Nalbone

1967 – SU Head Coach Loren Schoel
and Captain Gary MacLachlan

1968 – Head Coach Sanford and Captain Frank Doble

1967 – IRA finish line crowd

1967 – IRA Varsity race

1916 – IRA Champions Reunion in 1967

1969 – SU Varsity

L to R: Nils Peterson, Duane Hickling, Frank Doble, Charles Harris, Gary McKinney, Steve Rogers, Don Plath, Jeffrey Harriman, cox Richard Kortright

1971 – IRA SU Freshman eight final – Penn winning over Cornell and Navy with SU fourth

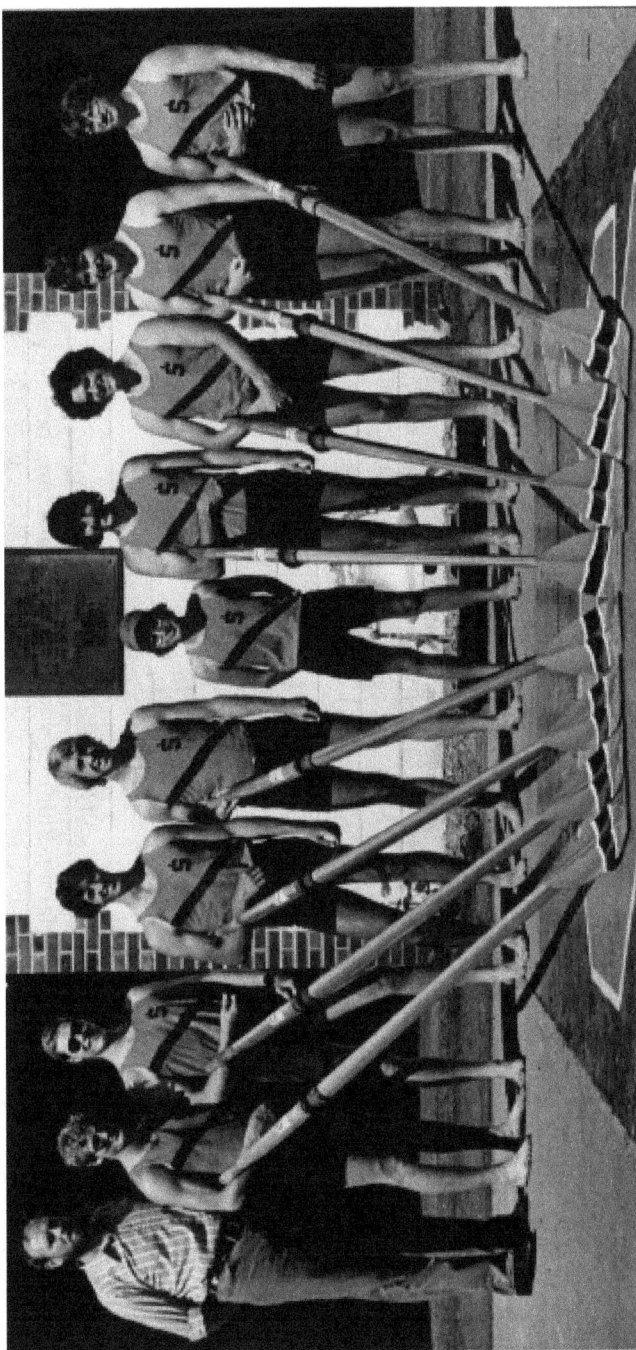

1975 – SU Men's Varsity

L to R: Head Coach Sanford, stroke Lyvers, Townsley, Evancie, Brown, cox Lukoff, Jordan, Watson, Jirak, Reid

1975 – SU Men's Varsity versus Rutgers
Stroke Kirchoff, Martin, Halbig, Plumb, Lyvers, Seany, Washburn, bow Watson, cox Hoffman

1976 – SU Men's Varsity eight

L to R: stroke Lyvers, Reid, Evancie, Purdy, cox Lukoff, Shamlian, Mogish, Brown, Townsley

1977 – IRA SU Freshman eight champions – Coach Drew Harrison, cox Ozzie Street and Stroke Art Sibley loft the Stewards Cup

Spring 1978 – First Intercollegiate Women's Crew Team

Back Row L to R: Debbie Grossman, Pauline Mojsiewicz, Irene Marx, Martha Mogish, Linda Eschenfelder, Beth Churchill, Lynne Della Pelle

Middle Row L to R: Mary Jo Dalrymple, Jill Fisher, Deborah Macy, Cathy Cohen, Maggie Matthews, Sharon Watson, Shari Hersh, Robbi Needham

Front Row L to R: Harli Diamond, Francie Johnson, Jane Levien, Karen Cunningham, Bonnie Hagemeister, Chris Kirkman

Spring 1978 – Syracuse Women's Varsity eight racing in front of the Ten Eyck Boathouse L to R: bow Cathy Cohen, Deborah Macy, Bonnie Hagemeister, Karen Cunningham, Linda Eschenfelder, Irene Marx, Shari Hersh, stroke Lynne Della Pelle, coxswain Francie Johnson

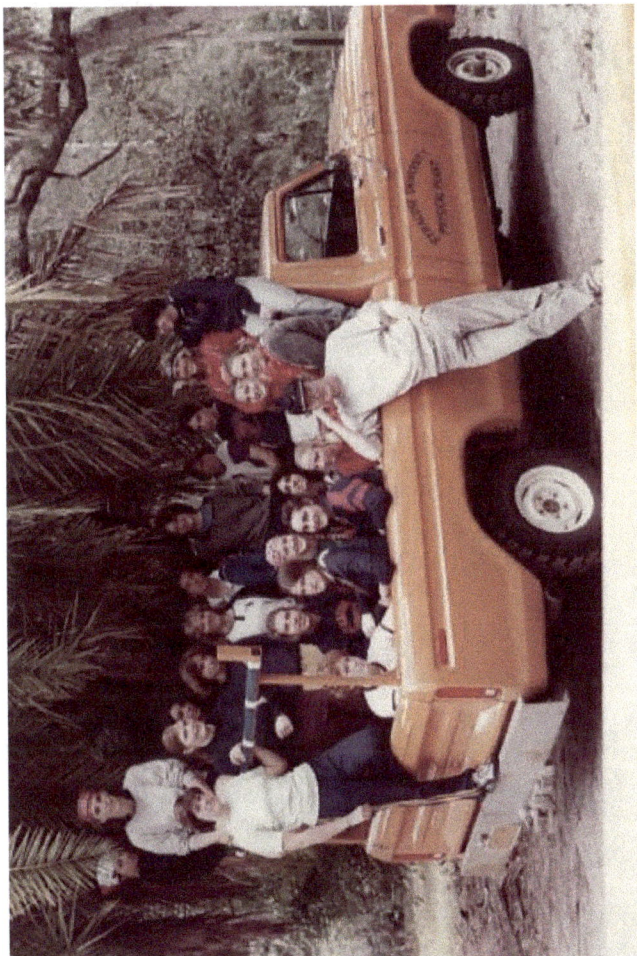

1979 – Women's Crew during winter training, Rollins College, Winter Park, Florida, with Head Coach Mark Lyvers (Photo by Robin Bogard Mowers)

1978 – SU Men's Varsity April 13, 1978
on Onondaga Lake

1978 – IRA SU Varisty eight pulling away

1978 – IRA SU Varsity eight championship crew post-race

1978 – IRA SU Varsity eight cox Ozzie Street above it all

1978 – IRA SU Freshman eight champions

L to R: Stroke Jacobi, cox Donabella, Buerigin, Darling, Ritter, Groch, Pistacchio, Feuer, bow Bickford, Coach Drew Harrison

1978 – IRA SU Varsity eight champions
L to R: Head Coach Bill Sanford. bow Henwood, Mogish, Shamlian, Townseley, cox Street, Purdy, Captiain Evancie, Reid, stroke Sibley

1980 – IRA Men's JV

1982 – SU Men's Captain Bryan Mahon

Liverpool HS graduate
and SARA Director Sheila
Roock a.k.a. Shelly Rock

SU Women's Head Coach
Debra Quinn

1983 – SU Women's EAWRC
four with bronze medal winner
Susan Church

1983 – SU Men's Crew cox Chris Colville front left

1985 – SU Women Crew with Coaches Deb Quinn and Gary Jordan

1985 – SU Women's Coach
Chris Lang at the helm

1986 – SU Men's Frosh Coach
Larry Laszlo and Head Coach
Bill Sanford

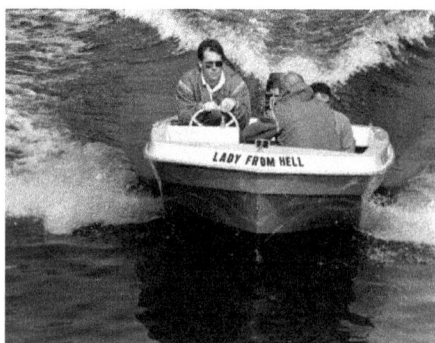

1987 – SU Men's Frosh
Coach Larry Laszlo in
the Lady from Hell

1987 – SU Women's eight

1988 – SU Chancellor Melvin Eggers speaks at the Ten Eyck Boathouse rededication

1988 – SU Assistant Athletics Director Doris Soladay, Bill Hider, Chancellor Melvin Eggers, Onondaga County Executive Nick Pirro at the Ten Eyck Boathouse rededication

1988 – Breuer Family boat dedication
L to R: Vladimir "Vic" '40 & Virginia "Bobbie" Breuer '42, Margaret "Peggy" Breuer Mooney '86, Catherine "Cathy" Cragg Breuer '73 & James "Jim" Breuer '72 with their son Andy, Men's Head Coach Bill Sanford, SU Chancellor Melvin Eggers

1989 – Fans cheer on the SU women

1990s – Colin Goodale and crew

1991 – SU Men's JV – 4 Totten 3 Butler 2 Lenahan
racing Rutgers

1991 – SU Women's JV cox Jane Park pays the price of
victory

1989 – SU Men's Varsity

1991 – SU Women's Varsity (photo by Steve Parker)

1992 – Fans cheering on SU's Women
from the Long Branch bridge

1990 – Men's crew racing Dartmouth

Stroke Pesot, Green, Ludden, Horn, McClimans, Smith, Schmidt, Stribrny, cox Heinstein

1990s – SU alum Charlie Roberts at the dedication of his eponymous shell

1993 – SU Women's varsity (photo by Steve Parker)

1995 – Women's novice crew row by their sign

L to R: Laura Graff, Carolyn Stephanik, Rachel Treadwell, Jen Tafuri, Erin Pollard, Jane Kramer

1995 – Men's JV working some things out
(photo by Steve Parker)

1995 – SU Men's Head Coach Bill Sanford
"A man and his megaphone"

1995 – SU Women's 2nd Novice eight – 8 Dent 7 Martin
6 Ashley (photo by Steve Parker)

1995 – SU Women's Crew
"The traditional celebration of victory"

1997 – Women's varsity

L to R: bow Treadwell, Blevins, Stephanik, Flindall, Carlson, McClellan, Pollard, stroke Panzarella, cox Rubinger

1998 – Men's JV then varsity at IRA

L to R: bow Kaplan, Jackson, Hillebrecht, Kaputa, Daskalakis, Michalowicz, Sera, stroke Markel, cox Krehbiel

1998 – Men's Varsity then JV at IRA
L to R: cox Lee, stroke Jones, Cellucci, Daughton, Bettini, Stratman, Kemezis, Bischoff, bow Michiels

1998 – Women's Varsity

L to R: cox Rubinger, stroke Wanf, Watkins, Tafuri, Ashley, Coffeen, Treadwell, Lollo, bow MacVane

1998 – SU Women practice on Onondaga Lake

2000 – SU Women headed out to Onondaga Lake

1998 – Otto joins the SU Women's Crew

1998 – Women's Varsity
L to R: Carlson, Modolo, Doyon, cox Karns

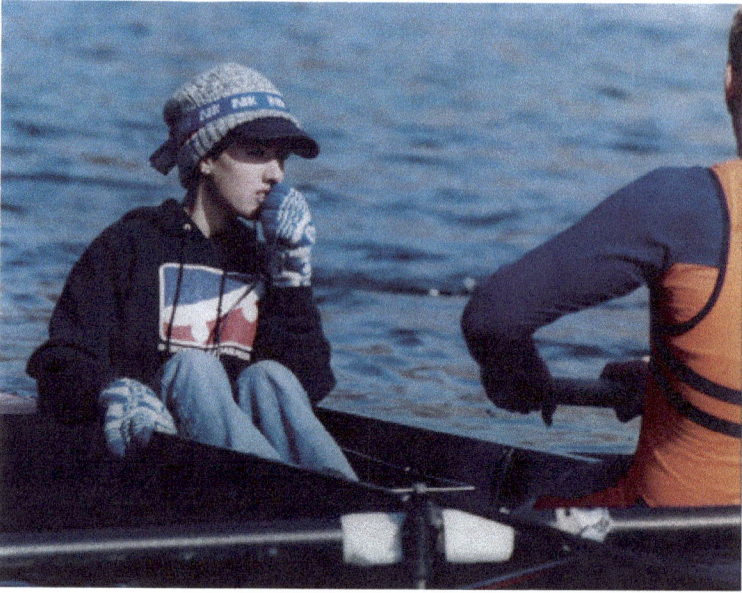

1999 – SU Men's cox Jess McNamara

2001 – JV cox Peter Romano gets some big air

1999 – SU Men's Varsity take on Boston University
L to R: bow Vande Vusse, Durham, White, Ring, Gryniuk,
Jackson, Hartsock, stroke Liwski, cox Heyer

2000 – Men's eight

2000 – SU Women at the south end of Onondaga Lake

2000 – SU Women race day on Onondaga Lake

2000 – SU Women's JV off the starting line on
Onondaga Lake

2000 – SU Women prepare to take on Penn at the Ten Eyck
Boathouse

2001 – SU Men's Head Coach Bill Sanford

2001 – SU Men's Varsity stroke Karl Sudar at the catch

2001 – SU Men's four at Henley

2001 – SU Men's four at Henley

2001 – SU Men's Varsity – L to R: cox Miller, stroke Sudar, Berster, Liwski, Heumann, Klein, Abbott, (Stratton, bow Merzig)

2003 – Anna Goodale in focus

2003 – SU Women in racing action

2003 – SU Men's Varsity
L to R: cox Eric Miller, stroke Andy Berster, Kevin Klein, Matt
Heumann, Chris Liwski, Steve Boselli, Andrew Wright, John
Merzig, bow Jason Bourcier

445

2003 – Goes Cup close up

2003 – Goes Cup racing in the rain

2003 – Goes Cup action

2003 – SU Men neck-and-neck with Navy at Goes Cup

2003 – SU Men's Varsity cox Eric Miller celebrates a win

2004 – SU Men's varsity in action

2004 – SU Women in a close race

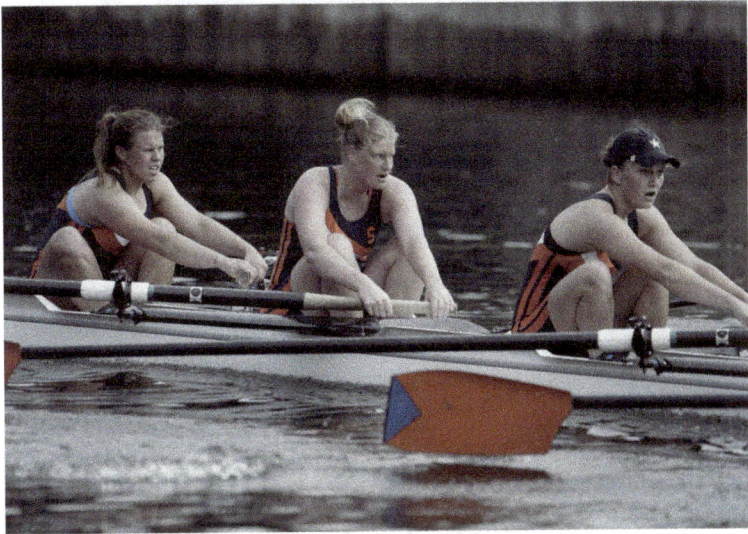

2004 – SU Women racing fiercely

2005 – SU Men's Head Coach Dave Reischman

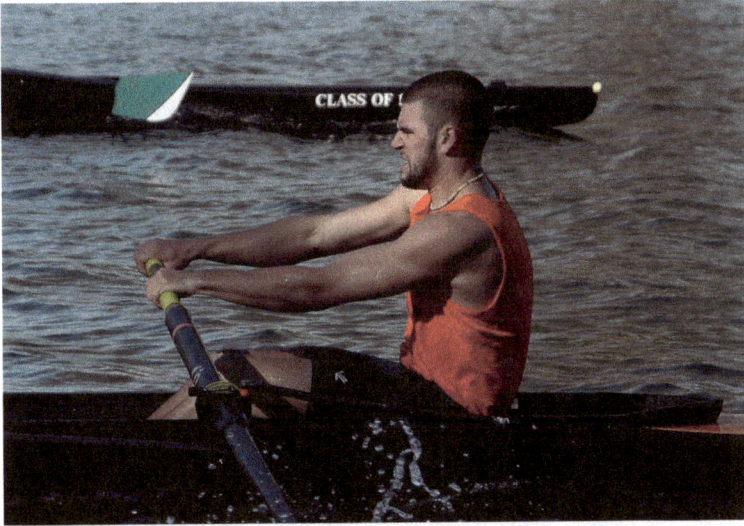

2005 – SU Men's crew edging ahead of Dartmouth

2005 – SU Men's Varsity – cox Chad Taylor, stroke Justin Stangel, Matt Morrow, Dan O'Shaughnessy, Joel Harrison, J.P. Geise, Andrew Cooley, Mike Beck, bow Tyler Page (photo by Steve Parker)

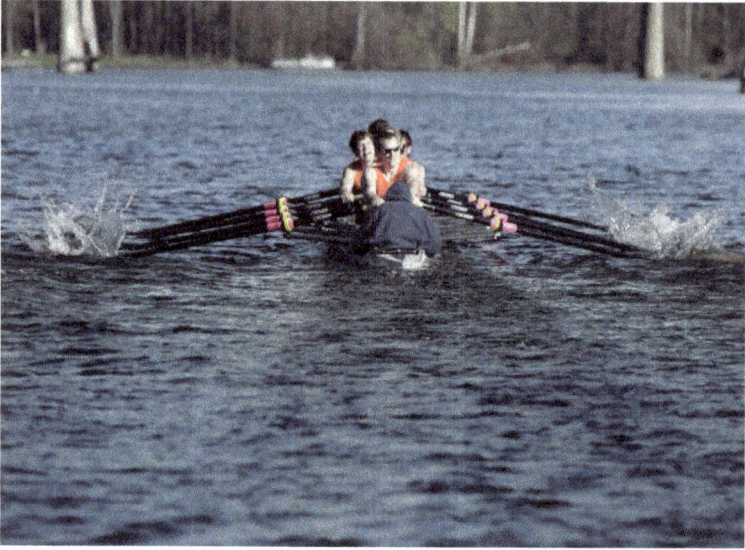

2005 – Packard Cup competition with SU Men's Varsity
putting it all into the oar

2005 – SU Men's Varsity racing Dartmouth

2005 – SU Women with the Orange Plus Trophy in hand

2005 – SU Women's Varsity on their way to the NCAAs

2006 – Syracuse University Rowing "generations"
L to R: Andrew Cooley, Doc Chamberlain, Charlie Roberts

2007 – SU Men's Varsity on their way to a
three-length margin over Dartmouth

2007 – SU Men's Varsity (photo by Steve Parker)

2008 – Varsities off the starting line
Boston U, SU and Columbia

2008 – Boston U, SU and Columbia after the start

2009 – Goes Cup competition with the Orange in the lead

2011 – SU Men's stroke Mike Gennaro and crew pull away from the Big Green

2011 – Goes Cup action

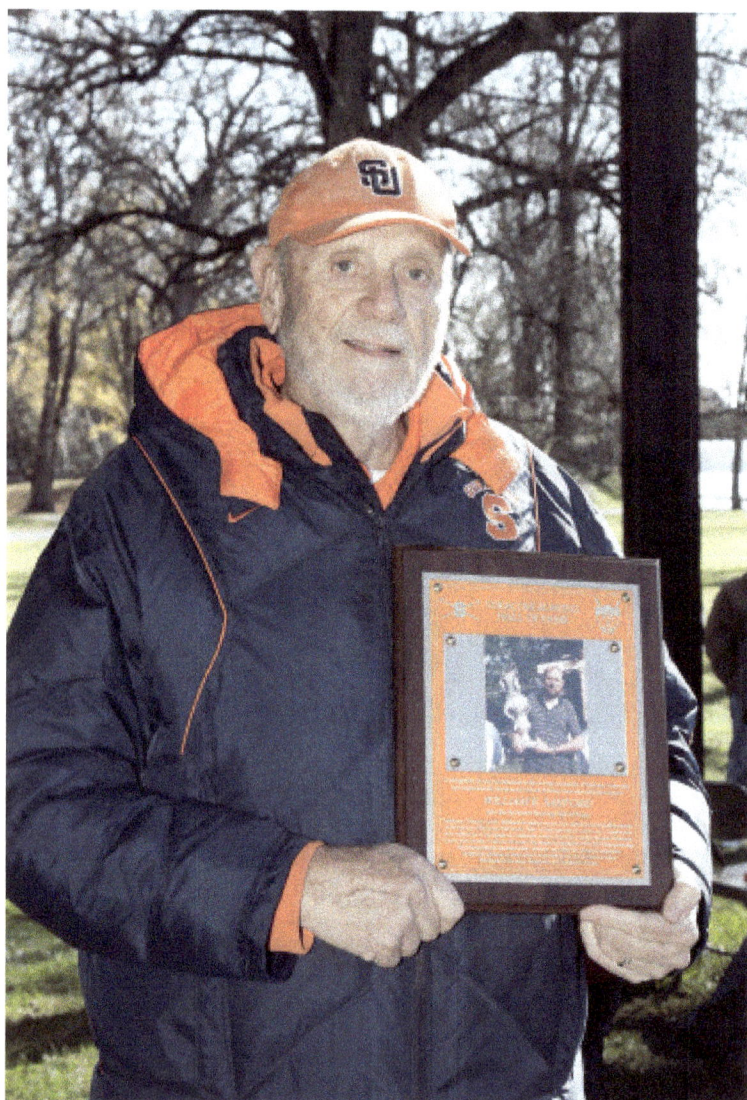

2011 – SU Men's Head Coach Bill Sanford with his
SU Crew Hall of Fame plaque

2011 – SU JV moves on Navy at the Goes Cup

2011 – SU Men – Goes Cup winners

2011 – SU Men's 3V in racing action

2011 – SU Head Coaches Justin Moore and Dave Reischman confer

2011 – SU Men's fall practice on Onondaga Lake

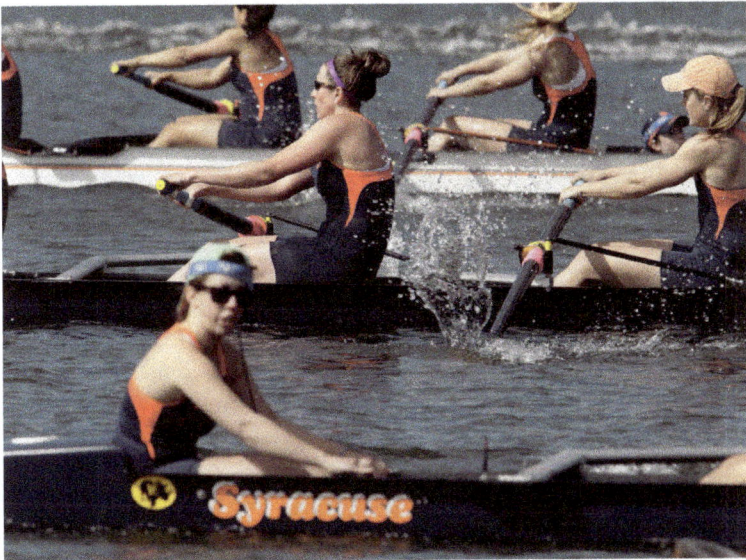

2011 – SU Women on Onondaga Lake

2011 – SU Men watching the action at the Syracuse Invitational

2011 – SU Women in action at the Syracuse Invitational

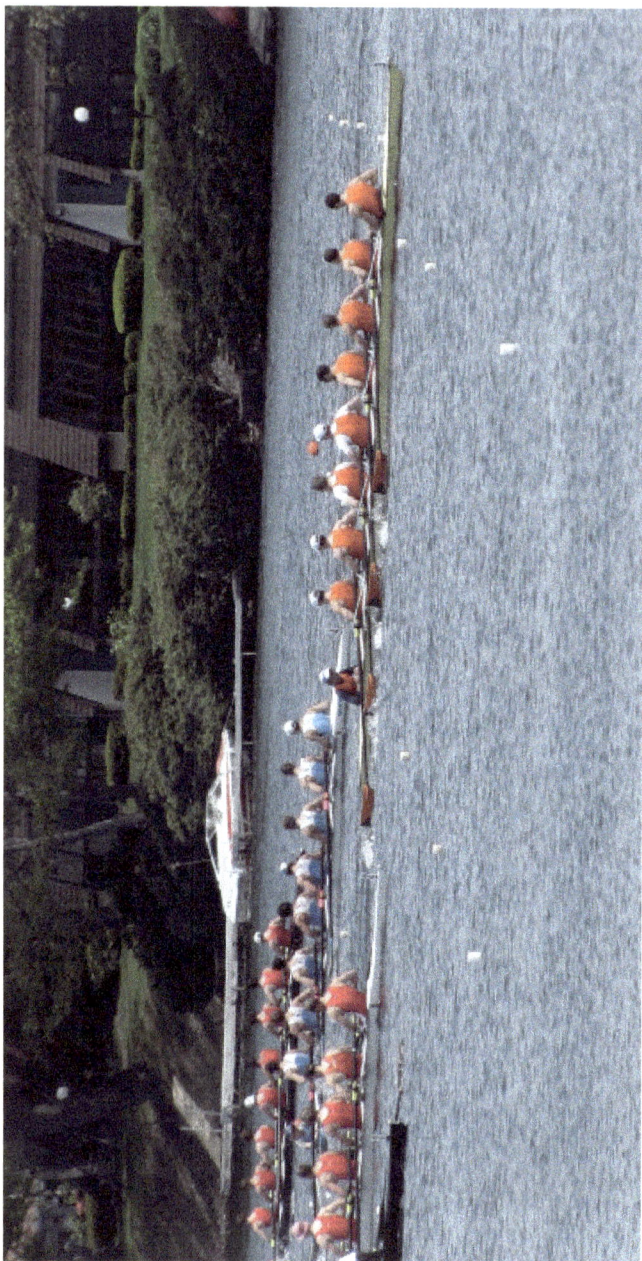

2012 – SU Men's Varsity eight in action at the Eastern Sprints

SU Women's Head Coach Justin Moore

Syracuse rowers' winter training

The "new" rowing tanks at Archbold

Index

469

188, 415
Quinn, Paul 45

R

Rademacher, John 239
Rayfield, Chuck 27
Reed, John 34, 35, 394
Reed, Roger 73, 79, 82, 84
Reelick, Kynan 351, 366, 367,
    374
Regan, Jimmy 151
Reid, Bill 16, 18, 22, 108, 335,
    403, 405, 413
Reinwald, Richard 84
Reischman, Dave 11, 266, 276,
    302, 303, 304, 305, 306,
    307, 308, 309, 310, 311,
    312, 313, 315, 316, 319,
    320, 322, 323, 324, 325,
    326, 327, 328, 329, 330,
    331, 332, 333, 334, 335,
    336, 337, 338, 339, 341,
    352, 353, 354, 355, 356,
    357, 358, 359, 360, 361,
    363, 364, 365, 366, 367,
    368, 369, 370, 371, 372,
    374, 375, 383, 384, 450,
    460
Remele, Jim 103
Rhodes, Jay 240
Richards, Ashton 163, 173
Ridgeley, Henry 80
Ring, Sean 439
Ritter, Rick 137, 141, 163, 171,
    412
Roberts, Charlie 275, 351, 427,
    454
Rogers, Eric 82, 84
Rogers, Steve 56, 59, 71, 72, 73,
    397, 401
Romano, Peter 11, 272, 302, 306,
    307, 438

Roock, Sheila 11, 134, 183, 276,
    415
Roop, Scott 176
Rosenberg, Al 59, 69, 70
Rosenthal, Dave 73, 80, 84
Rosenthal, Jonathan 181
Ross, Andrew 309, 329
Rossell, Bill 42, 394
Rothschild, John 36, 46
Rouen, Tom 11, 23, 60, 351
Rowe, Martha Mogish 11, 131,
    276
    see also Mogish, Martha
Rubinger, Joanne 432, 435
Rude, Tracy 191, 228, 229, 230,
    231, 232, 233
Rung, Kevin 119, 121
Russell, Jim 63
Russo, Brett 309
Russo, Will 306, 307, 308

S

Sacheck, Jen 11
Samios, Bill 117, 120
Samuels, Roger 270
Sanford, Bill 11, 15, 16, 17, 20,
    21, 22, 27, 28, 29, 30, 31,
    32, 34, 37, 43, 48, 52, 55,
    57, 58, 61, 62, 67, 68, 69,
    71, 72, 73, 74, 75, 76, 77,
    78, 80, 81, 85, 88, 89, 98,
    99, 103, 104, 105, 108,
    110, 113, 114, 115, 116,
    117, 119, 122, 123, 125,
    130, 138, 139, 140, 141,
    142, 145, 146, 147, 149,
    153, 154, 156, 157, 158,
    159, 164, 165, 168, 173,
    175, 176, 177, 178, 179,
    180, 181, 193, 194, 195,
    197, 198, 201, 202, 203,
    205, 208, 209, 211, 214,

476

479

www.ingramcontent.com/pod-product-compliance
Lightning Source LLC
Chambersburg PA
CBHW070943150426

42812CB00066B/3247/J